WESTMAR COLLEGE

History and Class Consciousness

GEORG LUKÁCS

History and Class Consciousness

Studies in Marxist Dialectics

Translated by Rodney Livingstone

THE MIT PRESS

CAMBRIDGE, MASSACHUSETTS

© 1968 by Hermann Luchterhand Verlag GmbH
Berlin and Neuwied
Translation © 1971 The Merlin Press Ltd
First published in this edition by
The Merlin Press Ltd

ISBN 0 262 12035 6 (hardcover)
ISBN 0 262 62020 0 (paperback)

Library of Congress catalog card number: 70–146824

Printed in Great Britain

Contents

For Gertrud Borstieber

Translator's Note

I have consulted both the French translation of 1960 by K. Axielos and J. Bois, Les Editions de Minuit, Paris, and the version of "What is Orthodox Marxism?" by Michael Harrington in *New International*, Summer 1957.

Preface to the New Edition (1967)

In an old autobiographical sketch (of 1933)[1] I called the story of my early development My Road to Marx. The writings collected in this volume encompass my years of apprenticeship in Marxism. In publishing again the most important documents of this period (1918–1930) my intention is to emphasise their experimental nature and on no account to suggest that they have any topical importance in the current controversies about the true nature of Marxism. In view of the great uncertainty prevailing with regard to its essential content and its methodological validity, it is necessary to state this quite firmly in the interests of intellectual integrity. On the other hand, if both they and the contemporary situation are scrutinised critically these essays will still be found to have a certain documentary value in the present debates. Hence the writings assembled here do more than simply illuminate the stages of my personal development; they also show the path taken by intellectual events generally and as long as they are viewed critically they will not be lacking in significance for an understanding of the present situation.

Of course, I cannot possibly describe my attitude towards Marxism around 1918 without briefly mentioning my earlier development. As I emphasised in the sketch I have just referred to, I first read Marx while I was still at school. Later, around 1908 I made a study of *Capital* in order to lay a sociological foundation for my monograph on modern drama.[2] At the time, then, it was Marx the 'sociologist' that attracted me—and I saw him through spectacles tinged by Simmel and Max Weber. I resumed my studies of Marx during World War I, but this time I was led to do so by my general philosophical interests and under the influence of Hegel rather than any contemporary thinkers. Of course, even Hegel's effect upon me was highly ambiguous. For, on the one hand, Kierkegaard had played a significant role in my early development and in the immediate pre-war years in Heidelberg I even planned an essay on his criticism of Hegel. On the other hand, the contradictions in my social and political views brought me intellectually into contact with Syndicalism and above all with the philosophy of Georges Sorel. I strove to go beyond bourgeois radicalism but found myself repelled by social-democratic theory (and especially Kautsky's version of it). My interest in Sorel was aroused by Ervin Szabó, the spiritual mentor of the Hungarian left-wing opposition in Social Democracy. During the war years I became acquainted with the works of Rosa Luxemburg. All this produced a highly contradictory amalgam of theories that was decisive for my thought during the war and the first few years after it.

I think that I would be departing from the truth if I were to attempt to iron out the glaring contradictions of that period by artificially constructing an organic development and fitting it into the correct pigeon-hole in the 'history of ideas'. If Faust could have two souls within his breast, why should not a normal person unite conflicting intellectual trends within himself when he finds himself changing from one class to another in the middle of a world crisis? In so far as I am able to recall those years, I, at least, find that my ideas hovered between the acquisition of Marxism and political activism on the one hand, and the constant intensification of my purely idealistic ethical preoccupations on the other.

I find this confirmed when I read the articles I wrote at the time. When I recall my none too numerous and none too important literary essays from that period I find that their aggressive and paradoxical idealism often outdoes that of my earlier works. At the same time the process of assimilating Marxism went on apace. If I now regard this disharmonious dualism as characteristic of my ideas at that period it is not my intention to paint it in black and white, as if the dynamics of the situation could be confined within the limits of a struggle between revolutionary good and the vestigial evil of bourgeois thought. The transition from one class to the class directly opposed to it is a much more complex business than that. Looking back at it now I see that, for all its romantic anti-capitalistic overtones, the ethical idealism I took from Hegel made a number of real contributions to the picture of the world that emerged after this crisis. Of course, they had to be dislodged from their position of supremacy (or even equality) and modified fundamentally before they could become part of a new, homogeneous outlook. Indeed, this is perhaps the moment to point out that even my intimate knowledge of capitalism became to a certain extent a positive element in the new synthesis. I have never succumbed to the error that I have often noticed in workers and petty-bourgeois intellectuals who despite everything could never free themselves entirely from their awe of the capitalist world. The hatred and contempt I had felt for life under capitalism ever since my childhood preserved me from this.

Mental confusion is not always chaos. It may strengthen the internal contradictions for the time being but in the long run it will lead to their resolution. Thus my ethics tended in the direction of praxis, action and hence towards politics. And this led in turn to economics, and the need for a theoretical grounding there finally brought me to the philosophy of Marxism. Of course, all these developments took place slowly and unevenly. But the direction I was taking began to become clear even during the war after the outbreak of the Russian Revolution. *The Theory of the Novel** was written at a time when I was still in a general state of despair (see my Preface to the New Edition[3]). It is no wonder, then, that the present appeared in it as a Fichtean condition of total degradation and that any hopes of a way out seemed to be a utopian mirage. Only the Russian Revolution really opened a window to the future; the fall of Czarism brought a glimpse of it, and with the collapse of capitalism it appeared in full view. At the time our knowledge of the facts and the principles underlying them was of the slightest and very unreliable. Despite this we saw—at last! at last!—a way for mankind to escape from war and capitalism. Of course, even when we recall this enthusiasm we must take care not to idealise the past. I myself—and I can speak here only for myself—experienced a brief transitional phase: my last hesitations before making my final, irrevocable choice, were marked by a misguided attempt at an apologia fortified with abstract and Philistine arguments. But the final decision could not be resisted for ever. The little essay *Tactics and Ethics* reveals its inner human motivations.

It is not necessary to waste many words on the few essays that were written at the time of the Hungarian Soviet Republic and the period leading up to it. Intellectually we were unprepared— and I was perhaps less prepared than anyone—to come to grips with the tasks that confronted us. Our enthusiasm was a very makeshift substitute for knowledge and experience. I need men-

---

* An English translation of this work is in preparation.

tion only one fact by way of illustration: we knew hardly anything of Lenin's theory of revolution and of the vital advances he had made in that area of Marxism. Only a few articles and pamphlets had been translated and made available at that time, and of those who had taken part in the Russian Revolution some (like Szamuely) had little talent for theory and others (like Béla Kun) were strongly influenced by the Russian left-wing opposition. It was not until my emigration to Vienna that I was able to make a thorough study of Lenin's theory. The result was that my thought of this period, too, contained an unresolved dualism. It was partly that I was unable to find the correct solution in principle to the quite catastrophic mistakes committed by the opportunists, such as their solution to the agrarian problem which went along purely social-democratic lines. And partly that my own intellectual predilections went in the direction of an abstract utopianism in the realm of cultural politics. Today, after an interval of nearly half a century, I am astounded to find how fruitful our activities were, relatively speaking. (Remaining on the theoretical level I should point out that the first version of the two essays, *What is Orthodox Marxism?* and *The Changing Function of Historical Materialism*, date from this period. They were revised for *History and Class Consciousness* but their basic orientation remains the same.)

My emigration to Vienna was the start of a period of study. And, in the first instance, this meant furthering my acquaintance with the works of Lenin. Needless to say, this study was not divorced from revolutionary activity for a single moment. What was needed above all was to breathe new life into the revolutionary workers' movement in Hungary and to maintain continuity: new slogans and policies had to be found that would enable it to survive and expand during the White Terror. The slanders of the dictatorship—whether purely reactionary or social-democratic was immaterial—had to be refuted. At the same time it was necessary to begin the process of Marxist self-criticism of the proletarian dictatorship. In addition we in Vienna found ourselves swept along by the current of the international revolutionary movement. The Hungarian emigration was perhaps the most numerous and the most divided at the time, but it was by no means the only one. There were many émigrés from Poland and the Balkans living in Vienna either temporarily or permanently. Moreover, Vienna was an international transit point, so that we were in continuous contact with German, French, Italian and other Communists. In such circumstances it is not surprising that a magazine called *Communism* was founded which for a time became a focal point for the ultra-left currents in the Third International. Together with Austrian Communists, Hungarian and Polish emigrants, who provided the inner core and the permanent membership, there were also sympathisers from the Italian ultra-left, like Bordiga and Terracini, and Dutch Communists like Pannekoek and Roland Holst.

In these circumstances it was natural that the dualism of my attitudes should not only have reached a climax but should also have crystallised out into a curious new practical and theoretical form. As a member of the inner collective of *Communism* I was active in helping to work out a new 'left-wing' political and theoretical line. It was based on the belief, very much alive at the time, that the great revolutionary wave that would soon sweep the whole world, or Europe at the very least, to socialism, had in no way been broken by the setbacks in Finland, Hungary and Munich. Events like the Kapp Putsch, the occupation of the factories in Italy, the Polish-Soviet War and even the March Action, strengthened our belief in the imminence of world revolution and the total transformation of the civilised world. Of course, in discussing this sectarianism of the early twenties we must not imagine anything like the sectarianism seen in Stalinist praxis. This aimed at protecting the given power relations against all reforms; its objectives were conservative and its methods bureaucratic. The sectarianism of the twenties had messianic, utopian aspirations and its methods were violently opposed to bureaucracy. The two trends have only the name in common and inwardly they represent two hostile extremes. (Of course, it is true that even in the Third International Zinoviev and his disciples introduced bureaucratic methods, just as it is true that Lenin's last years, at a time when he was already burdened by ill-health, were filled with anxiety about the problem of fighting the growing, spontaneously generated bureaucratisation of the Soviet Republic on the basis of proletatian democracy. But even here we perceive the distinction between the sectarians of then and now. My essay on questions of organisation in the Hungarian Party is directed against the theory and practice of Zinoviev's disciple, Béla Kun.)

Our magazine strove to propagate a messianic sectarianism by working out the most radical methods on every issue, and by proclaiming a total break with every institution and mode of life stemming from the bourgeois world. This would help to foster an undistorted class consciousness in the vanguard, in the Communist parties and in the Communist youth organisations. My polemical essay attacking the idea of participation in bourgeois parliaments is a good example of this tendency. Its fate—criticism at the hands of Lenin—enabled me to take my first step away from sectarianism. Lenin pointed to the vital distinction, indeed to the paradox, that an institution may be obsolete from the standpoint of world history—as e.g. the soviets had rendered parliaments obsolete—but that this need not preclude participation in it for tactical reasons; on the contrary. I at once saw the force of this criticism and it compelled me to revise my historical perspectives and to adjust them more subtly and less directly to the exigencies of day-to-day tactics. In this respect it was the beginning of a change in my views. Nevertheless this change took place within the framework of an essentially sectarian outlook. This became evident a year later when, uncritically, and in the spirit of sectarianism, I gave my approval to the March Action as a whole, even though I was critical of a number of tactical errors.

It is at this point that the objective internal contradictions in my political and philosophical views come into the open. On the international scene I was able to indulge all my intellectual passion for revolutionary messianism unhindered. But in Hungary, with the gradual emergence of an organised Communist movement, I found myself increasingly having to face decisions whose general and personal, long-term and immediate consequences I could not ignore and which I had to make the basis of yet further decisions. This had already been my position in the Soviet Republic in Hungary. There the need to consider other than messianic perspectives had often forced me into realistic decisions both in the People's Commissariat for Education and in the division where I was in charge politically. Now, however, the confrontation with the facts, the compulsion to search for what Lenin called 'the next link in the chain' became incomparably more urgent and intensive than ever before in my life. Precisely because the actual substance of such decisions seemed so empirical it had far-reaching consequences for my theoretical position. For this had now to be adjusted to objective situations and tendencies. If I wished to arrive at a decision that was correct

in principle I could never be content just to consider the immediate
state of affairs. I would have to seek out those often-concealed
mediations that had produced the situation and above all I would
have to strive to anticipate the factors that would probably
result from them and influence future praxis. I found myself
adopting an intellectual attitude dictated, by life itself, that
conflicted sharply with the idealism and utopianism of my
revolutionary messianism.

My dilemma was made even more acute by the fact that
opposed to me within the leadership of the Hungarian Party
was the group led by Zinoviev's disciple, Béla Kun, who subscribed
to a sectarianism of a modern bureaucratic type. In theory
it would have been possible to repudiate his views as those of a
pseudo-leftist. In practice, however, his proposals could only be
combated by an appeal to the highly prosaic realities of ordinary
life that were but distantly related to the larger perspectives of
the world revolution. At this point in my life, as so often, I had
a stroke of luck: the opposition to Béla Kun was headed by Eugen
Landler. He was notable not only for his great and above all
practical intelligence but also for his understanding of theoretical
problems so long as they were linked, however indirectly, with
the praxis of revolution. He was a man whose most deeply-
rooted attitudes were determined by his intimate involvement in
the life of the masses. His protest against Kun's bureaucratic
and adventurist projects convinced me at once, and when it
came to an open breach I was always on his side. It is not possible
to go into even the most important details of these inner party
struggles here, although there are some matters of theoretical interest. As far as I was concerned the breach meant that the methodological cleavage in my thought now developed into a division
between theory and practice. While I continued to support ultra-
left tendencies on the great international problems of revolution, as
a member of the leadership of the Hungarian Party I became the
most bitter enemy of Kun's sectarianism. This became particularly
obvious early in 1921. On the Hungarian front I followed Landler
in advocating an energetic anti-sectarian line while simultaneously
at the international level I gave theoretical support to the March
Action. With this the tension between the conflicting tendencies
reached a climax. As the divisions in the Hungarian Party became
more acute, as the movement of the radical workers in Hungary
began to grow, my ideas were increasingly influenced by the

theoretical tendencies brought into being by these events. However, they did not yet gain the upper hand at this stage despite the fact that Lenin's criticism had undermined my analysis of the March Action.

History and Class Consciousness was born in the midst of the crises of this transitional period. It was written in 1922. It consisted in part of earlier texts in a revised form; in addition to those already mentioned there was the essay on *Class Consciousness* of 1920. The two essays on Rosa Luxemburg and *Legality and Illegality* were included in the new collection without significant alterations. Only two studies, the most important ones, were wholly new: *Reification and the Consciousness of the Proletariat* and *Towards a Methodology of the Problem of Organisation.* (The latter was based on *Organisational Problems of the Revolutionary Movement,* an essay that had appeared in the magazine *The International* in 1921 immediately after the March Action.) *History and Class Consciousness* is, then, the final synthesis of the period of my development that began with the last years of the war. However, it is also in part the start of a transitional stage leading to a greater clarity, even though these tendencies could not mature properly.

This unresolved conflict between opposed intellectual trends which cannot always be easily labelled victorious or defeated makes it difficult even now to give a coherent critique of the book. However, the attempt must be made to isolate at least the dominant motifs. The book's most striking feature is that, contrary to the subjective intentions of its author, objectively it falls in with a tendency in the history of Marxism that has taken many different forms. All of them have one thing in common, whether they like it or not and irrespective of their philosophical origins or their political effects: they strike at the very roots of Marxian ontology. I refer to the tendency to view Marxism exclusively as a theory of society, as social philosophy, and hence to ignore or repudiate it as a theory of nature. Even before World War I Marxists as far apart as Max Adler and Lunacharsky defended views of this kind. In our day we find them emerging once more, above all in French Existentialism and its intellectual ambience— probably due in part to the influence of *History and Class Consciousness.* My book takes up a very definite stand on this issue. I argue in a number of places that nature is a societal category and the whole drift of the book tends to show that only a knowledge of society and the men who live in it is of relevance to philosophy.

The very names of the representatives of this tendency indicate
that it is not a clearly definable trend. I myself knew of Lunacharsky only by name and I always rejected Max Adler as a Kantian
and a Social Democrat. Despite this a close examination reveals
that they have a number of features in common. On the one hand,
it is demonstrable that it is the materialist view of nature that
brings about the really radical separation of the bourgeois and
socialist outlooks. The failure to grasp this blurs philosophical
debate and e.g. prevents the clear elaboration of the Marxist
concept of praxis. On the other hand, this apparent methodological upgrading of societal categories distorts their true epistemological functions. Their specific Marxist quality is weakened
and their real advance on bourgeois thought is often retracted
unconsciously.

I must confine myself here to a critique of *History and Class
Consciousness*, but this is not to imply that this deviation from
Marxism was less pronounced in the case of other writers with
a similar outlook. In my book this deviation has immediate
consequences for the view of economics I give there and fundamental confusions result, as in the nature of the case economics
must be crucial. It is true that the attempt is made to explain all
ideological phenomena by reference to their basis in economics
but, despite this, the purview of economics is narrowed down
because its basic Marxist category, labour as the mediator of
the metabolic interaction between society and nature, is missing.
Given my basic approach, such a consequence is quite natural.
It means that the most important real pillars of the Marxist
view of the world disappear and the attempt to deduce the
ultimate revolutionary implications of Marxism in as radical a
fashion as possible is deprived of a genuinely economic foundation. It is self-evident that this means the disappearance of
the ontological objectivity of nature upon which this process of
change is based. But it also means the disappearance of the interaction between labour as seen from a genuinely materialist
standpoint and the evolution of the men who labour. Marx's
great insight that "even production for the sake of production
means nothing more than the *development of the productive energies of
man, and hence the development of the wealth of human nature as an end
in itself*" lies outside the terrain which *History and Class Consciousness* is able to explore. Capitalist exploitation thus loses its objective
revolutionary aspect and there is a failure to grasp the fact that

"although this evolution of the species Man is accomplished at first at the expense of the majority of individual human beings and of certain human classes, it finally overcomes this antagonism and coincides with the evolution of the particular individual. Thus the higher development of individuality is only purchased by a historical process in which individuals are sacrificed."[4] In consequence, my account of the contradictions of capitalism as well as of the revolutionisation of the proletariat is unintentionally coloured by an overriding subjectivism.

This has a narrowing and distorting effect on the book's central concept of praxis. With regard to this problem, too, my intention was to base myself on Marx and to free his concepts from every subsequent bourgeois distortion and to adapt them to the requirements of the great revolutionary upsurge of the present. Above all I was absolutely convinced of one thing: that the purely contemplative nature of bourgeois thought had to be radically overcome. As a result the conception of revolutionary praxis in this book takes on extravagant overtones that are more in keeping with the current messianic utopianism of the Communist left than with authentic Marxist doctrine. Comprehensibly enough in the context of the period, I attacked the bourgeois and opportunistic currents in the workers' movement that glorified a conception of knowledge which was ostensibly objective but was in fact isolated from any sort of praxis; with considerable justice I directed my polemics against the over-extension and over-valuation of contemplation. Marx's critique of Feuerbach only reinforced my convictions. What I failed to realise, however, was that in the absence of a basis in real praxis, in labour as its original form and model, the over-extension of the concept of praxis would lead to its opposite: a relapse into idealistic contemplation. My intention, then, was to chart the correct and authentic class consciousness of the proletariat, distinguishing it from 'public opinion surveys' (a term not yet in currency) and to confer upon it an indisputably practical objectivity. I was unable, however, to progress beyond the notion of an 'imputed' [zugerechnet] class consciousness. By this I meant the same thing as Lenin in *What is to be done?* when he maintained that socialist class consciousness would differ from the spontaneously emerging trade-union consciousness in that it would be implanted in the workers 'from outside', i.e. "from outside the economic struggle and the sphere of the relations between workers and employers".[5] Hence, what I had intended subjectively, and what Lenin had arrived at as the result of an authentic Marxist analysis of a practical movement, was transformed in my account into a purely intellectual result and thus into something contemplative. In my presentation it would indeed be a miracle if this 'imputed' consciousness could turn into revolutionary praxis.

This transformation into its opposite of what was in itself a correct intention follows from the abstract and idealistic conception of praxis already referred to. This is seen clearly in the—once again not wholly misguided—polemic against Engels who had looked to experiment and industry for the typical cases in which praxis proves to be a criterion of theory. I have since come to realise that Engels' thesis is theoretically incomplete in that it overlooks the fact that the terrain of praxis while remaining unchanged in its basic structure has become much more extensive, more complex and more mediated than in the case of work. For this reason the mere act of producing an object may indeed become the foundation of the immediately correct realisation of a theoretical assumption. To this extent it can serve as a criterion of its truth or falsity. However, the task that Engels imposes here on immediate praxis of putting an end to the Kantian theory of the 'intangible thing-in-itself' is far from being solved. For work itself can easily remain a matter of pure manipulation, spontaneously or consciously by-passing the solution to the problem of the thing-in-itself and ignoring it either wholly or in part. History supplies us with instances where the correct action has been taken on the basis of false theories and in Engels' sense these cases imply a failure to understand the thing-in-itself. Indeed the Kantian theory itself in no way denies that experiments of this kind are objective and provide valuable knowledge. He only relegates them to the realm of mere appearances in which things-in-themselves remain unknown. And the neo-positivism of our own day aims at removing every question about reality (the thing-in-itself) from the purview of science, it rejects every question about the thing-in-itself as 'unscientific' and at the same time it acknowledges the validity of all the conclusions of technology and science. If praxis is to fulfil the function Engels rightly assigned to it, it must go beyond this immediacy while remaining praxis and developing into a comprehensive praxis.

My objections to Engels' solution were not without foundation. All the more mistaken was my chain of argument. It was quite wrong to maintain that 'experiment is pure contemplation'. My own account refutes this. For the creation of a situation in which the natural forces under investigation can function 'purely', i.e. without outside interference or subjective error, is quite comparable to the case of work in that it too implies the creation of a teleological system, admittedly of a special kind. In its essence it is therefore pure praxis. It was no less a mistake to deny that industry is praxis and to see in it "in a historical and dialectical sense only the object and not the subject of the natural laws of society". The half-truth contained in this sentence—and it is no more than a half-truth at best—applies only to the economic totality of capitalist production. But it is by no means contradicted by the fact that every single act in industrial production not only represents a synthesis of teleological acts of work but is also itself a teleological, i.e. practical, act in this very synthesis. It is in line with such philosophical misconceptions that *History and Class Consciousness* should begin its analysis of economic phenomena not with a consideration of work but only of the complicated structures of a developed commodity economy. This means that all prospects of advancing to decisive questions like the relation of theory to practice and subject to object are frustrated from the outset.

In these and similarly problematical premises we see the result of a failure to subject the Hegelian heritage to a thoroughgoing materialist reinterpretation and hence to transcend and preserve it. I would once again cite a central problem of principle. It is undoubtedly one of the great achievements of *History and Class Consciousness* to have reinstated the category of totality in the central position it had occupied throughout Marx's works and from which it had been ousted by the 'scientism' of the social-democratic opportunists. I did not know at the time that Lenin was moving in a similar direction. (The philosophical fragments were published nine years after the appearance of *History and Class Consciousness*.) But whereas Lenin really brought about a renewal of the Marxian method my efforts resulted in a— Hegelian—distortion, in which I put the totality in the centre of the system, overriding the priority of economics. "It is not the primacy of economic motives in historical explanation that constitutes the decisive difference between Marxism and bourgeois science, but the point of view of totality." This methodological paradox was intensified further by the fact that the totality was seen as the conceptual embodiment of the revolutionary principle in science. "The primacy of the category of totality is the bearer of the revolutionary principle in science." [6]

There is no doubt that such paradoxes of method played a not unimportant and in many ways very progressive role in the impact of *History and Class Consciousness* on later thought. For the revival of Hegel's dialectics struck a hard blow at the revisionist tradition. Already Bernstein had wished to eliminate everything reminiscent of Hegel's dialectics in the name of 'science'. And nothing was further from the mind of his philosophical opponents, and above all Kautsky, than the wish to undertake the defence of this tradition. For anyone wishing to return to the revolutionary traditions of Marxism the revival of the Hegelian traditions was obligatory. *History and Class Consciousness* represents what was perhaps the most radical attempt to restore the revolutionary nature of Marx's theories by renovating and extending Hegel's dialectics and method. The task was made even more important by the fact that bourgeois philosophy at the time showed signs of a growing interest in Hegel. Of course they never succeeded in making Hegel's breach with Kant the foundation of their analysis and, on the other hand, they were influenced by Dilthey's attempts to construct theoretical bridges between Hegelian dialectics and modern irrationalism. A little while after the appearance of *History and Class Consciousness* Kroner described Hegel as the greatest irrationalist of all time and in Löwith's later studies Marx and Kierkegaard were to emerge as parallel phenomena out of the dissolution of Hegelianism. It is by contrast with all these developments that we can best see the relevance of *History and Class Consciousness*. Another fact contributing to its importance to the ideology of the radical workers' movement was that whereas Plekhanov and others had vastly overestimated Feuerbach's role as an intermediary between Hegel and Marx, this was relegated to the background here. Anticipating the publication of Lenin's later philosophical studies by some years, it was nevertheless only somewhat later, in the essay on Moses Hess, that I explicitly argued that Marx followed directly from Hegel. However, this position is contained implicitly in many of the discussions in *History and Class Consciousness*.

In a necessarily brief summary it is not possible to undertake a concrete criticism of all the issues raised by the book, and to show how far the interpretation of Hegel it contained was a source of

confusion and how far it pointed towards the future. The contemporary reader who is qualified to criticise will certainly find
evidence of both tendencies. To assess the impact of the book
at that time, and also its relevance today, we must consider one
problem that surpasses in its importance all questions of detail.
This is the question of alienation, which, for the first time since
Marx, is treated as central to the revolutionary critique of capitalism and which has its theoretical and methodological roots in the
Hegelian dialectic. Of course the problem was in the air at the
time. Some years later, following the publication of Heidegger's
Being and Time (1927), it moved into the centre of philosophical debate. Even today it has not lost this position, largely because of the
influence of Sartre, his followers and his opponents. The philosophical problem raised above all by Lucien Goldmann when he
interpreted Heidegger's work in part as a polemical reply to
mine—which however was not mentioned explicitly—can be
left on one side here. The statement that the problem was in the
air is perfectly adequate, particularly as it is not possible to discuss
the reasons for this here and to lay bare the mixture of Marxist
and Existentialist ideas that were so influential after World War
II, especially in France. The question of who was first and who
influenced whom is not particularly interesting here. What is
important is that the alienation of man is a crucial problem of the
age in which we live and is recognised as such by both bourgeois
and proletarian thinkers, by commentators on both right and
left. Hence *History and Class Consciousness* had a profound impact
in youthful intellectual circles; I know of a whole host of good
Communists who were won over to the movement by this very
fact. Without a doubt the fact that this Marxist and Hegelian
question was taken up by a Communist was one reason why the
impact of the book went far beyond the limits of the party.

As to the way in which the problem was actually dealt with, it
is not hard to see today that it was treated in purely Hegelian
terms. In particular its ultimate philosophical foundation is
the identical subject-object that realises itself in the historical
process. Of course, in Hegel it arises in a purely logical and
philosophical form when the highest stage of absolute spirit is
attained in philosophy by abolishing alienation and by the return
of self-consciousness to itself, thus realising the identical subject-
object. In *History and Class Consciousness*, however, this process is
socio-historical and it culminates when the proletariat reaches

this stage in its class consciousness, thus becoming the identical subject-object of history. This does indeed appear to 'stand Hegel on his feet'; it appears as if the logico-metaphysical construction of the *Phenomenology of Mind* had found its authentic realisation in the existence and the consciousness of the proletariat. And this appears in turn to provide a philosophical foundation for the proletariat's efforts to form a classless society through revolution and to conclude the 'prehistory' of mankind. But is the identical subject-object here anything more in truth than a purely metaphysical construct? Can a genuinely identical subject-object be created by self-knowledge, however adequate, and however truly based on an adequate knowledge of society, i.e. however perfect that self-knowledge is? We need only formulate the question precisely to see that it must be answered in the negative. For even when the content of knowledge is referred back to the knowing subject, this does not mean that the act of cognition is thereby freed of its alienated nature. In the *Phenomenology of Mind* Hegel rightly dismisses the notion of a mystical and irrationalistic realisation of the identical subject-object, of Schelling's 'intellectual intuition', calling instead for a philosophical and rational solution to the problem. His healthy sense of reality induced him to leave the matter at this juncture; his very general system does indeed culminate in the vision of such a realisation but he never shows in concrete terms how it might be achieved. Thus the proletariat seen as the identical subject-object of the real history of mankind is no materialist consummation that overcomes the constructions of idealism. It is rather an attempt to out-Hegel Hegel, it is an edifice boldly erected above every possible reality and thus attempts objectively to surpass the Master himself.

Hegel's reluctance to commit himself on this point is the product of the wrong-headedness of his basic concept. For it is in Hegel that we first encounter alienation as the fundamental problem of the place of man in the world and *vis-à-vis* the world. However, in the term alienation he includes every type of objectification. Thus 'alienation' when taken to its logical conclusion is identical with objectification. Therefore, when the identical subject-object transcends alienation it must also transcend objectification at the same time. But as, according to Hegel, the object, the thing exists only as an alienation from self-consciousness, to take it back into the subject would mean the end of objective reality

and thus of any reality at all. *History and Class Consciousness* follows
Hegel in that it too equates alienation with objectification
[Vergegenständlichung] (to use the term employed by Marx
in the *Economic-Philosophical Manuscripts*). This fundamental and
crude error has certainly contributed greatly to the success
enjoyed by *History and Class Consciousness*. The unmasking of
alienation by philosophy was in the air, as we have remarked,
and it soon became a central problem in the type of cultural
criticism that undertook to scrutinise the condition of man in
contemporary capitalism. In the philosophical, cultural criticism
of the bourgeoisie (and we need look no further than Heidegger),
it was natural to sublimate a critique of society into a purely
philosophical problem, i.e. to convert an essentially social alienation into an eternal 'condition humaine', to use a term not coined
until somewhat later. It is evident that *History and Class Consciousness* met such attitudes half-way, even though its intentions had
been different and indeed opposed to them. For when I identified
alienation with objectification I meant this as a societal category
—socialism would after all abolish alienation—but its irreducible presence in class society and above all its basis in philosophy
brought it into the vicinity of the 'condition humaine'.

This follows from the frequently stressed false identification
of opposed fundamental categories. For objectification is indeed
a phenomenon that cannot be eliminated from human life in
society. If we bear in mind that every externalisation of an
object in practice (and hence, too, in work) is an objectification,
that every human expression including speech objectifies human
thoughts and feelings, then it is clear that we are dealing with a
universal mode of commerce between men. And in so far as this
is the case, objectification is a neutral phenomenon; the true is as
much an objectification as the false, liberation as much as enslavement. Only when the objectified forms in society acquire
functions that bring the essence of man into conflict with his
existence, only when man's nature is subjugated, deformed and
crippled can we speak of an objective societal condition of alienation and, as an inexorable consequence, of all the subjective
marks of an internal alienation. This duality was not acknowledged in *History and Class Consciousness*. And this is why it is so
wide of the mark in its basic view of the history of philosophy.
(We note in passing that the phenomenon of reification is closely
related to that of alienation but is neither socially nor conceptually

identical with it; here the two words were used synonymously.)

This critique of the basic concepts cannot hope to be comprehensive. But even in an account as brief as this mention must be made of my rejection of the view that knowledge is reflection. This had two sources. The first was my deep abhorrence of the mechanistic fatalism which was the normal concomitant of reflection theory in mechanistic materialism. Against this my messianic utopianism, the predominance of praxis in my thought rebelled in passionate protest—a protest that, once again, was not wholly misguided. In the second place I recognised the way in which praxis had its origins and its roots in work. The most primitive kind of work, such as the quarrying of stones by primeval man, implies a correct reflection of the reality he is concerned with. For no purposive activity can be carried out in the absence of an image, however crude, of the practical reality involved. Practice can only be a fulfilment and a criterion of theory when it is based on what is held to be a correct reflection of reality. It would be unrewarding at this point to detail the arguments that justify rejecting the analogy with photography which is so prevalent in the current debate on reflection theories.

It is, I believe, no contradiction that I should have spoken here so exclusively of the negative aspects of *History and Class Consciousness* while asserting that nevertheless the book was not without importance in its day. The very fact that all the errors listed here have their source not so much in the idiosyncracies of the author as in the prevalent, if often mistaken, tendencies of the age gives the book a certain claim to be regarded as representative. A momentous, world-historical change was struggling to find a theoretical expression. Even if a theory was unable to do justice to the objective nature of the great crisis, it might yet formulate a typical view and thus achieve a certain historical validity. This was the case, as I believe today, with *History and Class Consciousness*.

However, it is by no means my intention to pretend that all the ideas contained in the book are mistaken without exception. The introductory comments in the first essay, for example, give a definition of orthodoxy in Marxism which I now think not only objectively correct but also capable of exerting a considerable influence even today when we are on the eve of a Marxist renaissance. I refer to this passage: "Let us assume that recent research had proved once and for all that every one of Marx's individual theses was false. Even if this were to be proved every serious 'orthodox' Marxist would still be able to accept all such modern conclusions without reservation and hence dismiss every single one of Marx's theses—without being compelled for a single minute to renounce his orthodoxy. Orthodox Marxism, therefore, does not imply the uncritical acceptance of the results of Marx's investigations. It is not the 'belief' in this or that thesis, not the exegesis of a 'sacred' book. On the contrary, orthodoxy refers exclusively to *method*. It is the scientific conviction that dialectical Marxism is the road to truth and that its methods can be developed, expanded and deepened only along the lines laid down by its founders. It is the conviction, moreover, that all attempts to surpass or 'improve' it have led and must lead to over-simplification, triviality and eclecticism."[7]

And without feeling myself to be excessively immodest, I believe that a number of equally true ideas can be found in the book. I need only refer to the fact that I included the early works of Marx in the overall picture of his world-view I did this at a time when most Marxists were unwilling to see in them more than historical documents that were important only for his personal development. Moreover, *History and Class Consciousness* cannot be blamed if, decades later, the relationship was reversed so that the early works were seen as the products of the true Marxist philosophy, while the later works were neglected. Rightly or wrongly, I had always treated Marx's works as having an essential unity.

Nor do I wish to deny that in a number of places the attempt is made to depict the real nature and the movement of the dialectical categories. This points forward to a genuine Marxist ontology of existence in society. For example, the category of mediation is represented in this way: "Thus the category of mediation is a lever with which to overcome the mere immediacy of the empirical world and as such it is not anything (subjective) that has been foisted on to the objects from outside; it is no value judgement or 'Ought' as opposed to their 'Is'. *It is rather the manifestation of their authentic objective structure*."[8] And closely related to this is the discussion of the connection between genesis and history: "That genesis and history should coincide or, more exactly, that they should be different aspects of the same process, can only happen if two conditions are fulfilled. On the one hand, all the categories in which human existence is constructed must appear as the determinants of that existence itself (and not merely of the description of that existence). On the other hand their sequence, their coherence and their interconnections must appear as aspects of the historical process itself, as the structural physiognomy of the present. Thus the sequence and the inner coherence of the categories is neither purely logical, nor is it merely organised in conformity with the historical facts as they happen to be given." [9] This line of reasoning concludes, as is only logical, with a quotation from Marx's famous study of method, made in the fifties. Passages like this one which anticipate a genuine materialistic and dialectical reinterpretation of Marx are not infrequent.

If I have concentrated on my errors, there have been mainly practical reasons for it. It is a fact that *History and Class Consciousness* had a powerful effect on many readers and continues to do so even today. If it is the true arguments that achieve this impact, then all is well and the author's reaction is wholly uninteresting and irrelevant. Unfortunately I know it to be the case that, owing to the way society has developed and to the political theories this development has produced, it is precisely those parts of the book that I regard as theoretically false that have been most influential. For this reason I see it as my duty on the occasion of a reprint after more than 40 years to pronounce upon the book's negative tendencies and to warn my readers against errors that were hard to avoid then, perhaps, but which have long ceased to be so.

I have already said that *History and Class Consciousness* was in quite a definite sense the summation and conclusion of a period of development beginning in 1918–19. The years that followed showed this even more clearly. Above all my messianic utopianism lost (and was even seen to lose) its real grip on me. Lenin died in 1924. The party struggles that followed his death were concentrated increasingly on the debate about whether socialism could survive in one country. That it was possible in theory Lenin had affirmed long before. But the seemingly near prospect of world revolution made it appear particularly theoretical and abstract. The fact that it was now taken seriously proved that a world revolution could not be held to be imminent in these years. (Only with the slump in 1929 did it re-emerge from time to time as a possibility.) Moreover, after 1924 the Third International correctly defined the position of the capitalist world as one of 'relative stability'. These facts meant that I had to re-think my theoretical position. In the debates of the Russian Party I agreed with Stalin about the necessity for socialism in one country and this shows very clearly the start of a new epoch in my thought.

More immediately, this was brought about mainly by my experience in working for the Hungarian Party. The correct policy of the Landler faction began to bear fruit. The Party, working in conditions of strict illegality, steadily increased its influence on the left wing of the Social Democrats so that in 1924–25 it came to a split and the founding of a Workers' Party that would be radical and yet legal. This party was led illegally by Communists and for its strategic objective it had chosen the task of establishing democracy in Hungary. While the efforts of this party culminated in the call for a republic the Communist Party continued to pursue the aim of a dictatorship of the proletariat. At the time I was in agreement with this tactical policy but was increasingly tormented by a whole complex of unresolved problems concerning the theoretical justification of such a position.

These considerations began to undermine the bases of the ideas I had formed during the period 1917–24. A contributory factor was that the very obvious slowing-down of the tempo of the world-revolutionary ferment inevitably led to co-operation among the various left-wing movements so as to combat the increasingly strong growth of a reactionary movement. In the Hungary of Horthy this was an obvious necessity for any legal and left-wing radical workers' party. But even in the international movement there were similar tendencies. In 1922 the march on Rome had taken place and in Germany, too, the next few years brought a growth in National Socialism, an increasing concentration of all the forces of reaction. This put the problems of a United Front and a Popular Front on the agenda and these had to be discussed on the plane of theory as well as strategy and tactics. Moreover, few initiatives could be expected from the Third International which was being influenced more and more strongly by Stalinist tactics. Tactically it swung back and forth between right and left. Stalin himself intervened in the midst of this uncertainty with disastrous consequences when, around 1928, he described the Social Democrats as the 'twin brothers' of the Fascists. This put an end to all prospects of a United Front on the left. Although I was on Stalin's side on the central issue of Russia, I was deeply repelled by his attitude here. However, it did nothing to retard my gradual disenchantment with the ultra-left tendencies of my early revolutionary years as most of the left-wing groupings in the European parties were Trotskyite—a position which I always rejected. Of course, if I was against Ruth Fischer and Maslow in their attitude to German problems—and it was these with which I was always most concerned—this does not mean that I was in sympathy with Brandler and Thalheimer. To clear my own mind and to achieve a political and theoretical self-understanding I was engaged at the time on a search for a 'genuine' left-wing programme that would provide a third alternative to the opposing factions in Germany. But the idea of such a theoretical and political solution to the contradictions in the period of transition was doomed to remain a dream. I never succeeded in solving it to my own satisfaction and so I did not publish any theoretical or political contribution on the international level during this period.

The situation was different in the Hungarian movement. Landler died in 1928 and in 1929 the party prepared for its Second Congress. I was given the task of drafting the political theses for the Congress. This brought me face to face with my old problem in the Hungarian question: can a party opt simultaneously for two different strategic objectives (legally for a republic, illegally for a soviet republic)? Or looked at from another angle: can the party's attitude towards the form of the state be a matter of purely tactical expediency (i.e. with the illegal Communist movement as the genuine objective while the legal party is no more than a tactical manoeuvre)? A thorough analysis of the social and economic situation in Hungary convinced me more and more that Landler with his strategic policy in favour of a republic had instinctively touched on the central issue of a correct revolutionary plan for Hungary: even if the Horthy regime had undergone such a profound crisis as to create the objective conditions for a thorough-going revolution, Hungary would still be unable to make the transition directly to a soviet republic. Therefore, the legal policy of working for a republic had to be concretised to mean what Lenin meant in 1905 by a democratic dictatorship of the workers and peasants. It is hard for most people to imagine how paradoxical this sounded then. Although the Sixth Congress of the Third International did mention this as a possibility, it was generally thought to be historically impossible to take such a retrograde step, as Hungary had already been a soviet republic in 1919.

This is not the place to discuss all these different views. Particularly as the text of the theses can scarcely be held to have any great value as a theoretical document today, even though for me personally they changed the whole direction of my later development. But my analysis was inadequate both on the level of principle and of concrete detail. This was due in part to the fact that in order to make the chief matters of substance more acceptable I had treated the issues too generally and did not give suficient force to particulars. Even so they caused a great scandal in the Hungarian Party. The Kun group saw the theses as the purest opportunism; support for me from my own party was lukewarm. When I heard from a reliable source that Béla Kun was planning to expel me from the Party as a 'Liquidator', I gave up the struggle, as I was well aware of Kun's prestige in the International, and I published a 'Self-criticism'. I was indeed firmly convinced that I was in the right but I knew also—e.g. from the fate that had befallen Karl Korsch—that to be expelled from the Party meant that it would no longer be possible to participate actively in the struggle against Fascism. I wrote my self-criticism as an 'entry ticket' to such activity as I neither could nor wished to continue to work in the Hungarian movement in the circumstances.

How little this self-criticism was to be taken seriously can be gauged from the fact that the basic change in my outlook underlying the Blum Theses (which failed, however, to express it in an even remotely satisfactory fashion) determined from now on all my theoretical and practical activities. Needless to say, this is not the place to give even a brief account of these. As evidence that my claim is objectively verifiable and not merely the product of a wish-fulfilment, I may cite the comments made (in 1950) by Jószef Révai, the chief ideologist of the Party, with reference to the Blum Theses. He regards the literary views I held at the time as flowing directly from the Blum Theses. "Everyone familiar with the history of the Hungarian Communist Party knows that the *literary* views held by Comrade Lukács between 1945 and 1949 belong together with *political* views that he had formulated much earlier, in the context of political trends in Hungary and of the strategy of the Communist Party at the end of the twenties." [10]

This question has another, and for me a more important aspect, one which gives the change recorded here a much sharper definition. As the reader of these essays knows, my decision to take an active part in the Communist movement was influenced profoundly by ethical considerations. When I took this decision I did not suspect that I would be a politician for the next decade. However, circumstances would have it so. When, in February 1919, the Central Committee was arrested, I once again thought it my duty to accept the post offered to me in the semi-illegal committee set up to replace it. There then followed in inevitable sequence posts in the People's Commissariat for Education in the Soviet Republic and political People's Commissariat in the Red Army, illegal activity in Budapest, internal party conflict in Vienna and so on. Only then was I placed before a real alternative. My internal, private self-criticism came to the conclusion that if I was so clearly in the right, as I believed, and could still not avoid such a sensational defeat, then there must be grave defects in my practical political abilities. Therefore, I felt able to withdraw from my political career with a good conscience and concentrate once more on theoretical matters. I have never regretted this decision. (Nor is there any inconsistency in the fact that in 1956 I had once again to take on a ministerial post. I declared before accepting it that it was only for the interim, the period of acute crisis, and that as soon as the situation became more settled I would immediately resign.)

In pursuing the analysis of my theoretical activities in the narrow sense I have by-passed half a decade and can only now return to a more detailed discussion of the essays subsequent to *History and Class Consciousness*. This divergence from the correct chronological sequence is justified by the fact that, without my suspecting it in the least, the theoretical content of the Blum Theses formed the secret *terminus ad quem* of my development. The years of my apprenticeship in Marxism could only be held to have reached a conclusion when I really began to overcome the contradictory dualism that had characterised my thought since the last years of the war by confronting a particular question of importance involving the most diverse problems. I can now outline the course of this development up to the Blum Theses by pointing to my theoretical works dating from that period. I think that by establishing beforehand the terminal point of that development it becomes easier to give such an account. This is particu-

larly obvious when it is remembered that I devoted all my energy at this time to the practical problems of the Hungarian movement so that my contributions to theory consisted chiefly of occasional pieces.

The first and longest of these, an attempt to provide an intellectual portrait of Lenin, is literally an occasional piece. Immediately after Lenin's death my publisher asked me for a brief monograph about him; I complied and the little essay was completed within a few weeks. It represents an advance on *History and Class Consciousness* inasmuch as the need to concentrate on my great model helped me to put the concept of praxis into a clearer, more authentic, more natural and dialectical relationship with theory. Needless to say, my view of the world revolution was that of the twenties. However, partly because of my experience of the brief intervening period and partly because of the need to concentrate on Lenin's intellectual personality the most obviously sectarian features of *History and Class Consciousness* began to fade and were succeeded by others closer to reality. In a Postscript[11] that I recently wrote for a separate reissue of this little study I tried to show in somewhat greater detail than in the original what I still believe to be the healthy and relevant features of its basic argument. Above all I tried to see in Lenin neither a man who simply and straightforwardly followed in the footsteps of Marx and Engels, nor a pragmatic 'Realpolitiker' of genius. My aim was to clarify the authentic quality of his mind. Briefly this image of Lenin can be formulated as follows: his strength in theory is derived from the fact that however abstract a concept may be he always considers its implications for human praxis. Likewise in the case of every action which, as always with him, is based on the concrete analysis of the relevant situation, he always makes sure that his analysis can be connected organically and dialectically with the principles of Marxism. Thus he is neither a theoretician nor a practitioner in the strict sense of the word. He is a profound philosopher of praxis, a man who passionately transforms theory into practice, a man whose sharp attention is always focused on the nodal points where theory becomes practice, practice becomes theory. The fact that my old study still bears the marks of the twenties produces false emphases in my intellectual portrait of Lenin, especially as his critique of the present probed much deeper in his last period than that of his biographer. However, the main features are essentially correct as Lenin's theoretical

and practical life's work is objectively inseparable from the preparations of 1917 and their necessary consequences. Illumined by the spotlight of the twenties, this attempt to do justice to the specific nature of such a great man makes him appear slightly unfamiliar but not wholly unrecognisable.

Everything else that I wrote in the years that followed is not only outwardly adventitious (it consists largely of book reviews), but also inwardly. I was spontaneously searching for a new orientation and I tried to clarify my future direction by demarcating it off from the views of others. As far as substance is concerned the review of Bukharin is perhaps the most weighty of these works. (I would observe in passing for the benefit of the modern reader that in 1925 Bukharin was, after Stalin, the most important figure in the leadership of the Russian Party; the breach between them did not take place for another three years.) The most positive feature of this review is the way my views on economics become concretised. This can be seen above all in my polemic against an idea that had a wide currency among both vulgar-materialist Communists and bourgeois positivists. This was the notion that technology was the principle that objectively governed progress in the development of the forces of production. This evidently leads to historical fatalism, to the elimination of man and of social activity; it leads to the ideal that technology functions like a societal 'natural force' obedient to 'natural laws'. My criticism not only moved on a more concrete historical level than had been the case for most of *History and Class Consciousness*, but also I made less use of voluntaristic ideological counter-weights to oppose to this mechanistic fatalism. I tried to demonstrate that economic forces determined the course of society and hence of technology too. The same applies to my review of Wittfogel's book. Both analyses suffer from the same theoretical defect in that they both treat mechanistic vulgar-materialism and positivism as a single undifferentiated trend, and indeed the latter is for the most part assimilated into the former.

Of greater importance are the much more detailed discussions of the new editions of Lassalles's letters and the works of Moses Hess. Both reviews are dominated by the tendency to ground social criticism and the evolution of society more concretely in economics than I had ever been able to do in *History and Class Consciousness*. At the same time I tried to make use of the critique of idealism, of the continuation of the Hegelian dialectic for

B

enlarging our knowledge of the insights thus acquired. That is to say, I took up again the criticism that the young Marx had levelled in *The Holy Family* at the idealist thinkers who had allegedly refuted Hegel. Marx's criticism was that such thinkers believed subjectively that they were making an advance on Hegel, while objectively they simply represented a revival of Fichte's subjective idealism. Thus it is characteristic of the conservative aspects of Hegel's thought that his history of philosophy does not go beyond proving the necessity of the present. Subjectively, therefore, there was certainly something revolutionary about the impulses that lay behind Fichte's philosophy of history with its definition of the present as the 'age of total degradation' poised between the past and a future of which it claimed to have philosophical knowledge. Already in the review of Lassalle it is shown that this radicalism is purely imaginary and that as far as knowledge of the real movement of history is concerned Hegel's philosophy moves on an objectively higher plane than Fichte's. This is because the dynamics of Hegel's system of the social and historical mediating factors that produce the present is more real and less of an abstract intellectual construct than Fichte's manner of pointing towards the future. Lassalle's sympathy for such tendencies is anchored in the pure idealism of his overall view of the world; it refuses to concern itself with the worldliness that results from a view of history based on economics. In order to give full force to the distance separating Marx and Lassalle, I quoted in the review a statement made by Lassalle in the course of a conversation with Marx: "If you do not believe in the immortality of the categories, then you must believe in God." This sharp delineation of the retrograde features of Lassalle's thought was at the same time part of a theoretical polemic against currents in Social Democracy. For in contrast to the criticism Marx levelled at Lassalle, there was a tendency among the Social Democrats to make of Lassalle a co-founder of the socialist view of the world, on a par with Marx. I did not refer to them explicitly but I attacked the tendency as a bourgeois deviation. This helped to bring me closer to the real Marx on a number of issues than had been possible in *History and Class Consciousness*.

The discussion of Moses Hess had no such immediate political relevance. But having once taken up the ideas of the early Marx I felt a strong need to define my position against that of his contemporaries, the left wing that emerged from the ruins of

Hegelian philosophy and the True Socialists who were often closely associated with it. This also helped me to bring the philosophical definition of economic problems more forcefully into the foreground. My uncritical attitude towards Hegel had still not been overcome; my criticism of Hess, like *History and Class Consciousness*, is based on the supposed equation of objectification and alienation. The advance on my earlier position assumes a somewhat paradoxical form. On the one hand, I make use of those tendencies in Hegel which emphasise the point that economic categories are societal realities as a stick with which to beat Lassalle and the radical Young Hegelians. On the other hand, I launch a sharp attack on Feuerbach for his undialectical criticisms of Hegel. This last point leads to the position already affirmed: that Marx takes up the thread where Hegel left off; while the first leads to the attempt to define the relationship between economics and dialectics more closely. To take one example relating to the *Phenomenology*, emphasis is placed on Hegel's worldliness in his economic and social dialectics as opposed to the transcendentalism of every type of subjective idealism. In the same way alienation is regarded neither as "a mental construct nor as a 'reprehensible' reality" but "as the immediately given form in which the present exists on the way to overcoming itself in the historical process". This forms a link with an objective line of development stemming from *History and Class Consciousness* concerning mediation and immediacy in the evolution of society. The most important aspect of such ideas is that they culminate in the demand for a new kind of critique which is already searching explicitly for a direct link-up with Marx's *Critique of Political Economy*. Once I had gained a definite and fundamental insight into what was wrong with my whole approach in *History and Class Consciousness* this search became a plan to investigate the philosophical connections between economics and dialectics. My first attempt to put this plan into practice came early in the thirties, in Moscow and Berlin, with the first draft of my book on the young Hegel (which was not completed until autumn 1937).[12] Only now, thirty years later, am I attempting to discover a real solution to this whole problem in the ontology of social existence, on which I am currently engaged.

I am not in a position to document the extent to which these tendencies gained ground in the three years that separate the Hess essay from the Blum Theses. I just think it extremely unlikely that my practical work for the party, with its constant demands for concrete economic analysis, should have had no effect on my theoretical views on economics. At any rate, the great change in my views that is embodied in the Blum Theses took place in 1929 and it was with these new attitudes that I took up a research post at the Marx–Engels Institute at Moscow in 1930. Here I had two unexpected strokes of good luck: the text of the *Economic-Philosophical Manuscripts* had just been completely deciphered and I was able to read it. At the same time I made the acquaintance of Mikhail Lifschitz, and this proved to be the beginning of a life-long friendship. In the process of reading the Marx manuscript all the idealist prejudices of *History and Class Consciousness* were swept to one side. It is undoubtedly true that I could have found ideas similar to those which now had such an overwhelming effect on me in the works of Marx that I had read previously. But the fact is that this did not happen, evidently because I read Marx in the light of my own Hegelian interpretation. Hence only a completely new text could have such a shock effect. (Of course, an additional factor was that I had already undermined the socio-political foundations of that idealism in the Blum Theses.) However that may be, I can still remember even today the over-whelming effect produced in me by Marx's statement that objectivity was the primary material attribute of all things and relations. This links up with the idea already mentioned that objectification is a natural means by which man masters the world and as such it can be either a positive or a negative fact. By contrast, alienation is a special variant of that activity that becomes operative in definite social conditions. This completely shattered the theoretical foundations of what had been the particular achievement of *History and Class Consciousness*. The book became wholly alien to me just as my earlier writings had become by 1918–19. It suddenly became clear to me that if I wished to give body to these new theoretical insights I would have to start again from scratch.

It was my intention at the time to publish a statement of my new position. My attempt to do so proved a failure (the manuscript has since been lost). I was not much concerned about it then as I was intoxicated with the prospect of a new start. But I also realised that extensive research and many detours would be needed before I could hope to be inwardly in a position to correct the errors of *History and Class Consciousness* and to provide a scientific, Marxist account of the matters treated there. I have already mentioned one such detour: it lead from the study of Hegel via the projected work on economics and dialectics to my present attempt to work out an ontology of social being.

Parallel with this the desire arose in me to make use of my knowledge of literature, art and their theory to construct a Marxist aesthetics. This was the beginning of my collaboration with Mikhail Lifschitz. In the course of many discussions it became clear to us that even the best and most capable Marxists, like Plekhanov and Mehring, had not had a sufficiently profound grasp of the universal nature of Marxism. They failed, therefore, to understand that Marx confronts us with the necessity of erecting a systematic aesthetics on the foundations of dialectical materialism. This is not the place to describe Lifschitz' great achievements in the spheres of philosophy and philology. As far as I myself am concerned, I wrote an essay on the Sickingen debate between Marx/Engels and Lassalle.[13] In so doing the outlines of such a system became clearly visible, though naturally they were limited to a particular problem. After stubborn initial resistance, especially from the vulgar sociologists, this view has meanwhile gained widespread acceptance in Marxist circles. But it is not important to pursue the matter here any further. I would only point out that the general shift in my philosophical outlook that I have described became clearly apparent in my activities as a critic in Berlin from 1931 to 1933. For it was not just the problem of mimesis that occupied the forefront of my attention, but also the application of dialectics to the theory of reflection. This involved me in a critique of naturalistic tendencies. For all naturalism is based on the idea of the 'photographic' reflection of reality. The emphasis on the antithesis between realism and naturalism is absent from both bourgeois and vulgar-Marxist theories but is central to the dialectical theory of reflection and hence also to an aesthetics in the spirit of Marx.

Although these remarks do not belong here, strictly speaking, they were necessary to indicate the direction and the implications of the change brought about by my realisation that *History and Class Consciousness* was based on mistaken assumptions. It is these implications that give me the right to say that this was the point where my apprenticeship in Marxism and hence my whole youthful development came to an end.

All that remains is for me to offer some comments on my

notorious self-criticism of *History and Class Consciousness*. I must begin by confessing that having once discarded any of my works I remain indifferent to them for the whole of my life. A year after the publication of *The Soul and the Forms* (*Die Seele und die Formen*), for example, I wrote a letter of thanks to Margarethe Susmann for her review of the book. In it I observed that "both the book and its form had become quite alien to me". It had been the same with the *Theory of the Novel* and it was the same now in the case of *History and Class Consciousness*. I returned to the Soviet Union in 1933 with every prospect of frutful activity: the oppositional role of the magazine *Literaturni Kritik* on questions of literary theory in the years 1934–39 is well known. Tactically it was, however, necessary to distance myself publicly from *History and Class Consciousness* so that the real partisan warfare against official and semi-official theories of literature would not be impeded by counter-attacks in which my opponents would have been objectively in the right in my view, however narrow-minded they might otherwise be. Of course, in order to publish a self-criticism it was necessary to adopt the current official jargon. This is the only conformist element in the declaration I made at this time. It too was an entry-ticket to all further partisan warfare; the difference between this declaration and my earlier retraction of the Blum Theses is 'merely' that I sincerely did believe that *History and Class Consciousness* was mistaken and I think that to this day. When, later on, the errors enshrined in the book were converted into fashionable notions, I resisted the attempt to identify these with my own ideas and in this too I believe I was in the right. The four decades that have elapsed since the appearance of *History and Class Consciousness*, the changed situation in the struggle for a true Marxist method, my own production during this period, all these factors may perhaps justify my taking a less one-sided view now. It is not, of course, my task to establish how far particular, rightly-conceived tendencies in *History and Class Consciousness* really produced fruitful results in my own later activities and perhaps in those of others. That would be to raise a whole complex of questions whose resolution I may be allowed to leave to the judgement of history.

Budapest, March 1967.

NOTES

1 In *Georg Lukács zum siebzigsten Geburtstag*, Aufbau, Berlin, 1955; reprinted in G. Lukács, *Schriften zu Ideologie und Politik*, edited by P. Ludz, Luchterhand, Neuwied, 1967, pp. 323–9.

2 *Development of the Modern Drama*, 2 vols., Budapest, 1911 (in Hungarian).

3 Ibid. in German translation, 2nd Edition, Luchterhand, Neuwied, 1963, p. 5 and also the 3rd Edition, 1965.

4 *Theorien über den Mehrwert*, *II*, 1, Stuttgart, 1921, pp. 309 ff.

5 Lenin, *Werke*, Wien–Berlin, IV, II, pp. 216 ff.

6 Georg Lukács, *History and Class Consciousness*. See page 27 of this edition.

7 Ibid., see p. 1 of this edition.

8 Ibid., see p. 162 of this edition.

9 Ibid., see p. 159 of this edition.

10 Jószef Révai, *Literarische Studien*, Dietz, Berlin, 1926, p. 235.

11 Georg Lukács, *Lenin*, Luchterhand, Neuwied, 1967, pp. 87 ff.

12 Georg Lukács, *Der junge Hegel*, Works Vol. 8, Luchterhand, Neuwied 1967.

13 In *Internationale Literatur*, Vol. 3, No. 2, Moscow, 1933, pp. 95–126.

Preface

THE collection and publication of these essays in book form is not intended to give them a greater importance as a whole than would be due to each individually. For the most part they are attempts, arising out of actual work for the party, to clarify the theoretical problems of the revolutionary movement in the mind of the author and his readers. The exceptions to this are the two essays *Reification and the Consciousness of the Proletariat* and *Towards a Methodology of the Problem of Organisation* which were both written specially for this collection during a period of enforced leisure. They, too, are based on already existing occasional pieces. Although they have now been partly revised, no systematic attempt has been made to remove the traces of the particular circumstances in which they were written. In some cases a radical recasting of an essay would have meant destroying what I regard as its inner core of truth. Thus in the essay on *The Changing Function of Historical Materialism* we can still hear the echoes of those exaggeratedly sanguine hopes that many of us cherished concerning the duration and tempo of the revolution. The reader should not, therefore, look to these essays for a complete scientific system.

Despite this the book does have a definite unity. This will be found in the sequence of the essays, which for this reason are best read in the order proposed. However, it would perhaps be advisable for readers unversed in philosophy to put off the chapter on reification to the very end.

A few words of explanation—superfluous for many readers perhaps—are due for the prominence given in these pages to the presentation, interpretation and discussion of the theories of Rosa Luxemburg. On this point I would say, firstly, that Rosa Luxemburg, alone among Marx's disciples, has made a real advance on his life's work in both the content and method of his economic doctrines. She alone has found a way to apply them concretely to the present state of social development. Of course, in these pages, in pursuance of the task we have set ourselves, it is the methodological aspect of these questions that will be most heavily stressed. There will be no assessment of the economic content of the theory of accumulation, nor of Marx's economic theories as such: we shall confine our discussion to their methodological premisses and implications. It will in any case be obvious to the reader that the present writer upholds the validity of their content. Secondly, a detailed analysis of Rosa Luxemburg's thought is necessary because its seminal discoveries no less than its errors have had a decisive influence on the theories of Marxists outside Russia, above all in Germany. To some extent this influence persists to this day. For anyone whose interest was first aroused by these problems a truly revolutionary, Communist and Marxist position can be acquired only through a critical confrontation with the theoretical life's work of Rosa Luxemburg.

Once we take this path we discover that the writings and speeches of Lenin become crucial, *methodologically* speaking. It is not our intention to concern ourselves here with Lenin's political achievements. But just because our task is consciously one-sided and limited it is essential that we remind ourselves constantly of Lenin's importance *as a theoretician* for the development of Marxism. This has been obscured for many people by his overwhelming impact as a politician. The immediate practical importance of each of his utterances for the particular moment in which they are made is always so great as to blind some people to the fact that, in the last resort, he is only so effective in practice because of his greatness, profundity and fertility as a theoretician. His effectiveness rests on the fact that he has developed the *practical essence* of Marxism to a pitch of clarity and concreteness never before achieved. He has rescued this aspect of Marxism from an almost total oblivion and by virtue of this *theoretical action* he has once again placed in our hands the key to a right understanding of Marxist method.

For it is our task—and this is the fundamental conviction underlying this book—to understand the essence of Marx's method and to apply it correctly. In no sense do we aspire to 'improve' on it. If on a number of occasions certain statements of Engels' are made the object of a polemical attack this has been done, as every perceptive reader will observe, in the spirit of the system as a whole. On these particular points the author believes, rightly or wrongly, that he is defending orthodox Marxism against Engels himself.

We adhere to Marx's doctrines, then, without making any

attempt to diverge from them, to improve or correct them. The goal of these arguments is an *interpretation*, an exposition of Marx's theory *as Marx understood it*. But this 'orthodoxy' does not in the least strive to preserve what Mr. von Struve calls the 'aesthetic integrity' of Marx's system. On the contrary, our underlying premise here is the belief that in Marx's theory and method the *true method* by which to understand society and history has *finally* been discovered. This method is historical through and through. It is self-evident, therefore, that it must be constantly applied to itself, and this is one of the focal points of these essays. At the same time this entails taking up a substantive position with regard to the urgent problems of the present; for according to this view of Marxist method its pre-eminent aim is *knowledge of the present*. Our preoccupation with methodology in these essays has left little space for an analysis of the concrete problems of the present. For this reason the author would like to take this opportunity to state unequivocally that in his view the experiences of the years of revolution have provided a magnificent confirmation of all the essential aspects of orthodox (i.e. Communist) Marxism. The war, the crisis and the Revolution, not excluding the so-called slower tempo in the development of the Revolution and the new economic policy of Soviet Russia have not thrown up a single problem that cannot be solved by the dialectical method—and by that method *alone*. The concrete answers to particular practical problems lie outside the framework of these essays. The task they propose is to make us aware of Marxist method, to throw light on it as an unendingly fertile source of solutions to otherwise intractable dilemmas.

This is also the purpose of the copious quotations from the works of Marx and Engels. Some readers may indeed find them all too plentiful. But every quotation is also an interpretation. And it seems to the present writer that many very relevant aspects of the Marxist method have been unduly neglected, above all those which are indispensable for understanding the coherent structure of that method from the point of view of logic as well as content. As a consequence it has become difficult, if not almost impossible, to understand the life nerve of that method, namely the dialectic.

We cannot do justice to the concrete, historical dialectic without considering in some detail the founder of this method, Hegel, and his relation to Marx. Marx's warning not to treat Hegel as a 'dead dog' has gone unheeded even by many good

Marxists. (The efforts of Engels and Plekhanov have also been all too ineffectual.) Yet Marx frequently drew attention to this danger. Thus he wrote of Dietzgen: "It is his bad luck that he managed *not* to study Hegel." (Letter to Engels, 7.11.1868.) And in another letter (dated 11.1.1868) we read: "The gentlemen in Germany . . . think that Hegel's dialectic is a 'dead dog'. In this respect Feuerbach has much on his conscience." In a letter dated 14 January, 1858 he lays emphasis on the 'great benefits' he has derived for his method of procedure with the *Critique of Political Economy* from his rereading of Hegel's *Logic*. But we are not here concerned with the philological side of the relation between Marx and Hegel. Marx's view of the importance of Hegel's dialectic is of lesser moment here than the substantive significance of this method for Marxism. These statements which could be multiplied at will were quoted only because this significance had been underestimated even by Marxists. Too much reliance has been placed on the well-known passage in the preface to *Capital* which contains Marx's last public statement on the matter. I am referring here not to his account of the real content of their relationship, with which I am in complete agreement and which I have tried to spell out systematically in these pages. I am thinking exclusively of the phrase which talks of 'flirting' with Hegel's 'mode of expression'. This has frequently misled people into believing that for Marx the dialectic was no more than a superficial stylistic ornament and that in the interests of 'scientific precision' all traces of it should be eradicated systematically from the method of historical materialism. Even otherwise conscientious scholars like Professor Vorländer, for example, believed that they could prove that Marx had 'flirted' with Hegelian concepts 'in only two places', and then again in a 'third place'. Yet they failed to notice that a whole series of *categories of central importance and in constant use* stem *directly* from Hegel's *Logic*. We need only recall the Hegelian origin and the substantive and methodological importance of what is for Marx as fundamental a distinction as the one between immediacy and mediation. If this could go *unnoticed* then it must be just as true even today that Hegel is still treated as a 'dead dog', and this despite the fact that in the universities he has once again become *persona grata* and even fashionable. What would Professor Vorländer say if a historian of philosophy contrived *not to notice* in the works of a successor of Kant, however critical and original, that the 'synthetic unity of apperception', to take but one instance, was derived from the *Critique of Pure Reason*?

The author of these pages wishes to break with such views. He believes that today it is of *practical* importance to return in this respect to the traditions of Marx-interpretation founded by Engels (who regarded the 'German workers' movement' as the 'heir to classical German philosophy'), and by Plekhanov. He believes that all good Marxists should form, in Lenin's words "a kind of society of the materialist friends of the Hegelian dialectic".

But Hegel's position today is the reverse of Marx's own. The problem with Marx is precisely to take his method and his system *as we find them* and to demonstrate that they *form a coherent unity that must be preserved*. The opposite is true of Hegel. The task he imposes is to separate out from the complex web of ideas with its sometimes glaring contradictions all the *seminal elements* of his thought and rescue them *as a vital intellectual force for the present*. He is a more profitable and potent thinker than many people imagine. And as I see it, the more vigorously we set about the task of confronting this issue the more clearly we will discern his fecundity and his power as a thinker. But for this we must add (and it is a scandal that we should have to add it) that a greater knowledge of Hegel's writings is utterly indispensable. Of course we will no longer expect to discover his achievement in his total system. The system as we have it belongs to the past. Even this statement concedes too much for, in my view, a really incisive critic would have to conclude that he had to deal, not with an authentically organic and coherent system, but with a number of overlapping systems. The contradictions in method between the *Phenomenology* and the system itself are but one instance of this. Hegel must not be treated as a 'dead dog', but even so we must demolish the 'dead' architecture of the system in its historical form and release the extremely relevant and modern sides of his thought and help them once again to become a vital and effective force in the present.

It is common knowledge that Marx himself conceived this idea of writing a dialectics. "The true laws of dialectics are already to be found in Hegel, albeit in a mystical form. What is needed is to strip them of that form," he wrote to Dietzgen. I hope it is not necessary to emphasise that it is not my intention in these pages to propose even the sketchiest outline of a system of dialectics. My aim is to stimulate *discussion* and, as it were, to put the issue back on the agenda from the point of view of method. Hence, at every opportunity attention has been drawn as concretely as possible both to those points at which Hegelian categories have proved decisive for historical materialism and also to those places where Hegel and Marx part company. In this way it is to be hoped that material and, where possible, direction has been provided for the very necessary discussion of this problem. These considerations have also determined in part the detailed account of classical philosophy in Section II of the chapter on reification. (But only in part. For it seemed to me equally essential to examine the contradictions of bourgeois thought at the point where that thought received its highest philosophical expression.)

Discussions of the kind contained in these pages have the inevitable defect that they fail to fulfil the—justifiable—demand for a completely systematic theory, without offering any compensation in the way of popularity. I am only too aware of this failing. This account of the genesis and aim of these essays is offered less as an apology than as a stimulus—and this is the true aim of this work—to make the problem of dialectical method the focus of discussion as an urgent living problem. If these essays provide the beginning or even just the occasion for a genuinely profitable discussion of dialectical method, if they succeed in making dialectics generally known again, they will have fulfilled their function perfectly.

While dwelling on such shortcomings I should perhaps point out to the reader unfamiliar with dialectics one difficulty inherent in the nature of dialectical method relating to the definition of concepts and terminology. It is of the essence of dialectical method that concepts which are false in their abstract one-sidedness are later transcended (zur Aufhebung gelangen). The process of transcendence makes it inevitable that we should operate with these one-sided, abstract and false concepts. These concepts acquire their true meaning less by definition than by their function as aspects that are then transcended in the totality. Moreover, it is even more difficult to establish fixed meanings for concepts in Marx's improved version of the dialectic than in the Hegelian original. For if concepts are only the intellectual forms of historical realities then these forms, one-sided, abstract and false as they are, belong to the true unity as genuine aspects of it. Hegel's statements about this problem of terminology in the preface to the *Phenomenology* are thus even more true than Hegel himself realised when he said: "Just as the expressions 'unity of subject and object', of 'finite and infinite', of 'being and thought', etc., have the drawback that 'object' and 'subject' bear the same meaning as when *they exist outside that unity,* so that within the unity they mean something other than is implied by their expression: so, too, falsehood is not, *qua* false, any longer a moment of truth." In the pure historicisation of the dialectic this statement receives yet another twist: in so far as the 'false' is an aspect of the 'true' it is both 'false' and 'non-false'. When the professional demolishers of Marx criticise his 'lack of conceptual rigour' and his use of 'image' rather than 'definitions', etc., they cut as sorry a figure as did Schopenhauer when he tried to expose Hegel's 'logical howlers' in his Hegel critique. All that is proved is their total inability to grasp even the ABC of the dialectical method. The logical conclusion for the dialectician to draw from this failure is not that he is faced with a conflict between different scientific methods, but that he is in the presence of a *social phenomenon* and that by conceiving it as a socio-historical phenomenon he can at once refute it and transcend it dialectically.

Vienna, Christmas 1922.

What is Orthodox Marxism?

> The philosophers have only *interpreted* the
> world in various ways; the point, however,
> is to *change* it.
>
> Marx: *Theses on Feuerbach.*

THIS question, simple as it is, has been the focus of much discussion in both proletarian and bourgeois circles. But among intellectuals it has gradually become fashionable to greet any profession of faith in Marxism with ironical disdain. Great disunity has prevailed even in the 'socialist' camp as to what constitutes the essence of Marxism, and which theses it is 'permissible' to criticise and even reject without forfeiting the right to the title of 'Marxist'. In consequence it came to be thought increasingly 'unscientific' to make scholastic exegeses of old texts with a quasi-Biblical status, instead of fostering an 'impartial' study of the 'facts'. These texts, it was argued, had long been 'superseded' by modern criticism and they should no longer be regarded as the sole fount of truth.

If the question were really to be formulated in terms of such a crude antithesis it would deserve at best a pitying smile. But in fact it is not (and never has been) quite so straightforward. Let us assume for the sake of argument that recent research had disproved once and for all every one of Marx's individual theses. Even if this were to be proved, every serious 'orthodox' Marxist would still be able to accept all such modern findings without reservation and hence dismiss all of Marx's theses *in toto*—without having to renounce his orthodoxy for a single moment. Orthodox Marxism, therefore, does not imply the uncritical acceptance of the results of Marx's investigations. It is not the 'belief' in this or that thesis, nor the exegesis of a 'sacred' book. On the contrary, orthodoxy refers exclusively to *method*. It is the scientific conviction that dialectical materialism is the road to truth and that its methods can be developed, expanded and deepened only along the lines laid down by its founders. It is the conviction, moreover, that all attempts to surpass or 'improve' it have led and must lead to over-simplification, triviality and eclecticism.

1

1

Materialist dialectic is a revolutionary dialectic. This definition is so important and altogether so crucial for an understanding of its nature that if the problem is to be approached in the right way this must be fully grasped before we venture upon a discussion of the dialectical method itself. The issue turns on the question of theory and practice. And this not merely in the sense given it by Marx when he says in his first critique of Hegel that "theory becomes a material force when it grips the masses".[1] Even more to the point is the need to discover those features and definitions both of the theory and the ways of gripping the masses which convert the theory, the dialectical method, into a vehicle of revolution. We must extract the practical essence of the theory from the method and its relation to its object. If this is not done that 'gripping the masses' could well turn out to be a will o' the wisp. It might turn out that the masses were in the grip of quite different forces, that they were in pursuit of quite different ends. In that event, there would be no necessary connection between the theory and their activity, it would be a form that enables the masses to become conscious of their socially necessary or fortuitous actions, without ensuring a genuine and necessary bond between consciousness and action.

In the same essay[2] Marx clearly defined the conditions in which a relation between theory and practice becomes possible. "It is not enough that thought should seek to realise itself; reality must also strive towards thought." Or, as he expresses it in an earlier work:[3] "It will then be realised that the world has long since possessed something in the form of a dream which it need only take possession of consciously, in order to possess it in reality." Only when consciousness stands in such a relation to reality can theory and practice be united. But for this to happen the emergence of consciousness must become the *decisive step* which the historical process must take towards its proper end (an end constituted by the wills of men, but neither dependent on human whim, nor the product of human invention). The historical function of theory is to make this step a practical possibility. Only when a historical situation has arisen in which a class must understand society if it is to assert itself; only when the fact that a class understands itself means that it understands society as a whole and when, in consequence, the class becomes both the subject and the object of knowledge; in short, only when these conditions are all satisfied will the unity of theory and practice, the precondition of the revolutionary function of the theory, become possible.

Such a situation has in fact arisen with the entry of the proletariat into history. "When the proletariat proclaims the dissolution of the existing social order," Marx declares, "it does no more than disclose the secret of its own existence, for it is the effective dissolution of that order." [4] The links between the theory that affirms this and the revolution are not just arbitrary, nor are they particularly tortuous or open to misunderstanding. On the contrary, the theory is essentially the intellectual expression of the revolutionary process itself. In it every stage of the process becomes fixed so that it may be generalised, communicated, utilised and developed. Because the theory does nothing but arrest and make conscious each necessary step, it becomes at the same time the necessary premise of the following one.

To be clear about the function of theory is also to understand its own basis, i.e. dialectical method. This point is absolutely crucial, and because it has been overlooked much confusion has been introduced into discussions of dialectics. Engels' arguments in the *Anti-Dühring* decisively influenced the later life of the theory. However we regard them, whether we grant them classical status or whether we criticise them, deem them to be incomplete or even flawed, we must still agree that this aspect is nowhere treated in them. That is to say, he contrasts the ways in which concepts are formed in dialectics as opposed to 'metaphysics'; he stresses the fact that in dialectics the definite contours of concepts (and the objects they represent) are dissolved. Dialectics, he argues, is a continuous process of transition from one definition into the other. In consequence a one-sided and rigid causality must be replaced by interaction. But he does not even mention the most vital interaction, namely the *dialectical relation between subject and object in the historical process*, let alone give it the prominence it deserves. Yet without this factor dialectics ceases to be revolutionary, despite attempts (illusory in the last analysis) to retain 'fluid' concepts. For it implies a failure to recognise that in all metaphysics the object remains untouched and unaltered so that thought remains contemplative and fails to become practical; while for the dialectical method the central problem is *to change reality*.

If this central function of the theory is disregarded, the virtues of forming 'fluid' concepts become altogether problematic: a purely 'scientific' matter. The theory might then be accepted or rejected in accordance with the prevailing state of science without any modification at all to one's basic attitudes, to the question of whether or not reality can be changed. Indeed, as the so-called Machists among Marx's supporters have demonstrated, it even reinforces the view that reality with its 'obedience to laws', in the sense used by bourgeois, contemplative materialism and the classical economics with which it is so closely bound up, is impenetrable, fatalistic and immutable. That Machism can also give birth to an equally bourgeois voluntarism does not contradict this. Fatalism and voluntarism are only mutually contradictory to an undialectical and unhistorical mind. In the dialectical view of history they prove to be necessarily complementary opposites, intellectual reflexes clearly expressing the antagonisms of capitalist society and the intractability of its problems when conceived in its own terms.

For this reason all attempts to deepen the dialectical method with the aid of 'criticism' inevitably lead to a more superficial view. For 'criticism' always starts with just this separation between method and reality, between thought and being. And it is just this separation that it holds to be an improvement deserving of every praise for its introduction of true scientific rigour into the crude, uncritical materialism of the Marxian method. Of course, no one denies the right of 'criticism' to do this. But if it does so we must insist that it will be moving counter to the essential spirit of dialectics.

The statements of Marx and Engels on this point could hardly be more explicit. "Dialectics thereby reduced itself to the science of the general laws of motion—both in the external world and in the thought of man—two sets of laws which are identical *in substance*" (Engels).[5] Marx formulated it even more precisely. "In the study of economic categories, as in the case of every historical and social science, it must be borne in mind that . . . *the categories are therefore but forms of being, conditions of existence. . . .*"[6] If this meaning of dialectical method is obscured, dialectics must inevitably begin to look like a superfluous additive, a mere ornament of Marxist 'sociology' or 'economics'. Even worse, it will appear as an obstacle to the 'sober', 'impartial' study of the 'facts', as an empty construct in whose name Marxism does violence to the facts.

This objection to dialectical method has been voiced most clearly and cogently by Bernstein, thanks in part to a 'freedom from bias' unclouded by any philosophical knowledge. However, the very real political and economic conclusions he deduces from this desire to liberate method from the 'dialectical snares' of Hegelianism, show clearly where this course leads. They show that it is precisely the dialectic that must be removed if one wishes to found a thoroughgoing opportunistic theory, a theory of 'evolution' without revolution and of 'natural development' into Socialism without any conflict.

2

We are now faced with the question of the methodological implications of these so-called facts that are idolised throughout the whole of Revisionist literature. To what extent may we look to them to provide guide-lines for the actions of the revolutionary proletariat? It goes without saying that all knowledge starts from the facts. The only question is: which of the data of life are relevant to knowledge and in the context of which method?

The blinkered empiricist will of course deny that facts can only become facts within the framework of a system—which will vary with the knowledge desired. He believes that every piece of data from economic life, every statistic, every raw event already constitutes an important fact. In so doing he forgets that however simple an enumeration of 'facts' may be, however lacking in commentary, it already implies an 'interpretation'. Already at this stage the facts have been comprehended by a theory, a method; they have been wrenched from their living context and fitted into a theory.

More sophisticated opportunists would readily grant this despite their profound and instinctive dislike of all theory. They seek refuge in the methods of natural science, in the way in which science distills 'pure' facts and places them in the relevant contexts by means of observation, abstraction and experiment. They then oppose this ideal model of knowledge to the forced constructions of the dialectical method.

If such methods seem plausible at first this is because capitalism tends to produce a social structure that in great measure encourages such views. But for that very reason we need the dialectical method to puncture the social illusion so produced and help us to glimpse the reality underlying it. The 'pure' facts of the natural sciences arise when a phenomenon of the real world is placed (in thought or in reality) into an environment where its laws can be inspected without outside interference. This process is reinforced by reducing the phenomena to their purely quantitative essence, to their expression in numbers and numerical relations. Opportunists always fail to recognise that it is in the nature of capitalism to process phenomena in this way. Marx gives an incisive account[7] of such a 'process of abstraction' in the case of labour, but he does not omit to point out with equal vigour that he is dealing with a *historical* peculiarity of capitalist society. "Thus the most general abstractions commonly appear where there is the highest concrete development, where one feature appears to be shared by many, and to be common to all. Then it cannot be thought of any longer in one particular form."

But this tendency in capitalism goes even further. The fetishistic character of economic forms, the reification of all human relations, the constant expansion and extension of the division of labour which subjects the process of production to an abstract, rational analysis, without regard to the human potentialities and abilities of the immediate producers, all these things transform the phenomena of society and with them the way in which they are perceived. In this way arise the 'isolated' facts, 'isolated' complexes of facts, separate, specialist disciplines (economics, law, etc.) whose very appearance seems to have done much to pave the way for such scientific methods. It thus appears extraordinarily 'scientific' to think out the tendencies implicit in the facts themselves and to promote this activity to the status of science.

By contrast, in the teeth of all these isolated and isolating facts and partial systems, dialectics insists on the concrete unity of the whole. Yet although it exposes these appearances for the illusions they are—albeit illusions necessarily engendered by capitalism—in this 'scientific' atmosphere it still gives the impression of being an arbitrary construction.

The unscientific nature of this seemingly so scientific method consists, then, in its failure to see and take account of the *historical character* of the facts on which it is based. This is the source of more than one error (constantly overlooked by the practitioners of the method) to which Engels has explicitly drawn attention.[8] The nature of this source of error is that statistics and the 'exact' economic theory based upon them always lag behind actual developments. "For this reason, it is only too often necessary in current history, to treat this, the most decisive factor, as constant, and the economic situation existing at the beginning of the period concerned as given and unalterable for the whole period, or else to take notice of only those changes in the situation as arise out of the patently manifest events themselves and are therefore, likewise, patently manifest."

Thus we perceive that there is something highly problematic in the fact that capitalist society is predisposed to harmonise with scientific method, to constitute indeed the social premises of its exactness. If the internal structure of the 'facts' of their interconnections is essentially historical, if, that is to say, they are caught up in a process of continuous transformation, then we may indeed question when the greater scientific inaccuracy occurs. It is when I conceive of the 'facts' as existing in a form and as subject to laws concerning which I have a methodological certainty (or at least probability) that they no longer apply to these facts? Or is it when I consciously take this situation into account, cast a critical eye at the 'exactitude' attainable by such a method and concentrate instead on those points where this *historical* aspect, this decisive fact of change really manifests itself?

The historical character of the 'facts' which science seems to have grasped with such 'purity' makes itself felt in an even more devastating manner. As the products of historical evolution they are involved in continuous change. But in addition they are also *precisely in their objective structure the products of a definite historical epoch, namely capitalism.* Thus when 'science' maintains that the manner in which data immediately present themselves is an adequate foundation of scientific conceptualisation and that the actual form of these data is the appropriate starting point for the formation of scientific concepts, it thereby takes its stand simply and dogmatically on the basis of capitalist society. It uncritically accepts the nature of the object as it is given and the laws of that society as the unalterable foundation of 'science'.

In order to progress from these 'facts' to facts in the true meaning of the word it is necessary to perceive their historical conditioning as such and to abandon the point of view that would see them as immediately given: they must themselves be subjected to a historical and dialectical examination. For as Marx says:[9] "The finished pattern of economic relations as seen on the surface in their real existence and consequently in the ideas with which the agents and bearers of these relations seek to understand them, is very different from, and indeed quite the reverse of and antagonistic to their inner, essential but concealed core and the concepts corresponding to it."

If the facts are to be understood, this distinction between their real existence and their inner core must be grasped clearly and precisely. This distinction is the first premise of a truly scientific study which in Marx's words, "would be superfluous if the outward appearance of things coincided with their essence".[10] Thus we must detach the phenomena from the form in which they are immediately given and discover the intervening links which connect them to their core, their essence. In so doing, we shall arrive at an understanding of their apparent form and see it as the form in which the inner core necessarily appears. It is necessary because of the historical character of the facts, because they have grown in the soil of capitalist society. This twofold character, the simultaneous recognition and transcendence of immediate appearances is precisely the dialectical nexus.

In this respect, superficial readers imprisoned in the modes of thought created by capitalism, experienced the gravest difficulties in comprehending the structure of thought in *Capital*. For on the one hand, Marx's account pushes the capitalist nature of all economic forms to their furthest limits, he creates an intellectual milieu where they can exist in their purest form by positing a society 'corresponding to the theory', i.e. capitalist through and through, consisting of none but capitalists and proletarians. But conversely, no sooner does this strategy produce results, no sooner does this world of phenomena seem to be on the point of crystallising out into theory than it dissolves into a mere illusion, a distorted situation appears as in a distorting mirror which is, however, "only the conscious expression of an imaginary movement".

Only in this context which sees the isolated facts of social life as aspects of the historical process and integrates them in a *totality*, can knowledge of the facts hope to become knowledge of *reality*. This knowledge starts from the simple (and to the capitalist world), pure, immediate, natural determinants described above. It progresses from them to the knowledge of the concrete totality, i.e. to the conceptual reproduction of reality. This concrete totality is by no means an unmediated datum for thought.

"The concrete is concrete," Marx says,[11] "because it is a synthesis of many particular determinants, i.e. a unity of diverse elements."

Idealism succumbs here to the delusion of confusing the intellectual reproduction of reality with the actual structure of reality itself. For "in thought, reality appears as the process of synthesis, not as starting-point, but as outcome, although it is the real starting-point and hence the starting-point for perception and ideas."

Conversely, the vulgar materialists, even in the modern guise donned by Bernstein and others, do not go beyond the reproduction of the immediate, simple determinants of social life. They imagine that they are being quite extraordinarily 'exact' when they simply take over these determinants without either analysing them further or welding them into a concrete totality. They take the facts in abstract isolation, explaining them only in terms of abstract laws unrelated to the concrete totality. As Marx observes: "Crudeness and conceptual nullity consist in the tendency to forge arbitrary unmediated connections between things that belong together in an organic union."[12]

The crudeness and conceptual nullity of such thought lies primarily in the fact that it obscures the historical, transitory nature of capitalist society. Its determinants take on the appearance of timeless, eternal categories valid for all social formations. This could be seen at its crassest in the vulgar bourgeois economists, but the vulgar Marxists soon followed in their footsteps. The dialectical method was overthrown and with it the methodological supremacy of the totality over the individual aspects; the parts were prevented from finding their definition within the whole and, instead, the whole was dismissed as unscientific or else it degenerated into the mere 'idea' or 'sum' of the parts. With the totality out of the way, the fetishistic relations of the isolated parts appeared as a timeless law valid for every human society.

Marx's dictum: "The relations of production of every society form a whole"[13] is the methodological point of departure and the key to the *historical* understanding of social relations. All the isolated partial categories can be thought of and treated—in isolation—as something that is always present in every society. (If it cannot be found in a given society this is put down to 'chance' as the exception that proves the rule.) But the changes to which these individual aspects are subject give no clear and unambiguous picture of the real differences in the various stages of the evolution of society. These can really only be discerned in the context of the total historical process of their relation to society as a whole.

3

This dialectical conception of totality seems to have put a great distance between itself and reality, it appears to construct reality very 'unscientifically'. But it is the only method capable of understanding and reproducing reality. Concrete totality is, therefore, the category that governs reality.[14] The rightness of this view only emerges with complete clarity when we direct our attention to the real, material substratum of our method, viz. capitalist society with its internal antagonism between the forces and the relations of production. The methodology of the natural sciences which forms the methodological ideal of every fetishistic science and every kind of Revisionism rejects the idea of contradiction and antagonism in its subject matter. If, despite this, contradictions do spring up between particular theories, this only proves that our knowledge is as yet imperfect. Contradictions between theories show that these theories have reached their natural limits; they must therefore be transformed and subsumed under even wider theories in which the contradictions finally disappear.

But we maintain that in the case of social reality these contradictions are not a sign of the imperfect understanding of society; on the contrary, they belong to *the nature of reality itself and to the nature of capitalism*. When the totality is known they will not be transcended and *cease* to be contradictions. Quite the reverse, they will be seen to be necessary contradictions arising out of the antagonisms of this system of production. When theory (as the knowledge of the whole) opens up the way to resolving these contradictions it does so by revealing the *real tendencies* of social evolution. For these are destined to effect a *real* resolution of the contradictions that have emerged in the course of history.

From this angle we see that the conflict between the dialectical method and that of 'criticism' (or vulgar materialism, Machism, etc.) is a social problem. When the ideal of scientific knowledge is applied to nature it simply furthers the progress of science. But when it is applied to society it turns out to be an ideological weapon of the bourgeoisie. For the latter it is a matter of life and death to understand its own system of production in terms of eternally valid categories: it must think of capitalism as being predestined to eternal survival by the eternal laws of nature and reason. Conversely, contradictions that cannot be ignored must be shown to be purely surface phenomena, unrelated to this mode of production.

The method of classical economics was a product of this ideological need. But also its limitations as a science are a consequence of the structure of capitalist reality and the antagonistic character of capitalist production. When, for example, a thinker of Ricardo's stature can deny the "necessity of expanding the market along with the expansion of production and the growth of capital", he does so (unconsciously of course), to avoid the necessity of admitting that crises are inevitable. For crises are the most striking illustration of the antagonisms in capitalist production and it is evident that "the bourgeois mode of production implies a limitation to the free development of the forces of production".[15]

What was good faith in Ricardo became a consciously misleading apologia of bourgeois society in the writings of the vulgar economists. The vulgar Marxists arrived at the same results by seeking either the thorough-going elimination of dialectics from proletarian science, or at best its 'critical' refinement.

To give a grotesque illustration, Max Adler wished to make a critical distinction between dialectics as method, as the movement of thought on the one hand and the dialectics of being, as metaphysics on the other. His 'criticism' culminates in the sharp separation of dialectics from both and he describes it as a "piece of positive science" which "is what is chiefly meant by talk of real dialectics in Marxism". This dialectic might more aptly be called 'antagonism', for it simply "asserts that an opposition exists between the self-interest of an individual and the social forms in which he is confined".[16] By this stroke the objective economic antagonism as expressed in the *class struggle* evaporates, leaving only a conflict between the *individual and society*. This means that neither the emergence of internal problems, nor the collapse of capitalist society, can be seen to be necessary. The end-product, whether he likes it or not, is a Kantian philosophy of history. Moreover, the structure of bourgeois society is established as the universal form of society in general. For the central problem Max Adler tackles, of the real "dialectics or, better, antagonism" is nothing but one of the typical ideological forms of the capitalist social order. But whether capitalism is rendered immortal on economic or on ideological grounds, whether with naïve nonchalance, or with critical refinement is of little importance.

Thus with the rejection or blurring of the dialectical method history becomes unknowable. This does not imply that a more or less exact account of particular people or epochs cannot be given without the aid of dialectics. But it does put paid to attempts to understand history *as a unified process*. (This can be seen in the sociologically abstract, historical constructs of the type of Spencer and Comte whose inner contradictions have been convincingly exposed by modern bourgeois historians, most incisively by Rickert. But it also shows itself in the demand for a 'philosophy of history' which then turns out to have a quite inscrutable relationship to historical reality.) The opposition between the description of an aspect of history and the description of history as a unified process is not just a problem of scope, as in the distinction between particular and universal history. It is rather a conflict of method, of approach. Whatever the epoch or special topic of study, the question of a unified approach to the process of history is inescapable. It is here that the crucial importance of the dialectical view of totality reveals itself. For it is perfectly possible for someone to describe the essentials of an historical event and yet be in the dark about the real nature of that event and of its function in the historical totality, i.e. without understanding it as part of a unified historical process.

A typical example of this can be seen in Sismondi's treatment of the question of crisis.[17] He understood the immanent tendencies in the processes of production and distribution. But ultimately he failed because, for all his incisive criticism of capitalism, he remained imprisoned in capitalist notions of the objective and so necessarily thought of production and distribution as two independent processes, "not realising that the relations of distribution are only the relations of production *sub alia specia*". He thus succumbs to the same fate that overtook Proudhon's false dialectics; "he converts the various limbs of society into so many independent societies".[18]

We repeat: the category of totality does not reduce its various elements to an undifferentiated uniformity, to identity. The apparent independence and autonomy which they possess in the capitalist system of production is an illusion only in so far as they are involved in a dynamic dialectical relationship with one another and can be thought of as the dynamic dialectical aspects of an equally dynamic and dialectical whole. "The result we arrive at," says Marx, "is not that production, distribution, exchange and consumption are identical, but that they are all members of one totality, different aspects of a unit. . . . Thus a definite form of production determines definite forms of consumption, distribution and exchange as well as *definite relations between these different elements*. . . . A mutual interaction takes place between these various elements. This is the case with every organic body."[19]

But even the category of interaction requires inspection. If by interaction we mean just the reciprocal causal impact of two otherwise unchangeable objects on each other, we shall not have come an inch nearer to an understanding of society. This is the case with the vulgar materialists with their one-way causal sequences (or the Machists with their functional relations). After all, there is e.g. an interaction when a stationary billiard ball is struck by a moving one: the first one moves, the second one is deflected from its original path. The interaction we have in mind must be more than the interaction of *otherwise unchanging objects*. It must go further in its relation to the whole: for this relation determines the objective form of every object of cognition. Every substantial change that is of concern to knowledge manifests itself as a change in relation to the whole and through this as a change in the form of objectivity itself.[20] Marx has formulated this idea in countless places. I shall cite only one of the best-known passages:[21] "A negro is a negro. He only becomes a slave in certain circumstances. A cotton-spinning jenny is a machine for spinning cotton. Only in certain circumstances does it become capital. Torn from those circumstances it is no more capital than gold is money or sugar the price of sugar."

Thus the objective forms of all social phenomena change constantly in the course of their ceaseless dialectical interactions with each other. The intelligibility of objects develops in proportion as we grasp their function in the totality to which they belong. This is why only the dialectical conception of totality can enable us to understand *reality as a social process*. For only this conception dissolves the fetishistic forms necessarily produced by the capitalist mode of production and enables us to see them as mere illusions which are not less illusory for being seen to be necessary. These unmediated concepts, these 'laws' sprout just as inevitably from the soil of capitalism and veil the real relations between objects.

They can all be seen as ideas necessarily held by the agents of the capitalist system of production. They are, therefore, objects of knowledge, but the object which is known through them is not the capitalist system of production itself, but the ideology of its ruling class.

Only when this veil is torn aside does historical knowledge become possible. For the function of these unmediated concepts that have been derived from the fetishistic forms of objectivity is to make the phenomena of capitalist society appear as suprahistorical essences. The knowledge of the real, objective nature of a phenomenon, the knowledge of its historical character and the knowledge of its actual function in the totality of society form, therefore, a single, undivided act of cognition. This unity is shattered by the pseudo-scientific method. Thus only through the dialectical method could the distinction between constant and variable capital, crucial to economics, be understood. Classical economics was unable to go beyond the distinction between fixed and circulating capital. This was not accidental. For "variable capital is only a particular historical manifestation of the fund for providing the necessaries of life, or the labour-fund which the labourer requires for the maintenance of himself and his family, and which whatever be the system of social production, he must himself produce and reproduce. If the labour-fund constantly flows to him in the form of money that pays for his labour, it is because the product he has created moves constantly away from him in the form of capital. . . . The transaction is veiled by the fact that the product appears as a commodity and the commodity as money." [22]

The fetishistic illusions enveloping all phenomena in capitalist society succeed in concealing reality, but more is concealed than the historical, i.e. transitory, ephemeral nature of phenomena. *This* concealment is made possible by the fact that in capitalist society man's environment, and especially the categories of economics, appear to him immediately and necessarily in forms of objectivity which conceal the fact that they are the categories of the *relations of men with each other*. Instead they appear as things and the relations of things with each other. Therefore, when the dialectical method destroys the fiction of the immortality of the categories it also destroys their reified character and clears the way to a knowledge of reality. According to Engels in his discussion of Marx's *Critique of Political Economy*, "economics does not treat of things, but of the relations between persons and, in the last analysis, between classes; however, these relations are always *bound to things* and *appear as things*." [23]

It is by virtue of this insight that the dialectical method and its concept of totality can be seen to provide real knowledge of what goes on in society. It might appear as if the dialectic relations between parts and whole were no more than a construct of thought as remote from the true categories of social reality as the unmediated formulae of bourgeois economics. If so, the superiority of dialectics would be purely methodological. The real difference, however, is deeper and more fundamental.

At every stage of social evolution each economic category reveals a definite relation between men. This relation becomes conscious and is conceptualised. Because of this the inner logic of the movement of human society can be understood at once as the product of men themselves and of forces that arise from their relations with each other and which have escaped their control. Thus the economic categories become dynamic and dialectical in a double sense. As 'pure' economic categories they are involved in constant interaction with each other, and that enables us to understand any given historical cross-section through the evolution of society. But since they have arisen out of human relations and since they function in the process of the transformation of human relations, the actual process of social evolution becomes visible in their reciprocal relationship with the reality underlying their activity. That is to say, the production and reproduction of a particular *economic* totality, which science hopes to understand, is necessarily transformed into the process of production and reproduction of a particular *social* totality; in the course of this transformation, 'pure' economics are naturally transcended, though this does not mean that we must appeal to any transcendental forces. Marx often insisted upon this aspect of dialectics. For instance:[24] "Capitalist production, therefore, under its aspect of a continuous connected process or as a process of reproduction produces not only commodities, not only surplus value, but it also produces and reproduces the capitalist relation itself, on the one hand the capitalist and on the other, the labourer."

4

To posit oneself, to produce and reproduce oneself—that is

reality. Hegel clearly perceived this and expressed it in a way closely similar to that of Marx, albeit cloaked in abstraction and misunderstanding itself and thus opening the way to further misunderstanding. "What is actual is necessary in itself," he says in the *Philosophy of Right.* "Necessity consists in this that the whole is sundered into the different concepts and that this divided whole yields a fixed and permanent determinacy. However, this is not a fossilised determinacy but one which permanently recreates itself in its dissolution." [25] The deep affinities between historical materialism and Hegel's philosophy are clearly manifested here, for both conceive of theory as the *self-knowledge of reality.* Nevertheless, we must briefly point to the crucial difference between them. This is likewise located in the problem of reality and of the unity of the historical process.

Marx reproached Hegel (and, in even stronger terms, Hegel's successors who had reverted to Kant and Fichte) with his failure to overcome the duality of thought and being, of theory and practice, of subject and object. He maintained that Hegel's dialectic, which purported to be an inner, real dialectic of the historical process, was a mere illusion: in the crucial point he failed to go beyond Kant. His knowledge is no more than knowledge *about* an essentially alien material. It was not the case that this material, human society, came to know itself. As he remarks in the decisive sentences of his critique,[26] "Already with Hegel, the absolute spirit of history has its material in the masses, but only finds adequate expression in philosophy. But the philosopher appears merely as the instrument by which absolute spirit, which makes history, arrives at self-consciousness after the historical movement has been completed. The philosopher's role in history is thus limited to this subsequent consciousness, for the real movement is executed unconsciously by the absolute spirit. Thus the philosopher arrives *post festum.*" Hegel, then, permits "absolute spirit qua absolute spirit to make history only in appearance. . . . For, as absolute spirit does not appear in the mind of the philosopher in the shape of the creative world-spirit until after the event, it follows that it makes history only in the consciousness, the opinions and the ideas of the philosophers, only in the speculative imagination." Hegel's conceptual mythology has been definitively eliminated by the critical activity of the young Marx.

It is, however, not accidental that Marx achieved 'self-understanding' in the course of opposing a reactionary Hegelian movement reverting back to Kant. This movement exploited Hegel's obscurities and inner uncertainties in order to eradicate the revolutionary elements from his method. It strove to harmonise the reactionary content, the reactionary conceptual mythology, the vestiges of the contemplative dualism of thought and existence with the consistently reactionary philosophy which prevailed in the Germany of the day.

By adopting the progressive part of the Hegelian method, namely the dialectic, Marx not only cut himself off from Hegel's successors; he also split Hegel's philosophy in two. He took the historical tendency in Hegel to its logical extreme: he radically transformed all the phenomena both of society and of socialised man into historical problems: he concretely revealed the real substratum of historical evolution and developed a seminal method in the process. He measured Hegel's philosophy by the yardstick he had himself discovered and systematically elaborated, and he found it wanting. The mythologising remnants of the 'eternal values' which Marx eliminated from the dialectic belong basically on the same level as the philosophy of reflection which Hegel had fought his whole life long with such energy and bitterness and against which he had pitted his entire philosophical method, with its ideas of process and concrete totality, dialectics and history. In this sense Marx's critique of Hegel is the direct continuation and extension of the criticism that Hegel himself levelled at Kant and Fichte.[27] So it came about that Marx's dialectical method continued what Hegel had striven for but had failed to achieve in a concrete form. And, on the other hand, the corpse of the written system remained for the scavenging philologists and system-makers to feast upon.

It is at reality itself that Hegel and Marx part company. Hegel was unable to penetrate to the real driving forces of history. Partly because these forces were not yet fully visible when he created his system. In consequence he was forced to regard the peoples and their consciousness as the true bearers of historical evolution. (But he did not discern their real nature because of the heterogeneous composition of that consciousness. So he mythologised it into the 'spirit of the people'.) But in part he remained imprisoned in the Platonic and Kantian outlook, in the duality of thought and being, of form and matter, notwithstanding his very energetic efforts to break out. Even though he was the first

C

to discover the meaning of concrete totality, and even though his thought was constantly bent upon overcoming every kind of abstraction, matter still remained tainted for him with the '*stain* of the specific' (and here he was very much the Platonist). These contradictory and conflicting tendencies could not be clarified within his system. They are often juxtaposed, unmediated, contradictory and unreconciled. In consequence, the ultimate (apparent) synthesis had perforce to turn to the past rather than the future.[28] It is no wonder that from very early on bourgeois science chose to dwell on these aspects of Hegel. As a result the revolutionary core of his thought became almost totally obscure even for Marxists.

A conceptual mythology always points to the failure to understand a fundamental condition of human existence, one whose effects cannot be warded off. This failure to penetrate the object is expressed intellectually in terms of transcendental forces which construct and shape reality, the relations between objects, our relations with them and their transformations in the course of history in a mythological fashion. By recognising that "the production and reproduction of real life (is) in the last resort the decisive factor in history",[29] Marx and Engels gained a vantage point from which they could settle accounts with all mythologies. Hegel's absolute spirit was the last of these grandiose mythological schemes. It already contained the totality and its movement, even though it was unaware of its real character. Thus in historical materialism reason "which has always existed though not always in a rational form",[30] achieved that 'rational' form by discovering its real substratum, the basis from which human life will really be able to become conscious of itself. This completed the programme of Hegel's philosophy of history, even though at the cost of the destruction of his system. In contrast to nature in which, as Hegel emphasises,[31] "change goes in a circle, repeating the same thing", change in history takes place "in the concept as well as on the surface. It is the concept itself which is corrected."

5

The premise of dialectical materialism is, we recall: "It is not men's consciousness that determines their existence, but on the contrary, their social existence that determines their consciousness." Only in the context sketched above can this premise point beyond mere theory and become a question of praxis. Only when the core of existence stands revealed as a social process can existence be seen as the product, albeit the hitherto unconscious product, of human activity. This activity will be seen in its turn as the element crucial for the transformation of existence. Man finds himself confronted by purely natural relations or social forms mystified into natural relations. They appear to be fixed, complete and immutable entities which can be manipulated and even comprehended, but never overthrown. But also this situation creates the possibility of praxis in the individual consciousness. Praxis becomes the form of action appropriate to the isolated individual, it becomes his ethics. Feuerbach's attempt to supersede Hegel foundered on this reef: like the German idealists, and to a much greater extent than Hegel, he stopped short at the isolated individual of 'civil society'.

Marx urged us to understand 'the sensuous world', the object, reality, as human sensuous activity.[32] This means that man must become conscious of himself as a social being, as simultaneously the subject and object of the socio-historical process. In feudal society man could not yet see himself as a social being because his social relations were still mainly natural. Society was far too unorganised and had far too little control over the totality of relations between men for it to appear to consciousness as *the* reality of man. (The question of the structure and unity of feudal society cannot be considered in any detail here.) Bourgeois society carried out the process of socialising society. Capitalism destroyed both the spatio-temporal barriers between different lands and territories and also the legal partitions between the different 'estates' (Stände). In its universe there is a formal equality for all men; the economic relations that directly determined the metabolic exchange between men and nature progressively disappear. Man becomes, in the true sense of the word, a social being. Society becomes *the* reality for man.

Thus the recognition that society is reality becomes possible only under capitalism, in bourgeois society. But the class which carried out this revolution did so without consciousness of its function; the social forces it unleashed, the very forces that carried it to supremacy seemed to be opposed to it like a second nature, but a more soulless, impenetrable nature than feudalism ever was.[33] It was necessary for the proletariat to be born for social reality to become fully conscious. The reason for this is that the discovery of the class-outlook of the proletariat provided a vantage point from which to survey the whole of society. With the emergence of historical materialism there arose the theory of the "conditions for the liberation of the proletariat" and the doctrine of reality understood as the total process of social evolution. This was only possible because for the proletariat the total knowledge of its class-situation was a vital necessity, a matter of life and death; because its class situation becomes comprehensible only if the whole of society can be understood; and because this understanding is the inescapable precondition of its actions. Thus the unity of theory and practice is only the reverse side of the social and historical position of the proletariat. From its own point of view self-knowledge coincides with knowledge of the whole so that the proletariat is at one and the same time the subject and object of its own knowledge.

The mission of raising humanity to a higher level is based, as Hegel rightly observed[34] (although he was still concerned with nations), on the fact that these "stages of evolution exist as *immediate, natural principles*" and it devolves upon every nation (i.e. class) "endowed with such a *natural* principle to put it into practice". Marx concretises this idea with great clarity by applying it to social development:[35] "If socialist writers attribute this world-historical role to the proletariat it is not because they believe . . . that the proletariat are gods. Far from it. The proletariat can and must liberate itself because when the proletariat is fully developed, its humanity and even the appearance of its humanity has become totally abstract; because in the conditions of its life all the conditions of life of contemporary society find their most inhuman consummation; because in the proletariat man is lost to himself but at the same time he has acquired a theoretical consciousness of this loss, and is driven by the absolutely imperious dictates of his misery—the practical expression of this necessity—which can no longer be ignored or whitewashed, to rebel against this inhumanity. However, the proletariat cannot liberate itself without destroying the conditions of its own life. But it cannot do that without destroying *all* the inhuman conditions of life in contemporary society which exist in the proletariat in a concentrated form."

Thus the essence of the method of historical materialism is inseparable from the 'practical and critical' activity of the proletariat: both are aspects of the same process of social evolution. So, too, the knowledge of reality provided by the dialectical method is likewise inseparable from the class standpoint of the proletariat. The question raised by the Austrian Marxists of the methodological separation of the 'pure' science of Marxism from socialism is a pseudo-problem.[36] For, the Marxist method, the dialectical materialist knowledge of reality, can arise only from the point of view of a class, from the point of view of the struggle of the proletariat. To abandon this point of view is to move away from historical materialism, just as to adopt it leads directly into the thick of the struggle of the proleteriat.

Historical materialism grows out of the "immediate, natural" life-principle of the proletariat; it means the acquisition of total knowledge of reality from this one point of view. But it does not follow from this that this knowledge or this methodological attitude is the inherent or natural possession of the proletariat as a class (let alone of proletarian individuals). On the contrary. It is true that the proletariat is the conscious subject of total social reality. But the conscious subject is not defined here as in Kant, where 'subject' is defined as that which can never be an object. The 'subject' here is not a detached spectator of the process. The proletariat is more than just the active and passive part of this process: the rise and evolution of its knowledge and its actual rise and evolution in the course of history are just the two different sides of the same real process. It is not simply the case that the working class arose in the course of spontaneous, unconscious actions born of immediate, direct despair (the Luddite destruction of machines can serve as a primitive illustration of this), and then advanced gradually through incessant social struggle to the point where it "formed itself into a class". But it is no less true that proletarian consciousness of social reality, of its own class situation, of its own historical vocation and the materialist view of history are all products of this self-same process of evolution which historical materialism understands adequately and for what it really is for the first time in history.

Thus the Marxist method is equally as much the product of class warfare as any other political or economic product. In the same way, the evolution of the proletariat reflects the inner structure of the society which it was the first to understand. "Its result, therefore, appears just as constantly presupposed by it as its presuppositions appear as its results." [37] The idea of totality which we have come to recognise as the presupposition necessary to comprehend reality is the product of history in a double sense.

First, historical materialism became a formal, objective possibility only because economic factors created the proletariat, because the proletariat did emerge (i.e. at a particular stage of historical development), and because the subject and object of the knowledge of social reality were transformed. Second, this formal possibility became a real one only in the course of the evolution of the proletariat. If the meaning of history is to be found in the process of history itself and not, as formerly, in a transcendental, mythological or ethical meaning foisted on to recalcitrant material, this presupposes a proletariat with a relatively advanced awareness of its own position, i.e. a relatively advanced proletariat, and, therefore, a long preceding period of evolution. The path taken by this evolution leads from utopia to the knowledge of reality; from transcendental goals fixed by the first great leaders of the workers' movement to the clear perception by the Commune of 1871 that the working-class has "no ideals to realise", but wishes only "to liberate the elements of the new society". It is the path leading from the "class opposed to capitalism" to the class "for itself".

Seen in this light the revisionist separation of movement and ultimate goal represents a regression to the most primitive stage of the working-class movement. For the ultimate goal is not a 'state of the future' awaiting the proletariat somewhere independent of the movement and the path leading up to it. It is not a condition which can be happily forgotten in the stress of daily life and recalled only in Sunday sermons as a stirring contrast to workaday cares. Nor is it a 'duty', an 'idea' designed to regulate the 'real' process. The ultimate goal is rather that *relation to the totality* (to the whole of society seen as a process), through which every aspect of the struggle acquires its revolutionary significance. This relation informs every aspect in its simple and sober ordinariness, but only consciousness makes it real and so confers reality on the day-to-day struggle by manifesting its relation to the whole. Thus it elevates mere existence to reality. Do not let us forget either that every attempt to rescue the 'ultimate goal' or the 'essence' of the proletariat from every impure contact with—capitalist—existence leads ultimately to the same remoteness from reality, from 'practical, critical activity' and to the same relapse into the utopian dualism of subject and object, of theory and practice to which Revisionism has succumbed.[38]

WHAT IS ORTHODOX MARXISM?

The practical danger of every such dualism shows itself in the loss of any directive for *action*. As soon as you abandon the ground of reality that has been conquered and reconquered by dialectical materialism, as soon as you decide to remain on the 'natural' ground of existence, of the empirical in its stark, naked brutality, you create a gulf between the subject of an action and the milieux of the 'facts' in which the action unfolds so that they stand opposed to each other as harsh, irreconcilable principles. It then becomes impossible to impose the subjective will, wish or decision upon the facts or to discover in them any directive for action. A situation in which the 'facts' speak out unmistakably for or against a definite course of action has never existed, and neither can or will exist. The more conscientiously the facts are explored—in their isolation, i.e. in their unmediated relations—the less compellingly will they point in any one direction. It is self-evident that a merely subjective decision will be shattered by the pressure of uncomprehended facts acting automatically 'according to laws'.

Thus dialectical materialism is seen to offer the only approach to reality which can give action a direction. The self-knowledge, both subjective and objective, of the proletariat at a given point in its evolution is at the same time knowledge of the stage of development achieved by the whole society. The facts no longer appear strange when they are comprehended in their coherent reality, in the relation of all partial aspects to their inherent, but hitherto unelucidated roots in the whole: we then perceive the tendencies which strive towards the centre of reality, to what we are wont to call the ultimate goal. This ultimate goal is not an abstract ideal opposed to the process, but an aspect of truth and reality. It is the concrete meaning of each stage reached and an integral part of the concrete moment. Because of this, to comprehend it is to recognise the direction taken (unconsciously) by events and tendencies towards the totality. It is to know the direction that determines concretely the correct course of action at any given moment—in terms of the interest of the total process, viz. the emancipation of the proletariat.

However, the evolution of society constantly heightens the tension between the partial aspects and the whole. Just because the inherent meaning ef reality shines forth with an ever more resplendent light, the meaning of the process is embedded ever more deeply in day-to-day events, and totality permeates the spatio-temporal character of phenomena. The path to consciousness throughout the course of history does not become smoother but on the contrary ever more arduous and exacting. For this reason the task of orthodox Marxism, its victory over Revisionism and utopianism can never mean the defeat, once and for all, of false tendencies. It is an ever-renewed struggle against the insidious effects of bourgeois ideology on the thought of the proletariat. Marxist orthodoxy is no guardian of traditions, it is the eternally vigilant prophet proclaiming the relation between the tasks of the immediate present and the totality of the historical process. Hence the words of the *Communist Manifesto* on the tasks of orthodoxy and of its representatives, the Communists, have lost neither their relevance nor their value: "The Communists are distinguished from the other working-class parties *by this only*: 1. In the national struggles of the proletarians of the different countries, they point out and bring to the front the common interests of the *entire* proletariat, independent of nationality. 2. In the various stages of development which the struggle of the working class against the bourgeoisie has to pass through, they always and everywhere represent the interests of *the movement as a whole*."

March 1919.

NOTES

1 *The Critique of Hegel's Philosophy of Right*, in *Early Writings* edited by T. B. Bottomore, London, 1963, p. 52.
2 Ibid., p. 54.
3 *Nachlass* I, pp. 382–3. [*Correspondence of 1843*].
4 Ibid., p. 398. See also the essay on Class Consciousness.
5 *Feuerbach and the End of Classical German Philosophy*, in S.W. II, p. 350.
6 *A Contribution to the Critique of Political Economy*, translated by N. I. Stone, London, 1904 (my italics). It is of the first importance to realise that the method is limited here to the realms of history and society. The misunderstandings that arise from Engels' account of dialectics can in the main be put down to the fact that Engels—following Hegel's mistaken lead—extended the method to apply also to nature. However, the crucial determinants of dialectics—the interaction of subject and object, the unity of theory and practice, the historical changes in the reality underlying the categories as the root cause of changes in thought, etc.—are absent from our knowledge of nature. Unfortunately it is not possible to undertake a detailed analysis of these questions here.
7 Ibid., pp. 298–9.
8 Introduction to *The Class Struggles in France* in S.W. I, p. 110.

But it must be borne in mind that 'scientific exactitude' presupposes that the elements remain 'constant'. This had been postulated as far back as Galileo.

9 *Capital* III, p. 205. Similarly also pp. 47–8 and 307. The distinction between existence (which is divided into appearance, phenomenon and essence) and reality derives from Hegel's *Logic*. It is unfortunately not possible here to discuss the degree to which the conceptual framework of *Capital* is based on these distinctions. Similarly, the distinction between idea (Vorstellung) and concept (Begriff) is also to be found in Hegel.

10 *Capital* III, p. 797.

11 *A Contribution to political Economy*, p. 293.

12 Ibid., p. 273. The category of reflective connection also derives from Hegel's *Logic*. [See Explanatory Notes for this concept].

13 *The Poverty of Philosophy*, Moscow, n.d., p. 123.

14 We would draw the attention of readers with a greater interest in questions of methodology to the fact that in Hegel's logic, too, the relation of the parts to the whole forms the dialectical transition from existence to reality. It must be noted in this context that the question of the relation of internal and external also treated there is likewise concerned with the problem of totality. Hegel, *Werke* IV, pp. 156 ff. (The quotations from the Logic are all taken from the 2nd edition.)

15 Marx, *Theorien über den Mehrwert*, Stuttgart, 1905, II, II, pp. 305–9.

16 *Marxistische Probleme*, p. 77.

17 *Theorien über den Mehrwert*, III, pp. 55 and 93–4.

18 *The Poverty of Philosophy*, pp. 123–4.

19 *A Contribution to Political Economy*, pp. 291–2.

20 The very subtle nature of Cunow's opportunism can be observed by the way in which—despite his thorough knowledge of Marx's works—he substitutes the word 'sum' for the concept of the whole (totality) thus eliminating every dialectical relation. Cf. *Die Marxsche Geschichts-, Gesellschafts- und Staatstheorie*, Berlin, 1929, II, pp. 155–7.

21 *Wage Labour and Capital*, in S.W. I, p. 83.

22 *Capital* I, p. 568.

23 Cf. the essay on *Reification and the Consciousness of the Proletariat*.

24 *Capital* I, p. 578.

25 Hegel, *The Philosophy of Right*, trans. T. M. Knox, Oxford, 1942, p. 283.

26 *Nachlass* II, p. 187. [*The Holy Family*, Chapter 6].

27 It comes as no surprise that at the very point where Marx radically departs from Hegel, Cunow should attempt to correct Marx by appealing to Hegel as seen through Kantian spectacles. To Marx's purely historical view of the state he opposes the Hegelian state as 'an eternal value'. Its 'errors' are to be set aside as nothing more than 'historical matters' which do not 'determine the nature, the fate and the objectives of the state'. For Cunow, Marx is

inferior to Hegel on this point because he 'regards the question politically and not from the standpoint of the sociologist'. Cunow, op. cit. p. 308.

It is evident that all Marx's efforts to overcome Hegelian philosophy might never have existed in the eyes of the opportunists. If they do not return to vulgar materialism or to Kant they use the reactionary elements of Hegel's philosophy of the state to erase revolutionary dialectics from Marxism, so as to provide an intellectual immortalisation of bourgeois society.

28 Hegel's attitude towards national economy is highly significant in this context. (*Philosophy of Right*, § 189.) He clearly sees that the problem of chance and necessity is fundamental to it methodologically (very like Engels: *Origin of the Family* S.W. II, p. 293 and *Feuerbach*, etc. S.W. II, p. 354). But he is unable to see the crucial importance of the material reality underlying the economy, viz. the relation of men to each other; it remains for him no more than an 'arbitrary chaos' and its laws are thought to be 'similar to those of the planetary system'. Ibid. §. 189.

29 Engels, Letter to J. Bloch, 21 September 1890, S.W. II, p. 443.

30 *Nachlass* I, p. 381. [*Correspondence with Ruge (1843)*].

31 *The Philosophy of History*. Phil. Bibl. I. pp. 133–4.

32 *Theses on Feuerbach*, in S.W. II, pp. 364–7.

33 See the essay *Class Consciousness* for an explanation of this situation.

34 *The Philosophy of Right*, § 346–7.

35 *Nachlass* II, p. 133. [*The Holy Family*, Chapter 4].

36 Hilferding, *Finanzkapital*, pp. VIII–IX.

37 *Capital* III.

38 Cf. Zinoviev's polemics against Guesde and his attitude to the war in Stuttgart. *Gegen den Strom*, pp. 470–1. Likewise Lenin's book, "*Left-Wing*" *Communism—an Infantile Disorder*.

The Marxism of Rosa Luxemburg

> Economists explain how production takes place in the above-mentioned relations, but what they do not explain is how these relations themselves are produced, that is, the historical movement that gave them birth.
>
> Marx: *The Poverty of Philosophy.*

1

IT is not the primacy of economic motives in historical explanation that constitutes the decisive difference between Marxism and bourgeois thought, but the point of view of totality. The category of totality, the all-pervasive supremacy of the whole over the parts is the essence of the method which Marx took over from Hegel and brilliantly transformed into the foundations of a wholly new science. The capitalist separation of the producer from the total process of production, the division of the process of labour into parts at the cost of the individual humanity of the worker, the atomisation of society into individuals who simply go on producing without rhyme or reason, must all have a profound influence on the thought, the science and the philosophy of capitalism. Proletarian science is revolutionary not just by virtue of its revolutionary ideas which it opposes to bourgeois society, but above all because of its method. *The primacy of the category of totality is the bearer of the principle of revolution in science.*

The revolutionary nature of Hegelian dialectics had often been recognised as such before Marx, notwithstanding Hegel's own conservative applications of the method. But no one had converted this knowledge into a science of revolution. It was Marx who transformed the Hegelian method into what Herzen described as the 'algebra of revolution'. It was not enough, however, to give it a materialist twist. The revolutionary principle inherent in Hegel's dialectic was able to come to the surface less because of that than because of the validity of the method itself, viz. the concept of totality, the subordination of every part to the whole unity of history and thought. In Marx the dialectical method aims at understanding society as a whole. Bourgeois thought concerns itself with objects that arise either from the process of studying phenomena in isolation, or from the division of labour and specialisation in the different disciplines. It holds abstractions to be 'real' if it is naïvely realistic, and 'autonomous' if it is critical.

Marxism, however, simultaneously raises and reduces all specialisations to the level of aspects in a dialectical process. This is not to deny that the process of abstraction and hence the isolation of the elements and concepts in the special disciplines and whole areas of study is of the very essence of science. But what is decisive is whether this process of isolation is a means towards understanding the whole and whether it is integrated within the context it presupposes and requires, or whether the abstract knowledge of an isolated fragment retains its 'autonomy' and becomes an end in itself. In the last analysis Marxism does not acknowledge the existence of independent sciences of law, economics or history, etc.: there is nothing but a single, unified—dialectical and historical—science of the evolution of society as a totality.

The category of totality, however, determines not only the object of knowledge but also the subject. Bourgeois thought judges social phenomena consciously or unconsciously, naïvely or subtly, consistently from the standpoint of the individual.[1] No path leads from the individual to the totality; there is at best a road leading to aspects of particular areas, mere fragments for the most part, 'facts' bare of any context, or to abstract, special laws. The totality of an object can only be posited if the positing subject is itself a totality; and if the subject wishes to understand itself, it must conceive of the object as a totality. In modern society only the *classes* can represent this total point of view. By tackling every problem from this angle, above all in *Capital*, Marx supplied a corrective to Hegel who still wavered between the "great individual and the abstract spirit of the people." Although his successors understood him even less well here than on the issue of 'idealism' versus 'materialism' this corrective proved even more salutary and decisive.

Classical economics and above all its vulgarisers have always considered the development of capitalism from the point of view of the *individual capitalist*. This involved them in a series of insoluble contradictions and pseudo-problems. Marx's *Capital* represents a radical break with this procedure. Not that he acts the part of an agitator who treats every aspect exclusively from the proletarian standpoint. Such a one-sided approach would only result in a new vulgar economics with plus and minus signs reversed. His method is to consider the problems of the whole of capitalist society as problems of the classes constituting it, the classes being regarded as *totalities*. My aim in this essay is to point to methodological problems and so it is not possible to show here how Marx's method throws a completely new light on a whole series of problems, how new problems emerge which classical economics was unable even to glimpse, let alone solve, and how many of their pseudo-problems dissolve into thin air. My aim here is to elucidate as clearly as possible the two premises of a genuine application of the dialectical method as opposed to the frivolous use made of it by Hegel's traditionalist successors. These premises are the need to postulate a totality firstly as a posited object and then as a positing subject.

2

Rosa Luxemburg's major work *The Accumulation of Capital* takes up the problem at this juncture after decades of vulgarised Marxism. The trivialisation of Marxism and its deflection into a bourgeois 'science' was expressed first, most clearly and frankly in Bernstein's *Premises of Socialism*. It is anything but an accident that the chapter in this book which begins with an onslaught on the dialectical method in the name of exact 'science' should end by branding Marx as a Blanquist. It is no accident because the moment you abandon the point of view of totality, you must also jettison the starting point and the goal, the assumptions and the requirements of the dialectical method. When this happens revolution will be understood not as part of a process but as an isolated act cut off from the general course of events. If that is so it must inevitably seem as if the revolutionary aspects of Marx are really just a relapse into the primitive period of the workers' movement, i.e. Blanquism. The whole system of Marxism stands and falls with the principle that revolution is the product of a point of view in which the category of totality is dominant. Even in its opportunism Bernstein's criticism is much too opportunistic for all the implications of this position to emerge clearly.[2]

But even though the opportunists sought above all to eradicate the notion of the dialectical course of history from Marxism, they could not evade its ineluctable consequences. The economic development of the imperialist age had made it progressively more difficult to believe in their pseudo-attacks on the capitalist system and in the 'scientific' analysis of isolated phenomena in the name of the 'objective and exact sciences'. It was not enough to declare a political commitment for or against capitalism. One had to declare ones theoretical commitment also. One had to choose: either to regard the whole history of society from a Marxist point of view, i.e. as a totality, and hence to come to grips with the phenomenon of imperialism in theory and practice. Or else to evade this confrontation by confining oneself to the analysis of isolated aspects in one or other of the special disciplines. The attitude that inspires monographs is the best way to place a screen before the problem the very sight of which strikes terror into the heart of a Social-Democratic movement turned opportunist. By discovering 'exact' descriptions for isolated areas and 'eternally valid laws' for specific cases they have blurred the differences separating imperialism from the preceding age. They found themselves in a capitalist society 'in general'—and its existence seemed to them to correspond to the nature of human reason, and the 'laws of nature' every bit as much as it had seemed to Ricardo and his successors, the bourgeois vulgar economists.

It would be un-Marxist and undialectical to ask whether this theoretical relapse into the methodology of vulgar economics was the cause or the effect of this pragmatic opportunism. In the eyes of historical materialism the two tendencies belong together: they constitute the social ambience of Social Democracy before the War. The theoretical conflicts in Rosa Luxemburg's *Accumulation of Capital* can be understood only within that milieu.

The debate as conducted by Bauer, Eckstein and Co. did not turn on the truth or falsity of the solution Rosa Luxemburg proposed to the problem of the accumulation of capital. On the contrary, discussion centred on whether there was a real problem at all and in the event its existence was denied flatly and with the utmost vehemence. Seen from the standpoint of vulgar economics this is quite understandable, and even inevitable. For if it is treated as an isolated problem in economics and from the point of view of the individual capitalist it is easy to argue that no real problem exists.[3]

Logically enough the critics who dismissed the whole problem also ignored the decisive chapter of her book ("The historical determinants of Accumulation"). This can be seen from the way they formulated their key question. The question they posed was this: Marx's formulae were arrived at on the basis of a hypothetical society (posited for reasons of method) which consisted only of capitalists and workers. Were these formulae correct? How were they to be interpreted? The critics completely overlooked the fact that Marx posited this society for the sake of argument, i.e. to see the problem more clearly, before pressing forward to the larger question of the place of this problem within society as a whole. They overlooked the fact that Marx himself took this step with reference to so-called primitive accumulation, in Volume I of *Capital*. Consciously or unconsciously they suppressed the fact that on this issue *Capital* is an incomplete fragment which stops short at the point where this problem should be opened up. In this sense what Rosa Luxemburg has done is precisely to take up the thread where Marx left off and to solve the problem in his spirit.

By ignoring these factors the opportunists acted quite consistently. The problem is indeed superfluous from the standpoint of the individual capitalist and vulgar economics. As far as the former is concerned, economic reality has the appearance of a world governed by the eternal laws of nature, laws to which he has to adjust his activities. For him the production of surplus value very often (though not always, it is true) takes the form of an exchange with other individual capitalists. And the whole problem of accumulation resolves itself into a question of the manifold permutations of the formulae M–C–M and C–M–C in the course of production and circulation, etc. It thus becomes an isolated question for the vulgar economists, a question unconnected with the ultimate fate of capitalism as a whole. The solution to the problem is officially guaranteed by the Marxist 'formulae' which are correct in themselves and need only to be 'brought up to date'—a task performed e.g. by Otto Bauer. However, we must insist that economic reality can never be understood solely on the basis of these formulae because they are based on an abstraction (viz. the working hypothesis that society consists only of capitalists and workers). Hence they can serve only for clarification and as a springboard for an assault on the real problem. Bauer and his confreres misunderstood this just as surely as the disciples of Ricardo misunderstood the problematics of Marx in their day.

The Accumulation of Capital takes up again the methods and questions posed by the young Marx in *The Poverty of Philosophy.* In that work Marx had subjected to scrutiny the historical conditions that had made Ricardo's economics possible and viable. Similarly, Rosa Luxemburg applied the same method to the incomplete analyses in Volumes 2 and 3 of *Capital.* As the ideological representatives of capitalism in the ascendant, bourgeois economists were forced to identify the 'Laws of Nature' discovered by Adam Smith and Ricardo with the existing social order so as to be able to see capitalist society as the only form of society corresponding to the reason and the nature of man. Likewise here: Social Democracy was the ideological exponent of a workers' aristocracy turned petty bourgeois. It had a definite interest in the imperialist exploitation of the whole world in the last phase of capitalism but sought to evade its inevitable fate: the World War. It was compelled to construe the evolution of society as if it were possible for capitalist accumulation to operate in the rarified atmosphere of mathematical formulae, i.e. unproblematically and without a World War. In the upshot, their political insight and foresight compared very unfavourably with that of the great bourgeois and capitalist classes with their interest in imperialist exploitation together with its militarist consequences. However, it did enable them even then to take up their present theoretical position as guardians of the everlasting capitalist economic order; guardians against the fated catastrophic consequences towards which the true exponents of capitalist imperialism were drifting with open but unseeing eyes.

For a capitalist class in the ascendant the identification of Ricardo's 'Laws of Nature' with the existing social order had represented a means of ideological self-defence. Likewise here, the interpretation of Marx current in the Austrian school and especially its identification of Marx's abstractions with the totality of society represents a 'rational' means of self-defence for a capitalism in decline. And just as the young Marx's concept of totality cast a bright light upon the pathological symptoms of a still-flourishing capitalism, so too in the studies of Rosa Luxemburg we find the basic problems of capitalism analysed within the context of the historical process as a whole: and in her work we see how the last flowering of capitalism is transformed into a ghastly dance of death, into the inexorable march of Oedipus to his doom.

3

Rosa Luxemburg devoted a whole pamphlet (which was published posthumously) exclusively to the refutation of 'Marxist' vulgar economics. Both its approach and its method make it appear as a kind of natural appendage to the end of Section II of *The Accumulation of Capital* where it would take its place as the fourth round in her treatment of this crucial problem of capitalist development. Characteristically, the larger part of it is concerned with historical analysis. By this I mean more than the Marxian analysis of simple and expanded reproduction which forms the starting point of the whole study and the prelude to the conclusive solution of this problem. At the core of the work is what we can describe as the literary-historical examination of the great debates of the question of accumulation: the debate between Sismondi and Ricardo and his school; between Rodbertus and Kirchmann; between the Narodniki and the Russian Marxists.

The adoption of this approach does not place her outside the Marxist tradition. On the contrary, it implies a return to the pristine and unsullied traditions of Marxism: to Marx's own method. For his first, mature, complete and conclusive work, *The Poverty of Philosophy*, refutes Proudhon by reaching back to the true sources of his views, to Ricardo and Hegel. His analysis of where, how, and above all, why Proudhon *had* to misunderstand Hegel is the source of light that relentlessly exposes Proudhon's self-contradictions. It goes even further, and illuminates the dark places, unknown to Proudhon himself, from which these errors spring: the class relations of which his views are the theoretical expression. For as Marx says, "economic categories are nothing but the theoretical expressions, the abstractions of the social relations of production".[4] It is true that in his principal theoretical works he was prevented by the scope and wealth of the individual problems treated from employing a historical approach. But this should not obscure *the essential similarity in his approach. Capital* and *The Theories of Surplus Value* are in essence a single work whose internal structure points to the solution of the problem so brilliantly sketched in broad outline in *The Poverty of Philosophy*.

The question of the internal structuring of the problem leads us back to the central issue confronting the dialectical method: to the right understanding of the dominant position held by the concept of totality and hence to the philosophy of Hegel. On this essential point Marx never abandoned Hegel's philosophical method. And this was at all times—and most convincingly in *The Phenomenology of Mind*—both the history of philosophy and the philosophy of history. For the Hegelian—dialectical—identification of thought and existence, the belief in their unity as the unity and totality of a process is also, in essence, the philosophy of history of historical materialism.

Even Marx's materialist polemic against the 'ideological' view of history is aimed more at Hegel's followers than at the master himself, who on this point stood much closer to Marx than Marx may himself have realised from his position in the thick of the struggle against the fossilised 'idealisation' of the dialectical method. For the 'absolute' idealism of Hegel's followers implies the dissolution of the original system;[5] it implies the divorce of dialectics from the living stuff of history and this means ultimately the disruption of the dialectical unity of thought and existence. In the dogmatic materialism of Marx's epigones we find a repetition of the process dissolving the concrete totality of historical reality. And even if their method does not degenerate into the empty abstract schemata of Hegel's disciples, it does harden into a vulgar economics and a mechanical preoccupation with specialised sciences. If the purely ideological constructions of the Hegelians proved unequal to the task of understanding historical events, the Marxists have revealed a comparable inability to understand either the connections of the so-called 'ideological' forms of society and their economic base or the economy itself as a totality and as social reality.

Whatever the subject of debate, the dialectical method is concerned always with the same problem: knowledge of the historical process in its entirety. This means that 'ideological' and 'economic' problems lose their mutual exclusiveness and merge into one another. *The history of a particular problem turns into the history of problems.* The literary or scientific exposition of a problem appears as the expression of a social whole, of its possibilities, limits and problems. The approach of literary history is the one best suited to the problems of history. The history of philosophy becomes the philosophy of history.

It is therefore no accident that the two fundamental studies which inaugurate the theoretical rebirth of Marxism, Rosa Luxemburg's *The Accumulation of Capital* and Lenin's *State and Revolution*, both use the approach adopted by the young Marx. To ensure that the problems under consideration will arise before us dialectically, they provide what is substantially a literary-historical account of their genesis. They analyse the changes and reversals in the views leading up to the problem as it presents itself to them. They focus upon every stage of intellectual clarification or confusion and place it in the historical context conditioning it and resulting from it. This enables them to evoke with unparalleled vividness the *historical process* of which their own approach and their own solutions are the culmination. This method has absolutely nothing in common with the tradition in bourgeois science (to which social-democratic theoreticians also belong) of "taking the achievements of their forerunners into account". For there the distinction drawn between theory and history, and the lack of reciprocity between the separate disciplines leads to the disappearance of the problem of totality in the interests of greater specialisation. As a result, the history of a problem becomes mere theoretical and literary ballast. It is of interest only to the experts who inflate it to the point where it obscures the real problems and fosters mindless specialisation.

Reviving the literary and methodological traditions of Marx and Hegel, Lenin converts the history of his problem to an inner history of the European revolutions of the nineteenth century; and the literary-historical approach of Rosa Luxemburg grows into a history of the struggles of the capitalist system to survive and expand. The struggle was triggered off by the great crises of 1815 and 1818/19, the first great shocks sustained by a capitalism that was growing but was as yet undeveloped. The debate was introduced by Sismondi's *Nouveaux Principes d'Économie Politique*. Despite his reactionary purpose his work gives us our first insight into the dilemmas of capitalism. Ideologically, this undeveloped form of capitalism has recourse to attitudes as one-sided and wrong-headed as those of its opponents. While as a reactionary sceptic Sismondi deduces from the existence of crises the impossibility of accumulation, the advocates of the new system of production, their optimism unimpaired, deny that crises are inevitable and that there is in fact any dilemma at all.

If we look at the problem now we see that the social distribution of the questioners and the social significance of their answers has now been completely inverted. The present theme—even though it has not received the recognition it deserves—is the fate of the revolution and the doom of capitalism. The Marxist diagnosis has had a decisive impact on this change and this is itself symptomatic of the way in which the ideological leadership is slipping from the hands of the bourgeoisie. For while the petty bourgeois nature of the Narodniki shows itself blatantly in their theory, it is interesting to observe how the Russian 'Marxists' are developing more and more strongly into the ideological champions of capitalism. They view the prospects of the growth of capitalism in terms that show them to the worthy heirs to Say and MacCulloch. "Without doubt the 'legal' Russian Marxists have gained a victory", Rosa Luxemburg states,[6] "over their enemies, the Populists; but their victory goes too far. . . . The question is whether capitalism in general and Russian capitalism in particular is capable of growth and these Marxists have demonstrated this capability so thoroughly that in theory they have proved that it is possible for capitalism to last for ever. It is evident that if the limitless accumulation of capital can be assumed, then the limitless viability of capitalism must follow . . . . If the capitalist mode of production can ensure the unlimited increase in the forces of production and hence of economic progress, it will be invincible."

At this point the fourth and last round in the controversy about accumulation begins; it is the passage of arms between Otto Bauer and Rosa Luxemburg. The question of social optimism has now shifted. In Rosa Luxemburg's hands the doubts about the possibility of accumulation shed their absolute form. The problem becomes the *historical* one of the *conditions* of accumulation and thus it becomes certain that unlimited accumulation is not possible. Placed into its total social context accumulation becomes dialectical. It then swells into the dialectics of the whole capitalist system. As Rosa Luxemburg puts it:[7] "The moment the Marxian scheme of expanded reproduction corresponds to reality it points to the end, the historical limits of the movement of accumulation and therewith to the end of capitalist production. If accumulation is impossible then further growth in the forces of production is impossible too. And this means that the destruction of capitalism becomes an objective historical necessity. From this there follow the contradictory movements of the last, imperialist phase, which is the terminal phase in the historical career of capital." As doubt develops into certainty the petty bourgeois and reactionary elements disappear without a trace: *doubt turns to optimism and to the theoretical certainty of the coming social revolution.*

Through a comparable shift the opposed view, the faith in limitless accumulation is assailed by doubts, hesitations and petty bourgeois vacillations. Otto Bauer embraces this faith but with a marked falling off from the sunny, untroubled optimism of Say or Tugan-Baranovsky. Bauer and his associates work with a Marxist terminology, but their theory is essentially that of Proudhon. In the last analysis their attempts to solve the problem of accumulation, or rather their attempts to deny its existence, come to no more than Proudhon's endeavours to preserve the 'good sides' of capitalism while avoiding the 'bad sides'.[8] However, to recognise the existence of the problem of accumulation is to perceive that these 'bad sides' are an integral part of capitalism; and this in turn is to concede that imperialism, world war and world revolution are necessary factors in its evolution. But to admit this is not in the immediate interests of the classes whom the Centre Marxists have come to represent and who wish to believe in an advanced capitalism without any imperialist 'excrescences', and a 'well-regulated' production free of the 'disruptions' of war. According to Rosa Luxemburg,[9] "the essence of this position is the attempt to persuade the bourgeoisie that imperialism and militarism are damaging to itself even from the point of view of their own capitalist interests. It is hoped that by this manoeuvre the alleged handful of people who profit from imperialism will be isolated and that it will be possible to form a bloc consisting of the proletariat together with large sections of the bourgeoisie. This bloc will then be able to 'tame' imperialism and 'remove its sting'! Liberalism in decline directs its appeal away from the badly informed monarchy and towards a monarchy that is to be better informed. In the same way the 'Marxist Centre' appeals over the heads of a misguided bourgeoisie to one which is to be better instructed. . . ."

Bauer and his colleagues have made both an economic and ideological submission to capitalism. Their capitulation comes to the surface in their economic fatalism, in the belief that capitalism is as immortal as the 'laws of nature'. But as genuine petty bourgeois they are the ideological and economic appendages of capitalism. Their wish to see a capitalism without any 'bad sides' and without 'excrescences' means that their opposition to capitalism is the typically *ethical* opposition of the petty bourgeoisie.

4

Economic fatalism and the reformation of socialism through ethics are intimately connected. It is no accident that they reappear in similar form in Bernstein, Tugan-Baranovsky and Otto Bauer. This is not merely the result of the need to seek and find a subjective substitute for the objective path to revolution that they themselves have blocked. It is the logical consequence of the vulgar-economic point of view and of methodological individualism. The 'ethical' reformation of socialism is the subjective side of the missing category of totality which alone can provide an overall view. For the individual, whether capitalist or proletarian, his environment, his social milieu (including Nature which is the theoretical reflection and projection of that milieu) must appear the servant of a brutal and senseless fate which is eternally alien to him. This world can only be understood by means of a theory which postulates 'eternal laws of nature'. Such a theory endows the world with a rationality alien to man and human action can neither penetrate nor influence the world if man takes up a purely contemplative and fatalistic stance.

Within such a world only two possible modes of action commend themselves and they are both apparent rather than real ways of actively changing the world. Firstly, there is the exploitation for particular human ends (as in technology, for example) of the fatalistically accepted and immutable laws which are seen in the manner we have already described. Secondly, there is action directed wholly inwards. This is the attempt to change the world at its only remaining free point, namely man himself (ethics). But as the world becomes mechanised its subject, man, necessarily becomes mechanised too and so this ethics likewise remains abstract. Confronted by the totality of man in isolation from the world it remains merely normative and fails to be truly active in its creation of objects. It is only prescriptive and imperative in character. The logical nexus between Kant's *Critique of Pure Reason* and his *Critique of Practical Reason* is cogent and inescapable. And every 'Marxist' student of socio-economic realities who abandons the method of Hegel and Marx, i.e. the study of the historical process from a total point of view and who substitutes for it a 'critical' method which seeks unhistorical 'laws' in the special sciences will be forced to return to the abstract ethical imperatives of the Kantian school as soon as the question of action becomes imminent.

For the destruction of a totalising point of view disrupts *the unity of theory and practice*. Action, praxis—which Marx demanded before all else in his *Theses on Feuerbach*—is in essence the penetration and transformation of reality. But reality can only be understood and penetrated as a totality, and only a subject which is itself a totality is capable of this penetration. It was not for nothing that the young Hegel erected his philosophy upon the principle that "truth must be understood and expressed not merely as substance, but also as subject".[10] With this he exposed the deepest error and the ultimate limitation of Classical German philosophy. However, his own philosophy failed to live up to this precept and for much of the time it remained enmeshed in the same snares as those of his predecessors.

It was left to Marx to make the concrete discovery of 'truth as the subject' and hence to establish the unity of theory and practice. This he achieved by focusing the known totality upon the reality of the historical process and by confining it to this. By this means he determined both the knowable totality and the totality to be known. The scientific superiority of the standpoint of class (as against that of the individual) has become clear from the foregoing. Now we see the reason for this superiority: *only the class can actively penetrate the reality of society and transform it in its entirety*. For this reason, 'criticism' advanced from the standpoint of class is criticism from a total point of view and hence it provides the dialectical unity of theory and practice. In dialectical unity it is at once cause and effect, mirror and motor of the historical and dialectical process. The proletariat as the subject of thought in society destroys at one blow the dilemma of impotence: the dilemma created by the pure laws with their fatalism and by the ethics of pure intentions.

Thus for Marxism the knowledge that capitalism is historically conditioned (the problem of accumulation) becomes crucial. The reason for this is that only this knowledge, only the unity of theory and practice provide a real basis for social revolution and the total transformation of society. Only when this knowledge can be seen as the product of this process can we close the circle of the dialectical method—and this analysis, too, stems from Hegel.

As early as her first polemics with Bernstein, Rosa Luxemburg lays emphasis on this essential distinction between the total and the partial, the dialectical and the mechanical view of history (whether it be opportunistic or terrorist). "Here lies the chief difference," she explains,[11] "between the Blanquist coups d'état of a 'resolute minority' which always explode like pistol-shots and as a result always come at the wrong moment, and the conquest of the real power of a state by the broad, class-conscious mass of the people which itself can only be the product of the incipient collapse of bourgeois society and which therefore bears in itself the economic and political legitimation of its timely appearance." And in her last work[12] she writes in a similar vein: "The objective tendency of capitalism towards that goal suffices to aggravate the social and political conflicts within society to such an extent and so much earlier than was expected, that they must bring about the demise of the ruling system. But these social and political conflicts are themselves ultimately only the product of the *economic* instability of the capitalist system. Their increasing gravity springs from this source in exact proportion as that instability becomes acute."

The proletariat is, then, at one and the same time the product of the permanent crisis in capitalism and the instrument of those tendencies which drive capitalism towards crisis. In Marx's words: "The proletariat carries out the sentence which private property passes upon itself by its creation of a proletariat."[13] By recognising its situation it acts. By combating capitalism it discovers its own place in society.

But the class consciousness of the proletariat, the truth of the process 'as subject' is itself far from stable and constant; it does not advance according to mechanical 'laws'. It is the consciousness of the dialectical process itself: it is likewise a dialectical concept. For the active and practical side of class consciousness, its true essence, can only become visible in its authentic form when the historical process imperiously requires it to come into force, i.e. when an acute crisis in the economy drives it to action. At other times it remains theoretical and latent, corresponding to the latent and permanent crisis of capitalism:[14] it confronts the individual questions and conflicts of the day with its demands, but as 'mere' consciousness, as an 'ideal sum', in Rosa Luxemburg's phrase.

Marx had understood and described the proletariat's struggle for freedom in terms of the dialectical unity of theory and practice. This implied that consciousness cannot exist on its own either as 'pure' theory, or as a simple postulate, a simple imperative or norm of action. The postulate, too, must have a reality. That is to say, the moment when the class consciousness of the proletariat begins to articulate its demands, when it is 'latent and theoretical', must also be the moment when it creates a corresponding reality which will intervene actively in the total process.

The form taken by the class consciousness of the proletariat is the *Party*. Rosa Luxemburg had grasped the spontaneous nature of revolutionary mass actions earlier and more clearly than many others. (What she did, incidentally, was to emphasise another aspect of the thesis advanced earlier: that these actions are the necessary product of the economic process.) It is no accident, therefore, that she was also quicker to grasp the role of the party in the revolution.[15] For the mechanical vulgarisers the party was merely a form of organisation—and the mass movement, the revolution, was likewise no more than a problem of organisation.

Rosa Luxemburg perceived at a very early stage that the organisation is much more likely to be the effect than the cause of the revolutionary process, just as the proletariat can constitute itself as a class only in and through revolution. In this process which it can neither provoke nor escape, the Party is assigned the sublime role of *bearer of the class consciousness of the proletariat and the conscience of its historical vocation*. The superficially more active and 'more realistic' view allocates to the party tasks concerned predominantly or even exclusively with organisation. Such a view is then reduced to an unrelieved fatalism when confronted with the realities of revolution, whereas Rosa Luxemburg's analysis becomes the fount of true revolutionary activity. The Party must ensure that "in every phase and every aspect of the struggle the total sum of the available power of the proletariat that has already been unleashed should be mobilised and that is should be expressed in the fighting stance of the Party. The tactics of Social Democracy should always be more resolute and vigorous than required by the existing power relations, and never *less*." [16] It must immerse its own truth in the spontaneous mass movement and raise it from the depths of economic necessity, where it was conceived, on to the heights of free, conscious action. In so doing it will transform itself in the moment of the outbreak of revolution from a party that makes demands to one that imposes an effective reality.

This change from demand to reality becomes the lever of the truly class-oriented and truly revolutionary organisation of the proletariat. Knowledge becomes action, theory becomes battle slogan, the masses act in accordance with the slogans and join the ranks of the organised vanguard more consciously, more steadfastly and in greater numbers. The correct slogans give rise organically to the premisses and possibilities of even the technical organisation of the fighting proletariat.

Class consciousness is the 'ethics' of the proletariat, the unity of its theory and its practice, the point at which the economic necessity of its struggle for liberation changes dialectically into freedom. By realising that the party is the historical embodiment and the active incarnation of class consciousness, we see that it is also the incarnation of the ethics of the fighting proletariat. This must determine its politics. Its politics may not always accord with the empirical reality of the moment; at such times its slogans may be ignored. But the ineluctable course of history will give it its due. Even more, the moral strength conferred by the correct class consciousness will bear fruit in terms of practical politics.[17]

The true strength of the party is moral: it is fed by the trust of the spontaneously revolutionary masses whom economic conditions have forced into revolt. It is nourished by the feeling that the party is the objectification of their own will (obscure though this may be to themselves), that it is the visible and organised incarnation of their class consciousness. Only when the party has fought for this trust and earned it can it become the leader of the revolution. For only then will the masses spontaneously and instinctively press forward with all their energies towards the party and towards their own class consciousness.

By separating the inseparable, the opportunists have barred their own path to this knowledge, the active self-knowledge of the proletariat. Hence their leaders speak scornfully, in the authentic tones of the free-thinking petty bourgeoisie of the 'religious faith' that is said to lie at the roots of Bolshevism and revolutionary Marxism. The accusation is a tacit confession of their own impotence. In vain do they disguise their moth-eaten doubts, by cloaking their negativity in the spendid mantle of a cool and objective 'scientific method'. Every word and gesture betrays the despair of the best of them and the inner emptiness of the worst: their complete divorce from the proletariat, from its path and from its vocation. What they call faith and seek to deprecate by adding the epithet 'religious' is nothing more nor less than the certainty that capitalism is doomed and that—ultimately—the proletariat will be victorious. There can be no 'material' guarantee of this certitude. It can be guaranteed methodologically—by the dialectical method. And even this must be tested and proved by action, by the revolution itself, by living and dying for the revolution. A Marxist who cultivates the objectivity of the academic study is just as reprehensible as the man who believes that the victory of the world revolution can be guaranteed by the 'laws of nature'.

The unity of theory and practice exists not only *in* theory but also *for* practice. We have seen that the proletariat as a class can only conquer and retain a hold on class consciousness and raise itself to the level of its—objectively-given—historic task through conflict and action. It is likewise true that the party and the individual fighter can only really take possession of their theory if they are able to bring this unity into their praxis. The so-called religious faith is nothing more than the certitude that regardless of all temporary defeats and setbacks, the historical process will come to fruition *in our deeds and through our deeds*.

Here too the opportunists find themselves confronted by the dilemma posed by impotence. They argue that if the Communists foresee 'defeat' they must either desist from every form of action or else brand themselves as unscrupulous adventurers, catastrophe-mongers and terrorists. In their intellectual and moral degradation they are simply incapable of *seeing themselves and their action as an aspect of the totality and of the process*: the 'defeat' as the necessary prelude to victory.

It is characteristic of the unity of theory and practice in the life work of Rosa Luxemburg that the unity of victory and defeat, individual fate and total process is the main thread running through her theory and her life. As early as her first polemic against Bernstein[18] she argued that the necessarily 'premature' seizure of power by the proletariat was inevitable. She unmasked the resulting opportunist fear and lack of faith in revolution as "political nonsense which starts from the assumption that society progresses mechanically and which imagines a definite point in time external to and unconnected with the class struggle in which the class struggle will be won". It is this clear-sighted certitude that guides Rosa Luxemburg in the campaign she waged for the emancipation of the proletariat: its economic and political emancipation from physical bondage under capitalism, and its ideological emancipation from its spiritual bondage under opportunism. As she was the great spiritual leader of the proletariat her chief struggles were fought against the latter enemy—the more dangerous foe as it was harder to defeat. Her death at the hands of her bitterest enemies, Noske and Scheidemann, is, logically, the crowning pinnacle of her thought and life. Theoretically she had predicted the defeat of the January rising years before it took place; tactically she foresaw it at the moment of action. Yet she remained consistently on the side of the masses and shared their fate. That is to say, the unity of theory and practice was preserved in her actions with exactly the same consistency and with exactly the same logic as that which earned her the enmity of her murderers: the opportunists of Social Democracy.

January 1921.

NOTES

1 Marx has convincingly shown with reference to economic 'Robinsonades' that this is no accident but a consequence of the nature of bourgeois society. *A Critique of Political Economy* pp. 266 et seq.

2 Bernstein admits this himself. "It is quite true that because of the Party's requirements with regard to agitation I did not always take my principles to their logical conclusion." *Voraussetzungen des Sozialismus* IXth edition, p. 260.

3 Rosa Luxemburg demonstrates this conclusively with regard to her most serious critic, Otto Bauer, in her *Anti-critique*, p. 66 et seq.

4 *The Poverty of Philosophy*, p. 122.

5 On Hegel's relation to his successors see the excellent treatise by that Hegelian Lassalle: *Die Hegelsche und die Rosenkranzsche Logik*, Werke VI, Cassirer Verl. For the way in which Hegel misapplied his own system and was criticised on this point by Marx who then extended the system, see the essay: *What is orthodox Marxism?*

6 *Die Akkumulation des Kapitals*, 1st edition, p. 296.

7 Ibid. p. 393.

8 *The Poverty of Philosophy*. pp. 124–6.

9 *Antikritik*, p. 118.

10 *The Phenomenology of Mind*. Preface.

11 *Sozialreform oder Revolution?* p. 47.
12 *Antikritik*, p. 37.
13 *Nachlass* II, p. 132. [*The Holy Family*, chapter 4].
14 *Massenstreik*, 2nd edition, p. 48.
15 On the limitations of her view see the essays "Critical Observations on Rosa Luxemburg's 'Critique of the Russian Revolution' " and "Towards a Methodology of the Question of Organisation". In the present essay we are only concerned to present her point of view.
16 *Massenstreik* p. 38.
17 Cf. the fine passage in the Junius Pamphlet, Futurus Verlag, p. 92.
18 *Soziale Reform oder Revolution*, pp. 47-8.

Class Consciousness

> The question is not what goal is *envisaged* for the time being by this or that member of the proletariat, or even by the proletariat as a whole. The question is *what is the proletariat* and what course of action will it be forced historically to take in conformity with its own *nature*.
>
> Marx: *The Holy Family*.

MARX's chief work breaks off just as he is about to embark on the definition of class. This omission was to have serious consequences both for the theory and the practice of the proletariat. For on this vital point the later movement was forced to base itself on interpretations, on the collation of occasional utterances by Marx and Engels and on the independent extrapolation and application of their method. In Marxism the division of society into classes is determined by position within the process of production. But what, then, is the meaning of class consciousness? The question at once branches out into a series of closely interrelated problems. First of all, how are we to understand class consciousness (in theory)? Second, what is the (practical) function of class consciousness, so understood, in the context of the class struggle? This leads to the further question: is the problem of class consciousness a 'general' sociological problem or does it mean one thing for the proletariat and another for every other class to have emerged hitherto? And lastly, is class consciousness homogeneous in nature and function or can we discern different gradations and levels in it? And if so, what are their practical implications for the class struggle of the proletariat?

1

In his celebrated account of historical materialism[1] Engels proceeds from the assumption that although the essence of history consists in the fact that "nothing happens without a conscious purpose or an intended aim", to understand history it is necessary

46

to go further than this. For on the one hand, "the many individual wills active in history for the most part produce results quite other than those intended—often quite the opposite; *their motives, therefore, in relation to the total result are likewise of only secondary importance.* On the other hand, the further question arises: *what driving forces in turn stand behind these motives?* What are the historical causes which transform themselves into these motives in the brain of the actors?" He goes on to argue that these driving forces ought themselves to be determined, in particular those which "set in motion great masses, whole peoples and again whole classes of the people; and which create *a lasting action resulting in a great transformation.*" The essence of scientific Marxism consists, then, in the realisation that the real motor forces of history are independent of man's (psychological) consciousness of them.

At a more primitive stage of knowledge this independence takes the form of the belief that these forces belong, as it were, to nature and that in them and in their causal interactions it is possible to discern the 'eternal' laws of nature. As Marx says of bourgeois thought: "Man's reflections on the forms of social life and consequently also his scientific analysis of those forms, take a course directly opposite to that of their actual historical development. He begins post festum, with the results of the process of development ready to hand before him. The characters . . . have already acquired the stability of natural self-understood forms of social life, before man seeks to decipher not their historical character (for in his eyes they are immutable) but their meaning."[2]

This is a dogma whose most important spokesmen can be found in the political theory of classical German philosophy and in the economic theory of Adam Smith and Ricardo. Marx opposes to them a critical philosophy, a theory of theory and a consciousness of consciousness. This critical philosophy implies above all historical criticism. It dissolves the rigid, unhistorical, natural appearance of social institutions; it reveals their historical origins and shows therefore that they are subject to history in every respect including historical decline. Consequently history does not merely unfold *within* the terrain mapped out by these institutions. It does not resolve itself into the evolution of *contents*, of men and situations, etc., while the *principles* of society remain eternally valid. Nor are these institutions the *goal* to which all history aspires, such that when they are realised history will have fulfilled her mission and will then be at an end. On the contrary, history is precisely *the history of these institutions*, of the changes they undergo *as* institutions which bring men together in societies. Such institutions start by controlling economic relations between men and go on to permeate all human relations (and hence also man's relations with himself and with nature, etc.).

At this point bourgeois thought must come up against an insuperable obstacle, for its starting-point and its goal are always, if not always consciously, an apologia for the existing order of things or at least the proof of their immutability.[3] "Thus there has been history, but there is no longer any," [4] Marx observes with reference to bourgeois economics, a dictum which applies with equal force to all attempts by bourgeois thinkers to understand the process of history. (It has often been pointed out that this is also one of the defects of Hegel's philosophy of history.) As a result, while bourgeois thought is indeed able to conceive of history as a problem, it remains an *intractable* problem. Either it is forced to abolish the process of history and regard the institutions of the present as eternal laws of nature which for 'mysterious' reasons and in a manner wholly at odds with the principles of a rational science were held to have failed to establish themselves firmly, or indeed at all, in the past. (This is characteristic of bourgeois sociology.) Or else, everything meaningful or purposive is banished from history. It then becomes impossible to advance beyond the mere 'individuality' of the various epochs and their social and human representatives. History must then insist with Ranke that every age is "equally close to God", i.e. has attained an equal degree of perfection and that—for quite different reasons—there is no such thing as historical development.

In the first case it ceases to be possible to understand the *origin* of social institutions.[5] The objects of history appear as the objects of immutable, eternal laws of nature. History becomes fossilised in a *formalism* incapable of comprehending that the real nature of socio-historical institutions is that they consist of *relations between men*. On the contrary, men become estranged from this, the true source of historical understanding and cut off from it by an unbridgeable gulf. As Marx points out,[6] people fail to realise "that these definite social relations are just as much the products of men as linen, flax, etc.".

In the second case, history is transformed into the irrational rule of blind forces which is embodied at best in the 'spirit of the people' or in 'great men'. It can therefore only be described pragmatically but it cannot be rationally understood. Its only possible organisation would be aesthetic, as if it were a work of art. Or else, as in the philosophy of history of the Kantians, it must be seen as the instrument, senseless in itself, by means of which timeless, suprahistorical, ethical principles are realised.

Marx resolves this dilemma by exposing it as an illusion. The dilemma means only that the contradictions of the capitalist system of production are reflected in these mutually incompatible accounts of the same object. For in this historiography with its search for 'sociological' laws or its formalistic rationale, we find the reflection of man's plight in bourgeois society and of his helpless enslavement by the forces of production. "To them, *their own social action*", Marx remarks,[7] "takes the form of the action of objects which rule the producers instead of being ruled by them". This law was expressed most clearly and coherently in the purely natural and rational laws of classical economics. Marx retorted with the demand for a historical critique of economics which resolves the totality of the reified objectivities of social and economic life into *relations between men*. Capital and with it every form in which the national economy objectifies itself is, according to Marx, "not a thing but a social relation between persons mediated through things".[8]

However, by reducing the objectivity of the social institutions so hostile to man to relations between men, Marx also does away with the false implications of the irrationalist and individualist principle, i.e. the other side of the dilemma. For to eliminate the objectivity attributed both to social institutions inimical to man and to their historical evolution means the restoration of this objectivity to their underlying basis, to the relations between men; it does not involve the elimination of laws and objectivity independent of the will of man and in particular the wills and thoughts of individual men. It simply means that this objectivity is the self-objectification of human society at a particular stage in its development; its laws hold good only within the framework of the historical context which produced them and which is in turn determined by them.

It might look as though by dissolving the dilemma in this manner we were denying consciousness any decisive role in the process of history. It is true that the conscious reflexes of the different stages of economic growth remain historical facts of

D

great importance; it is true that while dialectical materialism is itself the product of this process, it does not deny that men perform their historical deeds themselves and that they do so consciously. But as Engels emphasises in a letter to Mehring,[9] this consciousness is false. However, the dialectical method does not permit us simply to proclaim the 'falseness' of this consciousness and to persist in an inflexible confrontation of true and false. On the contrary, it requires us to investigate this 'false consciousness' concretely as an aspect of the historical totality and as a stage in the historical process.

Of course bourgeois historians also attempt such concrete analyses; indeed they reproach historical materialists with violating the concrete uniqueness of historical events. Where they go wrong is in their belief that the concrete can be located in the empirical individual of history ('individual' here can refer to an individual man, class or people) and in his empirically given (and hence psychological or mass-psychological) consciousness. And just when they imagine that they have discovered the most concrete thing of all: *society as a concrete totality*, the system of production at a given point in history and the resulting division of society into classes—they are in fact at the furthest remove from it. In missing the mark they mistake something wholly abstract for the concrete. "These relations," Marx states, "are not those between one individual and another, but between worker and capitalist, tenant and landlord, etc. Eliminate these relations and you abolish the whole of society; your Prometheus will then be nothing more than a spectre without arms or legs. . . ."[10]

Concrete analysis means then: the relation to society *as a whole*. For only when this relation is established does the consciousness of their existence that men have at any given time emerge in all its essential characteristics. It appears, on the one hand, as something which is *subjectively* justified in the social and historical situation, as something which can and should be understood, i.e. as 'right'. At the same time, *objectively*, it by-passes the essence of the evolution of society and fails to pinpoint it and express it adequately. That is to say, objectively, it appears as a 'false consciousness'. On the other hand, we may see the same consciousness as something which fails *subjectively* to reach its self-appointed goals, while furthering and realising the *objective* aims of society of which it is ignorant and which it did not choose. This twofold dialectical determination of 'false consciousness' constitutes an analysis far removed from the naïve description of what men *in fact* thought, felt and wanted at any moment in history and from any given point in the class structure. I do not wish to deny the great importance of this, but it remains after all merely the *material* of genuine historical analysis. The relation with concrete totality and the dialectical determinants arising from it transcend pure description and yield the category of objective possibility. By relating consciousness to the whole of society it becomes possible to infer the thoughts and feelings which men would have in a particular situation if they were *able* to assess both it and the interests arising from it in their impact on immediate action and on the whole structure of society. That is to say, it would be possible to infer the thoughts and feelings appropriate to their objective situation. The number of such situations is not unlimited in any society. However much detailed researches are able to refine social typologies there will always be a number of clearly distinguished basic types whose characteristics are determined by the types of position available in the process of production. Now class consciousness consists in fact of the appropriate and rational reactions 'imputed' [zugerechnet] to a particular typical position in the process of production.[11] This consciousness is, therefore, neither the sum nor the average of what is thought or felt by the single individuals who make up the class. And yet the historically significant actions of the class as a whole are determined in the last resort by this consciousness and not by the thought of the individual—and these actions can be understood only by reference to this consciousness.

This analysis establishes right from the start the distance that separates class consciousness from the empirically given, and from the psychologically describable and explicable ideas which men form about their situation in life. But it is not enough just to state that this distance exists or even to define its implications in a formal and general way. We must discover, firstly, whether it is a phenomenon that differs according to the manner in which the various classes are related to society as a whole and whether the differences are so great as to produce *qualitative distinctions*. And we must discover, secondly, the *practical* significance of these different possible relations between the objective economic totality, the imputed class consciousness and the real, psychological thoughts of men about their lives. We must discover, in short, the *practical, historical function* of class consciousness.

Only after such preparatory formulations can we begin to exploit the category of objective possibility systematically. The first question we must ask is how far is it *in fact* possible to discern the whole economy of a society from inside it? It is essential to transcend the limitations of particular individuals caught up in their own narrow prejudices. But it is no less vital not to overstep the frontier fixed for them by the economic structure of society and establishing their position in it.[12] Regarded abstractly and formally, then, class consciousness implies a class-conditioned *unconsciousness* of ones own socio-historical and economic condition.[13] This condition is given as a definite structural relation, a definite formal nexus which appears to govern the whole of life. The 'falseness', the illusion implicit in this situation is in no sense arbitrary; it is simply the intellectual reflex of the objective economic structure. Thus, for example, "the value or price of labour-power takes on the appearance of the price or value of labour itself . . ." and "the illusion is created that the totality is paid labour. . . . In contrast to that, under slavery even that portion of labour which is paid for appears unpaid for." [14] Now it requires the most painstaking historical analysis to use the category of objective possibility so as to isolate the conditions in which this illusion can be exposed and a real connection with the totality established. For if from the vantage point of a particular class the totality of existing society is not visible; if a class thinks the thoughts imputable to it and which bear upon its interests right through to their logical conclusion and yet fails to strike at the heart of that totality, then such a class is doomed to play only a subordinate role. It can never influence the course of history in either a conservative or progressive direction. Such classes are normally condemned to passivity, to an unstable oscillation between the ruling and the revolutionary classes, and if perchance they do erupt then such explosions are purely elemental and aimless. They may win a few battles but they are doomed to ultimate defeat.

For a class to be ripe for hegemony means that its interests and consciousness enable it to organise the whole of society in accordance with those interests. The crucial question in every class struggle is this: which class possesses this capacity and this consciousness at the decisive moment? This does not preclude the use of force. It does not mean that the class-interests destined to prevail and thus to uphold the interests of society as a whole can be guaranteed an automatic victory. On the contrary, such a transfer of power can often only be brought about by the most ruthless use of force (as e.g. the primitive accumulation of capital). But it often turns out that questions of class consciousness prove to be decisive in just those situations where force is unavoidable and where classes are locked in a life-and-death-struggle. Thus the noted Hungarian Marxist Erwin Szabó is mistaken in criticising Engels for maintaining that the Great Peasant War (of 1525) was essentially a reactionary movement. Szabó argues that the peasants' revolt was suppressed *only* by the ruthless use of force and that its defeat was not grounded in socio-economic factors and in the class consciousness of the peasants. He overlooks the fact that the deepest reason for the weakness of the peasantry and the superior strength of the princes is to be sought in class consciousness. Even the most cursory student of the military aspects of the Peasants' War can easily convince himself of this.

It must not be thought, however, that all classes ripe for hegemony have a class consciousness with the same inner structure. Everything hinges on the extent to which they can become conscious of the actions they need to perform in order to obtain and organise power. The question then becomes: how far does the class concerned perform the actions history has imposed on it 'consciously' or 'unconsciously'? And is that consciousness 'true' or 'false'. These distinctions are by no means academic. Quite apart from problems of culture where such fissures and dissonances are crucial, in all practical matters too the fate of a class depends on its ability to elucidate and solve the problems with which history confronts it. And here it becomes transparently obvious that class consciousness is concerned neither with the thoughts of individuals, however advanced, nor with the state of scientific knowledge. For example, it is quite clear that ancient society was broken economically by the limitations of a system built on slavery. But it is equally clear that neither the ruling classes nor the classes that rebelled against them in the name of revolution or reform could perceive this. In consequence the practical emergence of these problems meant that the society was necessarily and irremediably doomed.

The situation is even clearer in the case of the modern bourgeoisie, which, armed with its knowledge of the workings of economics, clashed with feudal and absolutist society. For the bourgeoisie was quite unable to perfect its fundamental science, its own science of classes: the reef on which it foundered was its failure to discover even a theoretical solution to the problem of crises. The fact that a scientifically acceptable solution does exist is of no avail. For to accept that solution, even in theory, would be tantamount to observing society *from a class standpoint other than that of the bourgeoisie.* And no class can do that—unless it is willing to abdicate its power freely. Thus the barrier which converts the class consciousness of the bourgeoisie into 'false' consciousness is objective; it is the class situation itself. It is the objective result of the economic set-up, and is neither arbitrary, subjective nor psychological. The class consciousness of the bourgeoisie may well be able to reflect all the problems of organisation entailed by its hegemony and by the capitalist transformation and penetration of total production. But it becomes obscured as soon as it is called upon to face problems that remain within its jurisdiction but which point beyond the limits of capitalism. The discovery of the 'natural laws' of economics is pure light in comparison with mediaeval feudalism or even the mercantilism of the transitional period, but by an internal dialectical twist they became "natural laws based on the unconsciousness of those who are involved in them".[15]

It would be beyond the scope of these pages to advance further and attempt to construct a historical and systematic typology of the possible degrees of class consciousness. That would require—in the first instance—an exact study of the point in the total process of production at which the interests of the various classes are most immediately and vitally involved. Secondly, we would have to show how far it would be in the interest of any given class to go beyond this immediacy, to annul and transcend its immediate interest by seeing it as a factor within a totality. And lastly, what is the nature of the totality that is then achieved? How far does it really embrace the true totality of production? It is quite evident that the quality and structure of class consciousness must be very different if, e.g. it remains stationary at the separation of consumption from production (as with the Roman *Lumpen-proletariat*) or if it represents the formation of the interests of circulation (as with merchant capital). Although we cannot embark on a systematic typology of the various points of view it can be seen from the foregoing that these specimens of 'false' consciousness differ from each other both qualitatively, structurally and in a manner that is crucial for the activity of the classes in society.

2

It follows from the above that for pre-capitalist epochs and for the behaviour of many strata within capitalism whose economic roots lie in pre-capitalism, class consciousness is unable to achieve complete clarity and to influence the course of history consciously.

This is true above all because class interests in pre-capitalist society never achieve full (economic) articulation. Hence the structuring of society into castes and estates means that economic elements are *inextricably* joined to political and religious factors. In contrast to this, the rule of the bourgeoisie means the abolition of the estates-system and this leads to the organisation of society along class lines. (In many countries vestiges of the feudal system still survive, but this does not detract from the validity of this observation.)

This situation has its roots in the profound difference between capitalist and pre-capitalist economics. The most striking distinction, and the one that directly concerns us, is that pre-capitalist societies are much less *cohesive* than capitalism. The various parts are much more self-sufficient and less closely interrelated than in capitalism. Commerce plays a smaller role in society, the various sectors were more autonomous (as in the case of village communes) or else plays no part at all in the economic life of the community and in the process of production (as was true of large numbers of citizens in Greece and Rome). In such circumstances the state, i.e. the organised unity, remains insecurely anchored in the real life of society. One sector of society simply lives out its 'natural' existence in what amounts to a total independence of the fate of the state. "The simplicity of the organisation for production in these self-sufficient communities that constantly reproduce themselves in the same form, and when accidentally destroyed, spring up again on the spot and with the same name—this simplicity supplies the key to the secret of the immutability of Asiatic societies, an immutability in such striking contrast with the constant dissolution and refounding of Asiatic states, and the never-ceasing changes of dynasty. The structure of the economic elements of society remains untouched by the storm-clouds of the political sky." [16]

Yet another sector of society is—economically—completely parasitic. For this sector the state with its power apparatus is not, as it is for the ruling classes under capitalism, a means whereby to put into practice the principles of its economic power—if need be with the aid of force. Nor is it the instrument it uses to create the conditions for its economic dominance (as with modern colonialism). That is to say, the state is not a *mediation* of the economic control of society: it is that *unmediated dominance itself*. This is true not merely in cases of the straightforward theft of land or slaves, but also in so-called peaceful economic relations. Thus in connection with labour-rent Marx says: "Under such circumstances the surplus labour can be extorted from them for the benefit of the nominal landowner only by other than economic pressure." In Asia "rent and taxes coincide, or rather there is no tax other than this form of ground-rent".[17]

Even commerce is not able, in the forms it assumes in pre-capitalist societies, to make decisive inroads on the basic structure of society. Its impact remains superficial and the process of production above all in relation to labour, remains beyond its control. "A merchant could buy every commodity, but labour as a commodity he could not buy. He existed only on sufferance, as a dealer in the products of the handicrafts." [18]

Despite all this, every such society constitutes an economic unity. The only question that arises is whether this unity enables the individual sectors of society to relate to society as a whole in such a way that their imputed consciousness can assume an economic form. Marx emphasises[19] that in Greece and Rome the class struggle "chiefly took the form of a conflict between debtors and creditors". But he also makes the further, very valid point: "Nevertheless, the money-relationship—and the relationship of creditor to debtor is one of money—reflects only the deeper-lying antagonism between the economic conditions of existence." Historical materialism showed that this reflection was no more than a reflection, but we must go on to ask: was it at all possible—objectively—for the classes in such a society to become conscious of the economic basis of these conflicts and of the economic problems with which the society was afflicted? Was it not inevitable that these conflicts and problems should assume either natural, religious forms,[20] or else political and legal ones, depending on circumstances?

The division of society into estates or castes means in effect that conceptually and organisationally these 'natural' forms are established without their economic basis ever becoming conscious. It means that there is no mediation between the pure traditionalism of natural growth and the legal institutions it assumes.[21] In accordance with the looser economic structure of society, the political and legal institutions (here the division into estates, privileges, etc.), have different functions objectively and subjectively from those exercised under capitalism. In capitalism these institutions merely imply the stabilisation of purely economic forces so that—as Karner has ably demonstrated[22]—they frequently adapt themselves to changed economic structures without changing themselves in form or content. By contrast, in pre-capitalist societies legal institutions intervene *substantively* in the interplay of economic forces. In fact there are no purely economic categories to appear or to be given legal form (and according to Marx, economic categories are "forms of existence, determinations of life").[23] Economic and legal categories are objectively and *substantively so interwoven as to be inseparable*. (Consider here the instances cited earlier of labour-rent, and taxes, of slavery, etc.) In Hegel's parlance the economy has not even objectively reached the stage of being-for-itself. There is therefore no possible position within such a society from which the economic basis of all social relations could be made conscious.

This is not of course to deny the objective economic foundations of social institutions. On the contrary, the history of [feudal] estates shows very clearly that what in origin had been a 'natural' economic existence cast into stable forms begins gradually to disintegrate as a result of subterranean, 'unconscious' economic development. That is to say, it ceases to be a real unity. Their economic content destroys the unity of their juridical form. (Ample proof of this is furnished both by Engels in his analysis of the class struggles of the Reformation period and by Cunow in his discussion of the French Revolution.) However, despite this conflict between juridical form and economic content, the juridical (privilege-creating) forms retain a great and often absolutely crucial importance for the consciousness of estates in the process of disintegration. For the form of the estates conceals the connection between the—real but 'unconscious'—economic existence of the estate and the economic totality of society. It fixates consciousness directly on its privileges (as in the case of

the knights during the Reformation) or else—no less directly—on
the particular element of society from which the privileges eman-
ated (as in the case of the guilds).

Even when an estate has disintegrated, even when its members
have been absorbed economically into a number of different classes, it
still retains this (objectively unreal) ideological coherence.
For the relation to the whole created by the consciousness of
ones status is not directed to the real, living economic unity but
to a past state of society as constituted by the privileges accorded
to the estates. Status-consciousness—a real historical factor—
masks class consciousness; in fact it prevents it from emerging at
all. A like phenomenon can be observed under capitalism in the
case of all 'privileged' groups whose class situation lacks any
immediate economic base. The ability of such a class to adapt
itself to the real economic development can be measured by the
extent to which it succeeds in 'capitalising' itself, i.e. transforming
its privileges into economic and capitalist forms of control (as
was the case with the great landowners).

Thus class consciousness has quite a different relation to history
in pre-capitalist and capitalist periods. In the former case the
classes could only be deduced from the immediately given historical reality *by the methods of historical materialism*. In capitalism they
themselves constitute this immediately given historical *reality*. It is
therefore no accident that (as Engels too has pointed out) this
knowledge of history only became possible with the advent of
capitalism. Not only—as Engels believed—because of the greater
simplicity of capitalism in contrast to the 'complex and concealed
relations' of earlier ages. But primarily because only with capitalism does economic class interest emerge in all its starkness as the
motor of history. In pre-capitalist periods man could never become conscious (not even by virtue of an 'imputed' consciousness) of the "true driving forces which stand behind the motives
of human actions in history". They remained hidden behind
motives and were in truth the blind forces of history. Ideological
factors do not merely 'mask' economic interests, they are not
merely the banners and slogans: they are the parts, the components of which the real struggle is made. Of course, if historical
materialism is deployed to discover the *sociological meaning* of these
struggles, economic interests will doubtless be revealed as the
decisive *factors in any explanation*.

But there is still an unbridgeable gulf between this and capitalism where economic factors are not concealed 'behind' consciousness but are present *in* consciousness itself (albeit unconsciously or repressed). With capitalism, with the abolition of the feudal estates and with the creation of a society with a *purely economic* articulation, class consciousness arrived at the point where *it could become conscious.* From then on social conflict was reflected in an ideological struggle for consciousness and for the veiling or the exposure of the class character of society. But the fact that this conflict became possible points forward to the dialectical contradictions and the internal dissolution of pure class society. In Hegel's words, "When philosophy paints its gloomy picture a form of life has grown old. It cannot be rejuvenated by the gloomy picture, but only understood. Only when dusk starts to fall does the owl of Minerva spread its wings and fly."

3

Bourgeoisie and proletariat are the only pure classes in bourgeois society. They are the only classes whose existence and development are entirely dependent on the course taken by the modern evolution of production and only from the vantage point of these classes can a plan for the total organisation of society *even be imagined.* The outlook of the other classes (petty bourgeois or peasants) is ambiguous or sterile because their existence is not based exclusively on their role in the capitalist system of production but is indissolubly linked with the vestiges of feudal society. Their aim, therefore, is not to advance capitalism or to transcend it, but to reverse its action or at least to prevent it from developing fully. Their class interest concentrates on *symptoms of development* and not on development itself, and on elements of society rather than on the construction of society as a whole.

The question of consciousness may make its appearance in terms of the objectives chosen or in terms of action, as for instance in the case of the petty bourgeoisie. This class lives at least in part in the capitalist big city and every aspect of its existence is directly exposed to the influence of capitalism. Hence it cannot possibly remain wholly unaffected by the *fact* of class conflict between bourgeoisie and proletariat. But as a "transitional class in which the interests of two other classes become simultaneously blunted . . ." it will imagine itself "to be above all class antagonisms".[24] Accordingly it will search for ways whereby it will "not indeed eliminate the two extremes of capital and wage labour, but will weaken their antagonism and transform it into harmony".[25] In all decisions crucial for society its actions will be irrelevant and it will be forced to fight for both sides in turn but always without consciousness. In so doing its own objectives —which exist exclusively in its own consciousness—must become progressively weakened and increasingly divorced from social action. Ultimately they will assume purely 'ideological' forms. The petty bourgeoisie will only be able to play an active role in history as long as these objectives happen to coincide with the real economic interests of capitalism. This was the case with the abolition of the feudal estates during the French Revolution. With the fulfilment of this mission its utterances, which for the most part remain unchanged in form, become more and more remote from real events and turn finally into mere caricatures (this was true, e.g. of the Jacobinism of the Montagne 1848–51).

This isolation from society as a whole has its repercussions on the internal structure of the class and its organisational potential. This can be seen most clearly in the development of the peasantry. Marx says on this point:[26] "The small-holding peasants form a vast mass whose members live in similar conditions but without entering into manifold relations with each other. Their mode of production isolates them from one another instead of bringing them into mutual intercourse. . . . Every single peasant family . . . thus acquires its means of life more through exchange with nature than in intercourse with society. . . . In so far as millions of families live under economic conditions of existence that separate their mode of life, their interests and their culture from those of other classes and place them in opposition to them, they constitute a class. In so far as there is only a local connection between the small-holding peasants, and the identity of their interests begets no community, no national unity and no political organisation, they do not constitute a class." Hence *external* upheavals, such as war, revolution in the towns, etc. are needed before these masses can coalesce in a unified movement, and even then they are incapable of organising it and supplying it with slogans and a positive direction corresponding to their own interests.

Whether these movements will be progressive (as in the French Revolution of 1789 or the Russian Revolution of 1917), or reactionary (as with Napoleon's coup d'état) will depend on the position of the other classes involved in the conflict, and on the level of consciousness of the parties that lead them. For this reason, too, the *ideological* form taken by the class consciousness of the peasants changes its content more frequently than that of other classes: this is because it is always borrowed from elsewhere. Hence parties that base themselves wholly or in part on this class consciousness always lack really firm and secure support in critical situations (as was true of the Socialist Revolutionaries in 1917 and 1918). This explains why it is possible for peasant conflicts to be fought out under opposing flags. Thus it is highly characteristic of both Anarchism and the 'class consciousness' of the peasantry that a number of counter-revolutionary rebellions and uprisings of the middle and upper strata of the peasantry in Russia should have found the anarchist view of society to be a satisfying ideology. We cannot really speak of class consciousness in the case of these classes (if, indeed, we can even speak of them as classes in the strict Marxist sense of the term): for a full consciousness of their situation would reveal to them the hopelessness of their particularist strivings in the face of the inevitable course of events. Consciousness and self-interest then are *mutually incompatible* in this instance. And as class consciousness was defined in terms of the problems of imputing class interests the failure of their class consciousness to develop in the immediately given historical reality becomes comprehensible philosophically.

With the bourgeoisie, also, class consciousness stands in opposition to class interest. But here the antagonism is *not contradictory but dialectical*.

The distinction between the two modes of contradiction may be briefly described in this way: in the case of the other classes, a class consciousness is prevented from emerging by their position within the process of production and the interests this generates. In the case of the bourgeoisie, however, these factors combine to produce a class consciousness but one which is cursed by its very nature with the tragic fate of developing an insoluble contradiction at the very zenith of its powers. As a result of this contradiction it must annihilate itself.

The tragedy of the bourgeoisie is reflected historically in the fact that even before it had defeated its predecessor, feudalism, its new enemy, the proletariat, had appeared on the scene. Politically, it became evident when at the moment of victory, the 'freedom' in whose name the bourgeoisie had joined battle with feudalism, was transformed into a new repressiveness. Sociologically, the bourgeoisie did everything in its power to eradicate the fact of class conflict from the consciousness of society, even though class conflict had only emerged in its purity and became established as an historical fact with the advent of capitalism. Ideologically, we see the same contradiction in the fact that the bourgeoisie endowed the individual with an unprecedented importance, but at the same time that same individuality was annihilated by the economic conditions to which it was subjected, by the reification created by commodity production.

All these contradictions, and the list might be extended indefinitely, are only the reflection of the deepest contradictions in capitalism itself as they appear in the consciousness of the bourgeoisie in accordance with their position in the total system of production. For this reason they appear as dialectical contradictions in the class consciousness of the bourgeoisie. They do not merely reflect the inability of the bourgeoisie to grasp the contradictions inherent in its own social order. For, on the one hand, capitalism is the first system of production able to achieve a total economic penetration of society,[27] and this implies that in theory the bourgeoisie should be able to progress from this central point to the possession of an (imputed) class consciousness of the whole system of production. On the other hand, the position held by the capitalist class and the interests which determine its actions ensure that it will be unable to control its own system of production even in theory.

There are many reasons for this. In the first place, it only seems to be true that for capitalism production occupies the centre of class consciousness and hence provides the theoretical starting-point for analysis. With reference to Ricardo "who had been reproached with an exclusive concern with production", Marx emphasised [28] that he "defined distribution as the sole subject of economics". And the detailed analysis of the process by which capital is concretely realised shows in every single instance that the interest of the capitalist (who produces not goods but commodities) is necessarily confined to matters that must be peripheral in terms of production. Moreover, the capitalist, enmeshed in what is for him the decisive process of the expansion of capital, must have a standpoint from which the most important problems become quite invisible.[29]

The discrepancies that result are further exacerbated by the fact that there is an insoluble contradiction running through the internal structure of capitalism between the social and the individual principle, i.e. between the function of capital as private property and its objective economic function. As the *Communist Manifesto* states: "Capital is a social force and not a personal one." But it is a social force whose movements are determined by the individual interests of the owners of capital—who cannot see and who are necessarily indifferent to all the social implications of their activities. Hence the social principle and the social function implicit in capital can only prevail unbeknown to them and, as it were, against their will and behind their backs. Because of this conflict between the individual and the social, Marx rightly characterised the stock companies as the "negation of the capitalist mode of production itself".[30] Of course, it is true that stock companies differ only in inessentials from individual capitalists and even the so-called abolition of the anarchy in production through cartels and trusts only shifts the contradiction elsewhere, without, however, eliminating it. This situation forms one of the decisive factors governing the class consciousness of the bourgeoisie. It is true that the bourgeoisie acts as a class in the objective evolution of society. But it understands the process (which it is itself instigating) as something external which is subject to objective laws which it can only experience passively.

Bourgeois thought observes economic life consistently and necessarily from the standpoint of the individual capitalist and this naturally produces a sharp confrontation between the individual and the overpowering supra-personal 'law of nature' which propels all social phenomena.[31] This leads both to the antagonism between individual and class interests in the event of conflict (which, it is true, rarely becomes as acute among the ruling classes as in the bourgeoisie), and also to the logical impossibility of discovering theoretical and practical solutions to the problems created by the capitalist system of production.

"This sudden reversion from a system of credit to a system of hard cash heaps theoretical fright on top of practical panic; and the dealers by whose agency circulation is effected shudder before the impenetrable mystery in which their own economic relations are shrouded." [32] This terror is not unfounded, that is to say, it is much more than the bafflement felt by the individual capitalist when confronted by his own individual fate. The facts and the situations which induce this panic force something into the consciousness of the bourgeoisie which is too much of a brute fact for its existence to be wholly denied or repressed. But equally it is something that the bourgeoisie can never fully understand. For the recognisable background to this situation is the fact that "the *real barrier* of capitalist production is *capital itself*".[33] And if this insight were to become conscious it would indeed entail the self-negation of the capitalist class.

In this way the objective limits of capitalist production become the limits of the class consciousness of the bourgeoisie. The older 'natural' and 'conservative' forms of domination had left un-molested[34] the forms of production of whole sections of the people they ruled and therefore exerted by and large a traditional and unrevolutionary influence. Capitalism, by contrast, is a revolu-tionary form par excellence. *The fact that it must necessarily remain in ignorance of the objective economic limitations of its own system expresses itself as an internal, dialectical contradiction in its class consciousness.*

This means that *formally* the class consciousness of the bour-geoisie is geared to economic consciousness. And indeed the highest degree of unconsciousness, the crassest form of 'false consciousness' always manifests itself when the conscious mastery of economic phenomena appears to be at its greatest. From the point of view of the relation of consciousness to society this contradiction is expressed as the *irreconcilable antagonism between ideology and eco-nomic base.* Its dialectics are grounded in the irreconcilable antag-onism between the (capitalist) individual, i.e. the stereotyped individual of capitalism, and the 'natural' and inevitable process of development, i.e. the process not subject to consciousness. In consequence theory and practice are brought into irreconcilable opposition to each other. But the resulting dualism is anything but stable; in fact it constantly strives to harmonise principles that have been wrenched apart and thenceforth oscillate between a new 'false' synthesis and its subsequent cataclysmic disruption.

This internal dialectical contradiction in the class consciousness of the bourgeoisie is further aggravated by the fact that the objective limits of capitalism do not remain purely negative. That is to say that capitalism does not merely set 'natural' laws in motion that provoke crises which it cannot comprehend. On the contrary, those limits acquire a historical embodiment with its own consciousness and its own actions: the proletariat.

Most 'normal' shifts of perspective produced by the capitalist point of view in the image of the economic structure of society tend to "obscure and mystify the true origin of surplus value".[35] In the 'normal', purely theoretical view this mystification only attaches to the organic composition of capital, viz. to the place of the employer in the productive system and the economic function of interest, etc., i.e. it does no more than highlight the failure of observers to perceive the true driving forces that lie beneath the surface. But when it comes to practice this mystification touches upon the central fact of capitalist society: the class struggle.

In the class struggle we witness the emergence of all the hidden forces that usually lie concealed behind the façade of economic life, at which the capitalists and their apologists gaze as though transfixed. These forces appear in such a way that they cannot possibly be ignored. So much so that even when capitalism was in the ascendant and the proletariat could only give vent to its protests in the form of vehement spontaneous explosions, even the ideological exponents of the rising bourgeoisie acknowledged the class struggle as a basic fact of history. (For example, Marat and later historians such as Mignet.) But in proportion as the theory and practice of the proletariat made society conscious of this unconscious, revolutionary principle inherent in capitalism, the bourgeoisie was thrown back increasingly on to a conscious defensive. The dialectical contradiction in the 'false' consciousness of the bourgeoisie became more and more acute: the 'false' consciousness was converted into a mendacious consciousness. What had been at first an objective contradiction now became subjective also: the theoretical problem turned into a moral posture which decisively influenced every practical class attitude in every situation and on every issue.

Thus the situation in which the bourgeoisie finds itself determines the function of its class consciousness in its struggle to achieve control of society. The hegemony of the bourgeoisie really does embrace the whole of society; it really does attempt to organise the whole of society in its own interests (and in this it has had some success). To achieve this it was forced both to develop a coherent theory of economics, politics and society (which in itself presupposes and amounts to a 'Weltanschauung'), and also to make conscious and sustain its faith in its own *mission* to control and organise society. The tragic dialectics of the bourgeoisie can be seen in the fact that it is not only desirable but essential for it to clarify its own class interests on *every particular issue*, while at the same time such a clear awareness becomes fatal when it is extended to *the question of the totality*. The chief reason for this is that the rule of the bourgeoisie can only be the rule of a minority. Its hegemony is exercised not merely *by* a minority but *in the interest* of that minority, so the need to deceive the other classes and to ensure that their class consciousness remains amorphous is inescapable for a bourgeois regime. (Consider here the theory of the state that stands 'above' class antagonisms, or the notion of an 'impartial' system of justice.)

But the veil drawn over the nature of bourgeois society is indispensable to the bourgeoisie itself. For the insoluble internal contradictions of the system become revealed with increasing starkness and so confront its supporters with a choice. Either they must consciously ignore insights which become increasingly urgent or else they must suppress their own moral instincts in order to be able to support with a good conscience an economic system that serves only their own interests.

Without overestimating the efficacy of such ideological factors it must be agreed that the fighting power of a class grows with its ability to carry out its own mission with a good conscience and to adapt all phenomena to its own interests with unbroken confidence in itself. If we consider Sismondi's criticism of classical economics, German criticisms of natural law and the youthful critiques of Carlyle it becomes evident that from a very early stage the ideological history of the bourgeoisie was *nothing but a desperate resistance to every insight into the true nature of the society it had created and thus to a real understanding of its class situation.* When the *Communist Manifesto* makes the point that the bourgeoisie produces its own gravediggers this is valid ideologically as well as economically. The whole of bourgeois thought in the nineteenth century made the most strenuous efforts to mask the real foundations of bourgeois society; everything was tried: from the greatest falsifications of fact to the 'sublime' theories about the 'essence' of history and the state. But in vain: with the end of the century the issue was resolved by the advances of science and their corresponding effects on the consciousness of the capitalist elite.

This can be seen very clearly in the bourgeoisie's greater readiness to accept the idea of conscious organisation. A greater measure of concentration was achieved first in the stock companies and in the cartels and trusts. This process revealed the social character of capital more and more clearly without affecting the general anarchy in production. What it did was to confer near-monopoly status on a number of giant individual capitalists. Objectively, then, the social character of capital was brought into play with great energy but in such a manner as to keep its nature concealed from the capitalist class. Indeed this illusory elimination of economic anarchy successfully diverted their attention from the true situation. With the crises of the War and the post-war period this tendency has advanced still further: the idea of a 'planned' economy has gained ground at least among the more progressive elements of the bourgeoisie. Admittedly this applies only within quite narrow strata of the bourgeoisie and even there it is thought of more as a theoretical experiment than as a practical way out of the impasse brought about by the crises.

When capitalism was still expanding it rejected every sort of social organisation on the grounds that it was "an inroad upon such sacred things as the rights of property, freedom and unrestricted play for the initiative of the individual capitalist."[36] If we compare that with current attempts to harmonise a 'planned' economy with the class interests of the bourgeoisie, we are forced to admit that what we are witnessing is *the capitulation of the class consciousness of the bourgeoisie before that of the proletariat.* Of course, the section of the bourgeoisie that accepts the notion of a 'planned' economy does not mean by it the same as does the proletariat: it regards it as a last attempt to save capitalism by driving its internal contradictions to breaking-point. Nevertheless this means jettisoning the last theoretical line of defence. (As a strange counterpart to this we may note that *at just this point in time* certain sectors of the proletariat *capitulate before the bourgeoisie* and adopt this, the most problematic form of bourgeois organisation.)

With this the whole existence of the bourgeoisie and its culture is plunged into the most terrible crisis. On the one hand, we find the utter sterility of an ideology divorced from life, of a more or less conscious attempt at forgery. On the other hand, a cynicism no less terribly jejune lives on in the world-historical irrelevances and nullities of its own existence and concerns itself only with the defence of that existence and with its own naked self-interest. This ideological crisis is an unfailing sign of decay. The bourgeoisie has already been thrown on the defensive; however aggressive its *weapons* may be, it is fighting for self-preservation. *Its power to dominate has vanished beyond recall.*

4

In this struggle for consciousness historical materialism plays a crucial role. Ideologically no less than economically, the bourgeoisie and the proletariat are mutually interdependent. The same process that the bourgeoisie experiences as a permanent crisis and gradual dissolution appears to the proletariat, likewise in crisis-form, as the gathering of strength and the springboard to victory. Ideologically this means that the same growth of insight into the nature of society, which reflects the protracted death struggle of the bourgeoisie, entails a steady growth in the strength of the proletariat. For the proletariat the truth is a weapon that brings victory; and the more ruthless, the greater the victory. This makes more comprehensible the desperate fury with which bourgeois science assails historical materialism: for as soon as the bourgeoisie is forced to take up its stand on this terrain, it is lost. And, at the same time, this explains why the proletariat and *only* the proletariat can discern in the correct understanding of *the nature of society* a power-factor of the first, and perhaps decisive importance.

The unique function of consciousness in the class struggle of the proletariat has consistently been overlooked by the vulgar Marxists who have substituted a petty 'Realpolitik' for the great battle of principle which reaches back to the ultimate problems of the objective economic process. Naturally we do not wish to deny that the proletariat must proceed from the facts of a given situation. But it is to be distinguished from other classes by the fact that it goes beyond the contingencies of history; far from being driven forward by them, it is itself their driving force and impinges centrally upon the process of social change. When the vulgar Marxists detach themselves from this central point of view, i.e. from the point where a proletarian class consciousness arises, *they thereby place themselves on the level of consciousness of the bourgeoisie.* And that the bourgeoisie fighting on its own ground will prove superior to the proletariat both economically and ideologically can come as a surprise only to a vulgar Marxist. Moreover only a vulgar Marxist would infer from this fact, which after all derives exclusively from his own attitude, that the bourgeoisie *generally* occupies the stronger position. For quite apart from the very real force at its disposal, it is self-evident that the bourgeoisie *fighting on its own ground* will be both more experienced and more expert. Nor will it come as a surprise if the bourgeoisie automatically obtains the upper hand when its opponents abandon their own position for that of the bourgeoisie.

As the bourgeoisie has the intellectual, organisational and every other advantage, the superiority of the proletariat must lie exclusively in its ability to see society from the centre, as a coherent whole. This means that it is able to act in such a way as to change reality; in the class consciousness of the proletariat theory and practice coincide and so it can consciously throw the weight of its actions onto the scales of history—and this is the deciding factor. When the vulgar Marxists destroy this unity they cut the nerve that binds proletarian theory to proletarian action. They reduce theory to the 'scientific' treatment of the symptoms of social change and as for practice they are themselves reduced to being buffeted about aimlessly and uncontrollably by the various elements of the process they had hoped to master.

The class consciousness that springs from this position must exhibit the same internal structure as that of the bourgeoisie. But when the logic of events drives the same dialectical contradictions to the surface of consciousness the consequences for the proletariat are even more disastrous than for the bourgeoisie. For despite all the dialectical contradictions, despite all its objective falseness, the self-deceiving 'false' consciousness that we find in the bourgeoisie is at least in accord with its class situation. It cannot save the bourgeoisie from the constant exacerbation of these contradictions and so from destruction, but it can enable it to continue the struggle and even engineer victories, albeit of short duration.

But in the case of the proletariat such a consciousness not only has to overcome these internal (bourgeois) contradictions, but it also conflicts with the course of action to which the economic situation necessarily commits the proletariat (regardless of its own thoughts on the subject). The proletariat must act in a proletarian manner, but its own vulgar Marxist theory blocks its vision of the right course to adopt. The dialectical contradiction between necessary proletarian action and vulgar Marxist (bourgeois) theory becomes more and more acute. As the decisive battle in the class struggle approaches, the power of a true or false theory to accelerate or retard progress grows in proportion. The 'realm of freedom', the end of the 'pre-history of mankind' means precisely that the power of the objectified, reified relations between men begins to revert to *man*. The closer this process comes to its goal the more urgent it becomes for the proletariat to understand its own historical mission and the more vigorously and directly proletarian class consciousness will determine each of its actions. For the blind power of the forces at work will only advance 'automatically' to their goal of self-annihilation as long as that goal is not within reach. When the moment of transition to the 'realm of freedom' arrives this will become apparent just because the blind forces really will hurtle blindly towards the abyss, and only the conscious will of the proletariat will be able to save mankind from the impending catastrophe. In other words, when the final economic crisis of capitalism develops, *the fate of the revolution (and with it the fate of mankind) will depend on the ideological maturity of the proletariat, i.e. on its class consciousness.*

We have now determined the unique function of the class consciousness of the proletariat in contrast to that of other classes. The proletariat cannot liberate itself as a class without simultaneously abolishing class society as such. For that reason its consciousness, the last class consciousness in the history of mankind, must both lay bare the nature of society and achieve an increasingly inward fusion of theory and practice. 'Ideology' for the proletariat is no banner to follow into battle, nor is it a cover for its true objectives: it is the objective and the weapon itself. Every non-principled or unprincipled use of tactics on the part of the proletariat debases historical materialism to the level of mere 'ideology' and forces the proletariat to use bourgeois (or petty bourgeois) tactics. It thereby robs it of its greatest strength by forcing class consciousness into the secondary or inhibiting role of a bourgeois consciousness, instead of the active role of a proletarian consciousness.

5

The relationship between class consciousness and class situation is really very simple in the case of the proletariat, but the obstacles which prevent its consciousness being realised in practice are correspondingly greater. In the first place this consciousness is divided within itself. It is true that society as such is highly unified and that it evolves in a unified manner. But in a world where the reified relations of capitalism have the appearance of a natural environment it looks as if there is not a unity but a diversity of mutually independent objects and forces.

The most striking division in proletarian class consciousness and the one most fraught with consequences is the separation of the economic struggle from the political one. Marx repeatedly exposed[37] the fallacy of this split and demonstrated that it is in the nature of every economic struggle to develop into a political one (and vice versa). Nevertheless it has not proved possible to eradicate this heresy from the theory of the proletariat. The cause of this aberration is to be found in the dialectical separation of immediate objectives and ultimate goal and, hence, in the dialectical division within the proletarian revolution itself.

Classes that successfully carried out revolutions in earlier societies had their task made easier *subjectively* by this very fact of the discrepancy between their own class consciousness and the objective economic set-up, i.e. by their very unawareness of their own function in the process of change. They had only to use the power at their disposal to enforce their *immediate* interests while the social import of their actions was hidden from them and left to the 'ruse of reason' of the course of events.

But as the proletariat has been entrusted by history with the task of *transforming society consciously*, its class consciousness must develop a dialectical contradiction between its immediate interests and its long-term objectives, and between the discrete factors and the whole. For the discrete factor, the concrete situation with its concrete demands is by its very nature an integral part of the existing capitalist society; it is governed by the laws of that society and is subject to its economic structure. Only when the immediate interests are integrated into a total view and related to the final goal of the process do they become revolutionary, pointing concretely and consciously beyond the confines of capitalist society.

This means that subjectively, i.e. for the class consciousness of the proletariat, the dialectical relationship between immediate interests and objective impact on the whole of society is located *in the consciousness of the proletariat itself*. It does not work itself out as a purely objective process quite apart from all (imputed) consciousness—as was the case with all classes hitherto. Thus the revolutionary victory of the proletariat does not imply, as with former classes, *the immediate realisation of the socially given existence of the class*, but, as the young Marx clearly saw and defined, *its self-annihilation*. The *Communist Manifesto* formulates this distinction in this way: "All the preceding classes that got the upper hand, sought to fortify their already acquired status by subjecting society at large to their conditions of appropriation. The proletarians cannot become masters of the productive forces of society, except *by abolishing their own previous mode of appropriation*, and thereby every other previous mode of appropriation." (My italics.)

This inner dialectic makes it hard for the proletariat to develop its class consciousness in opposition to that of the bourgeoisie which by cultivating the crudest and most abstract kind of empiricism was able to make do with a superficial view of the world. Whereas even when the development of the proletariat was still at a very primitive stage it discovered that one of the elementary rules of class warfare was to advance beyond what was immediately given. (Marx emphasises this as early as his observations on the Weavers' Uprising in Silesia.)[38] For because of its situation this contradiction is introduced directly into the consciousness of the proletariat, whereas the bourgeoisie, from its situation, saw the contradictions confronting it as the outer limits of its consciousness.

Conversely, this contradiction means that 'false' consciousness is something very different for the proletariat than for every preceding class. Even correct statements about particular situations or aspects of the development of bourgeois class consciousness reveal, when related to the whole of society, the limits of that consciousness and unmask its 'falseness'. Whereas the proletariat *always aspires towards the truth* even in its 'false' consciousness and in its substantive errors. It is sufficient here to recall the social criticism of the Utopians or the proletarian and revolutionary extension of Ricardo's theory. Concerning the latter, Engels places great emphasis on the fact that it is "formally incorrect economically", but he adds at once: "What is false from a formal economic point of view can be true in the perspective of world history. . . . Behind the formal economic error may lie concealed a very true economic content." [39]

Only with the aid of this distinction can there be any resolution of the contradiction in the class consciousness of the proletariat; only with its aid can that contradiction become a conscious factor in history. For the objective aspiration towards truth which is immanent even in the 'false' consciousness of the proletariat does not at all imply that this aspiration can come to light without the active intervention of the proletariat. On the contrary, the mere aspiration towards truth can only strip off the veils of falseness and mature into historically significant and socially revolutionary knowledge by the potentiating of consciousness, by conscious action and conscious self-criticism. Such knowledge would of course be unattainable were it not for the objective aspiration, and here we find confirmation of Marx's dictum that "mankind only ever sets itself tasks which it can accomplish".[40] But the aspiration only *yields the possibility*. The accomplishment can only be the fruit of the *conscious* deeds of the proletariat.

The dialectical cleavage in the consciousness of the proletariat is a product of the same structure that makes the historical mission of the proletariat possible by pointing forward and beyond the existing social order. In the case of the other classes we found an antagonism between the class's self-interest and that of society, between individual deed and social consequences. This antagonism set an external limit to consciousness. Here, in the centre of proletarian class consciousness we discover an antagonism between momentary interest and ultimate goal. The outward victory of the proletariat can only be achieved if this antagonism is inwardly overcome.

As we stressed in the motto to this essay the existence of this conflict enables us to perceive that class consciousness is identical with neither the psychological consciousness of individual members of the proletariat, nor with the (mass-psychological) consciousness of the proletariat as a whole; but it is, on the contrary, *the sense, become conscious, of the historical role of the class*. This sense will objectify in particular interests of the moment which may only be omitted at the price of allowing the proletarian class struggle to slip back into the most primitive Utopianism. Every momentary interest may have either of two functions: either it will be a step towards the ultimate goal or else it will conceal it. Which of the two it will be depends *entirely upon the class consciousness of the proletariat and not on victory or defeat in isolated skirmishes*. Marx drew attention very early on[41] to this danger, which is particularly acute on the economic 'trade-union' front: "At the same time the working class ought not to exaggerate to themselves the ultimate consequences of these struggles. They ought not to forget that they are fighting with effects, but not with the causes of those effects..., that they are applying palliatives, not curing the malady. They ought, therefore, not to be exclusively absorbed in these unavoidable guerilla fights . . . instead of simultaneously trying to cure it, instead of using their organised forces as a lever for the final emancipation of the working class, that is to say, the ultimate abolition of the wages system."

We see here the source of every kind of opportunism which begins always with effects and not causes, parts and not the whole, symptoms and not the thing itself. It does not regard the particular interest and the struggle to achieve it as a means of education for the final battle whose outcome depends on closing the gap between the psychological consciousness and the imputed one. Instead it regards the particular as a valuable achievement in itself or at least as a step along the path towards the ultimate goal. In a word, opportunism *mistakes the actual, psychological state of consciousness of proletarians for the class consciousness of the proletariat.*

The practical damage resulting from this confusion can be seen in the great loss of unity and cohesiveness in proletarian praxis when compared to the unity of the objective economic tendencies. The superior strength of true, practical class consciousness lies in the ability to look beyond the divisive symptoms of the economic process to the unity of the total social system underlying it. In the age of capitalism it is not possible for the total system to become directly visible in external phenomena. For instance, the economic basis of a world crisis is undoubtedly unified and its coherence can be understood. But its actual appearance in time and space will take the form of a disparate succession of events in different countries at different times and even in different branches of industry in a number of countries.

When bourgeois thought "transforms the different limbs of society into so many separate societies"[42] it certainly commits a grave theoretical error. But the immediate practical consequences are nevertheless in harmony with the interests of capitalism. The bourgeoisie is unable in theory to understand more than the details and the symptoms of economic processes (a failure which will *ultimately* prove its undoing). In the short term, however, it is concerned above all to impose its mode of life upon the day-to-day actions of the proletariat. In this respect (and in this respect alone) its superiority in organisation is clearly visible, while the wholly different organisation of the proletariat, *its capacity for being organised as a class*, cannot become effective.

The further the economic crisis of capitalism advances, the more clearly this unity in the economic process becomes *comprehensible in practice*. It was there, of course, in so-called periods of normality, too, and was therefore visible from the class standpoint of the proletariat, but the gap between appearance and ultimate reality was too great for that unity to have any practical consequences for proletarian action.

In periods of crisis the position is quite different. The unity of the economic process now moves within reach. So much so that even capitalist theory cannot remain wholly untouched by it, though it can never fully adjust to it. In this situation the fate of the proletariat, and hence of the whole future of humanity, hangs on whether or not it will take *the step that has now become objectively possible*. For even if the particular symptoms of crisis appear separately (according to country, branch of industry, in the form of 'economic' or 'political' crisis, etc.), and even if in consequence the reflex of the crisis is fragmented in the immediate psychological consciousness of the workers, it is still possible and necessary to advance beyond this consciousness. And this is *instinctively* felt to be a necessity by larger and larger sections of the proletariat.

Opportunism had—as it seemed—merely served to inhibit the objective tendency until the crisis became acute. Now, however, it adopts a *course directly opposed to it*. Its aim now is to scotch the development of proletarian class consciousness in its progress from that which is merely given to that which conforms to the objective total process; even more, it hopes *to reduce the class consciousness of the proletariat to the level of* the psychologically given and thus to divert into the opposite direction what had hitherto been the purely instinctive tendency. As long as the unification of proletarian class consciousness was not a practical possibility this theory could—with some charity—be regarded as a mere error. But in this situation it takes on the character of a conscious deception (regardless of whether its advocates are psychologically conscious of this or not). In contrast with the right instincts of the proletariat it plays the same role as that played hitherto by capitalist theory: it denounces the correct view of the overall economic situation and the correct class consciousness of the proletariat together with its organised form, the Communist Party, as something unreal and inimical to the 'true' interests of the workers(i.e. their immediate, national or professional interests) and as something alien to their 'genuine' class consciousness (i.e. that which is psychologically given).

To say that class consciousness has no psychological reality does not imply that it is a mere fiction. Its reality is vouched for by its ability to explain the infinitely painful path of the proletarian revolution, with its many reverses, its constant return to its starting-point and the incessant self-criticism of which Marx speaks in the celebrated passage in *The Eighteenth Brumaire*.

Only the consciousness of the proletariat can point to the way that leads out of the impasse of capitalism. As long as this consciousness is lacking, the crisis remains permanent, it goes back to its starting-point, repeats the cycle until after infinite sufferings and terrible detours the school of history completes the education of the proletariat and confers upon it the leadership of mankind. But the proletariat is not given any choice. As Marx says, it must become a class not only "as against capital" but also "for itself"; [43] that is to say, the class struggle must be raised from the level of economic necessity to the level of conscious aim and effective class consciousness. The pacifists and humanitarians of the class struggle whose efforts tend whether they will or no to retard this lengthy, painful and crisis-ridden process would be horrified if they could but see what sufferings they inflict on the proletariat by extending this course of education. But the proletariat cannot abdicate its mission. The only question at issue is how much it has to suffer before it achieves ideological maturity, before it acquires a true understanding of its class situation and a true class consciousness.

Of course this uncertainty and lack of clarity are themselves the symptoms of the crisis in bourgeois society. As the product of capitalism the proletariat must necessarily be subject to the modes of existence of its creator. This mode of existence is inhumanity and reification. No doubt the very existence of the proletariat implies criticism and the negation of this form of life. But until the objective crisis of capitalism has matured and until the proletariat has achieved true class consciousness, and the ability to understand the crisis fully, it cannot go beyond the criticism of reification and so it is only negatively superior to its antagonist. Indeed, if it can do no more than negate some aspects of capitalism, if it cannot at least aspire to a critique of the whole, then it will not even achieve a negative superiority. This applies to the petty-bourgeois attitudes of most trade unionists. Such criticism from the standpoint of capitalism can be seen most strikingly in the separation of the various theatres of war. The bare fact of separation itself indicates that the consciousness of the proletariat is still fettered by reification. And if the proletariat finds the economic inhumanity to which it is subjected easier to understand than the political, and the political easier than the cultural, then all these separations point to the extent of the still unconquered power of capitalist forms of life in the proletariat itself.

The reified consciousness must also remain hopelessly trapped in the two extremes of crude empiricism and abstract utopianism. In the one case, consciousness becomes either a completely passive observer moving in obedience to laws which it can never control. In the other it regards itself as a power which is able of its own –subjective—volition to master the essentially meaningless motion of objects. We have already identified the crude empiricism of the opportunists in its relation to proletarian class consciousness. We must now go on to see utopianism as characteristic of the internal divisions within class consciousness. (The separation of empiricism from utopianism undertaken here for purely methodological reasons should not be taken as an admission that the two cannot occur together in particular trends and even individuals. On the contrary, they are frequently found together and are joined by an internal bond.)

The philosophical efforts of the young Marx were largely directed towards the refutation of the various false theories of consciousness (including both the 'idealism' of the Hegelian School and the 'materialism' of Feuerbach) and towards the discovery of a correct view of the role of consciousness in history. As early as the Correspondence of 1843 [with Ruge] he conceives of consciousness as immanent in history. Consciousness does not lie outside the real process of history. It does not have to be introduced into the world by philosophers; therefore to gaze down arrogantly upon the petty struggles of the world and to despise them is indefensible. "We only show it [the world] what its struggles are about and consciousness is a thing that it must needs acquire whether it will or not." What is needed then is only "to explain its own actions to it".[44] The great polemic against Hegel in *The Holy Family* concentrates mainly on this point.[45] Hegel's inadequacy is that he only seems to allow the absolute spirit to make history. The resulting otherworldliness of consciousness *vis-à-vis* the real events of history becomes, in the hands of Hegel's disciples, an arrogant—and reactionary—confrontation of 'spirit' and 'mass'. Marx mercilessly exposes the flaws and absurdities and the reversions to a pre-Heglian stage implicit in this approach.

Complementing this is his—aphoristic—critique of Feuerbach. The materialists had elaborated a view of consciousness as of something appertaining to this world. Marx sees it as merely one stage in the process, the stage of 'bourgeois society'. He opposes to it the notion of consciousness as 'practical critical activity' with the task of 'changing the world'.

This provides us with the philosophical foundation we need to settle accounts with the utopians. For their thought contains this very duality of social process and the consciousness of it. Consciousness approaches society from another world and leads it from the false path it has followed back to the right one. The utopians are prevented by the undeveloped nature of the proletarian movement from seeing the true bearer of historical movement in history itself, in the way the proletariat organises itself as a class and, hence, in the class consciousness of the proletariat. They are not yet able to "take note of what is happening before their very eyes and to become its mouthpiece".[46]

It would be foolish to believe that this criticism and the recognition that a post-utopian attitude to history has become *objectively possible* means that utopianism can be dismissed as a factor in the proletariat's struggle for freedom. This is true only for those stages of class consciousness that have really achieved the unity of theory and practice described by Marx, the real and practical intervention of class consciousness in the course of history and hence the practical understanding of reification. And this did not all happen at a single stroke and in a coherent manner. For there are not merely national and 'social' stages involved but there are also gradations within the class consciousness of workers in the same strata. The separation of economics from politics is the most revealing and also the most important instance of this. It appears that some sections of the proletariat have quite the right instincts as far as the economic struggle goes and can even raise them to the level of class consciousness. At the same time, however, when it comes to political questions they manage to persist in a completely utopian point of view. It does not need to be emphasised that there is no question here of a mechanical duality. The utopian view of the function of politics must impinge dialectically on their views about economics and, in particular, on their notions about the economy as a totality (as, for example, in the Syndicalist theory of revolution). In the absence of a real understanding of the interaction between politics and economics a war against the whole economic system, to say nothing of its reorganisation, is quite out of the question.

The influence enjoyed even today by such completely utopian theories as those of Ballod or of guild-socialism shows the extent to which utopian thought is still prevalent, even at a level where the direct life-interests of the proletariat are most nearly concerned and where the present crisis makes it possible to read off from history the correct course of action to be followed.

This syndrome must make its appearance even more blatantly where it is not yet possible to see society as a whole. This can be seen at its clearest in purely ideological questions, in questions of culture. These questions occupy an almost wholly isolated position in the consciousness of the proletariat; the organic bonds connecting these issues with the immediate life-interests of the proletariat as well as with society as a whole have not even begun to penetrate its consciousness. The achievement in this area hardly ever goes beyond the self-criticism of capitalism—carried out here by the proletariat. What is positive here in theory and practice is almost entirely utopian.

These gradations are, then, on the one hand, objective historical necessities, nuances in the objective possibilities of consciousness (such as the relative cohesiveness of politics and economics in comparison to cultural questions). On the other hand, where consciousness already exists as an objective possibility, they indicate degrees of distance between the psychological class consciousness and the adequate understanding of the total situation. *These* gradations, however, can no longer be referred back to socio-economic causes. *The objective theory of class consciousness is the theory of its objective possibility.* The stratification of the problems and economic interests *within* the proletariat is, unfortunately, almost wholly unexplored, but research would undoubtedly lead to discoveries of the very first importance. But however useful it would be to produce a typology of the various strata, we would still be confronted at every turn with the problem of whether it is actually possible to make the objective possibility of class consciousness into a reality. Hitherto this question could only occur to extraordinary individuals (consider Marx's completely non-utopian prescience with regard to the problems of dictatorship). Today it has become a real and relevant question for a whole class: the question of the inner transformation of the proletariat, of its development to the stage of its own objective historical mission. It is an ideological crisis which must be solved before a practical solution to the world's economic crisis can be found.

In view of the great distance that the proletariat has to travel ideologically it would be disastrous to foster any illusions. But it would be no less disastrous to overlook the forces at work within the proletariat which are tending towards the ideological defeat of capitalism. Every proletarian revolution has created workers' councils in an increasingly radical and conscious manner. When this weapon increases in power to the point where it becomes the organ of state, this is a sign that the class consciousness of the proletariat is on the verge of overcoming the bourgeois outlook of its leaders.

The revolutionary workers' council (not to be confused with its opportunist caricatures) is one of the forms which the consciousness of the proletariat has striven to create ever since its inception. The fact that it exists and is constantly developing shows that the proletariat already stands on the threshold of its own consciousness and hence on the threshold of victory. The workers' council spells the political and economic defeat of reification. In the period following the dictatorship it will eliminate the bourgeois separation of the legislature, administration and judiciary. During the struggle for control its mission is twofold. On the one hand, it must overcome the fragmentation of the proletariat in time and space, and on the other, it has to bring economics and politics together into the true synthesis of proletarian praxis. In this way it will help to reconcile the dialectical conflict between immediate interests and ultimate goal.

Thus we must never overlook the distance that separates the consciousness of even the most revolutionary worker from the authentic class consciousness of the proletariat. But even this situation can be explained on the basis of the Marxist theory of class struggle and class consciousness. *The proletariat only perfects itself by annihilating and transcending itself, by creating the classless society through the successful conclusion of its own class struggle.* The struggle for this society, in which the dictatorship of the proletariat is merely a phase, is not just a battle waged against an external enemy, the bourgeoisie. It is equally the struggle of the proletariat *against itself*: against the devastating and degrading effects of the capitalist system upon its class consciousness. The proletariat will only have won the real victory when it has overcome these effects within itself. The separation of the areas that should be united, the diverse stages of consciousness which the proletariat has reached in the various spheres of activity are a precise index of what has been achieved and what remains to be done. The proletariat must not shy away from self-criticism, for victory can only be gained by the truth and self-criticism must, therefore, be its natural element.

March 1920.

NOTES

1 *Feuerbach and the End of Classical German Philosophy*, S.W. II, pp. 354 ff.
2 *Capital* I, p. 75.
3 And also of the 'pessimism' which *perpetuates* the present state of affairs and represents it as the uttermost limit of human development just as much as does 'optimism'. In this respect (and in this respect alone) Hegel and Schopenhauer are on a par with each other.
4 *The Poverty of Philosophy*, p. 135.
5 Ibid., p. 117.
6 Ibid., p. 122.
7 *Capital* I, p. 75 (my italics). Cf. also Engels, *The Origin of the Family, Private Property and the State*, S.W. II, pp. 292–3.
8 *Capital* I, p. 766. Cf. also *Wage Labour and Capital*, S.W. II, p. 83; on machines see *The Poverty of Philosophy*, p. 149; on money, ibid., p. 89, etc.
9 *Dokumente des Sozialismus* II, p. 76.
10 *The Poverty of Philosophy*, p. 112.
11 In this context it is unfortunately not possible to discuss in greater detail some of the ramifications of these ideas in Marxism, e.g. the very important category of the 'economic persona'. Even less can we pause to glance at the relation of historical materialism to comparable trends in bourgeois thought (such as Max Weber's ideal types).
12 This is the point from which to gain an historical understanding of the great utopians such as Plato or Sir Thomas More. Cf. also Marx on Aristotle, *Capital* I, pp. 59–60.
13 "But although ignorant of this, yet he says it," Marx says of Franklin, *Capital* I, p. 51. And similarly: "They know not what they do, but they do it." Ibid., p. 74.
14 *Wages, Price and Profit*, S.W. I, pp. 388–9.
15 Engels, *Umriss zu einer Kritik der Nationalökonomie*, Nachlass I, p. 449.
16 *Capital* I, p. 358.
17 *Capital* III, p. 770 (my italics).
18 *Capital* I, pp. 358–9. This probably explains the politically reactionary role played by merchants' capital as opposed to industrial capital in the beginnings of capitalism. Cf. *Capital* III, p. 322.

E

19 *Capital* I, pp. 135–6.
20 Marx and Engels repeatedly emphasise the naturalness of these
    social formations, *Capital* I, pp. 339, 351, etc. The whole structure
    of evolution in Engels' *Origin of the Family* is based on this idea.
    I cannot enter here into the controversies on this issue—contro-
    versies involving Marxists too; I should just like to stress that here
    also I consider the views of Marx and Engels to be more profound
    and historically more correct than those of their 'improvers'.
21 Cf. *Capital* I, p. 339.
22 *Die soziale Funktion der Rechtsinstitute*, Marx-Studien, Vol. I.
23 *A Contribution to the Critique of Political Economy*, p. 302.
24 *The Eighteenth Brumaire of Louis Bonaparte*, S.W. I. p. 252.
25 Ibid., p. 249.
26 Ibid., pp. 302–3.
27 But no more than the tendency. It is Rosa Luxemburg's great
    achievement to have shown that this is not just a passing phase
    but that capitalism can only survive—economically—while it
    moves society in the direction of capitalism but has not yet fully
    penetrated it. ⸢This economic self-contradiction of any purely
    capitalist society is undoubtedly one of the reasons for the contra-
    dictions in the class consciousness of the bourgeoisie.
28 *A Contribution to the Critique of Political Economy*, p. 285.
29 *Capital* III, pp. 136, 307–8, 318, etc. It is self-evident that the
    different groups of capitalists, such as industrialists and merchants,
    etc., are differently placed; but the distinctions are not relevant
    in this context.
30 Ibid., p. 428.
31 On this point cf. the essay "The Marxism of Rosa Luxemburg".
32 *A Contribution to the Critique of Political Economy*, p. 198.
33 *Capital* III, pp. 245 and also 252.
34 This applies also to e.g. primitive forms of hoarding (see *Capital*
    I, p. 131) and even to certain expressions of (what is relatively)
    'pre-capitalist' merchants' capital. Cf. *Capital* III, p. 329.
35 *Capital* III, pp. 165 and also 151, 373–6, 383, etc.
36 *Capital* I, p. 356.
37 *The Poverty of Philosophy*, p. 197. Letters and extracts from letters
    to F. A. Sorge and others, p. 42, etc.
38 Nachlass II, p. 54. [Kritische Randglossen zu dem Artikel: Der
    König von Preussen und die Sozialreform.]
39 Preface to *The Poverty of Philosophy*, p. 197.
40 *A Contribution to the Critique of Political Economy*, p. 12.
41 *Wages, Price and Profit*, S.W. I, pp. 404–5.
42 *The Poverty of Philosophy*, pp. 123–4.
43 Ibid., p. 195.
44 Nachlass I, p. 382. [Correspondence with Ruge 1843.]
45 Cf. the essay "What is Orthodox Marxism?"
46 *The Poverty of Philosophy*, p. 140. Cf. also the *Communist Manifesto*,
    S.W. I, pp. 58–9.

Reification and the Consciousness of the Proletariat

> To be radical is to go to the root of the matter. For man, however, the root is man himself.
>
> Marx: *Critique of Hegel's*
> *Philosophy of Right.*

IT is no accident that Marx should have begun with an analysis of commodities when, in the two great works of his mature period, he set out to portray capitalist society in its totality and to lay bare its fundamental nature. For at this stage in the history of mankind there is no problem that does not ultimately lead back to that question and there is no solution that could not be found in the solution to the riddle of commodity-*structure*. Of course the problem can only be discussed with this degree of generality if it achieves the depth and breadth to be found in Marx's own analyses. That is to say, the problem of commodities must not be considered in isolation or even regarded as the central problem in economics, but as the central, structural problem of capitalist society in all its aspects. Only in this case can the structure of commodity-relations be made to yield a model of all the objective forms of bourgeois society together with all the subjective forms corresponding to them.

I

The Phenomenon of Reification

1

The essence of commodity-structure has often been pointed out. Its basis is that a relation between people takes on the character of a thing and thus acquires a 'phantom objectivity', an autonomy that seems so strictly rational and all-embracing as to conceal every trace of its fundamental nature: the relation between people. It is beyond the scope of this essay to discuss the central

83

importance of this problem for economics itself. Nor shall we consider its implications for the economic doctrines of the vulgar Marxists which follow from their abandonment of this starting-point.

Our intention here is to *base* ourselves on Marx's economic analyses and to proceed from there to a discusssion of the problems growing out of the fetish character of commodities, both as an objective form and also as a subjective stance corresponding to it. Only by understanding this can we obtain a clear insight into the ideological problems of capitalism and its downfall.

Before tackling the problem itself we must be quite clear in our minds that commodity fetishism is a *specific* problem of our age, the age of modern capitalism. Commodity exchange and the corresponding subjective and objective commodity relations existed, as we know, when society was still very primitive. What is at issue *here*, however, is the question: how far is commodity exchange together with its structural consequences able to influence the *total* outer and inner life of society? Thus the extent to which such exchange is the dominant form of metabolic change in a society cannot simply be treated in quantitative terms—as would harmonise with the modern modes of thought already eroded by the reifying effects of the dominant commodity form. The distinction between a society where this form is dominant, permeating every expression of life, and a society where it only makes an episodic appearance is essentially one of quality. For depending on which is the case, all the subjective and objective phenomena in the societies concerned are objectified in qualitatively different ways.

Marx lays great stress on the essentially episodic appearance of the commodity form in primitive societies: "Direct barter, the original natural form of exchange, represents rather the beginning of the transformation of use-values into commodities, than that of commodities into money. Exchange value has as yet no form of its own, but is still directly bound up with use-value. This is manifested in two ways. Production, in its entire organisation, aims at the creation of use-values and not of exchange values, and it is only when their supply exceeds the measure of consumption that use-values cease to be use-values, and become means of exchange, i.e. commodities. At the same time, they become commodities only within the limits of being direct use-values distributed at opposite poles, so that the commodities to be exchanged by their possessors must be use-values to both—each commodity to its non-possessor. As a matter of fact, the exchange of commodities originates not within the primitive communities, but where they end, on their borders at the few points where they come in contact with other communities. That is where barter begins, and from here it strikes back into the interior of the community, decomposing it."[1] We note that the observation about the disintegrating effect of a commodity exchange directed in upon itself clearly shows the qualitative change engendered by the dominance of commodities.

However, even when commodities have this impact on the internal structure of a society, this does not suffice to make them constitutive of that society. To achieve that it would be necessary —as we emphasized above—for the commodity structure to penetrate society in all its aspects and to remould it in its own image. It is not enough merely to establish an external link with independent processes concerned with the production of exchange values. The qualitative difference between the commodity as one form among many regulating the metabolism of human society and the commodity as the universal structuring principle has effects over and above the fact that the commodity relation as an isolated phenomenon exerts a negative influence at best on the structure and organisation of society. The distinction also has repercussions upon the nature and validity of the category itself. Where the commodity is universal it manifests itself differently from the commodity as a particular, isolated, non-dominant phenomenon.

The fact that the boundaries lack sharp definition must not be allowed to blur the qualitative nature of the decisive distinction. The situation where commodity exchange is not dominant has been defined by Marx as follows: "The quantitative ratio in which products are exchanged is at first quite arbitrary. They assume the form of commodities inasmuch as they are exchangeables, i.e. expressions of one and the same third. Continued exchange and more regular reproduction for exchange reduces this arbitrariness more and more. But at first not for the producer and consumer, but for their go-between, the merchant, who compares money-prices and pockets the difference. It is through his own movements that he establishes equivalence. Merchant's capital is originally merely the intervening movement between extremes which it does not control and between premises which it does not create."[2]

And *this* development of the commodity to the point where it becomes the dominant form in society did not take place until the advent of modern capitalism. Hence it is not to be wondered at that the personal nature of economic relations was still understood clearly on occasion at the start of capitalist development, but that as the process advanced and forms became more complex and less direct, it became increasingly difficult and rare to find anyone penetrating the veil of reification. Marx sees the matter in this way: "In preceding forms of society this economic mystification arose principally with respect to money and interest-bearing capital. In the nature of things it is excluded, in the first place, where production for the use-value, for immediate personal requirements, predominates; and secondly, where slavery or serfdom form the broad foundation of social production, as in antiquity and during the Middle Ages. Here, the domination of the producers by the conditions of production is concealed by the relations of dominion and servitude which appear and are evident as the direct motive power of the process of production."[3]

The commodity can only be understood in its undistorted essence when it becomes the universal category of society as a whole. Only in this context does the reification produced by commodity relations assume decisive importance both for the objective evolution of society and for the stance adopted by men towards it. Only then does the commodity become crucial for the subjugation of men's consciousness to the forms in which this reification finds expression and for their attempts to comprehend the process or to rebel against its disastrous effects and liberate themselves from servitude to the 'second nature' so created.

Marx describes the basic phenomenon of reification as follows: "A commodity is therefore a mysterious thing, simply because in it the social character of men's labour appears to them as an objective character stamped upon the product of that labour; because the relation of the producers to the sum total of their own labour is presented to them as a social relation, existing not between themselves, but between the products of their labour. This is the reason why the products of labour become commodities, social things whose qualities are at the same time perceptible and imperceptible by the senses. . . . It is only a definite social relation between men that assumes, in their eyes, the fantastic form of a relation between things."[4]

What is of central importance here is that because of this

situation a man's own activity, his own labour becomes something objective and independent of him, something that controls him by virtue of an autonomy alien to man. There is both an objective and a subjective side to this phenomenon. *Objectively* a world of objects and relations between things springs into being (the world of commodities and their movements on the market). The laws governing these objects are indeed gradually discovered by man, but even so they confront him as invisible forces that generate their own power. The individual can use his knowledge of these laws to his own advantage, but he is not able to modify the process by his own activity. *Subjectively*—where the market economy has been fully developed—a man's activity becomes estranged from himself, it turns into a commodity which, subject to the non-human objectivity of the natural laws of society, must go its own way independently of man just like any consumer article. "What is characteristic of the capitalist age," says Marx, "is that in the eyes of the labourer himself labour-power assumes the form of a commodity belonging to him. On the other hand it is only at this moment that the commodity form of the products of labour becomes general."[5]

Thus the universality of the commodity form is responsible both objectively and subjectively for the abstraction of the human labour incorporated in commodities. (On the other hand, this universality becomes historically possible because this process of abstraction has been completed.) *Objectively*, in so far as the commodity form facilitates the equal exchange of qualitatively different objects, it can only exist if that formal equality is in fact recognised—at any rate in *this* relation, which indeed confers upon them their commodity nature. *Subjectively*, this formal equality of human labour in the abstract is not only the common factor to which the various commodities are reduced; it also becomes the real principle governing the actual production of commodities.

Clearly, it cannot be our aim here to describe even in outline the growth of the modern process of labour, of the isolated, 'free' labourer and of the division of labour. Here we need only establish that labour, abstract, equal, comparable labour, measurable with increasing precision according to the time socially necessary for its accomplishment, the labour of the capitalist division of labour existing both as the presupposition and the product of capitalist production, is born only in the course of the development of the capitalist system. Only then does it become a category of society influencing decisively the objective form of things and people in the society thus emerging, their relation to nature and the possible relations of men to each other.[6]

If we follow the path taken by labour in its development from the handicraft via co-operation and manufacture to machine industry we can see a continuous trend towards greater rational-isation, the progressive elimination of the qualitative, human and individual attributes of the worker. On the one hand, the process of labour is progressively broken down into abstract, rational, specialised operations so that the worker loses contact with the finished product and his work is reduced to the mechanical repe-tition of a specialised set of actions. On the other hand, the period of time necessary for work to be accomplished (which forms the basis of rational calculation) is converted, as mechanisation and rationalisation are intensified, from a merely empirical average figure to an objectively calculable work-stint that confronts the worker as a fixed and established reality. With the modern 'psychological' analysis of the work-process (in Taylorism) this rational mechanisation extends right into the worker's 'soul': even his psychological attributes are separated from his total personality and placed in opposition to it so as to facili-tate their integration into specialised rational systems and their reduction to statistically viable concepts.[7]

We are concerned above all with the *principle* at work here: the principle of rationalisation based on what is and *can be calcu-lated*. The chief changes undergone by the subject and object of the economic process are as follows: (1) in the first place, the mathematical analysis of work-processes denotes a break with the organic, irrational and qualitatively determined unity of the product. Rationalisation in the sense of being able to predict with ever greater precision all the results to be achieved is only to be acquired by the exact breakdown of every complex into its ele-ments and by the study of the special laws governing production. Accordingly it must declare war on the organic manufacture of whole products based on the *traditional amalgam of empirical experi-ences of work*: rationalisation is unthinkable without specialisation.[8]

The finished article ceases to be the object of the work-process. The latter turns into the objective synthesis of rationalised special systems whose unity is determined by pure calculation and which must therefore seem to be arbitrarily connected with each other.

This destroys the organic necessity with which inter-related special operations are unified in the end-product. The unity of a product as a *commodity* no longer coincides with its unity as a use-value: as society becomes more radically capitalistic the increasing technical autonomy of the special operations involved in production is expressed also, as an economic autonomy, as the growing relativisation of the commodity character of a product at the various stages of production.[9] It is thus possible to separate forcibly the production of a use-value in time and space. This goes hand in hand with the union in time and space of special operations that are related to a set of heterogeneous use-values.

(2) In the second place, this fragmentation of the object of production necessarily entails the fragmentation of its subject. In consequence of the rationalisation of the work-process the human qualities and idiosyncrasies of the worker appear increasingly as *mere sources of error* when contrasted with these abstract special laws functioning according to rational predictions. Neither objectively nor in his relation to his work does man appear as the authentic master of the process; on the contrary, he is a mechanical part incorporated into a mechanical system. He finds it already pre-existing and self-sufficient, it functions independently of him and he has to conform to its laws whether he likes it or not.[10] As labour is progressively rationalised and mechanised his lack of will is reinforced by the way in which his activity becomes less and less active and more and more *contemplative*.[11] The contemplative stance adopted towards a process mechanically conforming to fixed laws and enacted independently of man's consciousness and impervious to human intervention, i.e. a perfectly closed system, must likewise transform the basic categories of man's immediate attitude to the world: it reduces space and time to a common denominator and degrades time to the dimension of space.

Marx puts it thus: "Through the subordination of man to the machine the situation arises in which men are effaced by their labour; in which the pendulum of the clock has become as accurate a measure of the relative activity of two workers as it is of the speed of two locomotives. Therefore, we should not say that one man's hour is worth another man's hour, but rather that one man during an hour is worth just as much as another man during an hour. Time is everything, man is nothing; he is at the most the incarnation of time. Quality no longer matters. Quantity alone decides everything: hour for hour, day for day. . . ."[12]

Thus time sheds its qualitative, variable, flowing nature; it freezes into an exactly delimited, quantifiable continuum filled with quantifiable 'things' (the reified, mechanically objectified 'performance' of the worker, wholly separated from his total human personality): in short, it becomes space.[13] In this environment where time is transformed into abstract, exactly measurable, physical space, an environment at once the cause and effect of the scientifically and mechanically fragmented and specialised production of the object of labour, the subjects of labour must likewise be rationally fragmented. On the one hand, the objectification of their labour-power into something opposed to their total personality (a process already accomplished with the sale of that labour-power as a commodity) is now made into the permanent ineluctable reality of their daily life. Here, too, the personality can do no more than look on helplessly while its own existence is reduced to an isolated particle and fed into an alien system. On the other hand, the mechanical disintegration of the process of production into its components also destroys those bonds that had bound individuals to a community in the days when production was still 'organic'. In this respect, too, mechanisation makes of them isolated abstract atoms whose work no longer brings them together directly and organically; it becomes mediated to an increasing extent exclusively by the abstract laws of the mechanism which imprisons them.

The internal organisation of a factory could not possibly have such an effect—even within the factory itself—were it not for the fact that it contained in concentrated form the whole structure of capitalist society. Oppression and an exploitation that knows no bounds and scorns every human dignity were known even to pre-capitalist ages. So too was mass production with mechanical, standardised labour, as we can see, for instance, with canal construction in Egypt and Asia Minor and the mines in Rome.[14] But mass projects of this type could never be *rationally mechanised*; they remained isolated phenomena within a community that organised its production on a different ('natural') basis and which therefore lived a different life. The slaves subjected to this exploitation, therefore, stood outside what was thought of as 'human' society and even the greatest and noblest thinkers of the time were unable to consider their fate as that of human beings.

As the commodity becomes universally dominant, this situation changes radically and qualitatively. The fate of the worker becomes the fate of society as a whole; indeed, this fate must become universal as otherwise industrialisation could not develop in this direction. For it depends on the emergence of the 'free' worker who is freely able to take his labour-power to market and offer it for sale as a commodity 'belonging' to him, a thing that he 'possesses'.

While this process is still incomplete the methods used to extract surplus labour are, it is true, more obviously brutal than in the later, more highly developed phase, but the process of reification of work and hence also of the consciousness of the worker is much less advanced. Reification requires that a society should learn to satisfy all its needs in terms of commodity exchange. The separation of the producer from his means of production, the dissolution and destruction of all 'natural' production units, etc., and all the social and economic conditions necessary for the emergence of modern capitalism tend to replace 'natural' relations which exhibit human relations more plainly by rationally reified relations. "The social relations between individuals in the performance of their labour," Marx observes with reference to pre-capitalist societies, "appear at all events as their own personal relations, and are not disguised under the shape of social relations between the products of labour."[15]

But this implies that the principle of rational mechanisation and calculability must embrace every aspect of life. Consumer articles no longer appear as the products of an organic process within a community (as for example in a village community). They now appear, on the one hand, as abstract members of a species identical by definition with its other members and, on the other hand, as isolated objects the possession or non-possession of which depends on rational calculations. Only when the whole life of society is thus fragmented into the isolated acts of commodity exchange can the 'free' worker come into being; at the same time his fate becomes the typical fate of the whole society.

Of course, this isolation and fragmentation is only apparent. The movement of commodities on the market, the birth of their value, in a word, the real framework of every rational calculation is not merely subject to strict laws but also presupposes the strict ordering of all that happens. The atomisation of the individual is, then, only the reflex in consciousness of the fact that the 'natural laws' of capitalist production have been extended to cover every manifestation of life in society; that—for the first time in history—the whole of society is subjected, or tends to be subjected, to a unified economic process, and that the fate of every member of society is determined by unified laws. (By contrast, the organic unities of pre-capitalist societies organised their metabolism largely in independence of each other).

However, if this atomisation is only an illusion it is a necessary one. That is to say, the immediate, practical as well as intellectual confrontation of the individual with society, the immediate production and reproduction of life—in which for the individual the commodity structure of all 'things' and their obedience to 'natural laws' is found to exist already in a finished form, as something immutably given—could only take place in the form of rational and isolated acts of exchange between isolated commodity owners. As emphasised above, the worker, too, must present himself as the 'owner' of his labour-power, as if it were a commodity. His specific situation is defined by the fact that his labour-power is his only possession. His fate is typical of society as a whole in that this self-objectification, this transformation of a human function into a commodity reveals in all its starkness the dehumanised and dehumanising function of the commodity relation.

2

This rational objectification conceals above all the immediate—qualitative and material—character of things as things. When use-values appear universally as commodities they acquire a new objectivity, a new substantiality which they did not possess in an age of episodic exchange and which destroys their original and authentic substantiality. As Marx observes: "Private property *alienates* not only the individuality of men, but also of things. The ground and the earth have nothing to do with ground-rent, machines have nothing to do with profit. For the landowner ground and earth mean nothing but ground-rent; he lets his land to tenants and receives the rent—a quality which the ground can lose without losing any of its inherent qualities such as its fertility; it is a quality whose magnitude and indeed existence depends on social relations that are created and abolished without any intervention by the landowner. Likewise with the machine."[16]

Thus even the individual object which man confronts directly, either as producer or consumer, is distorted in its objectivity by its commodity character. If that can happen then it is evident that this process will be intensified in proportion as the relations which man establishes with objects as objects of the life process are mediated in the course of his social activity. It is obviously not possible here to give an analysis of the whole economic structure of capitalism. It must suffice to point out that modern capitalism does not content itself with transforming the relations of production in accordance with its own needs. It also integrates into its own system those forms of primitive capitalism that led an isolated existence in pre-capitalist times, divorced from production; it converts them into members of the henceforth unified process of radical capitalism. (Cf. merchant capital, the role of money as a hoard or as finance capital, etc.)

These forms of capital are objectively subordinated, it is true, to the real life-process of capitalism, the extraction of surplus value in the course of production. They are, therefore, only to be explained in terms of the nature of industrial capitalism itself. But in the minds of people in bourgeois society they constitute the pure, authentic, unadulterated forms of capital. In them the relations between men that lie hidden in the immediate commodity relation, as well as the relations between men and the objects that should really gratify their needs, have faded to the point where they can be neither recognised nor even perceived.

For that very reason the reified mind has come to regard them as the true representatives of his societal existence. The commodity character of the commodity, the abstract, quantitative mode of calculability shows itself here in its purest form: the reified mind necessarily sees it as the form in which its own authentic immediacy becomes manifest and—as reified consciousness—does not even attempt to transcend it. On the contrary, it is concerned to make it permanent by 'scientifically deepening' the laws at work. Just as the capitalist system continuously produces and reproduces itself economically on higher and higher levels, the structure of reification progressively sinks more deeply, more fatefully and more definitively into the consciousness of man. Marx often describes this potentiation of reification in incisive fashion. One example must suffice here: "In interest-bearing capital, therefore, this automatic fetish, self-expanding value, money generating money, is brought out in its pure state and in this form it no longer bears the birth-marks of its origin. The social relation is consummated in the relation of a thing, of money, to itself. Instead of the actual transformation of money into capital, we see here only form without content. . . . It becomes a property of money to generate value and yield interest, much as it is an attribute of pear trees to bear pears. And the money-lender sells his money as just such an interest-bearing thing. But that is not all. The actually functioning capital, as we have seen, presents itself in such a light that it seems to yield interest not as functioning capital, but as capital in itself, as money-capital. This, too, becomes distorted. While interest is only a portion of the profit, i.e. of the surplus value, which the functioning capitalist squeezes out of the labourer, it appears now, on the contrary, as though interest were the typical product of capital, the primary matter, and profit, in the shape of profit of enterprise, were a mere accessory and by-product of the process of reproduction. Thus we get a fetish form of capital, and the conception of fetish capital. In M-M' we have the meaningless form of capital, the perversion and objectification of production relations in their highest degree, the interest-bearing form, the simple form of capital, in which it antecedes its own process of reproduction. It is the capacity of money, or of a commodity, to expand its own value independently of reproduction—which is a mystification of capital in its most flagrant form. For vulgar political economy, which seeks to represent capital as an independent source of value, of value creation, this form is naturally a veritable find, a form in which the source of profit is no longer discernible, and in which the result of the capitalist process of production—divorced from the process—acquires an independent existence."[17]

Just as the economic theory of capitalism remains stuck fast in its self-created immediacy, the same thing happens to bourgeois attempts to comprehend the ideological phenomenon of reification. Even thinkers who have no desire to deny or obscure its existence and who are more or less clear in their own minds about its humanly destructive consequences remain on the surface and make no attempt to advance beyond its objectively most derivative forms, the forms furthest from the real life-process of capitalism, i.e. the most external and vacuous forms, to the basic phenomenon of reification itself.

Indeed, they divorce these empty manifestations from their

real capitalist foundation and make them independent and permanent by regarding them as the timeless model of human relations in general. (This can be seen most clearly in Simmel's book,
The Philosophy of Money, a very interesting and perceptive work in
matters of detail.) They offer no more than a description of this
"enchanted, perverted, topsy-turvy world, in which Monsieur Le
Capital and Madame La Terre do their ghost-walking as social
characters and at the same time as mere things."[18] But they do
not go further than a description and their 'deepening' of the
problem runs in circles around the eternal manifestations of
reification.

The divorce of the phenomena of reification from their economic bases and from the vantage point from which alone they
can be understood, is facilitated by the fact that the [capitalist]
process of transformation must embrace every manifestation of
the life of society if the preconditions for the complete self-
realisation of capitalist production are to be fulfilled.

Thus capitalism has created a form for the state and a system of
law corresponding to its needs and harmonising with its own
structure. The structural similarity is so great that no truly perceptive historian of modern capitalism could fail to notice it.
Max Weber, for instance, gives this description of the basic lines
of this development: "Both are, rather, quite similar in their
fundamental nature. Viewed sociologically, a 'business-concern'
is the modern state; the same holds good for a factory: and this,
precisely, is what is specific to it historically. And, likewise, the
power relations in a business are also of the same kind. The relative independence of the artisan (or cottage craftsman), of the
landowning peasant, the owner of a benefice, the knight and vas-
sal was based on the fact that he himself owned the tools, supplies,
financial resources or weapons with the aid of which he fulfilled
his economic, political or military function and from which he
lived while this duty was being discharged. Similarly, the hier-
archic dependence of the worker, the clerk, the technical assistant,
the assistant in an academic institute *and* the civil servant and
soldier has a comparable basis: namely that the tools, supplies and
financial resources essential both for the business-concern and for
economic survival are in the hands, in the one case, of the entrepreneur and, in the other case, of the political master."[19]

He rounds off this account—very pertinently—with an analysis
of the cause and the social implications of this phenomenon:

"The modern capitalist concern is based inwardly above all on *calculation*. It requires for its survival a system of justice and an administration whose workings can be *rationally calculated*, at least in principle, according to fixed general laws, just as the probable performance of *a machine* can be calculated. It is as little able to tolerate the dispensing of justice according to the judge's sense of fair play *in individual cases* or any other irrational means or principles of administering the law . . . as it is able to endure a patriarchal administration that obeys the dictates of its own caprice, or sense of mercy and, for the rest, proceeds in accordance with an inviolable and sacrosanct, but irrational tradition. . . . What is specific to modern capitalism as distinct from the age-old capitalist forms of acquisition is that the strictly rational *organisation of work* on the basis of *rational technology* did not come into being *anywhere* within such irrationally constituted political systems nor could it have done so. For these modern businesses with their fixed capital and their exact calculations are much too sensitive to legal and administrative irrationalities. They could only come into being in the bureaucratic state with its rational laws where . . . the judge is more or less an automatic statute-dispensing machine in which you insert the files together with the necessary costs and dues at the top, whereupon he will eject the judgment together with the more or less cogent reasons for it at the bottom: that is to say, where the judge's behaviour is on the whole *predictable*."

The process we see here is closely related both in its motivation and in its effects to the economic process outlined above. Here, too, there is a breach with the empirical and irrational methods of administration and dispensing justice based on traditions tailored, subjectively, to the requirements of men in action, and, objectively, to those of the concrete matter in hand. There arises a rational systematisation of all statutes regulating life, which represents, or at least tends towards a closed system applicable to all possible and imaginable cases. Whether this system is arrived at in a purely logical manner, as an exercise in pure legal dogma or interpretation of the law, or whether the judge is given the task of filling the 'gaps' left in the laws, is immaterial for our attempt to understand the *structure* of modern legal reality. In either case the legal system is formally capable of being generalised so as to relate to every possible situation in life and it is susceptible to prediction and calculation. Even Roman Law, which comes closest to these developments while remaining, in modern terms, within the framework of pre-capitalist legal patterns, does not in this respect go beyond the empirical, the concrete and the traditional. The purely systematic categories which were necessary before a judicial system could become universally applicable arose only in modern times.[20]

It requires no further explanation to realise that the need to systematise and to abandon empiricism, tradition and material dependence was the need for exact calculation.[21] However, this same need requires that the legal system should confront the individual events of social existence as something permanently established and exactly defined, i.e. as a rigid system. Of course, this produces an uninterrupted series of conflicts between the unceasingly revolutionary forces of the capitalist economy and the rigid legal system. But this only results in new codifications; and despite these the new system is forced to preserve the fixed, change-resistant structure of the old system.

This is the source of the—apparently—paradoxical situation whereby the 'law' of primitive societies, which has scarcely altered in hundreds or sometimes even thousands of years, can be flexible and irrational in character, renewing itself with every new legal decision, while modern law, caught up in the continuous turmoil of change, should appear rigid, static and fixed. But the paradox dissolves when we realise that it arises only because the same situation has been regarded from two different points of view: on the one hand, from that of the historian (who stands 'outside' the actual process) and, on the other, from that of someone who experiences the effects of the social order in question upon his consciousness.

With the aid of this insight we can see clearly how the antagonism between the traditional and empirical craftsmanship and the scientific and rational factory is repeated in another sphere of activity. At every single stage of its development, the ceaselessly revolutionary techniques of modern production turn a rigid and immobile face towards the individual producer. Whereas the objectively relatively stable, traditional craft production preserves in the minds of its individual practitioners the appearance of something flexible, something constantly renewing itself, something produced by the producers.

In the process we witness, illuminatingly, how here, too, the *contemplative* nature of man under capitalism makes its appearance.

For the essence of rational calculation is based ultimately upon the recognition and the inclusion in one's calculations of the inevitable chain of cause and effect in certain events—independently of individual 'caprice'. In consequence, man's activity does not go beyond the correct calculation of the possible outcome of the sequence of events (the 'laws' of which he finds 'ready-made'), and beyond the adroit evasion of disruptive 'accidents' by means of protective devices and preventive measures (which are based in their turn on the recognition and application of similar laws). Very often it will confine itself to working out the probable effects of such 'laws' without making the attempt to intervene in the process by bringing other 'laws' to bear. (As in insurance schemes, etc.)

The more closely we scrutinise this situation and the better we are able to close our minds to the bourgeois legends of the 'creativity' of the exponents of the capitalist age, the more obvious it becomes that we are witnessing in all behaviour of this sort the structural analogue to the behaviour of the worker *vis-à-vis* the machine he serves and observes, and whose functions he controls while he contemplates it. The 'creative' element can be seen to depend at best on whether these 'laws' are applied in a—relatively—independent way or in a wholly subservient one. That is to say, it depends on the degree to which the contemplative stance is repudiated. The distinction between a worker faced with a particular machine, the entrepreneur faced with a given type of mechanical development, the technologist faced with the state of science and the profitability of its application to technology, is purely quantitative; it does not directly entail *any qualitative difference in the structure of consciousness*.

Only in this context can the problem of modern bureaucracy be properly understood. Bureaucracy implies the adjustment of one's way of life, mode of work and hence of consciousness, to the general socio-economic premises of the capitalist economy, similar to that which we have observed in the case of the worker in particular business concerns. The formal standardisation of justice, the state, the civil service, etc., signifies objectively and factually a comparable reduction of all social functions to their elements, a comparable search for the rational formal laws of these carefully segregated partial systems. Subjectively, the divorce between work and the individual capacities and needs of the worker produces comparable effects upon consciousness. This results in an inhuman, standardised division of labour analogous to that which we have found in industry on the technological and mechanical plane.[22]

It is not only a question of the completely mechanical, 'mindless' work of the lower echelons of the bureaucracy which bears such an extraordinarily close resemblance to operating a machine and which indeed often surpasses it in sterility and uniformity. It is also a question, on the one hand, of the way in which objectively all issues are subjected to an increasingly *formal* and standardised treatment and in which there is an ever-increasing remoteness from the qualitative and material essence of the 'things' to which bureaucratic activity pertains. On the other hand, there is an even more monstrous intensification of the one-sided specialisation which represents such a violation of man's humanity. Marx's comment on factory work that "the individual, himself divided, is transformed into the automatic mechanism of a partial labour" and is thus "crippled to the point of abnormality" is relevant here too. And it becomes all the more clear, the more elevated, advanced and 'intellectual' is the attainment exacted by the division of labour.

The split between the worker's labour-power and his personality, its metamorphosis into a thing, an object that he sells on the market is repeated here too. But with the difference that not every mental faculty is suppressed by mechanisation; only one faculty (or complex of faculties) is detached from the whole personality and placed in opposition to it, becoming a thing, a commodity. But the basic phenomenon remains the same even though both the means by which society instills such abilities and their material and 'moral' exchange value are fundamentally different from labour-power (not forgetting, of course, the many connecting links and nuances).

The specific type of bureaucratic 'conscientiousness' and impartiality, the individual bureaucrat's inevitable total subjection to a system of relations between the things to which he is exposed, the idea that it is precisely his 'honour' and his 'sense of responsibility' that exact this total submission,[23] all this points to the fact that the division of labour which in the case of Taylorism invaded the psyche, here invades the realm of ethics. Far from weakening the reified structure of consciousness, this actually strengthens it. For as long as the fate of the worker still appears to be an individual fate (as in the case of the slave in antiquity), the life of the ruling classes is still free to assume quite different forms. Not until the rise of capitalism was a unified economic structure, and hence a—formally—unified structure of consciousness that embraced the whole society, brought into being. This unity expressed itself in the fact that the problems of consciousness arising from wage-labour were repeated in the ruling class in a refined and spiritualised, but, for that very reason, more intensified form. The specialised 'virtuoso', the vendor of his objectified and reified faculties does not just become the [passive] observer of society; he also lapses into a contemplative attitude *vis-à-vis* the workings of his own objectified and reified faculties. (It is not possible here even to outline the way in which modern administration and law assume the characteristics of the factory as we noted above rather than those of the handicrafts.) This phenomenon can be seen at its most grotesque in journalism. Here it is precisely subjectivity itself, knowledge, temperament and powers of expression that are reduced to an abstract mechanism functioning autonomously and divorced both from the personality of their 'owner' and from the material and concrete nature of the subject matter in hand. The journalist's 'lack of convictions', the prostitution of his experiences and beliefs is comprehensible only as the apogee of capitalist reification.[24]

The transformation of the commodity relation into a thing of 'ghostly objectivity' cannot therefore content itself with the reduction of all objects for the gratification of human needs to commodities. It stamps its imprint upon the whole consciousness of man; his qualities and abilities are no longer an organic part of his personality, they are things which he can 'own' or 'dispose of' like the various objects of the external world. And there is no natural form in which human relations can be cast, no way in which man can bring his physical and psychic 'qualities' into play without their being subjected increasingly to this reifying process. We need only think of marriage, and without troubling to point to the developments of the nineteenth century we can remind ourselves of the way in which Kant, for example, described the situation with the naïvely cynical frankness peculiar to great thinkers.

"Sexual community", he says, "is the reciprocal use made by one person of the sexual organs and faculties of another . . . marriage . . . is the union of two people of different sexes with a view to the mutual possession of each other's sexual attributes for the duration of their lives."[25]

This rationalisation of the world appears to be complete, it seems to penetrate the very depths of man's physical and psychic nature. It is limited, however, by its own formalism. That is to say, the rationalisation of isolated aspects of life results in the creation of—formal—laws. All these things do join together into what seems to the superficial observer to constitute a unified system of general 'laws'. But the disregard of the concrete aspects of the subject matter of these laws, upon which disregard their authority as laws is based, makes itself felt in the incoherence of the system in fact. This incoherence becomes particularly egregious in periods of crisis. At such times we can see how the immediate continuity between two partial systems is disrupted and their independence from and adventitious connection with each other is suddenly forced into the consciousness of everyone. It is for this reason that Engels is able to define the 'natural laws' of capitalist society as the laws of chance.[26]

On closer examination the structure of a crisis is seen to be no more than a heightening of the degree and intensity of the daily life of bourgeois society. In its unthinking, mundane reality *that* life seems firmly held together by 'natural laws'; yet it can experience a sudden dislocation because the bonds uniting its various elements and partial systems are a chance affair even at their most normal. So that the pretence that society is regulated by 'eternal, iron' laws which branch off into the different special laws applying to particular areas is finally revealed for what it is: a pretence. The true structure of society appears rather in the independent, rationalised and formal partial laws whose links with each other are of necessity purely formal (i.e. their formal interdependence can be formally systematised), while as far as concrete realities are concerned they can only establish fortuitous connections.

On closer inspection this kind of connection can be discovered even in purely economic phenomena. Thus Marx points out—and the cases referred to here are intended only as an indication of the methodological factors involved, not as a substantive treatment of the problems themselves—that "the conditions of direct exploitation [of the labourer], and those of realising surplus-value, are not identical. They diverge not only in place and time, but also logically."[27] Thus there exists "an accidental rather than a necessary connection between the total amount of social labour applied to a social article" and "the volume whereby society seeks to satisfy the want gratified by the article in question."[28]

These are no more than random instances. It is evident that the whole structure of capitalist production rests on the interaction between a necessity subject to strict laws in all isolated phenomena and the relative irrationality of the total process. "Division of labour within the workshop implies the undisputed authority of the capitalist over men, who are but parts of a mechanism that belongs to him. The division of labour within society brings into contact independent commodity-producers who acknowledge no other authority than that of competition, of the coercion exerted by the pressure of their mutual interests."[29]

The capitalist process of rationalisation based on private economic calculation requires that every manifestation of life shall exhibit this very interaction between details which are subject to laws and a totality ruled by chance. It presupposes a society so structured. It produces and reproduces this structure in so far as it takes possession of society. This has its foundation already in the nature of speculative calculation, i.e. the economic practice of commodity owners at the stage where the exchange of commodities has become universal. Competition between the different owners of commodities would not be feasible if there were an exact, rational, systematic mode of functioning for the whole of society to correspond to the rationality of isolated phenomena. If a rational calculation is to be possible the commodity owner must be in possession of the laws regulating every detail of his production. The chances of exploitation, the laws of the 'market' must likewise be rational in the sense that they must be calculable according to the laws of probability. But they must not be governed by a law in the sense in which 'laws' govern individual phenomena; they must not under any circumstances be rationally organised through and through. This does not mean, of course, that there can be no 'law' governing the whole. But such a 'law' would have to be the 'unconscious' product of the activity of the different commodity owners acting independently of one another, i.e. a law of mutually interacting 'coincidences' rather than one of truly rational organisation. Furthermore, such a law must not merely impose itself despite the wishes of individuals, it may *not even be fully and adequately knowable*. For the complete knowledge of the whole would vouchsafe the knower a monopoly that would amount to the virtual abolition of the capitalist economy.

This irrationality, this—highly problematic—'systematisation' of the whole which diverges *qualitatively and in principle* from the

laws regulating the parts, is more than just a postulate, a presupposition essential to the workings of a capitalist economy. It is
at the same time the product of the capitalist division of labour.
It has already been pointed out that the division of labour disrupts every organically unified process of work and life and breaks
it down into its components. This enables the artificially isolated
partial functions to be performed in the most rational manner by
'specialists' who are specially adapted mentally and physically
for the purpose. This has the effect of making these partial functions autonomous and so they tend to develop through their own
momentum and in accordance with their own special laws independently of the other partial functions of society (or that part of
the society to which they belong).

As the division of labour becomes more pronounced and more
rational, this tendency naturally increases in proportion. For the
more highly developed it is, the more powerful become the claims
to status and the professional interests of the 'specialists' who are
the living embodiments of such tendencies. And this centrifugal
movement is not confined to aspects of a particular sector. It is
even more in evidence when we consider the great spheres of
activity created by the division of labour. Engels describes this
process with regard to the relation between economics and laws:
"Similarly with law. As soon as the new division of labour which
creates *professional lawyers* becomes necessary, another new and
independent sphere is opened up which, for all its essential
dependence on production and trade, still has also a special
capacity for reacting upon these spheres. In a modern state, law
must not only correspond to the general economic condition and
be its expression, but must also be an *internally coherent expression*
which does not, owing to inner contradictions, reduce itself to
nought. And in order to achieve this, the faithful reflection of
economic conditions suffers increasingly. . . ."[30] It is hardly
necessary to supplement this with examples of the inbreeding and
the interdepartmental conflicts of the civil service (consider the
independence of the military apparatus from the civil administration), or of the academic faculties, etc.

3

The specialisation of skills leads to the destruction of every
image of the whole. And as, despite this, the need to grasp the

whole—at least cognitively—cannot die out, we find that science, which is likewise based on specialisation and thus caught up in the same immediacy, is criticised for having torn the real world into shreds and having lost its vision of the whole. In reply to allegations that "the various factors are not treated as a whole" Marx retorts that this criticism is levelled "as though it were the text-books that impress this separation upon life and not life upon the text-books".[31] Even though this criticism deserves refutation in its naïve form it becomes comprehensible when we look for a moment from the outside, i.e. from a vantage point other than that of a reified consciousness, at the activity of modern science which is both sociologically and methodologically necessary and for that reason 'comprehensible'. Such a look will reveal (without constituting a 'criticism') that the more intricate a modern science becomes and the better it understands itself methodologically, the more resolutely it will turn its back on the ontological problems of its own sphere of influence and eliminate them from the realm where it has achieved some insight. The more highly developed it becomes and the more scientific, the more it will become a formally closed system of partial laws. It will then find that the world lying beyond its confines, and in particular the material base which it is its task to understand, *its own concrete underlying reality* lies, methodologically and in principle, *beyond its grasp.*

Marx acutely summed up this situation with reference to economics when he declared that "use-value as such lies outside the sphere of investigation of political economy".[32] It would be a mistake to suppose that certain analytical devices—such as we find in the 'Theory of Marginal Utility'—might show the way out of this impasse. It is possible to set aside objective laws governing the production and movement of commodities which regulate the market and 'subjective' modes of behaviour on it and to make the attempt to start from 'subjective' behaviour on the market. But this simply shifts the question from the main issue to more and more derivative and reified stages without negating the formalism of the method and the elimination from the outset of the concrete material underlying it. The formal act of exchange which constitutes the basic fact for the theory of marginal utility likewise suppresses use-value as use-value and establishes a relation of concrete equality between concretely unequal and indeed incomparable objects. It is this that creates the impasse.

Thus the subject of the exchange is just as abstract, formal and reified as its object. The limits of this abstract and formal method are revealed in the fact that its chosen goal is an abstract system of 'laws' that focuses on the theory of marginal utility just as much as classical economics had done. But the formal abstraction of these 'laws' transform economics into a closed partial system. And this in turn is unable to penetrate its own material substratum, nor can it advance from there to an understanding of society in its entirety and so it is compelled to view that substratum as an immutable, eternal 'datum'. Science is thereby debarred from comprehending the development and the demise, the social character of its own material base, no less than the range of possible attitudes towards it and the nature of its own formal system.

Here, once again, we can clearly observe the close interaction between a class and the scientific method that arises from the attempt to conceptualise the social character of that class together with its laws and needs. It has often been pointed out—in these pages and elsewhere—that the problem that forms the ultimate barrier to the economic thought of the bourgeoisie is the crisis. If we now—in the full awareness of our own one-sidedness—consider this question from a purely methodological point of view, we see that it is the very success with which the economy is totally rationalised and transformed into an abstract and mathematically orientated system of formal 'laws' that creates the methodological barrier to understanding the phenomenon of crisis. In moments of crisis the qualitative existence of the 'things' that lead their lives beyond the purview of economics as misunderstood and neglected things-in-themselves, as use-values, suddenly becomes the decisive factor. (Suddenly, that is, for reified, rational thought.) Or rather: these 'laws' fail to function and the reified mind is unable to perceive a pattern in this 'chaos'.

This failure is characteristic not merely of classical economics (which regarded crises as 'passing', 'accidental' disturbances), but of bourgeois economics *in toto*. The incomprehensibility and irrationality of crises is indeed a consequence of the class situation and interests of the bourgeoisie but it follows equally from their approach to economics. (There is no need to spell out the fact that for us these are both merely aspects of the same dialectical unity). This consequence follows with such inevitability that Tugan-Baranovsky, for example, attempts in his theory to draw the necessary conclusions from a century of crises by excluding consumption from economics entirely and founding a 'pure' economics based only on production. The source of crises (whose existence cannot be denied) is then found to lie in incongruities between the various elements of production, i.e. in purely quantitative factors. Hilferding puts his finger on the fallacy underlying all such explanations: "They operate only with economic concepts such as capital, profit, accumulation, etc., and believe that they possess the solution to the problem when they have discovered the quantitative relations on the basis of which either simple and expanded reproduction is possible, or else there are disturbances. They overlook the fact that there are qualitative conditions attached to these quantitative relations, that it is not merely a question of units of value which can easily be compared with each other but also use-values of a definite kind which must fulfil a definite function in production and consumption. Further, they are oblivious of the fact that in the analysis of the process of reproduction more is involved than just aspects of capital in general, so that it is not enough to say that an excess or a deficit of industrial capital can be 'balanced' by an appropriate amount of money-capital. Nor is it a matter of fixed or circulating capital, but rather of machines, raw materials, labour-power of a quite definite (technically defined) sort, if disruptions are to be avoided."[33]

Marx has often demonstrated convincingly how inadequate the 'laws' of bourgeois economics are to the task of explaining the true movement of economic activity *in toto*. He has made it clear that this limitation lies in the—methodologically inevitable—failure to comprehend use-value and real consumption. "Within certain limits, the process of reproduction may take place on the same or on an increased scale even when the commodities expelled from it have not really entered individual or productive consumption. The consumption of commodities is not included in the cycle of the capital from which they originated. For instance, as soon as the yarn is sold the cycle of the capital-value represented by the yarn may begin anew, regardless of what may next become of the sold yarn. So long as the product is sold, everything is taking its regular course from the standpoint of the capitalist producer. The cycle of the capital-value he is identified with is not interrupted. And if this process is expanded—which includes increased productive consumption of the means of production—this reproduction of capital may be accompanied by increased individual consumption (hence demand) on the part of the labourers, since this process is initiated and effected by productive consumption. Thus the production of surplus-value, and with it the individual consumption of the capitalist, may increase, the entire process of reproduction may be in a flourishing condition, and yet a large part of the commodities may have entered into consumption only in appearance, while in reality they may still remain unsold in the hands of dealers, may in fact still be lying in the market."[34]

It must be emphasised that this inability to penetrate to the real material substratum of science is not the fault of individuals. It is rather something that becomes all the more apparent the more science has advanced and the more consistently it functions— from the point of view of its own premises. It is therefore no accident, as Rosa Luxemburg has convincingly shown,[35] that the great, if also often primitive, faulty and inexact synoptic view of economic life to be found in Quesnay's "Tableau Economique", disappears progressively as the—formal—process of conceptualisation becomes increasingly exact in the course of its development from Adam Smith to Ricardo. For Ricardo the process of the total reproduction of capital (where this problem cannot be avoided) is no longer a central issue.

In jurisprudence this situation emerges with even greater clarity and simplicity—because there is a more conscious reification at work. If only because the question of whether the qualitative content can be understood by means of a rational, calculating approach is no longer seen in terms of a rivalry between two principles within the same sphere (as was the case with use-value and exchange value in economics), but rather, right from the start, as a question of form versus content. The conflict revolving around natural law, and the whole revolutionary period of the bourgeoisie was based on the assumption that the formal equality and universality of the law (and hence its rationality) was able at the same time to determine its content. This was expressed in the assault on the varied and picturesque medley of privileges dating back to the Middle Ages and also in the attack on the Divine Right of Kings. The revolutionary bourgeois class refused to admit that a legal relationship had a *valid* foundation merely because it existed *in fact*. "Burn your laws and make new ones!" Voltaire counselled; "Whence can new laws be obtained? From Reason!"[36]

The war waged against the revolutionary bourgeoisie, say, at the time of the French Revolution, was dominated to such an extent by this idea that it was inevitable that the natural law of the bourgeoisie could only be opposed by yet another natural law (see Burke and also Stahl). Only after the bourgeoisie had gained at least a partial victory did a 'critical' and a 'historical' view begin to emerge in both camps. Its essence can be summarised as the belief that the content of law is something purely factual and hence not to be comprehended by the formal categories of jurisprudence. Of the tenets of natural law the only one to survive was the idea of the unbroken continuity of the formal system of law; significantly, Bergbohm uses an image borrowed from physics, that of a 'juridical vacuum', to describe everything not regulated by law.[37]

Nevertheless, the cohesion of these laws is purely formal: *what* they express, "the content of legal institutions is never of a legal character, but always political and economic".[38] With this the primitive, cynically sceptical campaign against natural law that was launched by the 'Kantian' Hugo at the end of the eighteenth century, acquired 'scientific' status. Hugo established the juridical basis of slavery, among other things, by arguing that it "had been the law of the land for thousands of years and was acknowledged by millions of cultivated people".[39] In this naïvely cynical frankness the pattern which is to become increasingly characteristic of law in bourgeois society stands clearly revealed. When Jellinek describes the contents of law as metajuristic, when 'critical' jurists locate the study of the contents of law in history, sociology and politics what they are doing is, in the last analysis, just what Hugo had demanded: they are systematically abandoning the attempt to ground law in reason and to give it a rational content; law is henceforth to be regarded as a formal calculus with the aid of which the legal consequences of particular actions (*rebus sic stantibus*) can be determined as exactly as possible.

However, this view transforms the process by which law comes into being and passes away into something as incomprehensible to the jurist as crises had been to the political economist. With regard to the origins of law the perceptive 'critical' jurist Kelsen observes: "It is the great *mystery* of law and of the state that is consummated with the enactment of laws and for this reason it may be permissible to employ inadequate images in elucidating its nature."[40] Or in other words: "It is symptomatic of the nature

of law that a norm may be legitimate even if its origins are ini-
quitous. That is another way of saying that the legitimate origin
of a law cannot be written into the concept of law as one of its
conditions."[41] This epistemological clarification could also be a
factual one and could thereby lead to an advance in knowledge.
To achieve this, however, the other disciplines into which the
problem of the origins of law had been diverted would really
have to propose a genuine solution to it. But also it would be
essential really to penetrate the nature of a legal system which
serves purely as a means of calculating the effects of actions and of
rationally imposing modes of action relevant to a particular class.
In that event the real, material substratum of the law would at
one stroke become visible and comprehensible. But neither condition can be fulfilled. The law maintains its close relationship
with the 'eternal values'. This gives birth, in the shape of a philosophy of law to an impoverished and formalistic re-edition of
natural law (Stammler). Meanwhile, the real basis for the development of law, a change in the power relations between the classes,
becomes hazy and vanishes into the sciences that study it, sciences
which—in conformity with the modes of thought current in bourgeois society—generate the same problems of transcending their material substratum as we have seen in jurisprudence and economics.

The manner in which this transcendence is conceived shows
how vain was the hope that a comprehensive discipline, like philosophy, might yet achieve that overall knowledge which the particular sciences have so conspicuously renounced by turning away
from the material substratum of their conceptual apparatus. Such
a synthesis would only be possible if philosophy were able to
change its approach radically and concentrate on the concrete
material totality of what can and should be known. Only then
would it be able to break through the barriers erected by a formalism that has degenerated into a state of complete fragmentation.
But this would presuppose an awareness of the causes, the genesis
and the necessity of this formalism; moreover, it would not be
enough to unite the special sciences mechanically: they would
have to be transformed inwardly by an inwardly synthesising
philosophical method. It is evident that the philosophy of bourgeois society is incapable of this. Not that the desire for synthesis is
absent; nor can it be maintained that the best people have wel-
comed with open arms a mechanical existence hostile to life and a
scientific formalism alien to it. *But a radical change in outlook is not*

feasible on the soil of bourgeois society. Philosophy can attempt to assemble the whole of knowledge encyclopaedically (see Wundt). Or it may radically question the value of formal knowledge for a 'living life' (see irrationalist philosophies from Hamann to Bergson). But these episodic trends lie to one side of the main philosophical tradition. The latter acknowledges as given and necessary the results and achievements of the special sciences and assigns to philosophy the task of exhibiting and justifying the grounds for regarding as valid the concepts so constructed.

Thus philosophy stands in the same relation to the special sciences as they do with respect to empirical reality. The formalistic conceptualisation of the special sciences become for philosophy an immutably given substratum and this signals the final and despairing renunciation of every attempt to cast light on the reification that lies at the root of this formalism. The reified world appears henceforth quite definitively—and in philosophy, under the spotlight of 'criticism' it is potentiated still further—as the only possible world, the only conceptually accessible, comprehensible world vouchsafed to us humans. Whether this gives rise to ecstasy, resignation or despair, whether we search for a path leading to 'life' via irrational mystical experience, this will do absolutely nothing to modify the situation as it is in fact.

By confining itself to the study of the 'possible conditions' of the validity of the forms in which its underlying existence is manifested, modern bourgeois thought bars its own way to a clear view of the problems bearing on the birth and death of these forms, and on their real essence and substratum. Its perspicacity finds itself increasingly in the situation of that legendary 'critic' in India who was confronted with the ancient story according to which the world rests upon an elephant. He unleashed the 'critical' question: upon what does the elephant rest? On receiving the answer that the elephant stands on a tortoise 'criticism' declared itself satisfied. It is obvious that even if he had continued to press apparently 'critical' questions, he could only have elicited a third miraculous animal. He would not have been able to discover the solution to the real question.

II

The Antinomies of Bourgeois Thought

Modern critical philosophy springs from the reified structure

of consciousness. The specific problems of this philosophy are distinguishable from the problematics of previous philosophies by the fact that they are rooted in this structure. Greek philosophy constitutes something of an exception to this. This is not merely accidental, for reification did play a part in Greek society in its maturity. But as the problems and solutions of the philosophy of the Ancients were embedded in a wholly different society it is only natural that they should be qualitatively different from those of modern philosophy. Hence, from the standpoint of any adequate interpretation it is as idle to imagine that we can find in Plato a precursor of Kant (as does Natorp), as it is to undertake the task of erecting a philosophy on Aristotle (as does Thomas Aquinas). If these two ventures have proved feasible—even though arbitrary and inadequate—this can be accounted for in part by the use to which later ages are wont to put the philosophical heritage, bending it to their own purposes. But also further explanation lies in the fact that Greek philosophy was no stranger to certain aspects of reification, without having experienced them, however, as universal forms of existence; it had one foot in the world of reification while the other remained in a 'natural' society. Hence its problems can be applied to the two later traditions, although only with the aid of energetic re-interpretations.

1

Where, then, does the fundamental distinction lie? Kant has formulated the matter succinctly in the Preface to the *Critique of Pure Reason* with his well-known allusion to the "Copernican Revolution", a revolution which must be carried out in the realm of the problem of knowledge: "Hitherto, it has been assumed that all our knowledge must conform to the objects. . . . Therefore let us for once attempt to see whether we cannot reach a solution to the tasks of metaphysics by assuming that the objects must conform to our knowledge. . . .[1]" In other words, modern philosophy sets itself the following problem: it refuses to accept the world as something that has arisen (or e.g. has been created by God) independently of the knowing subject, and prefers to conceive of it instead as its own product.

This revolution which consists in viewing rational knowledge as the product of mind does not originate with Kant. He only

developed its implications more radically than his predecessors had done. Marx has recalled, in a quite different context, Vico's remark to the effect that "the history of man is to be distinguished from the history of nature by the fact that we have made the one but not the other".[2] In ways diverging from that of Vico who in many respects was not understood and who became influential only much later, the whole of modern philosophy has been preoccupied with this problem. From systematic doubt and the *Cogito ergo sum* of Descartes, to Hobbes, Spinoza and Leibniz there is a direct line of development whose central strand, rich in variations, is the idea that the object of cognition can be known by us for the reason that, and to the degree in which, it has been created by ourselves.[3] And with this, the methods of mathematics and geometry (the means whereby objects are constructed, created out of the formal presuppositions of objectivity in general) and, later, the methods of mathematical physics become the guide and the touchstone of philosophy, the knowledge of the world as a totality.

The question why and with what justification human reason should elect to regard just these systems as constitutive of its own essence (as opposed to the 'given', alien, unknowable nature of the content of those systems) never arises. It is assumed to be self-evident. Whether this assumption is expressed (as in the case of Berkeley and Hume) as scepticism, as doubt in the ability of 'our' knowledge to achieve universally valid results, or whether (as with Spinoza and Leibniz) it becomes an unlimited confidence in the ability of these formal systems to comprehend the 'true' essence of all things, is of secondary importance in this context. For we are not concerned to present a history of modern philosophy, not even in crude outline. We wish only to sketch the *connection* between the fundamental problems of this philosophy and the *basis in existence* from which these problems spring and to which they strive to return by the road of the understanding. However, the character of this existence is revealed at least as clearly by what philosophy does *not* find problematic as by what it does. At any rate it is advisable to consider the interaction between these two aspects. And if we do put the question in this way we then perceive that the salient characteristic of the whole epoch is the equation which appears naïve and dogmatic even in the most 'critical' philosophers, of formal, mathematical, rational knowledge both with knowledge in general and also with 'our' knowledge.

Even the most superficial glance at the history of human thought will persuade us that neither of the two equations is self-evidently true under all circumstances. This is most obviously apparent in the origins of modern thought where it was necessary to wage prolonged intellectual wars with the quite differently based thought of the Middle Ages before the new method and the new view of the nature of thought could finally prevail. This struggle, too, can obviously not be portrayed here. A familiarity with its dominant motifs can be assumed. These were the continuity of all phenomena (in contrast to the medieval distinction between the world 'beneath' the moon and the world 'above' it); the demand for immanent causal connections in contrast to views which sought to explain and connect phenomena from some transcendental point (astronomy versus astrology); the demand that mathematical and rational categories should be applied to all phenomena (in contrast to the qualitative approach of nature philosophy which experienced a new impetus in the Renaissance —Böhme, Fludd, etc.—and even formed the basis of Bacon's method. It can similarly be taken as read that the whole evolution of philosophy went hand in hand with the development of the exact sciences. These in turn interacted fruitfully with a technology that was becoming increasingly more rationalised, and with developments in production.[4]

These considerations are of crucial importance for our analysis. For rationalism has existed at widely different times and in the most diverse forms, in the sense of a formal system whose unity derives from its orientation towards that aspect of the phenomena that can be grasped by the understanding, that is created by the understanding and hence also subject to the control, the predictions and the calculations of the understanding. But there are fundamental distinctions to be made, depending on the *material* on which this rationalism is brought to bear and on the *role* assigned to it in the comprehensive system of human knowledge and human objectives. What is novel about modern rationalism is its increasingly insistent claim that it has discovered the *principle* which connects up all phenomena which in nature and society are found to confront mankind. Compared with this, every previous type of rationalism is no more than a *partial system*.

In such systems the 'ultimate' problems of human existence persist in an irrationality incommensurable with human understanding. The closer the system comes to these 'ultimate' questions

F

the more strikingly its partial, auxiliary nature and its inability to grasp the 'essentials' are revealed. An example of this is found in the highly rationalised techniques of Hindu asceticism,[5] with its ability to predict exactly all of its results. Its whole 'rationality' resides in the direct and immediate bond, related as means to ends, with an entirely supra-rational experience of the essence of the world.

Thus, here too, it will not do to regard 'rationalism' as something abstract and formal and so to turn it into a supra-historical principle inherent in the nature of human thought. We perceive rather that the question of whether a form is to be treated as a universal category or merely as a way of organising precisely delimited partial systems is essentially a *qualitative* problem. Nevertheless even the purely formal delimitation of this type of thought throws light on the necessary correlation of the rational and the irrational, i.e. on the inevitability with which every rational system will strike a frontier or barrier of irrationality. However, when—as in the case of Hindu asceticism—the rational system is conceived of as a partial system from the outset, when the irrational world which surrounds and delimits it—(in this case the irrational world comprises both the earthly existence of man which is unworthy of rationalisation and also the next world, that of salvation, which human, rational concepts cannot grasp)— is represented as independent of it, as unconditionally inferior or superior to it, this creates no technical problem for the rational system itself. It is simply the means to a—non-rational—end. The situation is quite different when rationalism claims to be the universal method by which to obtain knowledge of the whole of existence. In that event the necessary correlation with the principle of irrationality becomes crucial: it erodes and dissolves the whole system. This is the case with modern (bourgeois) rationalism.

The dilemma can be seen most clearly in the strange significance for Kant's system of his concept of the thing-in-itself, with its many iridescent connotations. The attempt has often been made to prove that the thing-in-itself has a number of quite disparate functions within Kant's system. What they all have in common is the fact that they each represent a limit, a barrier, to the abstract, formal, rationalistic, 'human' faculty of cognition. However, these limits and barriers seem to be so very different from each other that it is only meaningful to unify them by means of the—

admittedly abstract and negative—concept of the thing-in-itself if it is clear that, despite the great variety of effects, there is a unified explanation for these frontiers. To put it briefly, these problems can be reduced to two great, seemingly unconnected and even opposed complexes. There is, firstly, the problem of matter (in the logical, technical sense), the problem of the *content* of those forms with the aid of which 'we' know and are able to know the world because we have created it ourselves. And, secondly, there is the problem of the whole and of the ultimate substance of knowledge, the problem of those 'ultimate' objects of knowledge which are needed to round off the partial systems into a totality, a system of the perfectly understood world.

We know that in the *Critique of Pure Reason* it is emphatically denied that the second group of questions can be answered. Indeed, in the section on the *Transcendental Dialectic* the attempt is made to condemn them as questions falsely put, and to eliminate them from science.[6] But there is no need to enlarge on the fact that the question of totality is the constant centre of the transcendental dialectic. God, the soul, etc., are nothing but mythological expressions to denote the unified subject or, alternatively, the unified object of the totality of the objects of knowledge considered as perfect (and wholly known). The transcendental dialectic with its sharp distinction between phenomena and noumena repudiates all attempts by 'our' reason to obtain knowledge of the second group of objects. They are regarded as things-in-themselves as opposed to the phenomena that can be known.

It now appears as if the first complex of questions, that concerning the content of the forms, had nothing to do with these issues. Above all in the form sometimes given to it by Kant, according to which: "the sensuous faculty of intuition (which furnishes the forms of understanding with content) is in reality only a receptive quality, a capacity for being affected in a certain way by ideas. . . . The non-sensuous cause of these ideas is wholly unknown to us and we are therefore unable to intuit it as an object. . . . However, we can call the merely intelligible cause of phenomena in general the transcendental object, simply so that 'we' should have something which corresponds to sensuousness as receptivity."

He goes on to say of this object "that it is a datum in itself, antecedent to all experience".[7] But the problem of content goes much further than that of sensuousness, though unlike some particularly 'critical' and supercilious Kantians we cannot deny that the two are closely connected. For irrationality, the impossibility of reducing contents to their rational elements (which we shall discover again as a general problem in modern logic) can be seen at its crudest in the question of relating the sensuous content to the rational form. While the irrationality of other kinds of content is local and relative, the existence and the mode of being of sensuous contents remain absolutely irreducible.[8] But when the problem of irrationality resolves itself into the impossibility of penetrating any datum with the aid of rational concepts or of deriving them from such concepts, the question of the thing-in-itself, which at first seemed to involve the metaphysical dilemma of the relation between 'mind' and 'matter' now assumes a completely different aspect which is crucial both for methodology and for systematic theory.[9] The question then becomes: are the empirical facts—(it is immaterial whether they are purely 'sensuous' or whether their sensuousness is only the ultimate material substratum of their 'factual' essence)—to be taken as 'given' or can this 'givenness' be dissolved further into rational forms, i.e. can it be conceived as the product of 'our' reason? With this the problem becomes crucial for the possibility of the system in general.

Kant himself had already turned the problem explicitly in this direction. He repeatedly emphasises that pure reason is unable to make the least leap towards the synthesis and the definition of an object and so its principles cannot be deduced "directly from concepts but only indirectly by relating these concepts to something wholly contingent, namely *possible* experience";[10] in the *Critique of Judgement* this notion of 'intelligible contingency' both of the elements of possible experience and of all laws regulating and relating to it is made the central problem of systematisation. When Kant does this we see, on the one hand, that the two quite distinct delimiting functions of the thing-in-itself (viz. the impossibility of apprehending the whole with the aid of the conceptual framework of the rational partial systems and the irrationality of the contents of the individual concepts) are but two sides of the one problem. On the other hand, we see that this problem is in fact of central importance for any mode of thought that undertakes to confer universal significance on rational categories.

Thus the attempt to universalise rationalism necessarily issues in the demand for a system but, at the same time, as soon as one reflects upon the conditions in which a universal system is possible, i.e. as soon as the question of the system is consciously posed, it is seen that such a demand is incapable of fulfilment.[11] For a system in the sense given to it by rationalism—and any other system would be self-contradictory—can bear no meaning other than that of a co-ordination, or rather a supra- and subordination of the various partial systems of forms (and within these, of the individual forms). The connections between them must always be thought of as 'necessary', i.e. as visible in or 'created 'by the forms themselves, or at least by the principle according to which forms are constructed. That is to say, the correct positing of a principle implies—at least in its general tendency—the positing of the whole system determined by it; the consequences are contained in the principle, they can be deduced from it, they are predictable and calculable. The real evolution of the totality of postulates may appear as an 'infinite process', but this limitation means only that we cannot survey the whole system at once; it does not detract from the *principle* of systematisation in the least.[12] This notion of system makes it clear why pure and applied mathematics have constantly been held up as the methodological model and guide for modern philosophy. For the way in which their axioms are related to the partial systems and results deduced from them corresponds exactly to the postulate that systematic rationalism sets itself, the postulate, namely, that every given aspect of the system should be capable of being deduced from its basic principle, that it should be exactly predictable and calculable.

It is evident that the principle of systematisation is not reconcilable with the recognition of any 'facticity', of a 'content' which in principle cannot be deduced from the principle of form and which, therefore, has simply to be accepted as actuality. The greatness, the paradox and the tragedy of classical German philosophy lie in the fact that—unlike Spinoza—it no longer dismisses every donné as non-existent, causing it to vanish behind the monumental architecture of the rational forms produced by the understanding. Instead, while grasping and holding on to the irrational character of the actual contents of the concepts it strives to go beyond this, to overcome it and to erect a system. But from what has already been said it is clear what the problem of the actually given means for rationalism: viz. that it cannot be left to its own being and existence, for in that case it would remain ineluctably 'contingent'. Instead it must be wholly absorbed into the rational system of the concepts of the understanding.

At first sight we seem to be faced by an insoluble dilemma. For either the 'irrational' content is to be wholly integrated into the conceptual system, i.e. this is to be so constructed that it can be coherently applied to everything just as if there were no irrational content or actuality (if there is, it exists at best as a problem in the sense suggested above). In this event thought regresses to the level of a naïve, dogmatic rationalism: somehow it regards the mere actuality of the irrational contents of the concepts as non-existent. (This metaphysics may also conceal its real nature behind the formula that these contents are 'irrelevant' to know-ledge.) Alternatively we are forced to concede that actuality, con-tent, matter reaches right into the form, the structures of the forms and their interrelations and thus *into the structure of the system itself*.[13] In that case the system must be abandoned as a system. For then it will be no more than a register, an account, as well ordered as possible, of facts which are no longer linked rationally and so can no longer be made systematic even though the forms of their com-ponents are themselves rational.[14]

It would be superficial to be baffled by this abstract dilemma and the classical philosophers did not hesitate for a moment. They took the logical opposition of form and content, the point at which all the antitheses of philosophy meet, and drove it to extremes. This enabled them to make a real advance on their predecessors and lay the foundations of the dialectical method. They persisted in their attempts to construct a rational system in the face of their clear acknowledgement of and stubborn adher-ence to the irrational nature of the contents of their concepts (of the given world).

This system went in the direction of a dynamic relativisation of these antitheses. Here too, of course, modern mathematics provided them with a model. The systems it influenced (in par-ticular that of Leibniz) view the irrationality of the given world as a challenge. And in fact, for mathematics the irrationality of a given content only serves as a stimulus to modify and reinterpret the formal system with whose aid correlations had been established hitherto, so that what had at first sight appeared as a 'given' con-tent, now appeared to have been 'created'. Thus actuality was resolved into necessity. This view of reality does indeed represent a great advance on the dogmatic period (of 'holy mathematics').

But it must not be overlooked that mathematics was working with a concept of the irrational specially adapted to its own needs and homogeneous with them (and mediated by this concept it employed a similarly adapted notion of actuality, of existence). Certainly, the local irrationality of the conceptual content is to be found here too: but from the outset it is designed—by the method chosen and the nature of its axioms—to spring from as pure a position as possible and hence to be capable of being relativised.[15]

But this implies the discovery of a methodological model and not of the method itself. It is evident that the irrationality of existence (both as a totality and as the 'ultimate' material substratum underlying the forms), the irrationality of matter is qualitatively different from the irrationality of what we can call with Maimon, intelligible matter. Naturally this could not prevent philosophers from following the mathematical method (of construction, production) and trying to press even this matter into its forms. But it must never be forgotten that the uninterrupted 'creation' of content has a quite different meaning in reference to the material base of existence from what it involves in the world of mathematics which is a wholly constructed world. For the philosophers 'creation' means only the possibility of rationally comprehending the facts, whereas for mathematics 'creation' and the possibility of comprehension are identical. Of all the representatives of classical philosophy it was Fichte in his middle period who saw this problem most clearly and gave it the most satisfactory formulation. What is at issue, he says, is "the absolute projection of an object *of the origin of which no account can be given* with the result that *the space between projection and thing projected is dark and void*; I expressed it somewhat scholastically but, as I believe, very appropriately, as the projectio per hiatum irrationalem".[16]

Only with this problematic does it become possible to comprehend the parting of the ways in modern philosophy and with it the chief stages in its evolution. This doctrine of the irrational leaves behind it the era of philosophical 'dogmatism' or—to put it in terms of social history—the age in which the bourgeois class naïvely equated its own forms of thought, the forms in which it saw the world in accordance with its own existence in society, with reality and with existence as such.

The unconditional recognition of this problem, the renouncing of attempts to solve it leads directly to the various theories centr-

ing on the notion of fiction. It leads to the rejection of every
'metaphysics' (in the sense of ontology) and also to positing
as the aim of philosophy the understanding of the phenomena of
isolated, highly specialised areas by means of abstract rational
special systems, perfectly adapted to them and without making the
attempt to achieve a unified mastery of the whole realm of the
knowable. (Indeed any such attempt is dismissed as 'unscientific').
Some schools make this renunciation explicitly (e.g. Mach,
Avenarius, Poincaré, Vaihinger, etc.) while in many others it is
disguised. But it must not be forgotten that—as was demonstrated
at the end of Section I—the origin of the special sciences with
their complete independence of one another both in method
and subject matter entails the recognition that this problem
is insoluble. And the fact that these sciences are 'exact' is
due precisely to this circumstance. Their underlying material
base is permitted to dwell inviolate and undisturbed in its irrationality ('non-createdness', 'givenness') so that it becomes
possible to operate with unproblematic, rational categories in
the resulting methodically purified world. These categories are
then applied not to the real material substratum (even that of the
particular science) but to an 'intelligible' subject matter.

Philosophy—consciously—refrains from interfering with the
work of the special sciences. It even regards this renunciation as a
critical advance. In consequence its role is confined to the investigation of the formal presuppositions of the special sciences which
it neither corrects nor interferes with. And the problem which
they by-pass philosophy cannot solve either, nor even pose, for that
matter. Where philosophy has recourse to the structural assumptions lying behind the form-content relationship it either exalts
the 'mathematicising' method of the special sciences, elevating it
into the method proper to philosophy (as in the Marburg School),[17]
or else it establishes the irrationality of matter, as logically, the
'ultimate' fact (as do Windelband, Rickert and Lask). But in
both cases, as soon as the attempt at systematisation is made, the
unsolved problem of the irrational reappears in the problem of
totality. The horizon that delimits the totality that has been and
can be created here is, at best, culture (i.e. the culture of bourgeois
society). This culture cannot be derived from anything else and
has simply to be accepted on its own terms as 'facticity' in the
sense given to it by the classical philosophers.[18]

To give a detailed analysis of the various forms taken by the refusal to understand reality as a whole and as existence, would be to go well beyond the framework of this study. Our aim here was to locate the point at which there appears in the thought of bourgeois society the double tendency characteristic of its evolution. On the one hand, it acquires increasing control over the details of its social existence, subjecting them to its needs. On the other hand it loses—likewise progressively—the possibility of gaining intellectual control of society as a whole and with that it loses its own qualifications for leadership.

Classical German philosophy marks a unique transitional stage in this process. It arises at a point of development where matters have progressed so far that these problems can be raised to the level of consciousness. At the same time this takes place in a milieu where the problems can only appear on an intellectual and philosophical plane. This has the drawback that the concrete problems of society and the concrete solutions to them cannot be seen. Nevertheless, classical philosophy is able to think the deepest and most fundamental problems of the development of bourgeois society through to the very end—on the plane of philosophy. It is able—in thought—to complete the evolution of class. And—in thought—it is able to take all the paradoxes of its position to the point where the necessity of going beyond this historical stage in mankind's development can at least be seen as a problem.

2

Classical philosophy is indebted for its wealth, its depth and its boldness no less than its fertility for future thinkers to the fact that it narrowed the problem down, confining it within the realm of pure thought. At the same time it remains an insuperable obstacle even within the realm of thought itself. That is to say, classical philosophy mercilessly tore to shreds all the metaphysical illusions of the preceding era, but was forced to be as uncritical and as dogmatically metaphysical with regard to some of its own premises as its predecessors had been towards theirs. We have already made a passing reference to this point: it is the—dogmatic —assumption that the rational and formalistic mode of cognition is the only possible way of apprehending reality (or to put it in its most critical form: the only possible way for 'us'), in contrast to the facts which are simply given and alien to 'us'.

As we have shown, the grandiose conception that thought can

only grasp what it has itself created strove to master the world as a whole by seeing it as self-created. However, it then came up against the insuperable obstacle of the given, of the thing-in-itself. If it was not to renounce its understanding of the whole it had to take the road that leads inwards. It had to strive to find the subject of thought which could be thought of as producing existence without any *hiatus irrationalis* or transcendental thing-in-itself. The dogmatism alluded to above was partly a true guide and partly a source of confusion in this enterprise. It was a true guide inasmuch as thought was led beyond the mere acceptance of reality as it was given, beyond mere reflection and the conditions necessary for thinking about reality, to orientate itself beyond *mere contemplation* and mere intuition. It was a source of confusion since it prevented the same dogmatism from discovering its true antidote, the principle that would enable contemplation to be overcome, namely the *practical*. (The fact that *precisely for this reason* the given constantly re-emerges as untranscended in its irrationality will be demonstrated in the course of the following account.)

In his last important logical work[19] Fichte formulates the philosophical starting-point for this situation as follows: "We have seen all actual knowledge as being necessary, except for the form of 'is', on the assumption that there is one phenomenon that must doubtless remain as an absolute assumption for thought and concerning which doubt can only be resolved by an actual intuition. But with the distinction that we can perceive the definite and qualitative law in the content of one part of this fact, namely the ego–principle. Whereas for the *actual* content of this intuition of self we can merely perceive the fact that one must exist but cannot legislate for the existence of *this one* in particular. At the same time we note clearly that there can be no such law and that therefore, the qualitative law required for this definition is precisely the absence of law itself. Now, if the necessary is also that which is known *a priori* we have in this sense perceived all facticity *a priori*, not excluding the empirical since this we have deduced to be non-deducible."

What is relevant to our problem here is the statement that the subject of knowledge, the ego-principle, is known as to its content and, hence, can be taken as a starting-point and as a guide to method. In the most general terms we see here the origin of the philosophical tendency to press forward to a conception of the subject which can be thought of as the creator of the totality of content. And likewise in general, purely programmatic terms we see the origin of the search for a level of objectivity, a positing of the objects, where the duality of subject and object (the duality of thought and being is only a special case of this), is transcended, i.e. where subject and object coincide, where they are identical.

Obviously the great classical philosophers were much too perceptive and critical to overlook the empirically existing duality of subject and object. Indeed, they saw the basic structure of empirical data precisely in this split. But their demand, their programme was much more concerned with finding the nodal point, from which they could 'create', deduce and make comprehensible the duality of subject and object on the empirical plane, i.e. in its objective form. In contrast to the dogmatic acceptance of a merely given reality—divorced from the subject—they required that every datum should be understood as the product of the identical subject-object, and every duality should be seen as a special case derived from this pristine unity.

But this unity is *activity*. Kant had attempted in the *Critique of Practical Reason* (which has been much misunderstood and often falsely opposed to the *Critique of Pure Reason*) to show that the barriers that could not be overcome by theory (contemplation) were amenable to practical solutions. Fichte went beyond this and put the practical, action and activity in the centre of his unifying philosophical system. "For this reason," he says, "it is not such a trivial matter as it appears to some people, whether philosophy should begin from a fact or from an action (i.e. from pure activity which presupposes no object but itself creates it, so that *action* immediately becomes *deed*). For if it starts with the fact it places itself inside the world of existence and of finitude and will find it hard to discover the way that leads from there to the infinite and the suprasensual; if it begins from action it will stand at the point where the two worlds meet and from which they can both be seen at a glance."[20]

Fichte's task, therefore, is to exhibit the subject of the 'action' and, assuming its identity with the object, to comprehend every dual subject-object form as derived from it, as its product. But here, on a philosophically higher plane, we find repeated the same failure to resolve the questions raised by classical German philosophy. The moment that we enquire after the *concrete* nature of this identical subject-object, we are confronted with a dilemma. On the one hand, this configuration of consciousness can only be found really and concretely in the ethical act, in the relation of the ethically acting (individual) subject to itself. On the other hand, for the ethical consciousness of the acting individual the split between the self-generated, but wholly inwardly turning form (of the ethical imperative in Kant) and of the reality, the given, the empirical alien both to the senses and the understanding must become even more definitive than for the contemplative subject of knowledge.

It is well known that Kant did not go beyond the critical interpretation of ethical facts in the individual consciousness. This had a number of consequences. In the first place, these facts were thereby transformed into something merely there and could not be conceived of as having been 'created'.[21]

Secondly, this intensifies the 'intelligible contingency' of an 'external world' subject to the laws of nature. In the absence of a real, concrete solution the dilemma of freedom and necessity, of voluntarism and fatalism is simply shunted into a siding. That is to say, in nature and in the 'external world' laws still operate with inexorable necessity,[22] while freedom and the autonomy that is supposed to result from the discovery of the ethical world are reduced to a mere *point of view from which to judge* internal events. These events, however, are seen as being subject in all their motives and effects and even in their psychological elements to a fatalistically regarded objective necessity.[23]

Thirdly, this ensures that the hiatus between appearance and essence (which in Kant coincides with that between necessity and freedom) is not bridged and does not, therefore, give way to a manufactured unity with which to establish the unity of the world. Even worse than that: the duality is itself introduced into the subject. Even the subject is split into phenomenon and noumenon and the unresolved, insoluble and henceforth permanent conflict between freedom and necessity now invades its innermost structure.

Fourthly, in consequence of this, the resulting ethic becomes *purely formal and lacking in content.* As every content which is given to us belongs to the world of nature and is thus unconditionally subject to the objective laws of the phenomenal world, practical norms can only have bearing on the inward forms of action. The moment this ethic attempts to make itself concrete, i.e. to test its strength on concrete problems, it is forced to *borrow* the elements of content of these particular actions from the world of phenomena and from the conceptual systems that assimilate them and absorb their 'contingency'. The principle of creation collapses as soon as the first concrete content is to be created. And Kant's ethics cannot evade such an attempt. It does try, it is true, to find the formal principle which will both determine and preserve content—at least negatively—and to locate it in the principle of non-contradiction. According to this, every action contravening ethical norms contains a self-contradiction. For example, an essential quality of a deposit is that it should not be embezzled, etc. But as Hegel has pointed out quite rightly: "What if there were no deposit, where is the contradiction in that? For there to be no deposit would contradict yet other necessarily determined facts; just as the fact that a deposit is possible, is connected with other necessary facts and so it itself becomes necessary. But it is not permissible to involve other purposes and other material grounds; only the immediate form of the concept may decide which of the two assumptions is correct. But each of the opposed facts is as immaterial to the form as the other; either can be acceptable as a quality and this acceptance can be expressed as a law."[24]

Thus Kant's ethical analysis leads us back to the unsolved *methodological* problem of the thing-in-itself. We have already defined the philosophically significant side of this problem, its methodological aspect, as the relation between form and content, as the problem of the irreducibility of the factual, and the irrationality of matter. Kant's formalistic ethics, adapted to the consciousness of the individual, is indeed able to open up the possibility of a metaphysical solution to the problem of the thing-in-itself by enabling the concepts of a world seen as a totality, which had been destroyed by the transcendental dialectic, to reappear on the horizon as the postulates of practical reason. But from the point of view of method this subjective and practical solution remains imprisoned within the same barriers that proved so overwhelming to the objective and contemplative analysis in the *Critique of Pure Reason*.

This sheds light on a new and significant structural aspect of the whole complex of problems: in order to overcome the irrationality of the question of the thing-in-itself it is not enough that the attempt should be made to transcend the contemplative attitude. When the question is formulated more concretely it turns out that the essence of praxis consists in annulling *that indifference of form towards content* that we found in the problem of the thing-in-itself. Thus praxis can only be really established as a philosophical principle if, at the same time, a conception of form can be found whose basis and validity no longer rest on that pure rationality and that freedom from every definition of content. In so far as the principle of praxis is the prescription for changing reality, it must be tailored to the concrete material substratum of action if it is to impinge upon it to any effect.

Only this approach to the problem makes possible the clear dichotomy between praxis and the theoretical, contemplative and intuitive attitude. But also we can now understand the connection between the two attitudes and see how, with the aid of the principle of praxis, the attempt could be made to resolve the antinomies of contemplation. Theory and praxis in fact refer to the same objects, for every object exists as an immediate inseparable complex of form and content. However, the diversity of subjective attitudes orientates praxis towards what is qualitatively unique, towards the content and the material substratum of the object concerned. As we have tried to show, theoretical contemplation leads to the neglect of this very factor. For, theoretical clarification and theoretical analysis of the object reach their highest point just when they reveal at their starkest the formal factors liberated from all content (from all 'contingent facticity'). As long as thought proceeds 'naïvely', i.e. as long as it fails to reflect upon its activity and as long as it imagines it can derive the content from the forms themselves, thus ascribing active, metaphysical functions to them, or else regards as metaphysical and non-existent any material alien to form, this problem does not present itself. Praxis then appears to be consistently subordinated to the theory of contemplation.[25] But the very moment when this situation, i.e. when the indissoluble links that bind the contemplative attitude of the subject to the purely formal character of the object of knowledge become conscious, it is inevitable either that the attempt to find a solution to the problem of irrationality (the question of content, of the given, etc.) should be abandoned or that it should be sought in praxis.

It is once again in Kant that this tendency finds its clearest expression. When for Kant "existence is evidently not a real predicate, i.e. the concept of something that could be added to the concept of a thing",[26] we see this tendency with all its consequences at its most extreme. It is in fact so extreme that he is compelled to propose the dialectics of concepts in movement as the only alternative to his own theory of the structure of concepts. "For otherwise it would not be exactly the same thing that exists, but something more than I had thought in the concept and I would not be able to say that it is precisely the object of my concept that exists." It has escaped the notice of both Kant and the critics of his critique of the ontological argument that here—admittedly in a negative and distorted form arising from his purely contemplative viewpoint—Kant has hit upon the structure of true praxis as a way of overcoming the antinomies of the concept of existence. We have already shown how, despite all his efforts, his ethics leads back to the limits of abstract contemplation.

Hegel uncovers the methodological basis of this theory in his criticism of this passage.[27] "For this content regarded in isolation it is indeed a matter of indifference whether it exists or does not exist; there is no inherent distinction between existence and non-existence; this distinction does not concern it at all. . . . More generally, the abstractions existence and non-existence both cease to be abstract when they acquire a definite content; existence then becomes reality . . ." That is to say, the goal that Kant here sets for knowledge is shown to be the description of that structure of cognition that systematically isolates 'pure laws' and treats them in a systematically isolated and artificially homogeneous milieu. (Thus in the physical hypothesis of the vibrations of the ether the 'existence' of the ether would in fact add nothing to the concept.) But the moment that the object is seen as part of a concrete totality, the moment that it becomes clear that alongside the formal, delimiting concept of existence acknowledged by this pure contemplation other gradations of reality are possible and necessary to thought (being [*Dasein*], existence [*Existenz*], reality [*Realität*], etc. in Hegel), Kant's proof collapses: it survives only as the demarcation line of purely formal thought.

In his doctoral thesis Marx, more concrete and logical than Hegel, effected the transition from the question of existence and its hierarchy of meanings to the plane of historical reality and concrete praxis. "Didn't the Moloch of the Ancients hold sway? Wasn't the Delphic Apollo a real power in the life of the Greeks? In this context Kant's criticism is meaningless."[28] Unfortunately Marx did not develop this idea to its logical conclusion although in his mature works his *method* always operates with concepts of existence graduated according to the various levels of praxis.

The more conscious this Kantian tendency becomes the less avoidable is the dilemma. For, the ideal of knowledge represented by the purely distilled formal conception of the object of knowledge, the mathematical organisation and the ideal of necessary natural laws all transform knowledge more and more into the systematic and conscious contemplation of those purely formal connections, those 'laws' which function in—objective—reality *without the intervention of the subject*. But the attempt to eliminate every element of content and of the irrational affects not only the object but also, and to an increasing extent, the subject. The critical elucidation of contemplation puts more and more energy into its efforts to weed out ruthlessly from its own outlook every subjective and irrational element and every anthropomorphic tendency; it strives with ever increasing vigour to drive a wedge between the subject of knowledge and 'man', and to transform the knower into a pure and purely formal subject.

It might seem as if this characterisation of contemplation might be thought to contradict our earlier account of the problem of knowledge as the knowledge of what 'we' have created. This is in fact the case. But this very contradiction is eminently suited to illuminate the difficulty of the question and the possible solutions to it. For the contradiction does not lie in the inability of the philosophers to give a definitive analysis of the available facts. It is rather the intellectual expression of the objective situation itself which it is their task to comprehend. That is to say, the contradiction that appears here between subjectivity and objectivity in modern rationalist formal systems, the entanglements and equivocations hidden in their concepts of subject and object, the conflict between their nature as systems created by 'us' and their fatalistic necessity distant from and alien to man is nothing but the logical and systematic formulation of the modern state of society. For, on the one hand, men are constantly smashing, replacing and leaving behind them the 'natural', irrational and actually existing bonds, while, on the other hand, they erect around themselves in the reality they have created and 'made', a kind of second nature which evolves with exactly the same inexorable necessity as was the case earlier on with irrational forces of nature (more exactly: the social relations which appear in this form). "To them, their own social action", says Marx, "takes the form of the action of objects, which rule the producers instead of being ruled by them."

1. From this it follows that the powers that are beyond man's control assume quite a different character. Hitherto it had been that of the blind power of a—fundamentally—irrational fate, the point where the possibility of human knowledge ceased and where absolute transcendence and the realm of faith began.[29] Now, however, it appears as the ineluctable consequence of known, knowable, rational systems of laws, as a necessity which cannot ultimately and wholly be grasped, as was indeed recognised by the critical philosophers, unlike their dogmatic predecessors. In its parts, however—within the radius in which men live—it can increasingly be penetrated, calculated and predicted. It is anything but a mere chance that at the very beginning of the development of modern philosophy the ideal of knowledge took the form of universal mathematics: it was an attempt to establish a rational system of relations which comprehends the totality of the formal possibilities, proportions and relations of a rationalised existence with the aid of which every phenomenon—independently of its real and material distinctiveness—could be subjected to an exact calculus.[30]

This is the modern ideal of knowledge at its most uncompromising and therefore at its most characteristic, and in it the contradiction alluded to above emerges clearly. For, on the one hand, the basis of this universal calculus can be nothing other than the certainty that only a reality cocooned by such concepts can truly be controlled by us. On the other hand, it appears that even if we may suppose this universal mathematics to be entirely and consistently realised, 'control' of reality can be nothing more than the objectively correct contemplation of what is yielded—necessarily and without our intervention—by the abstract combinations of these relations and proportions. In this sense contemplation does seem to come close to the universal philosophical ideal of knowledge (as in Greece and India). What is peculiar to modern philosophy only becomes fully revealed when we critically examine the assumption that this universal system of combinations can be put into practice.

For it is only with the discovery of the 'intelligible contingency' of these laws that there arises the possibility of a 'free' movement within the field of action of such overlapping or not fully comprehended laws. It is important to realise that if we take action in the sense indicated above to mean changing reality, an orientation towards the qualitatively essential and the material substratum

of action, then the attitude under discussion will appear much
more contemplative than, for instance, the ideal of knowledge
held by Greek philosophers.[31] For this 'action' consists in predicting, in calculating as far as possible the probable effects of those
laws and the subject of the 'action' takes up a position in which
these effects can be exploited to the best advantage of his own purposes. It is therefore evident that, on the one hand, the more the
whole of reality is rationalised and the more its manifestations
can be integrated into the system of laws, the more such prediction becomes feasible. On the other hand, it is no less evident that
the more reality and the attitude of the subject 'in action' approxi-
mate to this type, the more the subject will be transformed into a
receptive organ ready to pounce on opportunities created by the
system of laws and his 'activity' will narrow itself down to the
adoption of a vantage point from which these laws function in his
best interests (and this without any intervention on his part).
The attitude of the subject then becomes purely contemplative
in the philosophical sense.

2. But here we can see that this results in the assimilation of all
human relations to the level of natural laws so conceived. It has
often been pointed out in these pages that nature is a social category. Of course, to modern man who proceeds immediately from
ready-made ideological forms and from their effects which dazzle
his eye and exercise such a profound effect on his whole intellectual
development, it must look as if the point of view which we have
just outlined consisted simply in applying to society an intellectual
framework derived from the natural sciences. In his youthful
polemic against Fichte, Hegel had already pointed out that his
state was "a machine", its substratum "an atomistic ... multitude
whose elements are ... a quantity of points. This absolute substantiality of the points founds an atomistic system in practical
philosophy in which, as in the atomism of nature, a mind alien
to the atoms becomes law."[32]

This way of describing modern society is so familiar and the
attempts to analyse it recur so frequently in the course of later
developments that it would be supererogatory to furnish further
proof of it. What is of greater importance is the fact that the
converse of this insight has not escaped notice either. After Hegel
had clearly recognised the bourgeois character of the 'laws of
nature',[33] Marx pointed out[34] that "Descartes with his definition
of animals as mere machines saw with the eyes of the manufac-

turing period, while in the eyes of the Middle Ages, animals were man's assistants"; and he adds several suggestions towards explaining the intellectual history of such connections. Tönnies notes the same connection even more bluntly and categorically: "A special case of abstract reason is *scientific* reason and its subject is the man who is objective, and who recognises relations, i.e. thinks in concepts. In consequence, scientific concepts which by their ordinary origin and their real properties are judgements by means of which complexes of feeling are given names, behave within science like commodities in society. They gather together within the system like commodities on the market. The supreme scientific concept which is no longer the name of anything real is like money. E.g. the concept of an atom, or of energy."[35]

It cannot be our task to investigate the question of priority or the historical and causal order of succession between the 'laws of nature' and capitalism. (The author of these lines has, however, no wish to conceal his view that the development of capitalist economics takes precedence.) What is important is to recognise clearly that all human relations (viewed as the objects of social activity) assume increasingly the objective forms of the abstract elements of the conceptual systems of natural science and of the abstract substrata of the laws of nature. And also, the subject of this 'action' likewise assumes increasingly the attitude of the pure observe of these—artificially abstract—processes, the attitude of the experimenter.

*   *   *

I may be permitted to devote a few words—as a sort of excursus —to the views expressed by Friedrich Engels on the problem of the thing-in-itself. In a sense they are of no immediate concern to us, but they have exercised such a great influence on the meaning given to the term by many Marxists that to omit to correct this might easily give rise to a misunderstanding. He says:[36] "The most telling refutation of this as of all other philosophical crotchets is practice, namely, experiment and industry. If we are able to prove the correctness of our conception of a natural process by making it ourselves, bringing it into being out of its conditions and making it serve our own purposes into the bargain, then there is an end to the ungraspable Kantian 'thing-in-itself'. The chemical substances produced in the bodies of plants and animals remained such 'things-in-themselves' until organic chemistry began to produce them one after another, whereupon the 'thing-in-itself' became a thing for us, as, for instance, alizarin, the colouring matter of the madder, which we no longer trouble to grow in the madder roots in the field, but produce much more cheaply and simply from coal tar."

Above all we must correct a terminological confusion that is almost incomprehensible in such a connoisseur of Hegel as was Engels. For Hegel the terms 'in itself' and 'for us' are by no means opposites; in fact they are *necessary correlatives*. That something exists merely 'in itself' means for Hegel that it merely exists 'for us'. The antithesis of 'for us or in itself'[37] is rather 'for itself', namely that mode of being posited where the fact that an object is thought of implies at the same time that the object is conscious of itself.[38] In that case, it is a complete misinterpretation of Kant's epistemology to imagine that the problem of the thing-in-itself could be a barrier to the possible concrete expansion of our knowledge. On the contrary, Kant who sets out from the most advanced natural science of the day, namely from Newton's astronomy, tailored his theory of knowledge precisely to this science and to its future potential. For this reason he necessarily assumes that the method was capable of *limitless expansion*. His 'critique' refers merely to the fact that even the complete knowledge of all phenomena would be no more than a knowledge of phenomena (as opposed to the things-in-themselves). Moreover, even the complete knowledge of the phenomena could never overcome the *structural limits* of this knowledge, i.e. in our terms, the antinomies of totality and of content. Kant has himself dealt sufficiently clearly with the question of agnosticism and of the relation to Hume (and to Berkeley who is not named but whom Kant has particularly in mind) in the section entitled 'The Refutation of Idealism'.[39]

But Engels' deepest misunderstanding consists in his belief that the behaviour of industry and scientific experiment constitutes praxis in the dialectical, philosophical sense. In fact, scientific experiment is contemplation at its purest. The experimenter creates an artificial, abstract milieu in order to be able to *observe* undisturbed the untrammelled workings of the laws under examination, eliminating all irrational factors both of the subject and the object. He strives as far as possible to reduce the material substratum of his observation to the purely rational 'product', to the 'intelligible matter' of mathematics. And when Engels speaks, in the context of industry, of the "product" which is made to serve "our purposes", he seems to have forgotton for a moment the fundamental structure of capitalist society which he himself had once formulated so supremely well in his brilliant early essay. There he had pointed out that capitalist society is based on "a natural law that is founded on the unconsciousness of those involved in it".[40] Inasmuch as industry sets itself 'objectives'—it is in the decisive, i.e. historical, dialectical meaning of the word, only the object, not the subject of the natural laws governing society.

Marx repeatedly emphasised that the capitalist (and when we speak of 'industry' in the past or present we can only mean the capitalist) is nothing but a puppet. And when, for example, he compares his instinct to enrich himself with that of the miser, he stresses the fact that "what in the miser is a mere idiosyncrasy, is, in the capitalist, the effect of the social mechanism, of which he is but one of the wheels. Moreover, the development of capitalist production makes it constantly necessary to keep increasing the amount of the capital invested in a given industrial undertaking, and competition makes the immanent laws of capitalist production to be felt as external coercive laws by each individual capitalist."[41] The fact, therefore, that 'industry', i.e. the capitalist as the incarnation of economic and technical progress, does not act but is acted upon and that his 'activity' goes no further than the correct observation and calculation of the objective working out of the natural laws of society, is a truism for Marxism and is elsewhere interpreted in this way by Engels also.

* * *

3. To return to our main argument, it is evident from all this that the attempt at a solution represented by the turn taken by critical philosophy towards the practical, does not succeed in resolving the antinomies we have noted. On the contrary it fixes them for eternity.[42] For just as objective necessity, despite the rationality and regularity of its manifestations, yet persists in a state of immutable contingency because its material substratum remains transcendental, so too the freedom of the subject which this device is designed to rescue, is unable, being an empty freedom, to evade the abyss of fatalism. "Thoughts without content are empty," says Kant programmatically at the beginning of the 'Transcendental Logic', "Intuitions without concepts are blind."[43] But the *Critique* which here propounds the necessity of an interpretation of form and content can do no more than offer

it as a methodological programme, i.e. for each of the discrete areas it can indicate the point where the real synthesis *should* begin, and where it *would* begin if its formal rationality *could* allow it to do more than predict formal possibilities in terms of formal calculations.

The freedom (of the subject) is neither able to overcome the sensuous necessity of the system of knowledge and the soullessness of the fatalistically conceived laws of nature, nor is it able to give them any meaning. And likewise the contents produced by reason, and the world acknowledged by reason are just as little able to fill the purely formal determinants of freedom with a truly living life. The impossibility of comprehending and 'creating' the union of form and content concretely instead of as the basis for a purely formal calculus leads to the insoluble dilemma of freedom and necessity, of voluntarism and fatalism. The 'eternal, iron' regularity of the processes of nature and the purely inward freedom of individual moral practice appear at the end of the *Critique of Practical Reason* as wholly irreconcilable and at the same time as the unalterable foundations of human existence.[44] Kant's greatness as a philosopher lies in the fact that in both instances he made no attempt to conceal the intractability of the problem by means of an arbitrary dogmatic resolution of any sort, but that he bluntly elaborated the contradiction and presented it in an undiluted form.

3

As everywhere in classical philosophy it would be a mistake to think that these discussions are no more than the problems of intellectuals and the squabbles of pedants. This can be seen most clearly if we turn back a page in the growth of this problem and examine it at a stage in its development when it had been less worked over intellectually, when it was closer to its social background and accordingly more concrete. Plekhanov strongly emphasises the intellectual barrier that the bourgeois materialism of the eighteenth century came up against and he puts it into perspective by means of the following antinomy: on the one hand, *man appears as the product* of his social milieu, whereas, on the other hand, "*the social milieu is produced* by 'public opinion', i.e. *by man*".[45] This throws light on the social reality underlying the antinomy which we encountered in the—seemingly—purely epistemological problem of production, in the systematic question of the subject of an 'action', of the 'creator' of a unified reality. Plekhanov's account shows no less clearly that the duality of the contemplative and the (individual) practical principles which we saw as the first achievement and as the starting-point for the later development of classical philosophy, leads towards this antinomy.

However, the naïver and more primitive analysis of Holbach and Helvetius permits a clearer insight into the life that forms the true basis of this antinomy. We observe, firstly, that following on the development of bourgeois society all social problems cease to transcend man and appear as the products of human activity in contrast to the view of society held by the Middle Ages and the early modern period (e.g. Luther). Secondly, it becomes evident that the man who now emerges must be the individual, egoistic bourgeois isolated artificially by capitalism and that his consciousness, the source of his activity and knowledge, is an individual isolated consciousness à la Robinson Crusoe.[46] But, thirdly, it is this that robs social action of its character as action. At first this looks like the after-effects of the sensualist epistemology of the French materialists (and Locke, etc.) where it is the case, on the one hand, that "his brain is nothing but wax to receive the imprint of every impression made in it" (Holbach according to Plekhanov, op. cit.) and where, on the other hand, only *conscious* action can count as activity. But examined more closely this turns out to be the simple effect of the situation of bourgeois man in the capitalist production process.

We have already described the characteristic features of this situation several times: man in capitalist society confronts a reality 'made' by himself (as a class) which appears to him to be a natural phenomenon alien to himself; he is wholly at the mercy of its 'laws', his activity is confined to the exploitation of the inexorable fulfilment of certain individual laws for his own (egoistic) interests. But even while 'acting' he remains, in the nature of the case, the object and not the subject of events. The field of his activity thus becomes wholly internalised: it consists on the one hand of the awareness of the laws which he uses and, on the other, of his awareness of his inner reactions to the course taken by events.

This situation generates very important and unavoidable problem-complexes and conceptual ambivalences which are decisive for the way in which bourgeois man understands himself in his relation to the world. Thus the word 'nature' becomes highly ambiguous. We have already drawn attention to the idea, formulated most lucidly by Kant but essentially unchanged since Kepler and Galileo, of nature as the "aggregate of systems of the laws" governing what happens. Parallel to this conception whose development out of the economic structures of capitalism has been shown repeatedly, there is another conception of nature, a *value concept*, wholly different from the first one and embracing a wholly different cluster of meanings.

A glance at the history of natural law shows the extent to which these two conceptions have become inextricably interwoven with each other. For here we can see that 'nature' has been heavily marked by the revolutionary struggle of the bourgeoisie: the 'ordered', calculable, formal and abstract character of the approaching bourgeois society appears natural by the side of the artifice, the caprice and the disorder of feudalism and absolutism. At the same time if one thinks of Rousseau, there are echoes of a quite different meaning wholly incompatible with this one. It concentrates increasingly on the feeling that social institutions (reification) strip man of his human essence and that the more culture and civilisation (i.e. capitalism and reification) take possession of him, the less able he is to be a human being. And with a reversal of meanings that never becomes apparent, nature becomes the repository of all these inner tendencies opposing the growth of mechanisation, dehumanisation and reification.

Nature thereby acquires the meaning of what has grown organically, what was not created by man, in contrast to the artificial structures of human civilisation.[47] But, at the same time, it can be understood as that aspect of human inwardness which has remained natural, or at least tends or longs to become natural once more. "They are what we once were," says Schiller of the forms of nature, "they are what we should once more become." But here, unexpectedly and indissolubly bound up with the other meanings, we discover a third conception of nature, one in which we can clearly discern the ideal and the tendency to overcome the problems of a reified existence. 'Nature' here refers to authentic humanity, the true essence of man liberated from the false, mechanising forms of society: man as a perfected whole who has inwardly overcome, or is in the process of overcoming, the dichotomies of theory and practice, reason and the senses, form and content; man whose tendency to create his own forms does not imply an abstract rationalism which ignores concrete content; man for whom freedom and necessity are identical.

With this we find that we have unexpectedly discovered what we had been searching for when we were held up by the irreducible duality of pure and practical reason, by the question of the subject of an 'action', of the 'creation' of reality as a totality. All the more as we are dealing with an attitude (whose ambivalence we recognise as being necessary but which we shall not probe any further) which need not be sought in some mythologising transcendent construct; it does not only exist as a 'fact of the soul', as a nostalgia inhabiting the consciousness, but it also possesses a very real and concrete field of activity where it may be brought to fruition, namely art. This is not the place to investigate the ever-increasing importance of aesthetics and the theory of art within the total world-picture of the eighteenth century. As everywhere in this study, we are concerned solely to throw light on the social and historical background which threw up these problems and conferred upon aesthetics and upon consciousness of art philosophical importance that art was unable to lay claim to in previous ages. This does not mean that art itself was experiencing an unprecedented golden age. On the contrary, with a very few exceptions the actual artistic production during this period cannot remotely be compared to that of past golden ages. What is crucial here is the theoretical and philosophical importance which the *principle of art* acquires in this period.

This principle is the creation of a concrete totality that springs from a conception of form orientated towards the concrete content of its material substratum. In this view form is therefore able to demolish the 'contingent' relation of the parts to the whole and to resolve the merely apparent opposition between chance and necessity. It is well known that Kant in the *Critique of Judgement* assigned to this principle the role of mediator between the otherwise irreconcilable opposites, i.e. the function of perfecting the system. But even at this early stage this attempt at a solution could not limit itself to the explanation and interpretation of the phenomenon of art. If only because, as has been shown, the principle thus discovered was, from its inception, indissolubly bound up with the various conceptions of nature so that its most obvious and appropriate function seemed to provide a principle for the solution of all insoluble problems both of contemplative theory and ethical practice. Fichte did indeed provide a succinct programmatic account of the use to which this principle was to be put: art "transforms the transcendental point of view into the common one",[48] that is to say, what was for transcendental philosophy a highly problematic postulate with which to explain the world, becomes in art perfect achievement: it proves that this postulate of the transcendental philosophers is necessarily anchored in the structure of human consciousness.

However, this proof involves a vital issue of methodology for classical philosophy which—as we have seen—was forced to undertake the task of discovering the subject of 'action' which could be seen to be the maker of reality in its concrete totality. For only if it can be shown that such a subjectivity can be found in the consciousness and that there can be a principle of form which is not affected by the problem of indifference *vis-à-vis* content and the resulting difficulties concerning the thing-in-itself, 'intelligible contingency', etc., only then is it methodologically possible to advance concretely beyond formal rationalism. Only then can a logical solution to the problem of irrationality (i.e. the relation of form to content) become at all feasible. Only then will it be possible to posit the world as conceived by thought as a perfected, concrete, meaningful system 'created' by us and attaining in us the stage of self-awareness. For this reason, together with the discovery of the principle of art, there arises also the problem of the 'intuitive understanding' whose content is not given but 'created'. This understanding is, in Kant's words,[49] spontaneous (i.e. active) and not receptive (i.e. contemplative) both as regards knowledge and intuitive perception. If, in the case of Kant himself, this only indicates the point from which it would be *possible* to complete and perfect the system, in the works of his successors this principle and the postulate of an intuitive understanding and an intellectual intuition becomes the cornerstone of systematic philosophy.

But it is in Schiller's aesthetic and theoretical works that we can see, even more clearly than in the systems of the philosophers (where for the superficial observer the pure edifice of thought sometimes obscures the living heart from which these problems arise), the need which has provided the impetus for these analyses as well as the function to be performed by the solutions offered. Schiller defines the aesthetic principle as the play-instinct (in contrast to the form-instinct and the content-instinct) and his analysis of this contains very valuable insights into the question of reification, as is indeed true of all his aesthetic writings). He formulates it as follows: "For it must be said once and for all that man only plays when he is a man in the full meaning of the word, and *he is fully human only when he plays.*"[50] By extending the aesthetic principle far beyond the confines of aesthetics, by seeing it as the key to the solution of the question of the meaning of man's existence in society, Schiller brings us back to the basic issue of classical philosophy. On the one hand, he recognises that social life has destroyed man as man. On the other hand, he points to the principle whereby *man having been socially destroyed, fragmented and divided between different partial systems is to be made whole again in thought.* If we can now obtain a clear view of classical philosophy we see both the magnitude of its enterprise and the fecundity of the perspectives it opens up for the future, but we see no less clearly the inevitability of its failure. For while earlier thinkers remained naïvely entangled in the modes of thought of reification, or at best (as in the cases cited by Plekhanov) were driven into objective contradictions, here the problematic nature of social life for capitalist man becomes fully conscious.

"When the power of synthesis", Hegel remarks, "vanishes from the lives of men and when the antitheses have lost their vital relation and their power of interaction and gain independence, it is then that philosophy becomes a felt need."[51] At the same time, however, we can see the limitations of this undertaking. Objectively, since question and answer are confined from the very start to the realm of pure thought. These limitations are objective in so far as they derive from the dogmatism of critical philosophy. Even where its method has forced it beyond the limits of the formal, rational and discursive understanding enabling it to become critical of thinkers like Leibniz and Spinoza its *fundamental systematic posture* still remains rationalistic. The dogma of rationality remains unimpaired and is by no means superseded.[52] The limitations are subjective since the principle so discovered reveals when it becomes conscious of itself the narrow confines of its own validity. For if man is fully human "only when he plays", we are indeed enabled to comprehend all the contents of life from this vantage point. And in the aesthetic mode, conceived as broadly as possible, they may be salvaged from the deadening effects of the mechanism of reification. But only *in so far* as these contents become aesthe-

tic. That is to say, either the world must be aestheticised, which
is an evasion of the real problem and is just another way in which
to make the subject purely contemplative and to annihilate
'action'. Or else, the aesthetic principle must be elevated into the
principle by which objective reality is shaped: but that would
be to mythologise the discovery of intuitive understanding.

From Fichte onwards it became increasingly necessary to
make the mythologising of the process of 'creation' into a central
issue, a question of life and death for classical philosophy; all the
more so as the critical point of view was constrained, parallel with
the antinomies which it discovered in the given world and our
relationship with it, to treat the subject in like fashion and to tear
it to pieces (i.e. its fragmentation in objective reality had to be
reproduced in thought, accelerating the process as it did so).
Hegel pours scorn in a number of places on Kant's 'soul-sack'
in which the different 'faculties' (theoretical, practical, etc.)
are lying and from which they have to be 'pulled out'. But there
is no way for Hegel to overcome this fragmentation of the subject
into independent parts whose empirical reality and even necessity
is likewise undeniable, other than by creating this fragmentation,
this disintegration out of a concrete, total subject. On this point
art shows us, as we have seen, the two faces of Janus, and with the
discovery of art it becomes possible either to provide yet another
domain for the fragmented subject or to leave behind the safe
territory of the concrete evocation of totality and (using art at
most by way of illustration) tackle the problem of 'creation' from
the side of the subject. The problem is then no longer—as it was
for Spinoza—to create an objective system of reality on the model
of geometry. It is rather *this* creation which is at once philosophy's
premise and its task. This creation is undoubtedly given ("There
are synthetic judgements a priori—how are they possible?" Kant
had once asked). But the task is to deduce the unity—which is not
given—of this disintegrating creation and to prove that it is the
product of a creating subject. In the final analysis then: to create
the subject of the 'creator'.

4

This extends the discussions to the point where it goes beyond
pure epistemology. The latter had aimed at investigating only the
'possible conditions' of those forms of thought and action which
are given in 'our' reality. Its cultural and philosophical tendency,

namely the impulse to overcome the reified disintegration of the subject and the—likewise reified—rigidity and impenetrability of its objects, emerges here with unmistakable clarity. After describing the influence Hamann had exercised upon his own development, Goethe gives a clear formulation to this aspiration: "Everything which man undertakes to perform, whether by word or deed, must be the product of all his abilities acting in concert; everything isolated is reprehensible."[54] But with the shift to a fragmented humanity in need of reconstruction (a shift already indicated by the importance of the problem of art), the different meanings assumed by the subjective 'we' at the different stages of development can no longer remain concealed. The fact that the problematics have become more conscious, that it is harder to indulge confusions and equivocations than was the case with the concept of nature only makes matters more difficult. The reconstitution of the unity of the subject, the intellectual restoration of man has consciously to take its path through the realm of disintegration and fragmentation. The different forms of fragmentation are so many necessary phases on the road towards a reconstituted man but they dissolve into nothing when they come into a true relation with a grasped totality, i.e. when they become dialectical.

"The antitheses," Hegel observes, "which used to be expressed in terms of mind and matter, body and soul, faith and reason, freedom and necessity, etc., and were also prominent in a number of more restricted spheres and concentrated all human interests in themselves, became transformed as culture advanced into contrasts between reason and the senses, intelligence and nature and, in its most general form, between absolute subjectivity and absolute objectivity. To transcend such ossified antitheses is the sole concern of reason. This concern does not imply hostility to opposites and restrictions in general; for the necessary course of evolution is *one* factor of life which advances by opposites: and the totality of life at its most intense is only possible as a new synthesis out of the most absolute separation."[55] The genesis, the creation of the creator of knowledge, the dissolution of the irrationality of the thing-in-itself, the resurrection of man from his grave, all these issues become concentrated henceforth on the question of *dialectical method*. For in this method the call for an intuitive understanding (for method to supersede the rationalistic principle of knowledge) is clearly, objectively and scientifically stated.

Of course, the history of the dialectical method reaches back deep into the history of rationalistic thought. But the turn it now takes distinguishes it qualitatively from all earlier approaches. (Hegel himself underestimates the importance of this distinction, e.g. in his treatment of Plato.) In all earlier attempts to use dialectics in order to break out of the limits imposed by rationalism there was a failure to connect the dissolution of rigid concepts clearly and firmly to the problem of the logic of the content, to the problem of irrationality.

Hegel in his *Phenomenology* and *Logic* was the first to set about the task of consciously recasting all problems of logic by grounding them in the qualitative material nature of their content, in matter in the logical and philosophical sense of the word.[56] This resulted in the establishment of a completely new logic of the *concrete concept*, the logic of totality—admittedly in a very problematic form which was not seriously continued after him.

Even more original is the fact that the subject is neither the unchanged observer of the objective dialectic of being and concept (as was true of the Eleatic philosophers and even of Plato), nor the practical manipulator of its purely mental possibilities (as with the Greek sophists): the dialectical process, the ending of a rigid confrontation of rigid forms, is enacted essentially *between the subject and the object*. No doubt, a few isolated earlier dialecticians were not wholly unaware of the different levels of subjectivity that arise in the dialectical process (consider for example the distinction between 'ratio' and 'intellectus' in the thought of Nicholas of Cusa). But this relativising process only refers to the possibility of different subject-object relations existing simultaneously or with one subordinated to the other, or at best developing dialectically from each other; they do not involve the relativising or the interpenetration of the subject and the object themselves. But only if that were the case, only if "the true [were understood] not only as substance but also as subject", only if the subject (consciousness, thought) were both producer and product of the dialectical process, only if, as a result the subject moved in a self-created world of which it is the conscious form and only if the world imposed itself upon it in full objectivity, only then can the problem of dialectics, and with it the abolition of the antitheses of subject and object, thought and existence, freedom and necessity, be held to be solved.

It might look as if this would take philosophy back to the great system-builders of the beginning of the modern age. The identity, proclaimed by Spinoza, of the order to be found in the realm of ideas with the order obtaining in the realm of things seems to come very close to this point of view. The parallel is all the more plausible (and made a strong impression on the system of the young Schelling) as Spinoza, too, found the basis of this identity in the object, in the substance. Geometric construction is a creative principle that can create only because it represents the factor of self-consciousness in objective reality. But here [in Hegel's argument] objectivity tends in every respect in the opposite direction to that given it by Spinoza for whom every subjectivity, every particular content and every movement vanishes into nothing before the rigid purity and unity of this substance. If, therefore, it is true that philosophy is searching for an identical order in the realms of ideas and things and that the ground of existence is held to be the first principle, and if it is true also that this identity should serve as an explanation of concreteness and movement, then it is evident that the meaning of substance and order in the realm of things must have undergone a fundamental change.

Classical philosophy did indeed advance to the point of this change in meaning and succeeded in identifying the substance, now appearing for the first time, in which philosophically the underlying order and the connections between things were to be found, namely *history*. The arguments which go to show that here and here alone is the concrete basis for genesis are extraordinarily diverse and to list them would require almost a complete recapitulation of our analysis up to this point. For in the case of almost every insoluble problem we perceive that the search for a solution leads us to history. On the other hand, we must discuss some of these factors at least briefly for even classical philosophy was not fully conscious of the *logical necessity* of the link between genesis and history and for social and historical reasons to be spelled out later, it could not become fully conscious of it.

The materialists of the eighteenth century were aware that history is an insuperable barrier to a rationalist theory of knowledge.[57] But in accordance with their own rationalistic dogma they interpreted this as an eternal and indestructible limit to human reason in general. The logical and methodological side of this fallacy can easily be grasped when we reflect that rationalist thought by concerning itself with the formal calculability of the contents of forms made abstract, *must define* these contents as *immutable*—within the system of relations obtaining at any given time. The evolution of the *real contents*, i.e. the problem of history, can only be accommodated by this mode of thought by means of a system of laws which strives to do justice to every *foreseeable possibility*.

How far this is practicable need not detain us here; what we find significant is the fact that thanks to this conclusion *the method itself* blocks the way to an understanding both of the quality and the concreteness of the contents and also of their evolution, i.e. of history: it is of the essence of such a law that within its jurisdiction nothing new can happen by definition and a system of such laws which is held to be perfect can indeed reduce the need to correct individual laws but cannot calculate what is novel. (The concept of the 'source of error' is just a makeshift to cover up for the fact that for rational knowledge process and novelty have the [unknowable] quality of things-in-themselves.) But if genesis, in the sense given to it in classical philosophy, is to be attained it is necessary to create a basis for it in a logic of contents which change. It is only in history, in the historical process, in the uninterrupted outpouring of what is qualitatively new that the requisite paradigmatic order can be found in the realm of things.[58]

For as long as this process and this novelty appear merely as an obstacle and not as the simultaneous result, goal and substratum of the method, the concepts—like the objects of reality as it is experienced—must preserve their encapsulated rigidity which only appears to be eliminated by the *juxtaposition* of other concepts. Only the historical process truly eliminates the—actual—autonomy of the objects and the concepts of objects with their resulting rigidity. As Hegel remarks with reference to the relation between body and soul: "Indeed, if both are presumed to be *absolutely independent* of each other they are as impenetrable for each other as any material is for any other and the presence of one can be granted only in the non-being, in the pores of the other; just as Epicurus assigned to the gods a dwelling place in the pores but was logical enough not to impose upon them any community with the world."[59] But historical evolution annuls the autonomy of the individual factors. By compelling the knowledge which ostensibly does these factors justice to construct its conceptual system upon content and upon what is qualitatively unique and new in the phenomena, it forces it at the same time to refuse to allow any of these elements to remain at the level of mere concrete uniqueness. Instead, the concrete totality of the historical world, the concrete and total historical process is the only point of view from which understanding becomes possible.

With this point of view the two main strands of the irrationality of the thing-in-itself and the concreteness of the individual content and of totality are given a positive turn and appear as a unity. This signals a change in the relation between theory and practice and between freedom and necessity. The idea that we have made reality loses its more or less fictitious character: we have—in the prophetic words of Vico already cited—made our own history and if we are able to regard the whole of reality as history (i.e. as *our* history, for there is no other), we shall have raised ourselves in fact to the position from which reality can be understood as our 'action'. The dilemma of the materialists will have lost its meaning for it stands revealed as a rationalistic prejudice, as a dogma of the formalistic understanding. This had recognised as deeds only those actions which were consciously performed whereas the historical environment we have created, the product of the historical process was regarded as a reality which influences us by virtue of laws alien to us.

Here in our newly-won knowledge where, as Hegel puts it in the *Phenomenology*, "the true becomes a Bacchantic orgy in which no one escapes being drunk", reason seems to have lifted the veil concealing the sacred mystery at Saïs and discovers, as in the parable of Novalis, that it is itself the solution to the riddle. But here, we find once again, quite concretely this time, the decisive problem of this line of thought: *the problem of the subject of the action, the subject of the genesis.* For the unity of subject and object, of thought and existence which the 'action' undertook to prove and to exhibit finds both its fulfilment and its substratum in the unity of the genesis of the determinants of thought and of the history of the evolution of reality. But to comprehend this unity it is necessary both to discover the site from which to resolve all these problems and also to exhibit *concretely* the 'we' which is the subject of history, that 'we' whose action is in fact history.

However, at this point classical philosophy turned back and lost itself in the endless labyrinth of conceptual mythology. It will be our task in the next section to explain why it was *unable*

G

to discover this concrete subject of genesis, the methodologically indispensable subject-object. At this stage it is only necessary to indicate what obstacle it encountered as a result of this aberrancy.

Hegel, who is in every respect the pinnacle of this development, also made the most strenuous search for this subject. The 'we' that he was able to find is, as is well known, the World Spirit, or rather, its concrete incarnations, the spirits of the individual peoples. Even if we—provisionally—ignore the mythologising and hence abstract character of this subject, it must still not be over-looked that, even if we accept all of Hegel's assumptions without demur, this subject remains incapable of fulfilling the methodo-logical and systematic function assigned to it, even from Hegel's own point of view. Even for Hegel, the spirit of a people can be no more than a 'natural' determinant of the World Spirit, i.e. one "which strips off its limitation only at a higher moment, namely at the moment when it *becomes conscious of its own essence* and it possesses its absolute truth only in this recognition and not immediately in its *existence*."[60]

From this follows above all that the spirit of a people only seems to be the subject of history, the doer of its deeds: for in fact it is the World Spirit that *makes use of* that 'natural character' of a people which corresponds to the actual requirements and to the idea of the World Spirit and accomplishes its deeds *by means of and in spite* of the spirit of the people.[61] But in this way the deed be-comes something transcendent for the doer himself and the free-dom that seems to have been won is transformed unnoticed into that specious freedom to reflect upon laws which themselves govern man, a freedom which in Spinoza a thrown stone would possess if it had consciousness. It is doubtless true that Hegel whose realistic genius neither could nor would disguise the truth about the nature of history as he found it did nevertheless seek to provide an explanation of it in terms of "the ruse of reason". But it must not be forgotten that "the ruse of reason" can only claim to be more than a myth if authentic reason can be discovered and demonstrated in a truly concrete manner. In that case it becomes a brilliant explanation for stages in history that have not yet be-come conscious. But these can only be understood and evaluated as stages from a standpoint already achieved by a reason that has discovered itself.

At this point Hegel's philosophy is driven inexorably into the arms of mythology. Having failed to discover the identical subject-object in history it was forced to go out beyond history and, there, to establish the empire of reason which has discovered itself. From that vantage point it became possible to understand history as a mere stage and its evolution in terms of "the ruse of reason". History is not able to form the living body of the total system: it becomes a part, an aspect of the totality that culminates in the 'absolute spirit', in art, religion and philosophy.

But history is much too much the natural, and indeed the uniquely possible life-element of the dialectical method for such an enterprise to succeed. On the one hand, history now intrudes, illogically but inescapably into the structure of those very spheres which according to the system were supposed to lie beyond its range.[62] On the other hand, this inappropriate and inconsistent approach to history deprives history itself of that essence which is so important precisely within the Hegelian system.

For, in the first place, its relation to reason will now appear to be accidental. "When, where and in what form such self-reproductions of reason make their appearance as philosophy is accidental," Hegel observes in the passage cited earlier concerning the "needs of philosophy".[63] But in the absence of necessity history relapses into the irrational dependence on the 'given' which it had just overcome. And if its relation to the reason that comprehends it is nothing more than that of an irrational content to a more general form for which the concrete *hic et nunc*, place, time and concrete content are contingent, then reason itself will succumb to all the antinomies of the thing-in-itself characteristic of pre-dialectical methods.

In the second place, the unclarified relation between absolute spirit and history forces Hegel to the assumption, scarcely comprehensible in view of this method, that *history has an end* and that in his own day and in his own system of philosophy the consummation and the truth of all his predecessors are to be found. This necessarily means that even in the more mundane and properly historical spheres, history must find its fulfilment in the restored Prussian state.

In the third place, genesis, detached from history, passes through its own development from logic through nature to spirit. But as the historicity of all categories and their movements intrudes decisively into the dialectical method and as dialectical genesis and history necessarily belong together objectively and only go their separate ways because classical philosophy was unable to complete its programme, this process which had been designed to be suprahistorical, inevitably exhibits a historical structure at every point. And since the method, having become abstract and contemplative, now as a result falsifies and does violence to history, it follows that history will gain its revenge and violate the method which has failed to integrate it, tearing it to pieces. (Consider in this context the transition from the logic to the philosophy of nature.)

In consequence, as Marx has emphasised in his criticism of Hegel, the demiurgic role of the 'spirit' and the 'idea' enters the realm of conceptual mythology.[64] Once again—and from the standpoint of Hegel's philosophy itself—it must be stated that the demiurge only seems to make history. But this semblance is enough to dissipate wholly the attempt of the classical philosophers to break out of the limits imposed on formal and rationalistic (bourgeois, reified) thought and thereby to restore a humanity destroyed by that reification. Thought relapses into the contemplative duality of subject and object.[65]

Classical philosophy did, it is true, take all the antinomies of its life-basis to the furthest extreme it was capable of in thought; it conferred on them the highest possible intellectual expression. But even for this philosophy they remain unsolved and insoluble. Thus classical philosophy finds itself historically in the paradoxical position that it was concerned to find a philosophy that would mean the end of bourgeois society, and to resurrect in thought a humanity destroyed in that society and by it. In the upshot, however, it did not manage to do more than provide a complete intellectual copy and the *a priori* deduction of bourgeois society. It is only the *manner* of this deduction, namely the dialectical method that points beyond bourgeois society. And even in classical philosophy this is only expressed in the form of an unsolved and insoluble antinomy. This antinomy is admittedly the most profound and the most magnificent intellectual expression of those antinomies which lie at the roots of bourgeois society and which are unceasingly produced and reproduced by it— albeit in confused and inferior forms. Hence classical philosophy had nothing but these unresolved antinomies to bequeath to succeeding (bourgeois) generations. The continuation of that course which at least in method started to point the way beyond these limits, namely the dialectical method as the true historical method was reserved for the class which was able to discover within itself on the basis of its life-experience the identical subject-object, the subject of action; the 'we' of the genesis: namely the proletariat.

III

The Standpoint of the Proletariat

In his early *Critique of Hegel's Philosophy of Right*, Marx gave a lapidary account of the special position of the proletariat in society and in history, and the standpoint from which it can function as the identical subject-object of the social and historical processes of evolution. "When the proletariat proclaims the dissolution of the previous world-order it does no more than reveal the secret of its own existence, for it represents the effective dissolution of that world-order." The self-understanding of the proletariat is therefore simultaneously the objective understanding of the nature of society. When the proletariat furthers its own class-aims it simultaneously achieves the conscious realisation of the—objective—aims of society, aims which would inevitably remain abstract possibilities and objective frontiers but for this conscious intervention.[1]

What change has been brought about, then, socially by this point of view and even by the possibility of taking up a point of view at all towards society? 'In the first instance' nothing at all. For the proletariat makes its appearance as the product of the capitalist social order. The forms in which it exists are—as we demonstrated in Section I—the repositories of reification in its acutest and direst form and they issue in the most extreme dehumanisation. Thus the proletariat shares with the bourgeoisie the reification of every aspect of its life. Marx observes: "The property-owning class and the class of the proletariat represent the same human self-alienation. But the former feels at home in this self-alienation and feels itself confirmed by it; it recognises alienation as its own instrument and in it it possesses the semblance of a human existence. The latter feels itself destroyed by this alienation and sees in it its own impotence and the reality of an inhuman existence."[2]

1

It would appear, then, that—even for Marxism—nothing has

changed in the objective situation. Only the 'vantage point from which it is judged' has altered, only 'the value placed on it' has acquired a different emphasis. This view does in fact contain a very essential grain of truth, one which must constantly be borne in mind if true insight is not to degenerate into its opposite.

To put it more concretely: the objective reality of social existence is *in its immediacy* 'the same' for both proletariat and bourgeoisie. But this does not prevent the *specific categories of mediation* by means of which both classes raise this immediacy to the level of consciousness, by means of which the merely immediate reality becomes for both the authentically objective reality, from being fundamentally different, thanks to the different position occupied by the two classes within the 'same' economic process. It is evident that once again we are approaching—this time from another angle—the fundamental problem of bourgeois thought, the problem of the thing-in-itself. The belief that the transformation of the immediately given into a truly understood (and not merely an immediately perceived) and *for that reason* really objective reality, i.e. the belief that the impact of the category of mediation upon the picture of the world is merely 'subjective', i.e. is no more than an 'evaluation' of a reality that 'remains unchanged', all this is as much as to say that objective reality has the character of a thing-in-itself.

It is true that the kind of knowledge which regards this 'evaluation' as merely 'subjective', as something which does not go to the heart of the facts, nevertheless claims to penetrate the essence of actuality. The source of its self-deception is to be found in its uncritical attitude to the fact that its own standpoint is conditioned (and above all that it is conditioned by the society underlying it). Thus—to take this view of history at its most developed and most highly articulated—we may consider Rickert's arguments with regard to the historian who studies "his own cultural environment". He claims that: "If the historian forms his concepts with an eye on the values of the community to which he himself belongs, the objectivity of his presentation will depend entirely on the accuracy of his factual material, and the question of whether this or that event in the past is crucial will not even arise. He will be immune from the charge of arbitrariness, as long as he relates, e.g. the history of art to the aesthetic values of his culture and the history of the state to its political values and, so long as he refrains from making unhistorical *value-judgements*, he will create a mode of historical narrative that is valid for all who regard political or aesthetic values as normative for the members of his community."[3]

By positing the materially unknown and only formally valid 'cultural values' as the founders of a 'value-related' historical objectivity, the subjectivity of the historian is, to all appearances, eliminated. However, this does no more than enthrone as the measure and the index of objectivity, the "cultural values" *actually* "prevailing in his community" (i.e. in his class). The arbitrariness and subjectivity are transformed from the material of the particular facts and from judgements on these into the criterion itself, into the "prevailing cultural values". And to judge or even investigate the validity of these values is not possible *within that framework*; for the historian the 'cultural values' become the thing-in-itself; a structural process analogous to those we observed in economics and jurisprudence in Section I.

Even more important, however, is the other side of the question, viz. that the thing-in-itself character of the form-content relation necessarily opens up the *problem of totality*. Here, too, we must be grateful to Rickert for the clarity with which he formulates his view. Having stressed the methodological need for a substantive theory of value for the philosophy of history, he continues: "Indeed, universal or world history, too, can only be written *in a unified manner* with the aid of a system of cultural values and to that extent it presupposes a substantive philosophy of history. For the rest, however, knowledge of a value system is irrelevant to the question of the scientific objectivity of purely empirical narrative."[4]

We must ask, however: is the distinction between historical monograph and universal history purely one of *scope* or does it also involve *method*? Of course, even in the former case history according to Rickert's epistemological ideal would be extremely problematic. For the 'facts' of history must remain—notwithstanding their 'value-attributes'—in a state of crude, uncomprehended facticity as every path to, or real understanding of them, of their real meaning, their real function in the historical process has been blocked *systematically* by methodically abandoning any claim to a knowledge of the totality. But, as we have shown,[5] the question of universal history is a problem of methodology that necessarily emerges in every account of even the smallest segment of history. For history as a totality (universal history) is neither the mechanical aggregate of individual historical events, nor is it a transcendent heuristic principle opposed to the events of history, a principle that could only become effective with the aid of a special discipline, the philosophy of history. The totality of history is itself a real historical power—even though one that has not hitherto become conscious and has therefore gone unrecognised—a power which is not to be separated from the reality (and hence the knowledge) of the individual facts without at the same time annulling their reality and their factual existence. It is the real, ultimate ground of their reality and their factual existence and hence also of their knowability even as individual facts.

In the essay referred to above we used Sismondi's theory of crisis to illustrate how the real understanding of a particular phenomenon can be thwarted by the misapplication of the category of totality, even when all the details have been correctly grasped. We saw there, too, that integration in the totality (which rests on the assumption that it is precisely the *whole* of the historical process that constitutes the authentic historical reality) does not merely affect our judgement of individual phenomena decisively. But also, as a result, the objective structure, the actual content of *the individual phenomenon—as* individual phenomenon—is changed fundamentally. The difference between this method which treats individual historical phenomena in isolation and one which regards them from a totalising point of view becomes even more apparent if we compare the function of the machine in the view of bourgeois economics and of Marx: "The contradictions and antagonisms inseparable from the capitalist employment of machinery, do not exist, they say, since they do not arise out of machinery, as such, but out of its capitalist employment! Since therefore machinery, considered alone shortens the hours of labour, but, when in the service of capital, lengthens them; since in itself it lightens labour, but when employed by capital, heightens the intensity of labour; since in itself it is a victory of man over the forces of Nature, but in the hands of capital, makes man the slave of those forces; since in itself it increases the wealth of the producers, but in the hands of capital, makes them paupers—for all these reasons and others besides, says the bourgeois economist without more ado, it is clear as noonday that all these contradictions are a mere semblance of the reality, and that, as a matter of fact, they have neither an actual nor a theoretical existence."[6]

Ignoring for the moment the aspect of bourgeois economics

that constitutes an apologia on class lines, let us examine the distinction solely from the point of view of method. We then observe that the bourgeois method is to consider the machine as an isolated unique thing and to view it simply as an existing 'individual' (for as a phenomenon of the process of economic development *the* machine as a class rather than the particular appliance constitutes the historical individual in Rickert's sense). We see further that to view the machine thus is to distort its true objective nature by representing its function in the capitalist production process as its 'eternal' essence, as the indissoluble component of its 'individuality'. Seen methodologically, this approach makes of every historical object a variable monad which is denied any interaction with other—similarly viewed—monads and which possesses characteristics that appear to be absolutely immutable essences. It does indeed retain an individual uniqueness but this is only the uniqueness of mere facticity, of being-just-so. The 'value-relation' does not at all affect this structure, for it does no more than make it possible to *select* from the infinite mass of such facticities. Just as these individual historical monads are only related to each other in superficial manner, one which attempts no more than a simple factual description, so too their relation to the guiding value principle remains purely factual and contingent.

And yet, as the really important historians of the nineteenth century such as Riegl, Dilthey and Dvořak could not fail to notice, the essence of history lies precisely in the changes undergone by those *structural forms* which are the focal points of man's interaction with environment at any given moment and which determine the objective nature of both his inner and his outer life. But this only becomes objectively possible (and hence can only be adequately comprehended) when the individuality, the uniqueness of an epoch or an historical figure, etc., is grounded in the character of these structural forms, when it is discovered and exhibited in them and through them.

However, neither the people who experience it nor the historian have direct access to immediate reality in these, its true structural forms. It is first necessary to search for them and to find them— and the path to their discovery is the path to a knowledge of the historical process in its totality. At first sight—and anyone who insists upon immediacy may never go beyond this 'first sight' his whole life long—it may look as if the next stages implied a purely intellectual exercise, a mere process of abstraction. But this is an illusion which is itself the product of the habits of thought and feeling of mere immediacy where the immediately given form of the objects, the fact of their existing here and now and in this particular way appears to be primary, real and objective, whereas their 'relations' seem to be secondary and subjective. For anyone who sees things in such immediacy every true change must seem incomprehensible. The undeniable fact of change must then appear to be a catastrophe, a sudden, unexpected turn of events that comes from outside and eliminates all mediations.[7] If change is to be understood at all it is necessary to abandon the view that objects are rigidly opposed to each other, it is necessary to elevate their interrelatedness and the interaction between these 'relations' and the 'objects' to the same plane of reality. The greater the distance from pure immediacy the larger the net encompassing the 'relations', and the more complete the integration of the 'objects' within the system of relations, the sooner change will cease to be impenetrable and catastrophic, the sooner it will become comprehensible.

But this will only be true if the road beyond immediacy leads in the direction of a greater concreteness, if the system of mediating concepts so constructed represents the "totality of the empirical"—to employ Lassalle's felicitous description of the philosophy of Hegel. We have already noted the methodological limits of formal, rational and abstract conceptual systems. In this context it is important only to hold on to the fact that it is not possible to use them to surpass the purely factual nature of historical facts. (The critical efforts of Rickert and of modern historiography also focus on this point and they too have successfully proved this.) The very most that can be achieved in this way is to set up a formal typology of the manifestations of history and society using historical facts as *illustrations*. This means that only a chance connection links the theoretical system to the objective historical reality that the theory is intended to comprehend. This may take the form of a naïve 'sociology' in search of 'laws' (of the Comte/Spencer variety) in which the insolubility of the task is reflected in the absurdity of the results. Or else the methodological intractability may be a matter of critical awareness from the beginning (as with Max Weber) and, instead, an auxiliary science of history is brought into being. But in either case the upshot is the same: the problem of facticity is pushed back into history once again and the purely historical standpoint remains unable to transcend its immediacy regardless of whether this is desired or not.

We have described the stance adopted by the historian in Rickert's sense (i.e. critically the most conscious type in the bourgeois tradition) as a prolongation of the state of pure immediacy. This appears to contradict the obvious fact that historical reality can only be achieved, understood and described in the course of a complicated process of mediation. However, it should not be forgotten that immediacy and mediation are themselves aspects of a dialectical process and that every stage of existence (and of the mind that would understand it) has its own immediacy in the sense given to it in the *Phenomenology* in which, when confronted by an immediately given object, "we should respond just as immediately or receptively, and therefore make no alteration to it, leaving it just as it presents itself".[8] To go beyond this immediacy can only mean the genesis, the 'creation' of the object. But this assumes that the forms of mediation in and through which it becomes possible to go beyond the immediate existence of objects as they are given, can be shown to be *the structural principles and the real tendencies of the objects themselves.*

In other words, intellectual genesis must be identical in principle with historical genesis. We have followed the course of the history of ideas which, as bourgeois thought has developed, has tended more and more to wrench these two principles apart. We were able to show that as a result of this duality in method, reality disintegrates into a multitude of irrational facts and over these a network of purely formal 'laws' emptied of content is then cast. And by devising an 'epistemology' that can go beyond the abstract form of the immediately given world (and its conceivability) the structure is made permanent and acquires a justification—not inconsistently—as being the necessary 'precondition of the possibility' of this world view. But unable to turn this 'critical' movement in the direction of a true creation of the object—in this case of the thinking subject—and indeed by taking the very opposite direction, this 'critical' attempt to bring the analysis of reality to its logical conclusion ends *by returning to the same immediacy that faces the ordinary man of bourgeois society in his everyday life. It has been conceptualised, but only immediately.*

Immediacy and mediation are therefore not only related and mutually complementary ways of dealing with the objects of reality. But corresponding to the dialectical nature of reality and the dialectical character of our efforts to come to terms with it, they are related dialectically. That is to say that every mediation must necessarily yield a standpoint from which the objectivity it creates assumes the form of immediacy. Now this is the relation of bourgeois thought to the social and historical reality of bourgeois society—illuminated and made transparent as it has been by a multiplicity of mediations. Unable to discover further mediations, unable to comprehend the reality and the origin of bourgeois society as the product of the same subject that has 'created' the comprehended totality of knowledge, *its ultimate point of view, decisive for the whole of its thought, will be that of immediacy.* For, in Hegel's words: "the mediating factor would have to be something in which both sides were one, in which consciousness would discern each aspect in the next, its purpose and activity in its fate, its fate in its purpose and activity, *its own essence in this necessity*".[9]

It may be hoped that our arguments up to this point have demonstrated with sufficient clarity that this particular mediation was absent and could not be otherwise than absent from bourgeois thought. In the context of economics this has been proved by Marx time and time again.[10] And he explicitly attributed the mistaken ideas of bourgeois economists concerning the economic processes of capitalism to the absence of mediation, to the systematic avoidance of the categories of mediation, to the immediate acceptance of secondary forms of objectivity, to the inability to progress beyond the stage of merely immediate cognition. In Section II we were able to point out as emphatically as possible the various intellectual implications flowing from the character of bourgeois society and the systematic limitations of its thought. We drew attention there to the antinomies (between subject and object, freedom and necessity, individual and society, form and content, etc.) to which such thought necessarily led. It is important to realise at this point that although bourgeois thought only landed in these antinomies after the very greatest mental exertions, it yet accepted their existential basis as self-evident, as a simply unquestionable reality. Which is to say: bourgeois thought entered into an unmediated relationship with reality as it was given.

Thus Simmel has this to say about the ideological structure of reification in consciousness: "And therefore now that these counter-tendencies have come into existence, they should at least strive towards an ideal of absolutely pure separation: every material content of life should become more and more material and impersonal so that the non-reifiable remnant may become all the more personal and all the more indisputably the property of the person."[11] In this way the very thing that should be understood and deduced with the aid of mediation becomes the accepted principle by which to explain all phenomena and is even elevated to the status of a value: namely the unexplained and inexplicable facticity of bourgeois existence as it is here and now acquires the patina of an eternal law of nature or a cultural value enduring for all time.

At the same time this means that history must abolish itself.[12] As Marx says of bourgeois economics: "Thus history existed once upon a time, but it does not exist any more." And even if this antinomy assumes increasingly refined forms in later times, so that it even makes its appearance in the shape of historicism, of historical relativism, this does not affect the basic problem, the abolition of history, in the slightest.

We see the unhistorical and antihistorical character of bourgeois thought most strikingly when we consider *the problem of the present as a historical problem*. It is unnecessary to give examples here. Ever since the World War and the World Revolution the total inability of every bourgeois thinker and historian to see the world-historical events of the present as universal history must remain one of the most terrible memories of every sober observer. This complete failure has reduced otherwise meritorious historians and subtle thinkers to the pitiable or contemptible mental level of the worst kind of provincial journalism. But it cannot always be explained simply as the result of external pressures (censorship, conformity to 'national' class interests, etc.). It is grounded also in a theoretical approach based upon unmediated contemplation which opens up an irrational chasm between the subject and object of knowledge, the same "dark and empty" chasm that Fichte described. This murky void was also present in our knowledge of the past, though this was obscured by the distance created by time, space and historical mediation. Here, however, it must appear fully exposed.

A fine illustration borrowed from Ernst Bloch will perhaps make this theoretical limitation clearer than a detailed analysis which in any case would not be possible here. When nature becomes landscape—e.g. in contrast to the peasant's unconscious living within nature—the artist's unmediated experience of the landscape (which has of course only achieved this immediacy after undergoing a whole series of mediations) presupposes a distance (spatial in this case) between the observer and the landscape. The observer stands outside the landscape, for were this not the case it would not be possible for nature to become a landscape at all. If he were to attempt to integrate himself and the nature immediately surrounding him in space within 'nature-seen-as-landscape', without modifying his aesthetic contemplative immediacy, it would then at once become apparent that landscape only *starts* to become landscape at a definite (though of course variable) distance from the observer and that only as an observer set apart in space can he relate to nature in terms of landscape at all.

This illustration is only intended to throw light on the theoretical situation, for it is only in art that the relation to landscape is expressed in an appropriate and unproblematic way, although it must not be forgotten that even in art we find the same unbridgeable gap opening up between subject and object that we find confronting us everywhere in modern life, and that art can do no more than shape this problematic without however finding a real solution to it. But as soon as history is forced into the present—and this is inevitable as our interest in history is determined in the last analysis by our desire to understand the present—this "pernicious chasm" (to use Bloch's expression) opens up.

As a result of its incapacity to understand history, the contemplative attitude of the bourgeoisie became polarised into two extremes: on the one hand, there were the 'great individuals' viewed as the autocratic makers of history, on the other hand, there were the 'natural laws' of the historical environment. They both turn out to be equally impotent—whether they are separated or working together—when challenged to produce an interpretation of the present in all its radical novelty.[13] The inner perfection of the work of art can hide this gaping abyss because in its perfected immediacy it does not allow any further questions to arise about a mediation no longer available to the point of view of contemplation. However, the present is a problem of history, a problem that refuses to be ignored and one which imperiously demands such mediation. It must be attempted. But in the course of these attempts we discover the truth of Hegel's remarks about one of the stages of self-consciousness that follow the definition of mediation already cited: "Therefore consciousness has become an enigma to itself as a result of the very experience which was to reveal its truth to itself; it does not regard the effects of its deeds as its own deeds: what happens to it is not the same experience *for it* as it is *in itself*; the transition is not merely a formal change of the same content and essence seen on the one hand as the content and essence of consciousness and on the other hand as the object or *intuited* essence of itself. *Abstract necessity*, therefore passes for the merely negative, uncomprehended *power of the universal* by which individuality is destroyed".

2

The historical knowledge of the proletariat begins with knowledge of the present, with the self-knowledge of its own social situation and with the elucidation of its necessity (i.e. its genesis). That genesis and history should coincide or, more exactly, that they should be different aspects of the same process, can only happen if two conditions are fulfilled. On the one hand, all the categories in which human existence is constructed must appear as the determinants of that existence itself (and not merely of the description of that existence). On the other hand, their succession, their coherence and their connections must appear as aspects of the historical process itself, as the structural components of the present. Thus the succession and internal order of the categories constitute neither a purely logical sequence, nor are they organised merely in accordance with the facts of history. "Their sequence is rather determined by the relation which they bear to one another in modern bourgeois society, and which is the exact opposite of what seems to be their natural order or the order of their historical development."[14]

This in turn assumes that the world which confronts man in theory and in practice exhibits a kind of objectivity which—if properly thought out and understood—need never stick fast in an immediacy similar to that of forms found earlier on. This objectivity must accordingly be comprehensible as a constant factor mediating between past and future and it must be possible to demonstrate that it is everywhere the product of man and of the development of society. To pose the question thus is to bring up the issue of the 'economic structure' of society. For, as Marx points out in his attack on Proudhon's pseudo-Hegelianism and vulgar

Kantianism for its erroneous separation of principle (i.e. category) from history: "When we ask ourselves why a particular principle was manifested in the eleventh or in the eighteenth century rather than in any other, we are necessarily forced to examine minutely what men were like in the eleventh century, what they were like in the eighteenth, what were their respective needs, their productive forces, their mode of production and their raw materials—in short, what were the relations between man and man which resulted from all these conditions of existence. To get to the bottom of all these questions—what is this but to draw up the real, profane history of men in every century and to present these men as both the authors and the actors of their own drama? But the moment we present men as the actors and authors of their own history, we arrive—by a detour—at the real starting-point, because we have abandoned those eternal principles of which we spoke at the outset."[15]

It would, however, be an error—an error which marks the point of departure of all vulgar Marxism—to believe that to adopt this standpoint is simply to accept the immediately given (i.e. the empirical) social structure. Moreover, the refusal to be content with this empirical reality, this going beyond the bounds of what is immediately given by no means signifies a straight-forward dissatisfaction with it and a straightforward—abstract—desire to alter it. Such a desire, such an evaluation of empirical reality would indeed be no more than subjective: it would be a 'value-judgement', a wish, a utopia. And even though to aspire to a utopia is to affirm the will in what is philosophically the more objective and distilled form of an 'ought' (Sollen) it does not imply that the tendency to accept empirical reality has been over-come. This applies, too, to the subjectivism of the impulse to initiate change which admittedly appears here in a philosophically sophisticated form.

For precisely in the pure, classical expression it received in the philosophy of Kant it remains true that the 'ought' presupposes an existing reality to which the category of 'ought' remains *inapplicable* in principle. Whenever the refusal of the subject simply to accept his empirically given existence takes the form of an 'ought', this means that the immediately given empirical reality receives affirmation and consecration at the hands of philosophy: it is philosophically immortalised. "Nothing in the world of phenomena can be explained by the concept of freedom,"

Kant states, "the guiding thread in that sphere must always be the mechanics of nature."[16]

Thus every theory of the 'ought' is left with a dilemma: either it must allow the—meaningless—existence of empirical reality to survive unchanged with its meaninglessness forming the basis of the 'ought'—for in a meaningful existence the problem of an 'ought' could not arise. This gives the 'ought' a purely subjective character. Or else, theory must presuppose a principle that transcends the concept of both what 'is' and what 'ought to be' so as to be able to explain the real impact of the 'ought' upon what 'is'. For the popular solution of an infinite progression [towards virtue, holiness], which Kant himself had already proposed, merely conceals the fact that the problem is insoluble. Philosophically it is not important to determine the time needed by the 'ought' in order to reorganise what 'is'. The task is to discover the principles by means of which it becomes *possible in the first place* for an 'ought' to modify existence. And it is just this that the theory rules out from the start by establishing the mechanics of nature as an unchangeable fact of existence, by setting up a strict dualism of 'ought' and 'is', and by creating the rigidity with which 'is' and 'ought' confront each other—a rigidity which this point of view can never eliminate. However, if a thing is theoretically impossible it cannot be first reduced to infinitesimal proportions and spread over an infinite process and then suddenly be made to reappear as a reality.

It is, however, no mere chance that in its attempt to find a way out of the contradictions created by the fact that history is simply given, bourgeois thought should have taken up the idea of an infinite progression. For, according to Hegel, this progression makes its appearance "everywhere where *relative* determinants are driven to the point where they become antithetical so that they are united inseparably whilst an independent existence is attributed to each *vis-à-vis* the other. This progression is, therefore, the *contradiction* that is never resolved but is always held to be simply present."[17] And Hegel has also shown that the methodological device that forms the logical first link in the infinite progression consists in establishing a purely quantitative relationship between elements that are and remain qualitatively incommensurable but in such a way that "each is held to be indifferent to this change".[18]

With this we find ourselves once more in the old antinomy of the thing-in-itself but in a new form: on the one hand 'is' and 'ought' remain rigidly and irreducibly antithetical; on the other hand, by forging a link between them, an external, illusory link that leaves their irrationality and facticity untouched, an area of apparent Becoming is created thanks to which growth and decay, the authentic theme of history, is really and truly thrust out into the darkness of incomprehensibility. For the reduction to quantitative terms must affect not only the basic elements of the process but also its individual stages, and the fact that this procedure makes it appear as if a gradual transition were taking place, goes unobserved. "But this gradualness only applies to the externals of change, not to their quality; the preceding quantitative situation, infinitely close to the succeeding one yet possesses a different existence qualitatively. . . . One would like to employ gradual transitions in order to make a change *comprehensible* to oneself; but the gradual change is precisely the trivial one, it is the reverse of the true qualitative change. In the gradualness the connection between the two realities is abolished—this is true whether they are conceived of as states or as independent objects—; it is assumed that . . . one is simply external to the other; in this way the very thing necessary to *comprehension* is removed. . . . With this growth and decay are altogether abolished, or else the In Itself, the inner state of a thing prior to its existence is transformed into *a small amount of external existence* and the essential or conceptual distinction is changed into a simple, external difference of magnitude."[19]

The desire to leave behind the immediacy of empirical reality and its no less immediate rationalist reflections must not be allowed to become an attempt to abandon immanent (social) reality. The price of such a false process of transcendence would be the reinstating and perpetuating of empirical reality with all its insoluble questions, but this time in a philosophically sublimated way. But in fact, to leave empirical reality behind can only mean that the objects of the empirical world are to be understood as aspects of a totality, i.e. as the aspects of a total social situation caught up in the process of historical change. Thus the category of mediation is a lever with which to overcome the mere immediacy of the empirical world and as such it is not something (subjective) foisted on to the objects from outside, it is no value-judgement or 'ought' opposed to their 'is'. *It is rather the manifestation of their authentic objective structure.* This can only become apparent in the visible objects of consciousness when the false attitude of bourgeois thought to objective reality has been abandoned. Mediation would not be possible were it not for the fact that the empirical existence of objects is itself mediated and only appears to be unmediated in so far as the awareness of mediation is lacking so that the objects are torn from the complex of their true determinants and placed in artificial isolation.[20]

Moreover, it must be borne in mind that the process by which the objects are isolated is not the product of chance or caprice. When true knowledge does away with the false separation of objects (and the even falser connections established by unmediated abstractions) it does much more than merely correct a false or inadequate scientific method or substitute a superior hypothesis for a defective one. It is just as characteristic of the social reality of the present that its objective form should be subjected to this kind of intellectual treatment as it is that the objective starting-point of such treatment should have been chosen. If, then, the standpoint of the proletariat is opposed to that of the bourgeoisie, it is nonetheless true that proletarian thought does not require a *tabula rasa*, a new start to the task of comprehending reality and one without any preconceptions. In this it is unlike the thought of the bourgeoisie with regard to the mediaeval forms of feudalism—at least in its basic tendencies. Just because its practical goal is the *fundamental* transformation of the whole of society it conceives of bourgeois society together with its intellectual and artistic productions as the *point of departure* for its own method.

The methodological function of the categories of mediation consists in the fact that with their aid those immanent meanings that necessarily inhere in the objects of bourgeois society but which are absent from the immediate manifestation of those objects as well as from their mental reflection in bourgeois thought, now become objectively effective and can therefore enter the consciousness of the proletariat. That is to say, if the bourgeoisie is held fast in the mire of immediacy from which the proletariat is able to extricate itself, this is neither purely accidental nor a purely theoretical scientific problem. The distance between these two theoretical positions is an expression of the differences between the social existence of the two classes.

Of course, the knowledge yielded by the standpoint of the proletariat stands on a higher scientific plane objectively; it does after all apply a method that makes possible the solution of problems which the greatest thinkers of the bourgeois era have vainly struggled to find and in its substance, it provides the adequate historical analysis of capitalism which must remain beyond the grasp of bourgeois thinkers. However, this attempt to grade the methods objectively in terms of their value to knowledge is itself a social and historical problem, an inevitable result of the types of society represented by the two classes and their place in history. It implies that the 'falseness' and the 'one-sidedness' of the bourgeois view of history must be seen as a necessary factor in the systematic acquisition of knowledge about society.[21]

But also, it appears that every method is necessarily implicated in the existence of the relevant class. For the bourgeoisie, method arises directly from its social existence and this means that mere immediacy adheres to its thought, constituting its outermost barrier, one that can not be crossed. In contrast to this the proletariat is confronted by the need to break through this barrier, to overcome it inwardly *from the very start* by adopting its own point of view. And as it is the nature of the dialectical method constantly to produce and reproduce its own essential aspects, as its very being constitutes the denial of any smooth, linear development of ideas, the proletariat finds itself *repeatedly* confronted with the problem of its own point of departure both in its efforts to increase its theoretical grasp of reality and to initiate practical historical measures. For the proletariat the barrier imposed by immediacy has become an inward barrier. With this the problem becomes clear; by putting the problem in this way the road to a possible answer is opened up.[22]

But it is no more than a possible answer. The proposition with which we began, viz. that in capitalist society reality is—immediately—the same for both the bourgeoisie and the proletariat, remains unaltered. But we may now add that this same reality employs the motor of class interests to keep the bourgeoisie imprisoned within this immediacy while forcing the proletariat to go beyond it. For the social existence of the proletariat is far more powerfully affected by the dialectical character of the historical process in which the mediated character of every factor receives the imprint of truth and authentic objectivity only in the mediated totality. For the proletariat to become aware of the dialectical nature of its existence is a matter of life and death, whereas the bourgeoisie uses the abstract categories of reflection, such as quantity and infinite progresssion, to conceal the dialectical structure of the historical process in daily life only to be confronted by unmediated catastrophes when the pattern is reversed. This is based—as we have shown—on the fact that the bourgeoisie always perceives the subject and object of the historical process and of social reality in a double form: in terms of his consciousness the single individual is a perceiving subject confronting the overwhelming objective necessities imposed by society of which only minute fragments can be comprehended. But in reality it is precisely the conscious activity of the individual that is to be found on the object-side of the process, while the subject (the class) cannot be awakened into consciousness and this activity must always remain beyond the consciousness of the—apparent—subject, the individual.

Thus we find the subject and object of the social process co-existing in a state of dialectical interaction. But as they always appear to exist in a rigidly twofold form, each external to the other, the dialectics remain unconscious and the objects retain their twofold and hence rigid character. This rigidity can only be broken by catastrophe and it then makes way for an equally rigid structure. This unconscious dialectic which is for that very reason unmanageable "breaks forth in their confession of naïve surprise, when what they have just thought to have defined with great difficulty as a thing suddenly appears as a social relation and then reappears to tease them again as a thing, before they have barely managed to define it as a social relation."[23]

For the proletariat social reality does not exist in this double form. It appears in the first instance as the pure *object* of societal events. In every aspect of daily life in which the individual worker imagines himself to be the subject of his own life he finds this to be an illusion that is destroyed by the immediacy of his existence. This forces upon him the knowledge that the most elementary gratification of his needs, "his own individual consumption, whether it proceed within the workshop or outside it, whether it be part of the process of reproduction or not, forms therefore an aspect of the production and the reproduction of capital; just as cleaning machinery does, whether it be done while the machinery is working or while it is standing idle".[24] The quantification of objects, their subordination to abstract mental categories makes its appearance in the life of the worker immediately as a process of abstraction of which he is the victim, and which cuts him off from his labour-power, forcing him to sell it on the market as a commodity, belonging to him. And by selling this, his only commodity, he integrates it (and himself: for his commodity is inseparable from his physical existence) into a specialised process that has been rationalised and mechanised, a process that he discovers already existing, complete and able to function without him and in which he is no more than a cipher reduced to an abstract quantity, a mechanised and rationalised tool.

Thus for the worker the reified character of the immediate manifestations of capitalist society receives the most extreme definition possible. It is true: for the capitalist also there is the same doubling of personality, the same splitting up of man into an element of the movement of commodities and an (objective and impotent) observer of that movement.[25] But for his consciousness it necessarily appears as an activity (albeit this activity is objectively an illusion), in which effects emanate from himself. This illusion blinds him to the true state of affairs, whereas the worker, who is denied the scope for such illusory activity, perceives the split in his being preserved in the brutal form of what is in its whole tendency a slavery without limits. He is therefore forced into becoming the object of the process by which he is turned into a commodity and reduced to a mere quantity.

But this very fact forces him to surpass the immediacy of his condition. For as Marx says, "Time is the place of human development".[26] The quantitative differences in exploitation which appear to the capitalist in the form of quantitative determinants of the objects of his calculation, must appear to the worker as the decisive, qualitative categories of his whole physical, mental and moral existence. The transformation of quantity into quality is not only a particular aspect of the dialectical process of development, as Hegel represents it in his philosophy of nature and, following him, Engels in the *Anti-Dühring*. But going beyond that, as we have just shown with the aid of Hegel's *Logic*, it means the emergence of the truly objective form of existence and the destruction of those confusing categories of reflection which had deformed true objectivity into a posture of merely immediate, passive, contemplation.

Above all, as far as labour-time is concerned, it becomes abundantly clear that quantification is a reified and reifying cloak spread over the true essence of the objects and can only be regarded as an objective form of reality inasmuch as the subject is uninterested in the essence of the object to which it stands in a contemplative or (seemingly) practical relationship. When Engels illustrates the transformation of quantity into quality by pointing to the example of water changing into solid or gaseous form[27] he is in the right so far as these points of transition are concerned. But this ignores the fact that when the point of view is changed even the transitions that had seemed to be purely quantitative now become qualitative. (To give an extremely trivial example, consider what happens when water is drunk; there is here a point at which 'quantitative' changes take on a qualitative nature.) The position is even clearer when we consider the example Engels gives from *Capital*. The point under discussion is the amount needed at a particular stage of production to transform a given sum into capital; Marx observes that it is at this point that quantity is changed into quality.[28]

Let us now compare these two series (the growth or reduction in the sum of money and the increase or decrease in labour-time) and examine their possible quantitative changes and their transformation into quality. We note that in the first case we are in fact confronted only by what Hegel calls a "knotted line of proportional relations". Whereas in the second case *every* change is one of quality in its innermost nature and although its quantitative appearance is forced on to the worker by his social environment, its essence for him lies in its qualitative implications. This second aspect of the change obviously has its origin in the fact that for the worker labour-time is not merely the objective form of the commodity he has sold, i.e. his labour-power (for in that form the problem for him, too, is one of the exchange of equivalents, i.e. a quantitative matter). But in addition it is the determining form of his existence as subject, as human being.

This does not mean that immediacy together with its consequences for theory, namely the rigid opposition of subject and object, can be regarded as having been wholly overcome. It is true that in the problem of labour-time, just because it shows reification at its zenith, we can see how proletarian thought is necessarily driven to surpass this immediacy. For, on the one hand, in his social existence the worker is immediately placed *wholly* on the side of the object: he appears to himself immediately as an object and not as the active part of the social process of labour. On the other hand, however, the role of object is no longer purely immediate. That is to say, it is true that the worker is objectively transformed into a mere object of the process of production by the methods of capitalist production (in contrast to those of slavery and servitude) i.e. by the fact that the worker is forced to objectify his labour-power over against his total personality and to sell it as a commodity. But because of the split between subjectivity and objectivity induced in man by the compulsion to objectify himself as a commodity, the situation becomes one that can be made conscious. In earlier, more organic forms of society, work is defined "as the direct function of a member of the social organism":[29] in slavery and servitude the ruling powers appear as the "immediate mainsprings of the production process" and this prevents labourers enmeshed in such a situation with their personalities undivided from achieving clarity about their social position. By contrast, "work which is represented as exchange value has for its premise the work of the isolated individual. It becomes social by assuming the form of its immediate antithesis, the form of abstract universality."

We can already see here more clearly and concretely the factors that create a dialectic between the social existence of the worker and the forms of his consciousness and force them out of their pure immediacy. Above all the worker can only become conscious of his existence in society when he becomes aware of himself as a commodity. As we have seen, his immediate existence integrates him as a pure, naked object into the production process. Once this immediacy turns out to be the consequence of a multiplicity of mediations, once it becomes evident how much it presupposes, then the fetishistic forms of the commodity system begin to dissolve: in the commodity the worker recognises himself and his own relations with capital. Inasmuch as he is incapable in practice of raising himself above the role of object his consciousness is the *self-consciousness of the commodity*; or in other words it is the self-knowledge, the self-revelation of the capitalist society founded upon the production and exchange of commodities.

By adding self-consciousness to the commodity structure a new element is introduced, one that is different in principle and in quality from what is normally described as consciousness 'of' an object. Not just because it is a matter of self-consciousness. For, as in the science of psychology, this might very well be consciousness 'of' an object, one which without modifying the way in which consciousness and object are related and thus without changing the knowledge so attained, might still 'accidentally' choose itself for an object. From this it would follow that knowledge acquired in this way must have the same truth-criteria as in the case of knowledge of 'other' objects. Even when in antiquity a slave, an *instrumentum vocale*, becomes conscious of himself as a slave this is not self-knowledge in the sense we mean here: for he can only attain to knowledge of an object which happens 'accidentally' to be himself. Between a 'thinking' slave and an 'unconscious' slave there is no real distinction to be drawn in an objective social sense. No more than there is between the possibility of a slave's becoming conscious of his own social situation and that of a 'free' man's achieving an understanding of slavery. The rigid epistemological doubling of subject and object remains unaffected and hence the perceiving subject fails to impinge upon the structure of the object despite his adequate understanding of it.

In contrast with this, when the worker knows himself as a commodity his knowledge is practical. *That is to say, this knowledge brings about an objective structural change in the object of knowledge.* In this consciousness and through it the special objective character of labour as a commodity, its 'use-value' (i.e. its ability to yield surplus produce) which like every use-value is submerged without a trace in the quantitative exchange categories of capitalism, now awakens and becomes *social reality*. The special nature of labour as a commodity which in the absence of this consciousness acts as an unacknowledged driving wheel in the economic process now objectifies itself by means of this consciousness. The specific nature of this kind of commodity had consisted in the fact that beneath the cloak of the thing lay a relation between men, that beneath the quantifying crust there was a qualitative, living core. Now that this core is revealed it becomes possible to recognise the fetish character *of every commodity* based on the commodity character of labour power: in every case we find its core, the relation between men, entering into the evolution of society.

Of course, all of this is only contained implicitly in the dialectical antithesis of quantity and quality as we meet it in the question of labour-time. That is to say, this antithesis with all its implications is only the *beginning* of the complex process of mediation whose goal is the knowledge of society as a historical totality. The dialectical method is distinguished from bourgeois thought not only by the fact that it alone can lead to a knowledge of totality; it is also significant that such knowledge is only attainable because the relationship between parts and whole has become fundamentally different from what it is in thought based on the categories of reflection. In brief, from this point of view, the essence of the dialectical method lies in the fact that in every aspect correctly grasped by the dialectic the whole totality is comprehended and that the whole method can be unravelled from every single aspect.[30] It has often been claimed—and not without a certain justification—that the famous chapter in Hegel's *Logic* treating of Being, Non-Being and Becoming contains the whole of his philosophy. It might be claimed with perhaps equal justification that the chapter dealing with the fetish character of the commodity contains within itself the whole of historical materialism and the whole self-knowledge of the proletariat seen as the knowledge of capitalist society (and of the societies that preceded it). [*Capital I*, Chapter 1, Section 4].

Obviously, this should not be taken to mean that the whole of history with its teeming abundance should be thought of as being superfluous. Quite the reverse. Hegel's programme: to see the absolute, the goal of his philosophy, as a *result* remains valid for Marxism with its very different objects of knowledge, and is even of greater concern to it, as the dialectical process is seen to be identical with the course of history. The theoretical point we are anxious to emphasise here is merely the structural fact that the single aspect is not a segment of a mechanical totality that could be put together out of such segments, for this would lead us to see knowledge as an infinite progression. It must be seen instead as containing the possibility of unravelling the whole abundance of the totality from within itself. But this in turn can only be done if the aspect is seen as aspect, i.e. as a point of transition to the totality; if every movement beyond the immediacy that had made the aspect an aspect of the dialectical process (whereas before it had been nothing more than the evident contradiction of two categories of thought) is not to freeze once more in a new rigidity and a new immediacy.

This reflection leads us back to our concrete point of departure. In the Marxist analysis of labour under capitalism that we have sketched above, we encountered the antithesis between the isolated individual and the abstract generality within which he finds mediated the relation between his work and society. And once again it is important to emphasise, that as in every immediate and abstract form of existence as it is simply given, here, too, we find bourgeoisie and proletariat placed in an immediately similar situation. But, here too, it appears that while the bourgeoisie remains enmeshed in its immediacy by virtue of its class role, the proletariat is driven by the specific dialectics of its class situation to abandon it. The transformation of all objects into commodities, their quantification into fetishistic exchange-values is more than an intensive process affecting the form of every aspect of life in this way (as we were able to establish in the case of labour-time). But also and inseparably bound up with this we find the extensive expansion of these forms to embrace the whole of society. For the capitalist this side of the process means an increase in the quantity of objects for him to deal with in his calculations and speculations. In so far as this process does acquire the semblance of a qualitative character, this goes no further than an aspiration towards the increased rationalisation, mechanisation and quantification of the world confronting him. (See the distinction between the dominance of merchant's capital and that of industrial capital, the capitalisation of agriculture, etc.) Interrupted abruptly now and again by 'irrational' catastrophes, the way is opened up for an infinite progression leading to the thorough-going capitalist rationalisation of society as a whole.

For the proletariat, however, the 'same' process means *its own emergence as a class*. In both cases a transformation from quantity to quality is involved. We need only consider the line of development leading from the mediaeval craft via simple co-operation and manufacture to the modern factory and we shall see the extent to which even for the bourgeoisie the qualitative changes stand out as milestones on the road. The *class meaning* of these changes lies precisely in the fact that the bourgeoisie regularly transforms each new qualitative gain back on to the quantitative level of yet another rational calculation. Whereas for the proletariat the 'same' development has a different class meaning: it means the *abolition of the isolated individual*, it means that workers can become conscious of the social character of labour, it means that the abstract, universal form of the societal principle as it is manifested can be increasingly concretised and overcome.

This enables us to understand why it is only in the proletariat that the process by which a man's achievement is split off from his total personality and becomes a commodity leads to a revolutionary consciousness. It is true, as we demonstrated in Section I, that the basic structure of reification can be found in all the social forms of modern capitalism (e.g. bureaucracy.) But this structure can only be made fully conscious in the work-situation of the proletarian. For his work as he experiences it directly possesses the naked and abstract form of the commodity, while in other forms of work this is hidden behind the façade of 'mental labour', of 'responsibility', etc. (and sometimes it even lies concealed behind 'patriarchal' forms). The more deeply reification penetrates into the soul of the man who sells his achievement as a commodity the more deceptive appearances are (as in the case of journalism). Corresponding to the objective concealment of the commodity form, there is the subjective element. This is the fact that while the process by which the worker is reified and becomes a commodity dehumanises him and cripples and atrophies his 'soul'—as long as he does not consciously rebel against it—it remains true that precisely his humanity and his soul are not changed into commodities. He is able therefore to objectify himself completely against his existence while the man reified in the bureaucracy, for instance, is turned into a commodity, mechanised and reified in the only faculties that might enable him to rebel against reification. Even his thoughts and feelings become reified. As Hegel says: "It is much harder to bring movement into fixed ideas than into sensuous existence."[31]

In the end this corruption assumes objective forms also. The worker experiences his place in the production process as ultimate but at the same time it has all the characteristics of the commodity (the uncertainties of day-to-day movements of the market). This stands in contrast to other groups which have both the appearance of stability (the routine of duty, pension, etc.) and also the—abstract—possibility of an *individual's* elevating himself into the ruling class. By such means a 'status-consciousness' is created that is calculated to inhibit effectively the growth of a class consciousness. Thus the purely abstract negativity in the life of the worker is objectively the most typical manifestation of reification, it is the constitutive type of capitalist socialisation. But for this very reason it is also *subjectively* the point at which this structure is raised to consciousness and where it can be breached in practice. As Marx says: "Labour . . . is no longer grown together with the individual into one particular determination";[32] once the false manifestations of this unmediated existence are abolished, the true existence of the proletariat as a class will begin.

3

It could easily appear at this point that the whole process is nothing more than the 'inevitable' consequence of concentrating masses of workers in large factories, of mechanising and standardising the processes of work and levelling down the standard of living. It is therefore of vital importance to see the truth concealed behind this deceptively one-sided picture. There is no doubt that the factors mentioned above are *the indispensable precondition* for the emergence of the proletariat as a class. *Without* them the proletariat would never have become a class and if they had not been continually intensified—by the natural workings of capitalism—it would never have developed into the decisive factor in human history.

Despite this it can be claimed without self-contradiction that we are not concerned here with an unmediated relation. What is unmediated is the fact that, in the words of the *Communist Manifesto*, "these labourers, who must sell themselves piecemeal, are a commodity, like every other article of commerce". And the fact that this commodity is able to become aware of its existence as a commodity does not suffice to eliminate the problem. For the unmediated consciousness of the commodity is, in conformity with the simple form in which it manifests itself, precisely an awareness of abstract isolation and of the merely abstract relationship—external to consciousness—to those factors that create it socially. I do not wish to enter here into a discussion of the conflict between the (immediate) interests of the individual and the (mediated) interests of the class that have been arrived at through experience and knowledge; nor shall I discuss the conflict between immediate and momentary interests as opposed to general long-term interests.

It is self-evident that immediacy must be abandoned at this point. If the attempt is made to attribute an immediate form of existence to class consciousness, it is not possible to avoid lapsing into mythology: the result will be a mysterious species-consciousness (as enigmatic as the 'spirits of the nations' in Hegel) whose relation to and impact upon the individual consciousness is wholly incomprehensible. It is then made even more incomprehensible by a mechanical and naturalistic psychology and finally appears as a demiurge governing historical movement.[33]

On the other hand, the growing class consciousness that has been brought into being through the awareness of a common situation and common interests is by no means confined to the working class. The unique element in its situation is that its surpassing of immediacy represents an *aspiration towards society in its totality* regardless of whether this aspiration remains conscious or whether it remains unconscious for the moment. This is the reason why its *logic* does not permit it to remain stationary at a relatively higher stage of immediacy but forces it to persevere in an uninterrupted movement towards this totality, i.e. to persist in the dialectical process by which immediacies are constantly annulled and transcended. Marx recognised this aspect of proletarian class consciousness very early on. In his comments on the revolt of the Silesian weavers he lays emphasis on its "conscious and theoretical character".[34] He sees in the 'Song of the Weavers' a "bold battle cry which does not even mention the hearth, factory or district but in which the proletariat immediately proclaims its opposition to private property in a forceful, sharp, ruthless and violent manner". Their action revealed their "superior nature" for "whereas every other movement turned initially only against the industrialist, the visible enemy, this one attacked also the hidden enemy, namely the banker."

We would fail to do justice to the theoretical significance of this view if we were to see in the attitude that Marx—rightly or wrongly—attributes to the Silesian weavers nothing more than their ability to see further than their noses and to give weight to considerations whether spatial or conceptual that were rather more remote. For this is something that can be said in varying degrees of almost every class in history. What is crucial is how to interpret the connection between these remoter factors and the structure of the objects immediately relevant to action. We must understand the importance of this remoteness for the consciousness of those initiating the action and for its relation to the existing state of affairs. And it is here that the differences between the standpoints of the bourgeoisie and the proletariat are thrown sharply into relief.

In bourgeois thought these remoter factors are simply incorporated into the rational calculation. They are conceived of as being similar to the factors that are within easy reach and which can be rationalised and quantified. The view that things as they appear can be accounted for by 'natural laws' of society is, according to Marx, both the highpoint and the 'insuperable barrier' of bourgeois thought. The notion of the laws of society undergoes changes in the course of history and this is due to the fact that it originally represented the principle of the overthrow of (feudal) reality. Later on, while preserving the same structure, it became the principle for conserving (bourgeois) reality. However, even the initial revolutionary movement was unconscious from a social point of view.

For the proletariat, however, this ability to go beyond the immediate in search of the 'remoter' factors means the *transformation of the objective nature of the objects of action*. At first sight it appears as if the more immediate objects are no less subject to this transformation than the remote ones. It soon becomes apparent, however, that in their case the transformation is even more visible and striking. For the change lies on the one hand in the practical interaction of the awakening consciousness and the objects from which it is born and of which it is the consciousness. And on the other hand, the change means that the objects that are viewed here as aspects of the development of society, i.e. of the dialectical totality become fluid: they become parts of a process. And as the innermost kernel of this movement is praxis, its point of departure is of necessity that of action; it holds the immediate objects of action firmly and decisively in its grip so as to bring about their total, structural transformation and thus the movement of the whole gets under way.

The category of totality begins to have an effect long before the whole multiplicity of objects can be illuminated by it. It operates by ensuring that actions which seem to confine themselves to particular objects, in both content and consciousness, yet preserve an aspiration towards the totality, that is to say: action is directed objectively towards a transformation of totality. We pointed out earlier in the context of a purely methodological discussion, that the various aspects and elements of the dialectical method contain the structure of the whole; we see the same thing here in a more concrete form, a form more closely orientated towards action. As history is essentially dialectical, this view of the way reality changes can be confirmed at every decisive moment of transition. Long before men become conscious of the decline of a particular economic system and the social and juridical forms associated with it, its contradictions are fully revealed in the objects of its day-to-day actions.

When, for example, the theory and practice of tragedy from Aristotle to the age of Corneille, regard family conflicts as providing the most fruitful subject-matter for tragedy, we glimpse lying behind this view—ignoring its technical merits such as concentration—the feeling that the great changes in society are being revealed here with a sensuous, practical vividness. This enables their contours to be drawn clearly whereas it is subjectively and objectively impossible to grasp their essence, to understand their origins and their place in the whole process. Thus an Aeschylus[35] or a Shakespeare draw pictures of family life that provide us with such penetrating and authentic portraits of the social upheavals of their age that it is only now, with the aid of historical materialism, that it has become at all possible for theory to do justice to these artistic insights.

The place in society and hence the viewpoint of the proletariat goes further than the example just cited in one vital qualitative way. The uniqueness of capitalism is to be seen precisely in its abolition of all 'natural barriers' and its transformation of all relations between human beings into purely social relations.[36] Bourgeois thought, however, remains enmeshed in fetishistic categories and in consequence the products of human relations become ossified, with the result that such thought trails behind objective developments. The abstract, rational categories of reflection which constitute the objectively immediate expression of this—the first—socialisation of the whole of human society, appear in the eyes of the bourgeoisie as something ultimate and indestructible. (For this reason bourgeois thought remains always in an unmediated relation to such categories.) The proletariat, however, stands at the focal point of this socialising process. On the one hand, this transformation of labour into a commodity removes every 'human' element from the immediate existence of the proletariat, on the other hand the same development progressively eliminates everything 'organic', every direct link with nature from the forms of society so that socialised man can stand revealed in an objectivity remote from or even opposed to humanity. It is just in this objectification, in this rationalisation and reification of all social forms that we see clearly for the first time how society is constructed from the relations of men with each other.

But we can see this only if we also remember that these human interrelations are, in Engels' words, "bound to objects" and that they "appear as objects", only if we do not forget for a single moment that these human interrelations are not direct relations between one man and the next. They are instead typical relations mediated by the objective laws of the process of production in such a way that these 'laws' necessarily become the forms in which human relations are directly manifested.

From this it follows, firstly, that man, who is the foundation and the core of all reified relations, can only be discovered by abolishing the immediacy of those relations. It is always necessary, therefore, to begin from this immediacy and from these reified laws. Secondly, these manifestations are by no means merely modes of thought, they are the forms in which contemporary bourgeois society is objectified. Their abolition, if it is to be a true abolition, cannot simply be the result of thought alone, it must also amount to their *practical* abolition as the *actual forms of social life*. Every kind of knowledge that aspires to remain pure knowledge is doomed to end up granting recognition to these forms once again. Thirdly, this praxis cannot be divorced from knowledge. A praxis which envisages a genuine transformation of these forms can only start to be effective if it intends to think out the process immanent in these forms to its logical conclusion, to become conscious of it and to make it conscious. "Dialectics", Hegel says, "is this *immanent* process of transcendence, in the course of which the one-sidedness and the limitation of the determinants of the understanding shows itself to be what it really is, namely their negation."[37]

The great advance over Hegel made by the scientific standpoint of the proletariat as embodied in Marxism lay in its refusal to see in the categories of reflection a 'permanent' stage of human knowledge and in its insistence that they were the necessary mould both of thought and of life in bourgeois society, in the reification of thought and life. With this came the discovery of dialectics in history itself. Hence dialectics is not imported into history from outside, nor is it interpreted in the light of history (as often occurs in Hegel), but is *derived* from history made conscious as its logical manifestation at this particular point in its development.

Fourthly, it is the proletariat that embodies this process of consciousness. Since its consciousness appears as the immanent product of the historical dialectic, it likewise appears to be dialectical. That is to say, this consciousness is nothing but the expression of historical necessity. The proletariat "has no ideals to realise". When its consciousness is put into practice it can only breathe life into the things which the dialectics of history have forced to a crisis;

H

it can never 'in practice' ignore the course of history, forcing on it what are no more than its own desires or knowledge. For it is itself nothing but the contradictions of history that have become conscious. On the other hand, however, a dialectical necessity is far from being the same thing as a mechanical, causal necessity. Marx goes on to say, following the passage already quoted: The working class "has only to *liberate* (my italics) the elements of the new society that have already grown within the womb of the disintegrating society of the bourgeoisie".

In addition to the mere contradiction—the automatic product of capitalism—a *new* element is required: the consciousness of the proletariat must become deed. But as the mere contradiction is raised to a consciously dialectical contradiction, as the act of becoming conscious turns into *a point of transition in practice*, we see once more in greater concreteness the character of proletarian dialectics as we have often described it: namely, since consciousness here is not the knowledge of an opposed object but is the self-consciousness of the object *the act of consciousness overthrows the objective form of its object.*

Only with this consciousness do we see the emergence of that profound irrationality that lurks behind the particular rationalistic disciplines of bourgeois society. This irrationality appears normally as an eruption, a cataclysm, and for that very reason it fails to alter the form and the arrangement of the objects on the surface. This situation, too, can be seen most easily in the simple events of everyday. The problem of labour-time has already been mentioned but only from the standpoint of the worker, where it was seen as the moment at which his consciousness emerges as the consciousness of the commodity (i.e. of the substantive core of bourgeois society). The instant that this consciousness arises and goes beyond what is immediately given we find in concentrated form the basic issue of the class struggle: the problem of *force*. For this is the point where the 'eternal laws' of capitalist economics fail and become dialectical and are thus compelled to yield up the decisions regarding the fate of history to the conscious actions of men. Marx elaborates this thought as follows: "We see then, that, apart from extremely elastic bounds, the nature of the exchange of commodities itself imposes no limit to the working day, no limit to surplus-labour. The capitalist maintains his right as a purchaser when he tries to make the working day as long as possible, and to make, whenever possible, two working days out of one. On the other hand, the peculiar nature of the commodity sold implies a limit to its consumption by the purchaser, and the labourer maintains his right as seller when he wishes to reduce the working day to one of definite normal duration. There is here, therefore, an antinomy, right against right, both equally bearing the seal of the law of exchanges. Between equal rights force decides. Hence it is that in the history of capitalist production, the determination of what is a working day, presents itself as the result of a struggle, a struggle between collective capital, i.e. the class of capitalists, and collective labour, i.e. the working class."[38]

But here, too, we must emphasise that force, which appears here concretely as the point at which capitalist rationalism becomes irrational, at which its laws fail to function, means something quite different for the bourgeoisie and for the proletariat. For the former, force is simply the continuation of its daily reality: it is true that it is no novelty but at the same time and for that very reason it is not able to resolve any single one of the contradictions the bourgeoisie has created itself. For the latter, on the other hand, its use, its efficacy, its potentiality and its intensity depend upon the degree to which the immediacy of the given has been overcome. No doubt, the fact that it is possible to go beyond the given, the fact that this consciousness is so great and so profound is itself a product of history. But what is historically possible cannot be achieved simply by a straightforward progression of the immediately given (with its 'laws'), but only by a consciousness of the whole of society acquired through manifold mediations, and by a clear aspiration to realise the dialectical tendencies of history. And the series of mediations may not conclude with unmediated contemplation: it must direct itself to the qualitatively new factors arising from the dialectical contradictions: it must be a movement of mediations advancing from the present to the future.[39]

This in turn presupposes that the rigidly reified existence of the objects of the social process will dissolve into mere illusion, that the dialectic, which is self-contradictory, a logical absurdity as long as there is talk of the change of one 'thing' into another 'thing' (or of one thing-like concept into another), should test itself on every object. That is to say, its premise is that *things should be shown to be aspects of processes*. With this we reach the limits of the dialectics of the Ancients, the point at which they diverge from materialist and historical dialectics. (Hegel, too, marks the point of transition, i.e. he, too, combines elements of both views in a not fully clarified manner.) The dialectics of the Eleatic philosophers certainly lay bare the contradictions underlying movement but the moving object is left unaffected. Whether the arrow is flying or at rest its objective nature as an arrow, as a thing remains untouched amidst the dialectical turmoil. It may be the case, as Heraclitus says, that one cannot step into the same river twice; but as the eternal flux is and does not become, i.e. does not bring forth anything qualitatively new, it is just a becoming that confronts the rigid existence of the *individual objects*. As a theory of the whole eternal becoming eternal being; behind stands revealed as the flowing river stands an unchanging essence, even though it may express itself in the incessant transformations of the individual objects.[40]

Opposed to this is the Marxian dialectical process where the objective forms of the objects are themselves transformed into a process, a flux. Its revolutionary character appears quite clearly in the simple process of the reproduction of capital. The simple "repetition or continuity imbues the process with quite novel characteristics or rather causes the disappearance of some apparent characteristics which it possessed as an isolated discontinuous process". For "quite apart from all accumulation, the mere continuity of the process of production, in other words simple reproduction, sooner or later, and of necessity, converts every capital into accumulated capital, or capitalised surplus-value. Even if that capital was originally acquired by the personal labour of its employer, it sooner or later becomes value appropriated without an equivalent, the unpaid labour of others materialised either in money or in some other object."[41]

Thus the knowledge that social facts are not objects but relations between men is intensified to the point where facts are wholly dissolved into processes. But if their Being appears as a Becoming this should not be construed as an abstract universal flux sweeping past, it is no vacuous *durée réelle* but the unbroken production and reproduction of those relations that, when torn from their context and distorted by abstract mental categories, can appear to bourgeois thinkers as things. Only at this point does the consciousness of the proletariat elevate itself to the self-consciousness of society in its historical development. By becoming aware of the commodity relationship the proletariat can only become conscious of itself as the object of the economic process. For the commodity *is* produced and even the worker in his quality as commodity, as an immediate producer is at best a mechanical driving wheel in the machine. But if the reification of capital is dissolved into an unbroken process of its production and reproduction, it is possible for the proletariat to discover that it is itself the *subject* of this process even though it is in chains and is for the time being unconscious of the fact. As soon, therefore, as the ready-made, immediate reality is abandoned the question arises: "Does a worker in a cotton factory produce merely cotton textiles? No, he produces capital. He produces values which serve afresh to command his labour and by means of it to create new values."[42]

4

This throws an entirely new light on the problem of reality. If, in Hegel's terms, Becoming now appears as the truth of Being, and process as the truth about things, then this means that the *developing tendencies of history constitute a higher reality than the empirical 'facts'*. It is doubtless true that in capitalist society the past dominates the present—as indeed we have shown elsewhere.[43] But this only means that there is an antagonistic process that is not guided by a consciousness but is instead driven forward by its own immanent, blind dynamic and that this process stands revealed in all its immediate manifestations as the rule of the past over the present, the rule of capital over labour. It follows that any thinker who bases his thought on such ideas will be trapped in the frozen forms of the various stages. He will nevertheless stand helpless when confronted by the enigmatic forces thrown up by the course of events, and the actions open to him will never be adequate to deal with this challenge.

This image of a frozen reality that nevertheless is caught up in an unremitting, ghostly movement at once becomes meaningful when this reality is dissolved into the process of which man is the driving force. This can be seen only from the standpoint of the proletariat because the meaning of these tendencies is the abolition of capitalism and so for the bourgeoisie to become conscious of them would be tantamount to suicide. Moreover, the 'laws' of the reified reality of capitalism in which the bourgeoisie is compelled to live are only able to prevail over the heads of those who seem to be its active embodiments and agents. The average profit rate is the paradigm of this situation. Its relation to individual capitalists whose actions are determined by this unknown and unknowable force shows all the symptoms of Hegel's 'ruse of reason'. The fact that these individual 'passions', despite which these tendencies prevail, assume the form of the most careful, farsighted and exact calculations does not affect this conclusion in the least; on the contrary, it reinforces it still further. For the fact that there exists the illusion of a rationalism perfected in every detail—dictated by class interests and hence subjectively based—makes it even more evident that this rationalism is unable to grasp the meaning of the overall process as it really is. Moreover, the situation is not attenuated by the fact that we are not confronted here by a unique event, a catastrophe, but by the unbroken production and reproduction of the same relation whose elements are converted into empirical facts and incorporated in reified form in the web of rational calculation. It only shows the strength of the dialectical antagonism controlling the phenomena of capitalist society.

The conversion of social-democratic ideas into bourgeois ones can always be seen at its clearest in the jettisoning of the dialectical method. As early as the Bernstein Debate it was clear that the opportunists had to take their stand 'firmly on the facts' so as to be able to ignore the general trends[44] or else to reduce them to the status of a subjective, ethical imperative. In like fashion the manifold misunderstandings in the debate on accumulation should be seen as part of the same phenomenon. Rosa Luxemburg was a genuine dialectician and so she realised that it was not possible for a purely capitalist society to exist as a tendency of history, as a tendency which inevitably determines the actions of men—unbeknown to them—long before it had itself become 'fact'. Thus the economic impossibility of accumulation in a purely capitalist society does not show itself by the 'cessation' of capitalism once the last non-capitalist has been expropriated, but by actions that force upon the capitalist class the awareness that this (empirically still remote) state of affairs is on its way: actions such as feverish colonialisation, disputes about territories providing raw materials or markets, imperialism and world war. For dialectical trends do not constitute an infinite progression that gradually nears its goal in a series of quantitative stages. They are rather expressed in terms of an unbroken *qualitative revolution* in the structure of society (the composition of the classes, their relative strengths, etc.) The ruling class of the moment attempts to meet the challenge of these changes in the only way open to it, and on matters of detail it does appear to meet with some success. But in reality the blind and unconscious measures that seem to it to be so necessary simply hasten the course of events that destroy it.

The difference between 'fact' and tendency has been brought out on innumerable occasions by Marx and placed in the foreground of his studies. After all, the basic thought underlying his *magnum opus*, the retranslation of economic objects from things back into processes, into the changing relations between men, rests on just this idea. But from this it follows further that the question of theoretical priority, the location within the system (i.e. whether original or derivative) of the particular forms of the economic structure of society depends on their distance from this retranslation. Upon this is based the prior importance of industrial capital over merchant capital, money-dealing capital, etc. And this priority is expressed historically by the fact that these derivative forms of capital, that do not themselves determine the production process, are only capable of performing the negative function of dissolving the original forms of production. However, the question of "whither this process of dissolution will lead, in other words, what new mode of production will replace the old, does not depend on commerce, but on the character of the old mode of production itself".[45]

On the other hand, merely from the point of view of theory it would appear that the 'laws governing these forms are in fact only determined by the 'contingent' empirical movements of supply and demand and that they are not the expression of any universal social trend. As Marx points out in a discussion of interest: "Competition does not, in this case, determine the deviations from the rule. There is rather no law of division except that enforced by competition."[46]

In this theory of reality which allots a higher place to the prevailing trends of the total development than to the facts of the empirical world, the antithesis we stressed when considering the particular questions raised by Marxism (the antithesis between movement and final goal, evolution and revolution, etc.) acquires its authentic, concrete and scientific shape. For only this analysis permits us to investigate the concept of the 'fact' in a truly concrete manner, i.e. in the *social context* in which it has its origin and its existence. The direction to be taken by such an investigation has been outlined elsewhere,[47] although only with reference to the relation between the 'facts' and the concrete totality to which they belong and in which they become 'real'.

But now it becomes quite clear that the social development and its intellectual reflex that was led to form 'facts' from a reality that had been undivided (originally, in its autochthonous state) did indeed make it possible to subject nature to the will of man. At the same time, however, they served to conceal the socio-historical grounding of these facts in relations between men "so as to raise strange, phantom powers against them".[48] For the ossifying quality of reified thought with its tendency to oust the process is exemplified even more clearly in the 'facts' than in the 'laws' that would order them. In the latter it is still possible to detect a trace of human activity even though it often appears in a reified and false subjectivity. But in the 'facts' we find the crystal-lisation of the essence of capitalist development into an ossified, impenetrable thing alienated from man. And the form assumed by this ossification and this alienation converts it into a founda-tion of reality and of philosophy that is perfectly self-evident and immune from every doubt. When confronted by the rigidity of these 'facts' every movement seems like a movement *impinging on* them, while every tendency to change them appears to be a merely subjective principle (a wish, a value judgement, an ought). Thus only when the theoretical primacy of the 'facts' has been broken, only when *every phenomenon is recognised to be a process*, will it be understood that what we are wont to call 'facts' consists of processes. Only then will it be understood that the facts are noth-ing but the parts, the *aspects* of the total process that have been broken off, artificially isolated and ossified. This also explains why the total process which is uncontaminated by any trace of reification and which allows the process-like essence to prevail *in all its purity* should represent the authentic, higher reality. Of course, it also becomes clear why in the reified thought of the bourgeoisie the 'facts' have to play the part of its highest fetish in both theory and practice. This petrified factuality in which everything is frozen into a 'fixed magnitude',[49] in which the reality that just happens to exist persists in a totally senseless, unchanging way precludes any theory that could throw light on even this immediate reality.

This takes reification to its ultimate extreme: it no longer points dialectically to anything beyond itself: its dialectic is mediated only be the reification of the immediate forms of pro-

duction. But with that a climax is reached in the conflict between existence in its immediacy together with the abstract
categories that constitute its thought, on the one hand, and a vital
societal reality on the other. For these forms (e.g. interest) appear
to capitalist thinkers as the fundamental ones that determine all
the others and serve as paradigms for them. And likewise, every
decisive turn of events in the production process must more or
less reveal that the true categorical structure of capitalism has
been turned completely upside down.

Thus bourgeois thought remains fixated on these forms which
it believes to be immediate and original and from there it attempts
to seek an understanding of economics, blithely unaware that the
only phenomenon that has been formulated is its own inability to
comprehend its own social foundations. Whereas for the proletariat
the way is opened to a complete penetration of the forms of reification. It achieves this by starting with what is dialectically the
clearest form (the immediate relation of capital and labour). It
then relates this to those forms that are more remote from the
production process and so includes and comprehends them, too,
in the dialectical totality.[50]

5

Thus man has become the measure of all (societal) things. The
conceptual and historical foundation for this has been laid by the
methodological problems of economics: by dissolving the fetishistic objects into processes that take place among men and are
objectified in concrete relations between them; by deriving the
indissoluble fetishistic forms from the primary forms of human
relations. At the conceptual level the structure of the world of
men stands revealed as a system of dynamically changing relations
in which the conflicts between man and nature, man and man (in
the class struggle, etc.) are fought out. The structure and the
hierarchy of the categories are the index of the degree of clarity to
which man has attained concerning the foundations of his existence in these relations, i.e. the degree of consciousness of himself.

At the same time this structure and this hierarchy are the
central theme of history. History is no longer an enigmatic flux
to which men and things are subjected. It is no longer a thing to
be explained by the intervention of transcendental powers or
made meaningful by reference to transcendental values. History

is, on the one hand, the product (albeit the unconscious one) of man's own activity, on the other hand it is the succession of those processes in which the forms taken by this activity and the relations of man to himself (to nature, to other men) are overthrown. So that if—as we emphasised earlier on—the categories describing the structure of a social system are not immediately historical, i.e. if the empirical succession of historical events does not suffice to explain the origins of a particular form of thought or existence, then it can be said that despite this, or better, because of it, any such conceptual system will describe in its totality a definite stage in the society as a whole.

And the nature of history is precisely that every definition degenerates into an illusion: *history is the history of the unceasing overthrow of the objective forms that shape the life of man.* It is therefore not possible to reach an understanding of particular forms by studying their successive appearances in an empirical and historical manner. This is not because they transcend history, though this is and must be the bourgeois view with its addiction to thinking about isolated 'facts' in isolated mental categories. The truth is rather that these particular forms are not immediately connected with each other either by their simultaneity or by their consecutiveness. What connects them is their place and function in the totality and by rejecting the idea of a 'purely historical' explanation the notion of history as a universal discipline is brought nearer. When the problem of connecting isolated phenomena has become a problem of categories, by the same dialectical process every problem of categories becomes transformed into a historical problem. Though it should be stressed: it is transformed into a problem of universal history which now appears—more clearly than in our introductory polemical remarks—simultaneously as a problem of method and a problem of our knowledge of the present.

From this standpoint alone does history really become a history of mankind. For it contains nothing that does not lead back ultimately to men and to the relations between men. It is because Feuerbach gave this new direction to philosophy that he was able to exercise such a decisive influence on the origins of historical materialism. However, by transforming philosophy into 'anthropology' he caused man to become frozen in a fixed objectivity and thus pushed both dialectics and history to one side. And precisely this is the great danger in every 'humanism' or anthropological point of view.[51] For if man is made the measure of all things, and if with the aid of that assumption all transcendence is to be eliminated without man himself being measured against this criterion, without applying the same 'standard' to himself or —more exactly—without making man himself dialectical, then man himself is made into an absolute and he simply puts himself in the place of those transcendental forces he was supposed to explain, dissolve and systematically replace. At best, then, a dogmatic metaphysics is superseded by an equally dogmatic relativism.

This dogmatism arises because the failure to make man dialectical is complemented by an equal failure to make reality dialectical. Hence relativism moves within an essentially static world. As it cannot become conscious of the immobility of the world and the rigidity of its own standpoint it inevitably reverts to the dogmatic position of those thinkers who likewise offered to explain the world from premises they did not consciously acknowledge and which, therefore, they adopted uncritically. For it is one thing to relativise the truth about an individual or a species in an ultimately static world (masked though this stasis may be by an illusory movement like the "eternal recurrence of the same things" or the biological or morphological 'organic' succession of periods). And it is quite another matter when *the concrete, historical function and meaning* of the various 'truths' is revealed within a unique, concretised historical process. Only in the former case can we accurately speak of relativism. But in that case it inevitably becomes dogmatic. For it is only meaningful to speak of relativism where an 'absolute' is in some sense assumed. The weakness and the half-heartedness of such 'daring thinkers' as Nietzsche or Spengler is that their relativism only abolishes the absolute in appearance.

For, from the standpoint of both logic and method, the 'systematic location' of the absolute is to be found just where the apparent movement stops. The absolute is nothing but the fixation of thought, it is the projection into myth of the intellectual failure to understand reality concretely as a historical process. Just as the relativists have only appeared to dissolve the world into movement, so too they have only appeared to exile the absolute from their systems. Every 'biological' relativism, etc., that turns its limits into 'eternal' limits thereby involuntarily reintroduces the absolute, the 'timeless' principle of thought. And as long as the absolute survives in a system (even unconsciously) it will prove logically stronger than all attempts at relativism. For it represents the highest principle of thought attainable in an undialectical universe, in a world of ossified things and a logical world of ossified concepts. So that *here* both *logically and methodologically* Socrates must be in the right as against the sophists, and logic and value theory must be in the right as against pragmatism and relativism.

What these relativists are doing is to take the present philosophy of man with its social and historical limits and to allow these to ossify into an 'eternal' limit of a biological or pragmatic sort. Actuated either by doubt or despair they thus stand revealed as a *decadent version* of the very rationalism or religiosity they mean to oppose. Hence they may sometimes be a not unimportant *symptom* of the inner weakness of the society which produced the rationalism they are 'combating'. But they are significant only as symptoms. It is always the culture they assail, the culture of the class that has not yet been broken, that embodies the authentic spiritual values.

Only the dialectics of history can create a radically new situation. This is not only because it relativises all limits, or better, because it puts them in a state of flux. Nor is it just because all those forms of existence that constitute the counterpart of the absolute are dissolved into processes and viewed as concrete manifestations of history so that the absolute is not so much denied as endowed with *its concrete historical shape and treated as an aspect of the process itself.*

But, in addition to these factors, it is also true that the historical process is something unique and its dialectical advances and reverses are an incessant struggle to reach higher stages of the truth and of the (societal) *self-knowledge of man.* The 'relativisation' of truth in Hegel means that the higher factor is always the truth of the factor beneath it in the system. This does not imply the destruction of 'objective' truth at the lower stages but only that it means something different as a result of being integrated in a more concrete and comprehensive totality. When Marx makes dialectics the essence of history, the movement of thought also becomes just a part of the overall movement of history. History becomes the history of the objective forms from which man's environment and inner world are constructed and which he strives to master in thought, action and art, etc. (Whereas relativism always works with rigid and immutable objective forms.)

In the period of the "pre-history of human society" and of the struggles between classes the only possible function of truth is to establish the various possible attitudes to an essentially uncomprehended world in accordance with man's needs in the struggle to master his environment. Truth could only achieve an 'objectivity' relative to the standpoint of the individual classes and the objective realities corresponding to it. But as soon as mankind has clearly understood and hence *restructured* the foundations of its existence truth acquires a wholly novel aspect. When theory and practice are united it becomes possible to change reality and when this happens the absolute and its 'relativistic' counterpart will have played their historical role for the last time. For as the result of these changes we shall see the disappearance of that reality which the absolute and the relative expressed in like manner.

This process *begins* when the proletariat becomes conscious of its own class point of view. Hence it is highly misleading to describe dialectical materialism as 'relativism'. For although they share a common premise: man as the measure of all things, they each give it a different and even contradictory interpretation. The beginning of a 'materialist anthropology' in Feuerbach is in fact only a beginning and one that is in itself capable of a number of continuations. Marx took up Feuerbach's suggestion and thought it out to its logical conclusion. In the process he takes issue very sharply with Hegel: "Hegel makes of man a man of self-consciousness instead of making self-consciousness the self-consciousness of man, i.e. of real man as he lives in the real world of objects by which he is conditioned."[52]

Simultaneously, however, and this is moreover at the time when he was most under the influence of Feuerbach, he sees man historically and dialectically, and both are to be understood in a double sense. (1) He never speaks of man in general, of an abstractly absolutised man: he always thinks of him as a link in a concrete totality, in a society. The latter must be explained from the standpoint of man but only after man has himself been integrated in the concrete totality and has himself been made truly concrete. (2) Man himself is the objective foundation of the historical dialectic and the subject-object lying at its roots, and as such he is decisively involved in the dialectical process. To formulate it in the initial abstract categories of dialectics: *he both is and at the same time is not.* Religion, Marx says, in the Critique of Hegel's *Philosophy of Right*, "is the realisation in phantasy of the essence of man *because the essence of man does not possess any true reality.*"[53] And as this non-existent man is to be made the measure of all things, the true demiurge of history, his non-being must at once become the concrete and historically dialectical form of critical knowledge of the present in which man is necessarily condemned to non-existence. The negation of his being becomes concretised, then, in the understanding of bourgeois society. At the same time—as we have already seen—the dialectics of bourgeois society and the contradictions of its abstract categories stand out clearly when measured against the nature of man. Following the criticism of Hegel's theory of consciousness we have just quoted, Marx announces his own programme in these terms: "It must be shown how the state and private property, etc., transform men into abstractions, or that they are the products of abstract man instead of being the reality of individual, concrete men." And the fact that in later years Marx adhered to this view of the abstract non-existence of man can be seen from the well-known and oft-quoted words from the Preface to the *Critique of Political Economy* in which bourgeois society is described as the last manifestation of the "pre-history of human society".

It is here that Marx's 'humanism' diverges most sharply from all the movements that seem so similar to it at first glance. Others have often recognised and described how capitalism violates and destroys everything human. I need refer only to Carlyle's *Past and Present* whose descriptive sections received the approval and in part the enthusiastic admiration of the young Engels. In such accounts it is shown, on the one hand, that it is not possible to be human in bourgeois society, and, on the other hand, that man as he exists is opposed without mediation—or what amounts to the same thing, through the mediations of metaphysics and myth—to this non-existence of the human (whether this is thought of as something in the past, the future or merely an imperative).

But this does no more than present the problem in a confused form and certainly does not point the way to a solution. The solution can only be discovered by seeing these two aspects as they appear in the concrete and real process of capitalist development, namely inextricably bound up with one another: i.e. the categories of dialectics must be applied to man as the measure of all things in a manner that also includes simultaneously a complete description of the economic structure of bourgeois society and a correct knowledge of the present. For otherwise, any description will inevitably succumb to the dilemmas of empiricism and utopianism, of voluntarism and fatalism, even though it may give an accurate account of matters of detail. At best it will not advance beyond crude facticity on the one hand, while on the other it will confront the immanent course of history with alien and hence subjective and arbitrary demands.

This is without exception the fate that has befallen all those systems that start with man as their premise and strive in theory to solve the problems of his existence while in practice they seek to liberate him from them. This duality can be seen in all attempts of the type of the Christianity of the Gospels. Society as it actually exists is left unscathed. It makes no difference whether this takes the form of "giving to Caesar the things which are Caesar's", of Luther's sanctification of the powers that be, or of Tolstoy's "resist not evil". For as long as society, as it is, is to be declared sacrosanct it is immaterial with what emotional force or what metaphysical and religious emphasis this is done. What is crucial is that reality as it seems to be should be thought of as something man cannot change and its unchangeability should have the force of a moral imperative.

There are two aspects of the utopian counterpart to this ontology. The first is seen in God's annihilation of empirical reality in the Apocalypse, which can on occasion be absent (as with Tolstoy) without materially affecting the situation. The second lies in the utopian view of man as a 'saint' who can achieve an inner mastery over the external reality that cannot be eliminated. As long as such a view survives with all its original starkness its claims to offer a 'humanistic' solution to man's problems are self-refuting. For it is forced to deny humanity to the vast majority of mankind and to exclude them from the 'redemption' which alone confers meaning upon a life which is meaningless on the level of empirical experience. In so doing it reproduces the inhumanity of class society on a metaphysical and religious plane, in the next world, in eternity—of course with the signs reversed, with altered criteria and with the class structure stood on its head. And the most elementary study of any monastic order as it advances from a community of 'saints' to the point where it becomes an economic and political power at the side of the ruling class will make it abundantly clear that every relaxation of the utopian's requirements will mean an act of adaptation to the society of the day.

But the 'revolutionary' utopianism of such views cannot break out of the inner limits set to this undialectical 'humanism'. Even the Anabaptists and similar sects preserve this duality. On the one hand, they leave the objective structure of man's empirical existence unimpaired (consumption communism), while on the other hand they expect that reality will be changed by awakening man's inwardness which, independent of his concrete historical life, has existed since time immemorial and must now be brought to life—perhaps through the intervention of a transcendental deity.

They, too, start from the assumption of man as he exists and an empirical world whose structure is unalterable. That this is the consequence of their historical situation is self-evident, but needs no further discussion in this context. It was necessary to emphasise it only because it is no accident that it was the revolutionary religiosity of the sects that supplied the ideology for capitalism in its purest forms (in England and America). For the union of an inwardness, purified to the point of total abstraction and stripped of all traces of flesh and blood, with a transcendental philosophy of history does indeed correspond to the basic ideological structure of capitalism. It could even be maintained that the equally revolutionary Calvinist union of an ethics in which man has to prove himself (interiorised asceticism) with a thorough-going transcendentalism with regard to the objective forces that move the world and control the fate of man (*deus absconditus* and predestination) contain the bourgeois reified consciousness with its things-in-themselves in a mythologised but yet quite pure state.[54]

In the actively revolutionary sects the elemental vigour of a Thomas Münzer seems at first glance to obscure the irreducible quality and unsynthesised amalgam of the empirical and the utopian. But closer inspection of the way in which the religious and utopian premises of the theory *concretely impinge* upon Münzer's actions will reveal the same 'dark and empty chasm', the same 'hiatus irrationalis' between theory and practice that is everywhere apparent where a subjective and hence undialectical utopia directly assaults historical reality with the intention of changing it. Real actions then appear—precisely in their objective, revolutionary sense—wholly independent of the religious utopia: the latter can neither lead them in any real sense, nor can it offer concrete objectives or concrete proposals for their realisation.

When Ernst Bloch claims[55] that this union of religion with socio-economic revolution points the way to a deepening of the 'merely economic' outlook of historical materialism, he fails to notice that his deepening simply by-passes the real depth of historical materialism. When he then conceives of economics as a concern with objective things to which soul and inwardness are to be opposed, he overlooks the fact that the real social revolution can only mean the restructuring of the real and concrete life of man. He does not see that what is known as economics is nothing but the system of forms objectively defining this real life. The revolutionary sects were forced to evade this problem because in their historical situation such a restructuring of life and even of the definition of the problem was objectively impossible. But it will not do to fasten upon their weakness, their inability to discover the Archimedean point from which the whole of reality can be overthrown, and their predicament which forces them to aim too high or too low and to see in these things a sign of greater depth.

The individual can never become the measure of all things. For when the individual confronts objective reality he is faced by a complex of ready-made and unalterable objects which allow him only the subjective responses of recognition or rejection. Only the class can relate to the whole of reality in a practical revolutionary way. (The 'species' cannot do this as it is no more than an individual that has been mythologised and stylised in a spirit of contemplation.) And the class, too, can only manage it when it can see through the reified objectivity of the given world to the process that is also its own fate. For the individual, reification and hence determinism (determinism being the idea that things are necessarily connected) are irremovable. Every attempt to achieve 'freedom' from such premises must fail, for 'inner freedom' presupposes that the world cannot be changed. Hence, too, the cleavage of the ego into 'is' and 'ought', into the intelligible and the empirical ego, is unable to serve as the foundation for a dialectical process of becoming, even for the individual subject. The problem of the external world and with it the structure of the external world (of things) is referred to the category of the empirical ego. Psychologically and physiologically the latter is subject to the same deterministic laws as apply to the external world in the narrow sense. The intelligible ego becomes a transcendental idea (regardless of whether it is viewed as a metaphysical existent or an ideal to be realised). It is of the essence of this idea that it should preclude a dialectical interaction with the empirical components of the ego and *a fortiori* the possibility that the intelligible ego should recognise itself in the empirical ego. The impact of such an idea upon the empirical reality corresponding to it produces the same riddle that we described earlier in the relationship between '*is*' and '*ought*'.

This discovery makes it quite clear why all such views must end in mysticism and conceptual mythologies. Mythologies are always born where two terminal points, or at least two stages in a movement, have to be regarded as terminal points without its being possible to discover any concrete mediation between them and the movement. This is equally true of movements in the empirical world and of indirectly mediated movements of thought designed to encompass the totality. This failure almost always has the appearance of involving simultaneously the unbridgeable distance between the movement and the thing moved, between movement and mover, and between mover and thing moved. But mythology inevitably adopts the structure of the problem whose opacity had been the cause of its own birth. This insight confirms once again the value of Feuerbach's 'anthropological' criticism.

And thus there arises what at first sight seems to be the paradoxical situation that this projected, mythological world seems closer to consciousness than does the immediate reality. But the paradox dissolves as soon as we remind ourselves that we must abandon the standpoint of immediacy and solve the problem if immediate reality is to be mastered in truth. Whereas mythology is simply *the reproduction in imagination of the problem in its insolubility*. Thus immediacy is merely reinstated on a higher level. The desert beyond God which, according to Master Eckhart, the soul must seek in order to find the deity is nearer to the isolated individual soul than is its concrete existence within the concrete totality of a human society which from this background must be indiscernible even in its general outlines. Thus for reified man a robust causal determinism is more accessible than those mediations that could lead him out of his reified existence. But to posit the individual man as the measure of all things is to lead thought into the labyrinths of mythology.

Of course, 'indeterminism' does not lead to a way out of the difficulty for the individual. The indeterminism of the modern pragmatists was in origin nothing but the acquisition of that margin of 'freedom' that the conflicting claims and irrationality of the reified laws can offer the individual in capitalist society. It ultimately turns into a mystique of intuition which leaves the fatalism of the external reified world even more intact than before. Jacobi had rebelled in the name of 'humanism' against the tyranny of the 'law' in Kant and Fichte, he demanded that "laws should be made for the sake of man, not man for the sake of the law". But we can see that where Kant had left the established order untouched in the name of rationalism, Jacobi did no more than offer to glorify the same empirical, merely existing reality in the spirit of irrationalism.[56]

Even worse, having failed to perceive that man in his negative immediacy was a moment in a dialectical process, such a philosophy, when consciously directed toward the restructuring of society, is forced to distort the social reality in order to discover the positive side, man as he exists, in one of its manifestations. In support of this we may cite as a typical illustration the well-known passage in Lassalle's *Bastiat-Schulze*: "There is no *social way* that leads out of this social situation. The vain efforts of *things* to behave like *human beings* can be seen in the English strikes whose melancholy outcome is familiar enough. *The only* way out for the workers is to be found in *that* sphere *within which* they can still be *human beings*, i.e. in the *state*. Hence the instinctive but infinite hatred which the liberal bourgeoisie bears the concept of the state in its every manifestation."[57]

It is not our concern here to pillory Lassalle for his material and historical misconceptions. But it is important to establish that the abstract and absolute separation of the state from the economy and the rigid division between man as thing on the one hand and man as man on the other, is not without consequences. (1) It is responsible for the birth of a fatalism that cannot escape from immediate empirical facticity (we should think here of Lassalle's *Iron Law of Wages*). And (2) the 'idea' of the state is divorced from the development of capitalism and is credited with a completely utopian function, wholly alien to its concrete character. And this means that every path leading to a change in this reality is systematically blocked. Already the mechanical separation between economics and politics precludes any really effective action encompassing society in its totality, for this itself is based on the mutual interaction of both these factors. For a fatalism in economics would prohibit any thorough-going economic measure, while a state utopianism would either await a miracle or else pursue a policy of adventurous illusions.

This disintegration of a dialectical, practical unity into an inorganic aggregate of the empirical and the utopian, a clinging to the 'facts' (in their untranscended immediacy) and a faith in illusions as alien to the past as to the present is characteristic in increasing measure of the development of social democracy. We have only to consider it in the light of our systematic analysis of reification in order to establish that such a posture conceals a total capitulation before the bourgeoisie—and this notwithstanding the apparent 'socialism' of its policies. For it is wholly within the class interests of the bourgeoisie to separate the individual spheres of society from one another and to fragment the existence of men correspondingly. Above all we find, justified in different terms but essential to social democracy nevertheless, this very dualism of economic fatalism and ethical utopianism as applied to the 'human' functions of *the state*. It means inevitably that the proletariat will be drawn on to the territory of the bourgeoisie and naturally the bourgeoisie will maintain its superiority.[58]

The danger to which the proletariat has been exposed since its appearance on the historical stage was that it might remain imprisoned in its immediacy together with the bourgeoisie. With the growth of social democracy this threat acquired a real political organisation which artificially cancels out the mediations so laboriously won and forces the proletariat back into its immediate existence where it is merely a component of capitalist society and not *at the same time* the motor that drives it to its doom and destruction. Thus the proletariat submits to the 'laws' of bourgeois society either in a spirit of supine fatalism (e.g. towards the natural laws of production) or else in a spirit of 'moral' affirmation (the state as an ideal, a cultural positive). It is doubtless true that these 'laws' are part of an objective dialectic inaccessible to the reified consciousness and as such lead to the downfall of capitalism.[59] But as long as capitalism survives, such a view of society corresponds to the elementary class interests of the bourgeoisie. It derives every practical advantage from revealing aspects of the structure of immediate existence (regardless of how many insoluble problems may be concealed behind these abstract reflected forms) while veiling the overall unified dialectical structure.

On this territory, social democracy must inevitably remain in the weaker position. This is not just because it renounces of its own free will the historical mission of the proletariat to point to the way out of the problems of capitalism that the bourgeoisie cannot solve, nor is it because it looks on fatalistically as the 'laws' of capitalism drift towards the abyss. But social democracy must concede defeat on every particular issue also. For when confronted by the overwhelming resources of knowledge, culture and routine which the bourgeoisie undoubtedly possesses and will continue to possess as long as it remains the ruling class, the only effective superiority of the proletariat, its only decisive weapon is its ability to see the social totality as a concrete historical totality; to see the reified forms as processes between men; to see the immanent meaning of history that only appears negatively in the contradictions of abstract forms, to raise its positive side to consciousness and to put it into practice. With the ideology of social democracy the proletariat falls victim to all the antinomies of reification that we have hitherto analysed in such detail. The important role increasingly played in this ideology by 'man' as a value, an ideal, an imperative, accompanied, of course, by a growing 'insight' into the necessity and logic of the actual economic process, is only one symptom of this relapse into the reified immediacy of the bourgeoisie. For the unmediated juxtaposition of natural laws and imperatives is the logical expression of immediate societal existence in bourgeois society.

6

Reification is, then, the necessary, immediate reality of every person living in capitalist society. It can be overcome only by *constant and constantly renewed efforts to disrupt the reified structure of existence by concretely relating to the concretely manifested contradictions of the total development, by becoming conscious of the immanent meanings of these contradictions for the total development.* But it must be emphasided that (1) the structure can be disrupted only if the immanent contradictions of the process are made conscious. Only when the consciousness of the proletariat is able to point out the road along which the dialectics of history is objectively impelled, but which it cannot travel unaided, will the consciousness of the proletariat awaken to a consciousness of the process, and only then will the proletariat become the identical subject-object of history whose praxis will change reality. If the proletariat fails to take this step the contradiction will remain unresolved and will be reproduced by the dialectical mechanics of history at a higher level, in an altered form and with increased intensity. It is in *this* that the objective necessity of history consists. The deed of the proletariat can never be more than to take the *next step*[60] in the process. Whether it is 'decisive' or 'episodic' depends on the concrete circumstances, but in this context, where we are concerned with our knowledge of the structure, it does not much matter as we are talking about an unbroken process of such disruptions.

(2) Inseparable from this is the fact that the relation to totality does not need to become explicit, the plenitude of the totality does not need to be consciously integrated into the motives and objects of action. What is crucial is that there should be an aspiration towards totality, that action should serve the purpose, described above, in the totality of the process. Of course, with the mounting capitalist socialisation of society it becomes increasingly possible and hence necessary to integrate the content of each specific event into the totality of contents.[61] (World economics and world politics are much more immediate forms of existence today than they were in Marx's time.) However, this does not in the least contradict what we have maintained here, namely that the decisive actions can involve an—apparently—trivial matter. For here we can see in operation the truth that in the dialectical totality the individual elements incorporate the structure of the whole. This was made clear on the level of theory by the fact that e.g. it was possible to gain an understanding of the whole of bourgeois society from its commodity structure. We now see the same state of affairs in practice, when the fate of a whole process of development can depend on a decision in an—apparently—trivial matter.

Hence (3) when judging whether an action is right or wrong it is essential to relate it to its function in the total process. Proletarian thought is practical thought and as such is strongly pragmatic. "The proof of the pudding is in the eating," Engels says, providing an idiomatic gloss on Marx's second *Thesis on Feuerbach*: "The question whether human thinking can pretend to objective truth is not a theoretical but a practical question. Man must prove the truth, i.e. the reality and power, the 'this-sidedness' of his thinking in practice. The dispute over the reality or non-reality of thinking that is isolated from practice is a purely scholastic question." This pudding, however, is the making of the proletariat into a class: the process by which its class consciousness becomes real in practice. This gives a more concrete form to the proposition that the proletariat is the identical subject-object of the historical process, i.e. the first subject in history that is (objectively) capable of an adequate social consciousness. It turns out that the contradictions in which the antagonisms of the mechanics of history are expressed are only capable of an objective social solution in practice if the solution is at the same time a new, practically-won consciousness on the part of the proletariat.[62] Whether an action is functionally right or wrong is decided ultimately by the evolution of proletarian class consciousness.

The eminently practical nature of this consciousness is to be seen (4) in that an adequate, correct consciousness means a change in its own objects, and in the first instance, in itself. In Section II of this essay we discussed Kant's view of the ontological proof of God's existence, of the problem of existence and thought, and we quoted his very logical argument to the effect that if existence were a true predicate, then "I could not say that precisely the object of my concept exists". Kant was being very consistent when he denied this. At the same time it is clear that from the standpoint of the proletariat the empirically given reality of the objects does dissolve into processes and tendencies; this process is no single, unrepeatable tearing of the veil that masks the process but the unbroken alternation of ossification, contradiction and movement; and thus the proletariat represents the true reality, namely the tendencies of history awakening into consciousness. We must therefore conclude that Kant's seemingly paradoxical statement is a precise description of what actually follows from every functionally correct action of the proletariat.

This insight alone puts us in a position to see through the last vestiges of the reification of consciousness and its intellectual form, the problem of the thing-in-itself. Even Friedrich Engels has put the matter in a form that may easily give rise to misunderstandings. In his account of what separates Marx and himself from the school of Hegel, he says: "We comprehend the concepts in our heads once more materialistically—as reflections of real things instead of regarding the real things as reflections of this or that stage of the absolute concept."[63]

But this leaves a question to be asked and Engels not only asks it but also answers it on the following page quite in agreement with us. There he says: "that the world is not to be comprehended

as a complex of ready-made *things*, but as a complex of *processes*".
But if there are no things, what is 'reflected' in thought? We
cannot hope to offer even an outline of the history of the 'reflection theory' even though we could only unravel the full implications of this problem with its aid. In the theory of 'reflection' we
find the theoretical embodiment of the duality of thought and
existence, consciousness and reality, that is so intractable to the
reified consciousness. And from *that point of view* it is immaterial
whether things are to be regarded as reflections of concepts or
whether concepts are reflections of things. In both cases the duality
is firmly established.

Kant's grandiose and very cogent attempt to overcome this
duality *by logic*, his theory of the synthetic function of consciousness in the creation of the domain of theory could not arrive at
any *philosophical* solution to the question. For his duality was merely
banished from logic to reappear in perpetuity in the form of the
duality of phenomenon and the thing-in-itself. And in these terms
it remained an insoluble philosophical problem. The later history
of his theory shows how very unsatisfactory his solution was. To
see Kant's epistemology as scepticism and agnosticism is of course
a misunderstanding. But it is one that has at least one root in the
theory itself—not, be it admitted, in the logic but in the relation
between the logic and the metaphysics, in the relation between
thought and existence.

It must be clearly understood that every contemplative stance
and thus every kind of 'pure thought' that must undertake the
task of knowing an object outside itself raises the problem of
subjectivity and objectivity. The object of thought (as something
outside) becomes something alien to the subject. This raises the
problem of whether thought corresponds to the object! The
'purer' the cognitive character of thought becomes and the more
'critical' thought is, the more vast and impassable does the
abyss appear that yawns between the 'subjective' mode of thought
and the objectivity of the (existing) object. Now it is possible—
as with Kant—to view the object of thought as something
'created' by the forms of thought. But this does not suffice to solve
the problem of existence, and Kant, by removing it from the
sphere of epistemology, creates this philosophical situation for
himself: even his excogitated objects must correspond to some
'reality' or other. But this reality is treated as a thing-in-itself and
placed outside the realm of that which can be known by the

'critical' mind. It is with respect to *this* reality (which is the authentic, the metaphysical reality for Kant, as his ethics shows) that his position remains one of scepticism and agnosticism. This remains true however unsceptical was the solution he found for epistemological objectivity and the immanent theory of truth.

It is, therefore, no accident that it is from Kant that the various agnostic trends have taken their cue (one has only to think of Maimon or Schopenhauer). It is even less of an accident that Kant himself was responsible for the reintroduction into philosophy of the principle that is most violently opposed to his own synthetic principle of 'creation' (Erzeugung), namely the Platonic theory of ideas. For this theory is the most extreme attempt to rescue the objectivity of thought and its correspondence with its object, without having to resort to empirical and material reality to find a criterion for the correspondence.

Now it is evident that every consistent elaboration of the theory of ideas requires a principle that both links thought with the objects of the world of ideas and also connects these with the objects of the empirical world (recollection, intellectual intuition, etc.). But this in turn leads the theory of thought to transcend the limits of thought itself: and it becomes psychology, metaphysics or the history of philosophy. Thus instead of a solution to the problem we are left with complexities that have been doubled or tripled. And the problem remains without a solution. For the insight that a correspondence or relationship of 'reflection' cannot in principle be established between heterogeneous objects is precisely the driving force behind every view of the type of the Platonic theory of ideas. This undertakes to prove that the same ultimate essence forms the core of the objects of thought as well as of thought itself. Hegel gives an apt description of the basic philosophical theme of the theory of recollection from this standpoint when he says that it provides a myth of man's fundamental situation: "in him lies the truth and the only problem is to make it conscious".[64] But how to prove this identity in thought and existence of the ultimate substance?—above all when it has been shown that they are completely heterogeneous in the way in which they present themselves to the intuitive, contemplative mind? It becomes necessary to invoke metaphysics and with the aid of its overt or concealed mythical mediations thought and existence can once again be reunited. And this despite the fact that their separation is not merely the starting-point of 'pure' thought but also a factor that constantly informs it whether it likes it or not.

The situation is not improved in the slightest when the mythology is turned on its head and thought is deduced from empirical material reality. Rickert once described materialism as an inverted Platonism. And he was right in so doing. As long as thought and existence persist in their old, rigid opposition, as long as their own structure and the structure of their interconnections remain unchanged, then the view that thought is a product of the brain and hence must correspond to the objects of the empirical world is just such a mythology as those of recollection and the world of Platonic ideas. It is a mythology for it is incapable of explaining the *specific* problems that arise here by reference to *this principle*. It is forced to leave them unsolved, to solve them with the 'old' methods and to reinstate the mythology as a key to the whole unanalysed complex.[65] But as will already be clear, it is not possible to eliminate the distinction by means of an infinite progression. For that produces either a pseudo-solution or else the theory of reflection simply reappears in a different guise.[66]

Historical thought perceives the correspondence of thought and existence in their—immediate, but no more than immediate— rigid, reified structure. This is precisely the point at which non-dialectical thought is confronted by this insoluble problem. From the fact of this rigid confrontation it follows (1) that thought and (empirical) existence cannot reflect each other, but also (2) that the critierion of correct thought can only be found in the realm of reflection. As long as man adopts a stance of intuition and contemplation he can only relate to his own thought and to the objects of the empirical world in an immediate way. He accepts both as ready-made—produced by historical reality. As he wishes only to know the world and not to change it he is forced to accept both the empirical, material rigidity of existence and the logical rigidity of concepts as unchangeable. His mythological analyses are not concerned with the concrete origins of this rigidity nor with the real factors inherent in them that could lead to its elimination. They are concerned solely to discover how the *unchanged nature* of these data could be conjoined whilst leaving them unchanged and how to explain them *as such*.

The solution proposed by Marx in his *Theses on Feuerbach* is to transform philosophy into praxis. But, as we have seen, this praxis has its objective and structural preconditions and complement in the view that reality is a "complex of processes". That is to say, in the view that the movements of history represent the true reality; not indeed a transcendental one, but at all events a higher one than that of the rigid, reified facts of the empirical world, from which they arise. For the reflection theory this means that thought and consciousness are orientated towards reality but, at the same time, the criterion of truth is provided by relevance to reality. This reality is by no means identical with empirical existence. This reality is not, it becomes.

The process of Becoming is to be understood in a twofold sense. (1) In this Becoming, in this tendency, in this process the true nature of the object is revealed. This is meant in the sense that—as in the case of the instances we have cited and which could easily be multiplied—the transformation of things into a process provides a *concrete* solution to all the *concrete* problems created by the paradoxes of existent objects. The recognition that one cannot step into the same river twice is just an extreme way of highlighting the unbridgeable abyss between concept and reality. It does nothing to increase our concrete knowledge of the river.

In contrast with this, the recognition that capital as a process can only be accumulated, or rather accumulating, capital, provides the positive, concrete solution to a whole host of positive, concrete problems of method and of substance connected with capital. Hence only by overcoming the—theoretical—duality of philosophy and special discipline, of methodology and factual knowledge can the way be found by which to annul the duality of thought and existence. Every attempt to overcome the duality dialectically in logic, in a system of thought stripped of every concrete relation to existence, is doomed to failure. (And we may observe that despite many other opposing tendencies in his work, Hegel's philosophy was of this type.) For every pure logic is Platonic: it is thought released from existence and hence ossified. Only by conceiving of thought as a form of reality, as a factor in the total process can philosophy overcome its own rigidity dialectically and take on the quality of Becoming.[67]

(2) Becoming is also the mediation between past and future. But it is the mediation between the concrete, i.e. historical past, and the equally concrete, i.e. historical future. When the concrete here and now dissolves into a process it is no longer a continuous, intangible moment, immediacy slipping away;[68] it is the focus of the deepest and most widely ramified mediation, the focus of

decision and of the birth of the new. As long as man concent-
trates his interest contemplatively upon the past *or* future, both
ossify into an alien existence. And between the subject and the
object lies the unbridgeable "pernicious chasm" of the present.
Man must be able to comprehend the present as a becoming. He
can do this by seeing in it the tendencies out of whose dialectical
opposition he can *make* the future. Only when he does this will the
present be a process of becoming, that belongs to *him*. Only he
who is willing and whose mission it is to create the future can see
the present in its concrete truth. As Hegel says: "Truth is not to
treat objects as alien."[69]

But when the truth of becoming is the future that is to be created
but has not yet been born, when it is the new that resides in the
tendencies that (with our conscious aid) will be realised, then the
question whether thought is a reflection appears quite senseless.
It is true that reality is the criterion for the correctness of thought.
But reality is not, it becomes—and to become the participation of
thought is needed. We see here the fulfilment of the programme
of classical philosophy: the principle of genesis means in fact that
dogmatism is overcome (above all in its most important historical
incarnation: the Platonic theory of reflection). But only concrete
(historical) becoming can perform the function of such a genesis.
And consciousness (the practical class consciousness of the proletariat) is a necessary, indispensable, integral part of that process
of becoming.

Thus thought and existence are not identical in the sense that
they 'correspond' to each other, or 'reflect' each other, that they
'run parallel' to each other or 'coincide' with each other (all
expressions that conceal a rigid duality). Their identity is that
they are aspects of one and the same real historical and dialectical
process. What is 'reflected' in the consciousness of the proletariat
is the new positive reality arising out of the dialectical contradictions of capitalism. And this is by no means the invention of the
proletariat, nor was it 'created' out of the void. It is rather the
inevitable consequence of the process in its totality; one which
changed from being an abstract possibility to a concrete reality
only after it had become part of the consciousness of the proletariat
and had been made practical by it. And this is no mere formal
transformation. For a possibility to be realised, for a tendency to
become actual, what is required is that the objective components
of a society should be transformed; their functions must be changed

and with them the structure and content of every individual object.

But it must never be forgotten: *only the practical class consciousness of the proletariat* possesses this ability to transform things. Every contemplative, purely cognitive stance leads ultimately to a divided relationship to its object. Simply to transplant the structure we have discerned here into any stance other than that of proletarian action—for only the class can be practical in its relation to the total process—would mean the creation of a new conceptual mythology and a regression to the standpoint of classical philosophy refuted by Marx. For every purely cognitive stance bears the stigma of immediacy. That is to say, it never ceases to be confronted by a whole series of ready-made objects that cannot be dissolved into processes. Its dialectical nature can survive only in the tendency towards praxis and in its orientation towards the actions of the proletariat. It can survive only if it remains critically aware of its own tendency to immediacy inherent in every non-practical stance and if it constantly strives to explain critically the mediations, the relations to the totality as a process, to the actions of the proletariat as a class.

The practical character of the thought of the proletariat is born and becomes real as the result of an equally dialectical process. In this thought self-criticism is more than the self-criticism of its object, i.e. the self-criticism of bourgeois society. It is also a critical awareness of how much of its own practical nature has really become manifest, which stage of the genuinely practicable is objectively possible and how much of what is objectively possible has been made real. For it is evident that however clearly we may have grasped the fact that society consists of processes, however thoroughly we may have unmasked the fiction of its rigid reification, this does not mean that we are able to annul the 'reality' of this fiction in capitalist society *in practice*. The moments in which this insight *can* really be converted into practice are determined by developments in society. Thus proletarian thought is in the first place merely a *theory of praxis* which only gradually (and indeed often spasmodically) transforms itself into *a practical theory* that overturns the real world. The individual stages of this process cannot be sketched in here. They alone would be able to show how proletarian class consciousness evolves dialectically (i.e. how the proletariat becomes a class). Only then would it be possible to throw light on the intimate dialectical process of interaction between the socio-historical situation and the class consciousness of the proletariat. Only then would the statement that the proletariat is the identical subject-object of the history of society become truly concrete.[70]

Even the proletariat can only overcome reification as long as it is oriented towards practice. And this means that there can be no single act that will eliminate reification in all its forms at one blow; it means that there will be a whole host of objects that at least in appearance remain more or less unaffected by the process. This is true in the first instance of nature. But it is also illuminating to observe how a whole set of social phenomena become dialecticised by a different path than the one we have traced out to show the nature of the dialectics of history and the process by which the barriers of reification can be shattered. We have observed, for instance, how certain works of art are extraordinarily sensitive to the qualitative nature of dialectical changes without their becoming conscious of the antagonisms which they lay bare and to which they give artistic form.

At the same time we observed other societal phenomena which contain inner antagonisms but only in an abstract form, i.e. their inner contradictions are merely the secondary effects of the inner contradictions of other, more primary phenomena. This means that these last contradictions can only become visible if mediated by the former and can only become dialectical when they do. (This is true of interest as opposed to profit.) It would be necessary to set forth the whole system of these qualitative gradations in the dialectical character of the different kinds of phenomena before we should be in a position to arrive at the concrete totality of the categories with which alone true knowledge of the present is possible. The hierarchy of these categories would determine at the same time the point where system and history meet, thus fulfilling Marx's postulate (already cited) concerning the categories that "their sequence is determined by the relations they have to each other in modern bourgeois society".

In every consciously dialectical system of thought, however, any sequence is itself dialectical—not only for Hegel, but also as early as Proclus. Moreover, the dialectical deduction of categories cannot possibly involve a simple juxtaposition or even the succession of identical forms. Indeed, if the method is not to degenerate into a rigid schematicism, even identical formal patterns must not be allowed to function in a repetitively mechanical way (thus, the famous triad: thesis, antithesis and synthesis). When the dialectical method becomes rigid, as happens frequently in Hegel, to say nothing of his followers, the only control device and the only protection is the concrete historical method of Marx. But it is vital that we should draw all the conclusions possible from this situation. Hegel himself distinguishes between negative and positive dialectics.[71] By positive dialectics he understands the growth of a particular content, the elucidation of a concrete totality. In the process, however, we find that he almost always advances from the determinants of reflection to the positive dialectics even though his conception of nature, for example, as "otherness", as the idea in a state of "being external to itself"[72] directly precludes a positive dialectics. (It is here that we can find one of the theoretical sources for the frequently artificial constructs of his philosophy of nature.) Nevertheless, Hegel does perceive clearly at times that the dialectics of nature can never become anything more exalted than a dialectics of movement witnessed by the detached observer, as the subject cannot be integrated into the dialectical process, at least not at the stage reached hitherto. Thus he emphasises that Zeno's antinomies reached the same level as those of Kant,[73] with the implication that it is not possible to go any higher.

From this we deduce the necessity of separating the merely objective dialectics of nature from those of society. For in the dialectics of society the subject is included in the reciprocal relation in which theory and practice become dialectical with reference to one another. (It goes without saying that the growth of *knowledge* about nature is a social phenomenon and therefore to be included in the second dialectical type.) Moreover, if the dialectical method is to be consolidated concretely it is essential that the different types of dialectics should be set out in concrete fashion. It would then become clear that the Hegelian distinction between positive and negative dialectics as well as the different levels of intuition, representation and concept [Anschauung, Vorstellung, Begriff]—(a terminology that need not be adhered to) are only some of the possible types of distinction to be drawn. For the others the economic works of Marx provide abundant material for a clearly elaborated analysis of structures. However, even to outline a typology of these dialectical forms would be well beyond the scope of this study.

Still more important than these systematic distinctions is the fact that even the objects in the very centre of the dialectical process can only slough off their reified form after a laborious process. A process in which the seizure of power by the proletariat and even the organisation of the state and the economy on socialist lines are only stages. They are, of course, extremely important stages, but they do not mean that the ultimate objective has been achieved. And it even appears as if the decisive crisis-period of capitalism may be characterised by the tendency to intensify reification, to bring it to a head. Roughly in the sense in which Lassalle wrote to Marx: "Hegel used to say in his old age that directly before the emergence of something qualitatively new, the old state of affairs gathers itself up into its original, purely general, essence, into its simple totality, transcending and absorbing back into itself all those marked differences and peculiarities which it evinced when it was still viable."[74] On the other hand, Bukharin, too, is right when he observes that in the age of the dissolution of capitalism, the fetishistic categories collapse and it becomes necessary to have recourse to the 'natural form' underlying them.[75] The contradiction between these two views is, however, only apparent. For the contradiction has two aspects: on the one hand, there is the increasing undermining of the forms of reification—one might describe it as the cracking of the crust because of the inner emptiness—their growing inability to do justice to the phenomena, even as isolated phenomena, even as the objects of reflection and calculation. On the other hand, we find the quantitative increase of the forms of reification, their empty extension to cover the whole surface of manifest phenomena. And the fact that these two aspects together are in conflict provides the key signature to the decline of bourgeois society.

As the antagonism becomes more acute two possibilities open up for the proletariat. It is given the opportunity to substitute its own positive contents for the emptied and bursting husks. But also it is exposed to the danger that for a time at least it might adapt itself ideologically to conform to these, the emptiest and most decadent forms of bourgeois culture.

History is at its least automatic when it is the consciousness of the proletariat that is at issue. The truth that the old intuitive, mechanistic materialism could not grasp turns out to be doubly true for the proletariat, namely that it can be transformed and liberated only by its own actions, and that "the educator must himself be educated". The objective economic evolution could do no more than create the position of the proletariat in the production process. It was this position that determined its point of view. But the objective evolution could only give the proletariat the opportunity and the necessity to change society. Any transformation can only come about as the product of the—free—action of the proletariat itself.

NOTES ON SECTION I

1 *A Contribution to the Critique of Political Economy*, p. 53.
2 *Capital* III, p. 324.
3 *Capital* III, p. 810.
4 *Capital* I, p. 72. On this antagonism cf. the purely economic distinction between the exchange of goods in terms of their value and the exchange in terms of their cost of production. *Capital* III, p. 174.
5 *Capital* I, p. 170.
6 Cf. *Capital* I, pp. 322, 345.
7 This whole process is described systematically and historically in *Capital* I. The facts themselves can also be found in the writings of bourgeois economists like Bücher, Sombart, A. Weber and Gottl among others—although for the most part they are not seen in connection with the problem of reification.
8 *Capital* I, p. 384.
9 *Capital* I, p. 355 (note).
10 That this should appear so is fully justified from the point of view of the *individual* consciousness. As far as class is concerned we would point out that this subjugation is the product of a lengthy struggle which enters upon a new stage with the organisation of the proletariat into a class—but on a higher plane and with different weapons.
11 *Capital* I, pp. 374–6, 423–4, 460, etc. It goes without saying that this 'contemplation' can be more demanding and demoralizing than 'active' labour. But we cannot discuss this further here.
12 *The Poverty of Philosophy*, pp. 58–9.
13 *Capital* I, p. 344.
14 Cf. Gottl: *Wirtschaft und Technik*, Grundriss der Sozialökonomik II, 234 et seq.
15 *Capital* I, p. 77.
16 This refers above all to capitalist private property. *Der heilige Max. Dokumente des Sozialismus* III, 363. Marx goes on to make a number of very fine observations about the effects of reification upon language. A philological study from the standpoint of historical materialism could profitably begin here.
17 *Capital* III, pp. 384–5.
18 Ibid., p. 809.

I

19 *Gesammelte politische Schriften*, Munich, 1921, pp. 140–2. Weber's reference to the development of English law has no bearing on our problem. On the gradual ascendancy of the principle of economic calculation, see also A. Weber, *Standort der Industrien*, especially p. 216.

20 Max Weber, *Wirtschaft und Gesellschaft*, p. 491.

21 Ibid., p. 129.

22 If we do not emphasise the class character of the state in *this* context, this is because our aim is to understand reification as a *general* phenomenon constitutive of the *whole* of bourgeois society. But for this the question of class would have to begin with the machine. On this point see Section III.

23 Cf. Max Weber, *Politische Schriften*, p. 154.

24 Cf. the essay by A. Fogarasi in *Kommunismus*, Jg. II, No. 25/26.

25 *Die Metaphysik der Sitten*, Pt. I, § 24.

26 *The Origin of the Family*, in S. W. II, p. 293.

27 *Capital* III, p. 239.

28 Ibid., p. 183.

29 *Capital* I, p. 356.

30 Letter to Conrad Schmidt in S.W. II, pp. 447–8.

31 *A Contribution to the Critique of Political Economy*, p. 276.

32 Ibid., p. 21.

33 *Finanzkapital*, 2nd edition, pp. 378–9.

34 *Capital* II, pp. 75–6.

35 *Die Akkumulation des Kapitals*, 1st edition, pp. 78–9. It would be a fascinating task to work out the links between this process and the development of the great rationalist systems.

36 Quoted by Bergbohm, *Jurisprudenz und Rechtsphilosphie*, p. 170.

37 Ibid., p. 375.

38 Preuss, *Zur Methode der juristischen Begriffsbildung*. In Schmollers Jahrbuch, 1900, p. 370.

39 *Lehrbuch des Naturrechts*, Berlin, 1799, § 141. Marx's polemic against Hugo (Nachlass I, pp. 268 et seq.) is still on Hegelian lines.

40 *Hauptprobleme der Staatsrechtslehre*, p. 411 (my italics).

41 F. Somlo, *Juristiche Grundlehre*, p. 117.

NOTES ON SECTION II

1 Reclam, p. 17.

2 *Capital* I, p. 372 (note).

3 Cf. Tönnies, *Hobbes' Leben und Lehre* and especially Ernst Cassirer, *Das Erkenntnisproblem in der Philosophie und Wissenschaft der neueren Zeit*. We shall return to the conclusions of this book which are of value for us because they have been arrived at from a completely different point of view and yet describe the same process, showing the impact of the rationalism of mathematics and the 'exact' sciences upon the origins of modern thought.

4 *Capital* I, p. 486. See also Gottl, op. cit., pp. 238–45, for the

contrast with antiquity. For this reason the concept of 'rational-ism' must not be employed as an unhistorical abstraction, but it is always necessary precisely to determine the object (or sphere of life) to which it is to be related, and above all to define the objects to which it is *not* related.

5 Max Weber, *Gesammelte Aufsätze zur Religionssoziologie* II, pp. 165–70. A like structure can be found in the development of all the 'special' sciences in India: a highly advanced technology in particular branches without reference to a rational totality and without any *attempt* to rationalise the *whole* and to confer universal validity upon the rational categories. Cf. also Ibid., pp. 146–7, 166–7. The situation is similar with regard to the 'rationalism' of Confucianism. Op. cit. I, p. 527.

6 In this respect Kant is the culmination of the philosophy of the eighteenth century. Both the line from Locke to Berkeley and Hume and also the tradition of French materialism move in this direction. It would be beyond the scope of this inquiry to outline the different stages of this development with its various divergent strands.

7 *Kritik der reinen Vernunft*, pp. 403–4. Cf. also pp. 330 et seq.

8 Feuerbach also connected the problem of the absolute trans-cendence of sensuousness (by the understanding) with a contradic-tion in the existence of God. "The proof of the existence of God goes beyond the bounds of reason; true enough; but in the same sense in which seeing, hearing, smelling go beyond the bounds of reason." *Das Wesen des Christentums*, Reclam., p. 303. See Cassirer, op. cit. II, p. 608, for similar arguments in Hume and Kant.

9 This problem is stated most clearly by Lask: "For subjectivity" (i.e. for the logically subjective status of judgement), "it is by no means self-evident, but on the contrary it is the whole task of the philosopher to ascertain the categories into which logical form divides when applied to a particular subject-matter or, to put it differently, to discover which subjects form the particular province of the various categories." *Die Lehre vom Urteil*, p. 162.

10 *Die Kritik der reinen Vernunft*, p. 564.

11 This is not the place to show that neither Greek philosophy (with the possible exception of quite late thinkers, such as Proclus) nor mediaeval philosophy were acquainted with the idea of a 'system' in our sense. The problem of systems originates in modern times, with Descartes and Spinoza and from Leibniz and Kant onwards it becomes an increasingly conscious metho-dological postulate.

12 The idea of "infinite understanding", of intellectual intuition, etc., is *partly* designed as an epistemological solution to this difficulty. However, Kant had already perceived quite clearly that this problem leads on to the one we are about to discuss.

13 Once again it is Lask who perceives this most clearly and un-compromisingly. Cf. *Die Logik der Philosophie*, pp. 60–2. But he does not draw all the consequences of his line of reasoning, in

particular that of the impossibility of a rational system in principle.

14 We may point for example to Husserl's phenomenological method in which the whole terrain of logic is ultimately transformed into a 'system of facts' of a higher order. Husserl himself regards this method as purely descriptive. Cf. *Ideen zu einer reinen Phänomenologie* in Vol. I of his *Jahrbuch*, p. 113.

15 This fundamental tendency of Leibniz's thought attains maturity in the philosophy of Maimon where it appears in the form of the dissolution of the problem of the thing-in-itself and of "intelligible chance"; from here a path leads directly to Fichte and through him to later developments. The problem of the irrationality of mathematics is analysed incisively in an essay by Rickert, "Das Eine, die Einheit und das Eins," in *Logos* II, p. 1.

16 *Die Wissenschaftslehre* of 1804, Lecture XV, *Werke* (Neue Ausgabe) IV, p. 288. My italics. The problem is put similarly—though with varying degrees of clarity—by later 'critical' philosophers. Most clearly of all by Windelband when he defines existence as "content independent of form". In my opinion his critics have only obscured his paradox without providing a solution to the problem it contains.

17 This is not the place to offer a critique of particular philosophical schools. By way of proof of the correctness of this sketch I would only point to the relapse into natural law (which methodologically belongs to the pre-critical period) observable—in substance, though not in terminology—in the works of Cohen and also of Stammler whose thought is related to that of the Marburg School.

18 Rickert, one of the most consistent representatives of this school of thought, ascribes no more than a formal character to the cultural values underlying historiography, and it is precisely this fact that highlights the whole situation. On this point see Section III.

19 *Transcendentale Logik*, Lecture XXIII, Werke VI, p. 335. Readers unfamiliar with the terminology of classical philosophy are reminded that Fichte's concept of the ego has nothing to do with the empirical ego.

20 Second Introduction to the *Wissenschaftslehre*, Werke III, p. 52. Although Fichte's terminology changes from one work to the next, this should not blind us to the fact that he is always concerned with the same *problem*.

21 Cf. *Die Kritik der praktischen Vernunft*, Philisophische Bibliothek, p. 72.

22 "Now nature is in the common view the existence of things subject to laws." Ibid., p. 57.

23 Ibid., pp. 125-6.

24 *Über die wissenschaftliche Behandlungsarten des Naturrechts*, Werke I, pp. 352-3. Cf. ibid., p. 351. "For it is the absolute abstraction from every subject-matter of the will; every content posits a heteronomy of the free will." Or, with even greater clarity, in

the *Phenomenology of Hind*: "For pure duty is . . . absolutely indifferent towards every content and is compatible with every content." Werke II, p. 485.

25 This is quite clear in the case of the Greeks. But the same structure can be seen in the great systems at the beginning of the modern age, above all in Spinoza.

26 *Die Kritik der reinen Vernunft*, pp. 472–3.

27 Hegel, Werke III, pp. 78 et seq.

28 Nachlass I, p. 117. [*Fragments on The Difference between The Democritean and Epicurean philosophies of nature*].

29 From this ontological situation it becomes possible to understand the point of departure for the belief, so alien to modern thought in 'natural' states, e.g. the "credo ut intellegam" of Anselm of Canterbury, or the attitude of Indian thought ("Only by him whom he chooses will he be understood," it has been said of Atman). Descartes' systematic scepticism, which was the starting-point of *exact* thought, is no more than the sharpest formulation of this antagonism that was very consciously felt at the birth of the modern age. It can be seen again in every important thinker from Galileo to Bacon.

30 For the history of this universal mathematics, see Cassirer, op. cit. I, pp. 446, 563; II, 138, 156 et seq. For the connection between this mathematicisation of reality and the bourgeois 'praxis' of calculating the anticipated results of the 'laws', see Lange, *Geschichte des Materialismus* (Reclam) I, pp. 321–32 on Hobbes, Descartes and Bacon.

31 For the Platonic theory of ideas was indissolubly linked—with what right need not be discussed here—both with the totality and the qualitative existence of the given world. Contemplation means at the very least the bursting of the bonds that hold the 'soul' imprisoned within the limitations of the empirical. The Stoic ideal of ataraxy is a much better instance of this quite pure contemplation, but it is of course devoid of the paradoxical union with a feverish and uninterrupted 'activity'.

32 *Die Differenz des Fichteschen und Schellingschen Systems*, Werke I, p. 242. Every such 'atomic' theory of society only represents the ideological reflection of the purely bourgeois point of view; this was shown conclusively by Marx in his critique of Bruno Bauer, Nachlass II, p. 227. But this is not to deny the 'objectivity' of such views: they are in fact the necessary forms of consciousness that reified man has of his attitude towards society.

33 Hegel, Werke IX, p. 528.

34 *Capital* I, 390 (footnote).

35 *Gemeinschaft und Gesellschaft*, 3rd edition, p. 38.

36 *Ludwig Feuerbach and the End of Classical German Philosophy* in S.W. II, p. 336.

37 E.g. the *Phenomenology of Mind*, Preface, Werke II, p. 20; and also ibid., pp. 67–8, 451, etc.

38 Marx employs this terminology in the important, oft-quoted

passage about the proletariat (it is to be found in these pages too). *The Poverty of Philosophy*, p. 195. For this whole question, see also the relevant passages in the *Logik*, especially in Vol. III, pp. 127 et. seq., 166 et seq., and Vol. IV, pp. 120 et seq., and see also the critique of Kant in a number of places.

39 *Die Kritik der reinen Vernunft*, pp. 208 et seq.

40 Nachlass I, p. 449. [*An Outline of a Critique of National Economy*].

41 *Capital* I, p. 592, etc. Cf. also the essay on "Class Consciousness" for the question of the 'false consciousness' of the bourgeoisie.

42 It is this that provokes repeated attacks from Hegel. But in addition Goethe's rejection of the Kantian ethic points in the same direction although Goethe's motives and hence his terminology are different. That Kant's ethics is faced with the task of solving the problem of the thing-in-itself can be seen in innumerable places, e.g. the *Grundlegung der Metaphysik der Sitten*, Philosophische Bibliothek, p. 87; *Kritik der praktischen Vernunft*, p. 123.

43 *Die Kritik der reinen Vernunft*, p. 77.

44 Cf. also the essay "The Marxism of Rosa Luxemburg" on the question of the methodological interrelatedness of these two principles.

45 *Beiträge zur Geschichte des Materialismus*, pp. 54 et seq., 122 et seq. How near Holbach and Helvetius came to the problem of the thing-in-itself—admittedly in a more naïve form—can likewise be seen there on pp. 9, 51, etc.

46 The history of the stories à la Robinson cannot be undertaken here. I refer the reader to Marx's comments (*A Contribution to the Critique of Political Economy*, pp. 266 et seq., and to Cassirer's subtle remarks about the role of Robinson Crusoe in Hobbes' epistemology. Op. cit. II, pp. 61 et seq.

47 On this point cf. especially *Die Kritik der Urteilskraft* § 42. Via Schiller the illustration of the real and the imitated nightingale strongly influenced later thinkers. It would be of absorbing interest to follow through the historical development leading from German Romanticism via the historical school of law, Carlyle, Ruskin, etc., in the course of which the concept of 'organic growth' was converted from a protest against reification into an increasingly reactionary slogan. To do so, however, would be outside the scope of this work. Here it is only the *structure of the objects* that need concern us: namely the fact that what would seem to be the highpoint of the interiorisation of nature really implies the abandonment of any true understanding of it. To make moods [Stimmung] into the content presupposes the existence of unpenetrated and impenetrable objects (things-in-themselves) just as much as do the laws of nature.

48 *Das System der Sittenlehre*, 3. Hauptstück, § 31, Werke II, p. 747. It would be both interesting and rewarding to show how the so rarely understood Nature philosophy of the classical epoch necessarily springs from this state of affairs. It is not by chance that Goethe's Nature philosophy arose in the course of a conflict

with Newton's 'violation' of nature. Nor was it an accident that it set the pattern for all later developments. But both phenomena can only be understood in terms of the relation between man, nature and art. This also explains the methodological return to the qualitative Nature philosophy of the Renaissance as being the first assault upon a mathematical conception of nature.

49 *Die Kritik der Urteilskraft,* § 77.

50 *On the Aesthetic Education of Man,* 15th Letter.

51 *Die Differenz des Fichteschen und Schellingschen Systems,* Werke I, p. 174.

52 It is in his opposition *to this* that we can locate the substantive core in Schelling's later philosophy. However, his mythologising approach now became wholly reactionary. Hegel represents—as we shall show—the absolute consummation of rationalism, but this means that he can be superseded only by an interrelation of thought and existence that *has ceased to be contemplative,* by the *concrete* demonstration of the identical subject-object. Schelling made the absurd attempt to achieve this by going in the reverse direction and so to reach a purely intellectual solution. He thus ended up, like all the epigones of classical philosphy, in a reactionary mythology that glorified an empty irrationality.

53 It is not possible to examine the question in detail here, but I should like to point out that this is the point at which to begin an analysis of the problematics of Romanticism. Familiar, but seldom understood concepts, such as 'irony' spring from this situation. In particular the incisive questions posed by Solger who has wrongly been allowed to slide into oblivion, place him together with Friedrich Schlegel as a pioneer of the dialectical method between Schelling and Hegel, a position in some ways comparable to that occupied by Maimon in between Kant and Fichte. The role of mythology in Schelling's aesthetics becomes clearer with this in mind. There is an obvious connection between such problems and the conception of nature as a mood. The truly critical, metaphysically non-hypostatised, artistic view of the world leads to an even greater fragmentation of the unity of the subject and thus to an increase in the symptoms of alienation; this has been borne out by the later evolution of consistently modern views of art (Flaubert, Konrad Fiedler, etc.) On this point cf. my essay, *Die Subjekt-Objekt-Beziehung in der Ästhetik,* Logos, Jahrgang IV.

54 *Dichtung und Wahrheit,* Book 12. The subterranean influence of Hamann is much greater than is usually supposed.

55 Werke I, pp. 173–4. The *Phenomenology* is an attempt—unsurpassed hitherto, even by Hegel—to develop such a method.

56 Lask, the most ingenious and logical of the modern Neo-Kantians, clearly perceives this development in Hegel's Logic. "In this respect, too, the critic must admit that Hegel is in the right: irrationality can be overcome *if and only if* dialectically changing concepts are acceptable." *Fichtes Idealismus und die Geschichte,* p. 67.

57   Cf. Plekhanov, op. cit., pp. 9, 51, etc. But *methodologically* only
     formalistic rationalism is confronted by an insoluble problem at
     this point. Setting aside the *substantive* scientific value of mediaeval
     solutions to these questions, it is indubitable that the Middle Ages
     did not see any problem here, let alone an insoluble one. We may
     compare Holbach's statement, quoted by Plekhanov, that we
     cannot know "whether the chicken preceded the egg, or the egg
     the chicken" with e.g. the statement of Master Eckhard, "Nature
     makes the man from the child and the chicken from the egg;
     God makes the man before the child and the chicken before the
     egg" (Sermon of the noble man). Needless to say, we are here
     concerned *exclusively* with the contrast in *methodology*. On the basis
     of this methodological limitation as the result of which history is
     made to appear as a thing-in-itself, Plekhanov has rightly judged
     these materialists to be naïve idealists in their approach to history.
     Zu Hegels 60. Todestag, Neue Zeit X. I. 273.

58   Here too we can do no more than refer in passing to the history
     of this problem. The opposed positions were clearly established
     very early on. I would point to e.g. Friedrich Schlegel's critique
     of Condorcet's attempt (1795) to provide a rationalist explanation
     of history (as it were, of the type of Comte or Spencer). "*The
     enduring qualities* of man are the subject of pure science, but *the
     changing aspects of man*, both as an individual and in the mass, are
     the subject of a scientific history of mankind." *Prosaische Jugend-
     schriften*, Vienna, 1906. Vol. II, p. 52.

59   *Die Encyclopädie*, § 309. For us, of course, *only* the methodological
     aspect has any significance. Nevertheless, we must emphasise
     that all formal, rationalist concepts exhibit this same reified
     impenetrability. The modern substitution of functions for things
     does not alter this situation in the least, as concepts of function
     do not at all differ from thing-concepts in the only area that matters,
     i.e. the form-content relationship. On the contrary, they take
     their formal, rationalist structure to its extreme logical conclusion.

60   Hegel, Werke II, p. 267.

61   *Die Philosophie des Rechts*, § 345–7. *Encyclopädie*, § 548–52.

62   In the last versions of the system history represents the transition
     from the philosophy of right to the absolute spirit. (In the Pheno-
     menology the relation is more complex but methodologically
     just as ambiguous and undefined.) 'Absolute spirit' is the truth
     of the preceding moment, of history and therefore, in accordance
     with Hegel's logic, it would have to have annulled and preserved
     history within itself. However, in the dialectical method history
     cannot be so transcended and this is the message at the end of
     Hegel's *Philosophy of History* where at the climax of the system,
     at the moment where the 'absolute spirit' realises itself, history
     makes its reappearance and points beyond philosophy in its
     turn: "That the determinants of thought had this importance
     is a further insight that does not belong within the history of
     philosophy. These concepts are the simplest revelation of the

spirit of the world: this in its most concrete form is history."
Werke XV, p. 618.

63   Werke I, p. 174. Needless to say, Fichte places an even heavier
emphasis on chance.
64   Cf. the essay "What is orthodox Marxism?"
65   With this the Logic itself becomes problematic. Hegel's postulate
that the concept is "reconstituted being" (Werke V, 30) is only
possible on the assumption of the real creation of the identical
subject-object. A failure at this point means that the concept
acquires a Kantian, idealistic emphasis which is in conflict with
its dialectical function. To show this in detail would be well
beyond the scope of this study.

NOTES ON SECTION III

1   Cf. "What is orthodox Marxism?", "Class Consciousness" and
"The Changing Function of Historical Materialism". In view
of the fact that the themes in these essays are so closely interrelated
it has regrettably not always been possible to avoid repetition.
2   Nachlass II, p. 132. [*The Holy Family*, Chapter 4.]
3   *Grenzen der naturwissenschaftlichen Begriffsbildung*, 2nd ed., p. 562.
4   Ibid., pp. 606–7.
5   Cf. "What is orthodox Marxism?"
6   *Capital* I, p. 441.
7   For eighteenth century materialism, see Plekhanov, op. cit.,
p. 51. In Section I we have shown how this belief underlies the
bourgeois theory of crisis, the theory of the origin of law, etc.
In history itself anyone can easily understand that an approach
that is not world-historical and that does not relate to the overall
development must necessarily interpret the most important
turning-points of history as senseless cataclysms as their causes
lie outside its scheme. This can be seen, e.g. in the Germanic
Migrations, in the downward trend of German history from the
Renaissance on, etc.
8   Hegel's Werke II, p. 73.
9   Ibid., p. 275.
10   Cf. e.g. *Capital* III, pp. 336, 349–50, 370–1, 374–6, 383–4.
11   *Die Philosophie des Geldes*, p. 531.
12   *The Poverty of Philosophy*, p. 135.
13   I would refer the reader once again to Plekhanov's statement of
the dilemma confronting older forms of materialism. As Marx
showed in his critique of Bruno Bauer (Nachlass II, pp. 178 et seq.)
every bourgeois view of history logically ends up by mechanising
the 'masses' and irrationalising the hero. However, exactly
the same dualism can be found in such thinkers as Carlyle or
Nietzsche. Even a cautious thinker like Rickert, (despite some
reservations, e.g. op. cit., p. 380) is inclined to regard 'milieu'
and the 'movements of masses' as subject to natural laws and to

see only the isolated personality as a historical individual. Op. cit., pp. 444, 460-1.

14   *A Contribution to the Critique of Political Economy*, p. 304.

15   *The Poverty of Philosophy*, pp. 128-9.

16   *Die Kritik der praktischen Vernunft*, pp. 38-9, Cf. ibid., pp. 24, 123; *Die Grundlegung der Metaphysik der Sitten*, pp. 4, 38. Cf. also Hegel's critique, Werke III, pp. 133 et seq.

17   Werke III, p. 147.

18   Ibid., p. 262.

19   Ibid., pp. 432-5. Plehkanov deserves the credit for having pointed to the importance of this side of Hegel's Logic for the distinction between evolution and revolution as early as 1891 (Neue Zeit X/I, pp. 280 et seq.). Regrettably his insight was neglected by later theorists.

20   On the methodological side of this question, see above all the first part of Hegel's *Philosophy of Religion*. In particular, Werke XI, pp. 158-9. "There is no immediate knowledge. Immediate knowledge is where we have no *consciousness* of mediation; but it is mediated for all that." Similarly in the Preface to the Phenomenology: "The true is not an *original* unity as such or an *immediate* one, but only this *reconstituting* equality or reflection in otherness in itself." Werke II, p. 15.

21   Engels in fact accepted the Hegelian theory of the false (which has its finest definition in the Preface to the Phenomenology, Werke II, p. 30 et seq.). Cf. his analysis of the role of 'evil' in history, *Feuerbach and the End of Classical German Philosophy*, in S.W. II, p. 345 et seq. This refers, of course, only to the truly original representatives of bourgeois thought. Epigones, eclectics and simple partisans of the interests of a declining class belong in quite a different category.

22   On this distinction between the proletariat and the bourgeoisie, see the essay on "Class Consciousness".

23   *A Contribution to the Critique of Political Economy*, p. 31.

24   *Capital* I, p. 572.

25   All so-called theories of abstinence are based on this. We may mention especially the importance attributed by Max Weber to 'inner worldly asceticism' in the origins of the 'spirit' of capitalism. Marx, too, confirms this fact when he points out that for the capitalist "his own private consumption is a robbery perpetrated on accumulation, just as in book-keeping by double entry, the private expenditure of the capitalist is placed on the debtor side of his account against his capital". *Capital* I, p. 592.

26   *Wages, Price and Profit* in S.W. I, p. 398.

27   *Anti-Dühring*, p. 141.

28   *Capital* I, p. 309.

29   *A Contribution to the Critique of Political Economy*, p. 29.

30   Thus Marx writes to Engels: "These gentry, the economists, have hitherto overlooked the extremely simple point that the form: *20 yards of linen = 1 coat* is only the undeveloped basis of

20 yards of linen = £2, and that therefore the *simplest form of a commodity*, in which its value is not yet expressed as a relation to all other commodities but only as something *differentiated* from the commodity in its natural form, contains *the whole secret of the money form* and with it, in embryo, of *all the bourgeois forms of the product of labour*. (22 June, 1867). *Selected Correspondence*, Moscow, n.d., p. 228. On this point see also the magisterial analysis of the distinction between exchange value and price in *A Contribution to the Critique of Political Economy* where it is shown that in this distinction "all the tempests that threaten the commodity in the real process of circulation are concentrated", p. 80.

31 Werke II, p. 27.

32 *A Contribution to the Critique of Political Economy*, p. 299.

33 Thus Marx says of Feuerbach's use of the term 'species'—and all such views fail to advance beyond Feuerbach and many indeed do not go as far—that "it can be understood only as the inward dumb generality which *naturally* unites the many individuals". *6th Thesis on Feuerbach*.

34 Nachlass II, p. 54. [*Critical Notes on "The King of Prussia and Social Reform"*.] We are interested here solely in the methodical implications. Mehring's question (ibid., p. 30) about the extent to which Marx overestimated the consciousness of the Weavers' Uprising does not concern us here. *Methodologically* he has provided a perfect description of the development of revolutionary class consciousness in the proletariat and his later views (in the *Manifesto, Eighteenth Brumaire*, etc.) about the difference between bourgeois and proletarian revolutions are wholly in line with this.

35 We have in mind here Bachofen's analysis of the *Orestia* and of its significance for the history of social development. The fact that Bachofen's ideological timidity prevented him from going further than the correct interpretation of the drama is additional proof of the rightness of the views set out here.

36 On this point cf. Marx's analysis of the industrial reserve army and surplus-population. *Capital* I, pp. 628 et seq.

37 *Encyclopädie*, § 15.

38 *Capital* I, pp. 234–5. Cf. also *Wages, Price and Profit*, S.W. I, pp. 401–2.

39 Cf. what is said on the 'post festum' nature of the consciousness of the bourgeoisie in the essays "The Changing Function of Historical Materialism" and "What is Orthodox Marxism?"

40 A detailed examination of this question is not possible here although this distinction would enable us to differentiate clearly between the ancient and the modern world, because Heraclitus' self-annulling conception of the object bears the closest resemblance to the reified structure of modern thought. This alone would clearly reveal the limitation of the thought of the Ancients, viz. their inability to grasp dialectically their own societal existence in the present and hence also in history, as a limitation of classical

society. In various other contexts, but always in a way that leads to the same methodological goal, Marx has made the same point about Aristotle's 'economics'. Hegel's and Lassalle's overestimation of the modernity of Heraclitus' dialectics has symptomatic importance for their own. This only means, however, that this limitation of the thought of the 'Ancients' (the ultimately uncritical attitude towards the historical conditioning of the formations from which thought arises) remains decisive for them, too, and then emerges in the contemplative and speculative character of their thought, as opposed to a material and practical one.

41 *Capital* I, pp. 570, 572–3. Here too, as we have already emphasised, the change from quantity to quality is seen to be a characteristic of *every single* moment. The quantified moments only remain quantitative when regarded separately. Seen as aspects of a process they appear as qualitative changes in the economic structure of capital.

42 *Wage, Labour and Capital*, S.W. I, p. 86.

43 Cf. "The Changing Function of Historical Materialism". On fact and reality see the essay "What is Orthodox Marxism?"

44 Cf. the dispute about the disappearance or increase of the medium-sized firms in Rosa Luxemburg, *Soziale Reform oder Revolution*, pp. 11 et seq.

45 *Capital* III, p. 326.

46 Ibid., pp. 349–50. The rate of interest is thus "given as a fixed magnitude, like the price of commodities on the market" and the general profit rate is expressly contrasted with it as an opposing tendency. Ibid., p. 359. We see here the fundamental issue dividing us from bourgeois thought.

47 Cf. the essay "What is Orthodox Marxism?".

48 *Origin of the Family*, S.W. II, p. 92.

49 Cf. Marx's comments on Bentham, *Capital* I, pp. 609–10.

50 A fine elucidation of the different stages can be found in *Capital* III, pp. 806 et seq.

51 Modern pragmatism provides a model illustration of this.

52 Nachlass II (*The Holy Family*, chap. 8), p. 304.

53 Nachlass I, p. 384. (*Critique of Hegel's Philosophy of Right* in Bottomore, Early Writings, p. 43.) The italics are mine.

54 On this point, see Max Weber's essays in Vol. I of his Sociology of Religion. Whether we accept his causal interpretation or not is irrelevant to a judgement of his factual material. On the connection between Calvinism and capitalism, see also Engels' remarks in *Über historischen Materialismus*, Neue Zeit XI, I. p. 43. The same structure of ethics and existence is still active in the Kantian system. Cf. e.g. the passage in the *Critique of Practical Reason*, p. 120, which sounds wholly in line with Franklin's acquisitive Calvinist ethics. An analysis of the profound similarities would lead us too far away from our theme.

55 *Thomas Münzer*, pp. 73 et seq.

56 Werke III, pp. 37–8. Except that there is also an echo of the

nostalgia—here of no importance—for natural social formations.
Cf. Hegel's methodologically correct negative criticisms in
Glauben und Wissen, Werke I, pp. 105 et seq. His positive conclu-
sions, of course, amount to much the same thing.

57 Lassalle, Werke, Cassirer Verlag, V, pp. 275–6. The extent to
which Lassalle, by exalting a notion of the state founded in natural
law, moves on to the terrain of the bourgeoisie, can be seen not
only in the development of particular theories of natural law
that have deduced the impropriety of every organised movement
of the proletariat from the very idea of 'freedom' and the 'dignity
of man'. (Cf. e.g. Max Weber, *Wirtschaft und Gesellschaft*, p. 497,
on American natural law.) But also C. Hugo, the cynical founder
of the historical school of law arrives at a similar theoretical
construction—though he does so in order to prove the opposite
of Lassalle—viz. the view that it is possible to devise certain
rights that transform men into a commodity without negating
their 'human dignity' in other spheres. *Naturrecht*, § 144.

58 Cf. the essay "Class Consciousness".

59 These views can be found in an undiluted form in Kautsky's
latest programmatic statement. One need not go beyond the
rigid, mechanical separation of politics and economics to see
that he is treading the same mistaken path as Lassalle. His
conception of democracy is too familiar to require a fresh analysis
here. And as for his economic fatalism, it is symptomatic that even
where Kautsky admits that it is impossible to make concrete
predictions about the economic phenomenon of crises it remains
self-evident for him that the course of events will unfold according
to the laws of the capitalist economy, p. 57.

60 Lenin's achievement is that he rediscovered this side of Marxism
that points the way to an understanding of its *practical* core. His
constantly reiterated warning to seize the 'next link' in the chain
with all one's might, that link on which the fate of the totality
depends in that one moment, his dismissal of all utopian demands,
i.e. his 'relativism' and his 'Realpolitik': all these things are
nothing less than the practical realisation of the young Marx's
Theses on Feuerbach.

61 It must now be self-evident that totality is a problem of category
and in particular a problem of revolutionary action. It is obvious
that we cannot regard a method as authentically totalising if it
deals with 'all problems' in a substantive manner (which is, of
course, an impossibility) while remaining contemplative. This is
to be referred above all to the social-democratic treatment of
history in which a plethora of material is designed constantly to
divert attention from social action.

62 Cf. the essay "Towards a Methodology of the Problem of Organisation".

63 *Feuerbach and the End of Classical German Philosophy*, S.W. II, p. 350.

64 Hegel, Werke XI, p. 160.

65 This rejection of the metaphysical import of bourgeois materialism

does not affect our historical evaluation of it: it was the ideological form of the bourgeois revolution, and as such it remains of *practical relevance* as long as the bourgeois revolution remains relevant (including its relevance as an aspect of the proletarian revolution). On this point, see my essays on "Moleschott", "Feuerbach" and "Atheism" in the Rote Fahne, Berlin; and above all Lenin's comprehensive essay "Under the Banner of Marxism", The Communist International, 1922, No. 21.

66 Lask has very logically introduced a distinction between an antecedent and subsequent region ['vorbildlich' and 'nach-bildlich'] (Die Lehre vom Urteil.) This does indeed enable him to eliminate pure Platonism, the reflective duality of idea and reality—in the spirit of criticism—but it then experiences a logical resurrection.

67 Purely logical and systematic studies simply refer to the historical point at which we find ourselves: they signify our temporary inability to grasp and represent the totality of categoric problems as the problems of a historical reality in the process of revolution-ising itself.

68 Cf. on this point Hegel's *Phenomenology*, especially Werke II, pp. 73 et seq., where this problem receives its profoundest analysis. See also Ernst Bloch's theory of the "opacity of the lived moment" and his theory of "knowledge that has not yet become conscious".

69 Hegel, Werke XII, p. 207.

70 On the relationship between a theory of praxis to a practical theory, see the interesting essay by Josef Révai in *Kommunismus* I, Nos. 46-9, "The Problem of Tactics", even though I am not in agreement with all his conclusions.

71 *Encyclopädie*, §16.

72 Ibid., § 192.

73 Hegel, Werke XIII, pp. 299 et seq.

74 Letter dated 12 December, 1851. Ed. G. Mayer, p. 41.

75 Bukharin, *Ökonomie der Transformationsperiode*, pp. 50-1.

The Changing Function of Historical Materialism

*A Lecture given at the inauguration of the Institute for
Research into Historical Materialism in Budapest*

THE victory gained by the proletariat evidently confronts it with
the task of perfecting as far as possible the intellectual weapons
which have hitherto enabled it to hold its own in the class struggle.
Among these weapons historical materialism is, of course, pre-
eminent.

Historical materialism was one of the proletariat's most potent
weapons at a time when it was oppressed and now that it is preparing to rebuild society and culture anew it is natural to take
the method over into the new age. If only for this reason it was
necessary to found this Institute with the aim of applying the
methods of historical materialism to the historical sciences as a
whole. Up to now historical materialism was doubtless a superb
weapon but from a scientific point of view it was hardly more than
a programme, an indication of the way in which history ought to
be written. Now, however, a further task devolves upon it: the
whole of history really has to be re-written; the events of the past
have to be sorted, arranged and judged from the point of view of
historical materialism. We must strive to turn historical materialism
into the authentic method for carrying out concrete historical
research and for historiography in general.

But here we must answer the question why this has only now
become possible. A superficial answer would be to claim that the
time was only now ripe for converting historical materialism into
a scientific method because it was only now that the proletariat
had seized power and with it control of the physical and intellectual forces without which this could not be achieved and which
society as it was would never have made available to it. However,
much deeper underlying factors than the fact of naked power
place the proletariat of today in a position to organise science
as it thinks fit. These deeper factors are closely connected with the
profound change in function resulting from the dictatorship of
the proletariat, i.e. from the fact that the class struggle is now
waged from above and not from below. This change in function

affects all the organs of the proletariat, its whole emotional and intellectual outlook, its class situation and its class consciousness. It is absolutely imperative for us to discuss these factors today as we inagurate this Institute.

What is historical materialism? It is no doubt a scientific method by which to comprehend the events of the past and to grasp their true nature. In contrast to the historical methods of the bourgeoisie, however, it also permits us to view the present historically and hence scientifically so that we can penetrate beneath the surface and perceive the profounder historical forces which in reality control events.

Historical materialism has, therefore, a much greater value for the proletariat than that of a method of historical research. It is one of the most important of all its weapons. For the class struggle of the proletariat signifies at the same time the awakening of its class consciousness. And this awakening followed everywhere from an understanding of the true situation, of the actually existing historical connections. And it is this that gives the class struggle of the proletariat its special place among other class struggles, namely that it obtains its sharpest weapon from the hand of true science, from its clear insight into reality. Whereas in the class struggles of the past the most varied ideologies, religious, moral and other forms of 'false consciousness' were decisive, in the case of the class struggle of the proletariat, the war for the liberation of the last oppressed class, the revelation of the unvarnished truth became both a war-cry and the most potent weapon. By laying bare the springs of the historical process historical materialism became, in consequence of the class situation of the proletariat, an instrument of war.

The most important function of historical materialism is to deliver a precise judgement on the capitalist social system, to unmask capitalist society. Throughout the class struggle of the proletariat, therefore, historical materialism has constantly been used at every point, where, by means of all sorts of ideological frills, the bourgeoisie had concealed the true situation, the state of the class struggle; it has been used to focus the cold rays of science upon these veils and to show how false and misleading they were and how far they were in conflict with the truth. For this reason the chief function of historical materialism did not lie in the elucidation of pure scientific knowledge, but in the field of action. Historical materialism did not exist for its own sake, it existed so that the proletariat could understand a situation and so that, armed with this knowledge, it could act accordingly.

In the capitalist era, then, historical materialism was an instrument of war. In consequence, the resistance offered to historical materialism by bourgeois thought was by no means simply a matter of narrow-mindedness. It was the expression of the bourgeoisie's correct class instinct as embodied in bourgeois historiography. It would be suicidal for the bourgeoisie to grant recognition to historical materialism. Any member of the bourgeoisie who admitted the scientific truth of historical materialism would thereby abandon his own class consciousness and with it the strength needed to defend the interests of his own class effectively. On the other hand, it would be no less suicidal for the proletariat to remain satisfied with the scientific value of historical materialism and to see in it nothing more than an instrument of knowledge. The essence of the class struggle of the proletariat can in fact be defined by its union of theory and practice so that knowledge leads to action without transition.

The survival of the bourgeoisie rests on the assumption that it never obtains a clear insight into the social preconditions of its own existence. A glance at the history of the nineteenth century reveals a profound and continuous parallel between the gradual growth of this self-knowledge and the decline of the bourgeoisie. At the end of the eighteenth century the bourgeoisie was ideologically strong and unbroken. The same thing was still true at the beginning of the nineteenth century when its ideology, the idea of bourgeois freedom and democracy had not yet been undermined from within by the natural workings of economics, and when the bourgeoisie could still hope, and moreover hope in good faith that this democratic, bourgeois freedom and the supremacy of economics would one day lead to the salvation of all mankind.

The glory and the pathos of this faith does more than fill the history of the first bourgeois revolutions—above all the Great French Revolution. It is this, too, which confers upon the great scientific pronouncements of the bourgeois class (e.g. the economics of Adam Smith and Ricardo) their forthrightness and the strength to strive for the truth and to reveal what they have discovered without cloaking it.

The history of bourgeois ideology is the history of the destruction of this faith in its mission to save the world by making the whole of society bourgeois. From the time of Sismondi's theory of

crisis and Carlyle's social criticism the process by which bourgeois ideology has undermined itself develops with constantly
increasing intensity. What began as the reactionary feudal
criticism of emergent capitalism develops increasingly, with
the criticism between mutually hostile ruling classes into the
self-criticism of the bourgeoisie and finally turns into its bad conscience when criticism is progressively concealed and kept secret.
As Marx observes: "The bourgeoisie had a true insight into the
fact that all the weapons which it had forged against feudalism
turned their points against itself, that all the means of education
which it had produced rebelled against its own civilisation, that
all the gods which it had created had fallen away from it."[1]

For this reason the idea of class struggle is openly expressed
twice in the history of bourgeois ideology. It is one of the determining factors in its 'heroic' period, in its vigorous struggle for
social hegemony (above all in France where political and ideological conflicts were most acute), and it recurs in its last period of
crisis and dissolution. The social theory of the great employers'
associations, for example, is often the frank and even cynical
expression of a class point of view. The final, imperialist, phase of
capitalism is generally given to modes of self-expression that
ideologically tear down veils and that produce in the ruling circles
of the bourgeoisie an ever more explicit description of 'what is the
case'. (Consider, for example, the ideology of the power-state in
imperialist Germany and also the fact that the economy of the
war and the post-war periods has forced the theoreticians of the
bourgeoisie to see economic forms as consisting of something more
than purely fetishistic relations and to concede that there is a
connection between economics and the gratification of human
wants.)

This is not to say that the limitations imposed on the bourgeoisie by its place in the process of production could be overcome, or that, like the proletariat, the bourgeoisie could henceforth start from a position of a true knowledge of the real driving
forces of history. On the contrary, this lucidity with regard to
individual problems or phases only makes the blindness *vis-à-vis*
the totality stand out more clearly. For this 'lucidity' is on the one
hand for 'internal use only'; the same progressive group of the
bourgeoisie which saw through the economic ramifications of
imperialism more clearly than many 'socialists' knows very well
that this knowledge would be highly dangerous for sections of its

own class, to say nothing of society as a whole. (Consider in this context the metaphysics of history that tends to accompany imperialist theories of power.) But if this does in part point to a conscious deception it does, on the other hand, indicate something rather more than a simple deception. That is to say, the amalgam of 'clear insight' in the case of individual economic problems, with a fantastic and chaotic metaphysical view of the state, of society and of the historical process as a whole is the inevitable consequence of the class situation of the bourgeoisie and from this not even the more conscious strata are exempted. But whereas at the period of its ascendency the extreme limits of its understanding of society were still obscure and unconscious, today the objective disintegration of capitalist society is reflected in the total incoherence and irreconcilability of opinions joined together in one ideology.

In this we find expressed a—mostly unconscious and certainly unacknowledged—ideological capitulation to historical materialism. For the economic theories now being developed no longer have a purely bourgeois base, as they did in the age of classical economics. Precisely in countries like Russia where the growth of capitalism came relatively late and where, in consequence, there was a direct need for theoretical backing it turned out that the theory that did emerge bore a strongly 'Marxist' character. (Struve, Tugan-Baranovski, etc.) But the same phenomenon was observable at the same time in Germany (e.g. Sombart) and in other countries. And the theories of war-economy and planned economies show that this tendency is becoming stronger.

There is no contradiction in the fact that simultaneously—say, from Bernstein onwards—a section of socialist theory came more and more strongly under bourgeois influence. For even at the time clear-sighted Marxists realised that there was no question here of a conflict of aims within the workers' movement. With increasing frequency leading 'comrades' have crossed over openly into the bourgeois camp (the cases of Briand and Millerand, Parvus and Lensch are only the most notorious instances) and however this is to be judged from the standpoint of the proletariat, its meaning for the bourgeoisie is unmistakable: namely that it is incapable of defending its own position ideologically and with its own resources. It not only needs these renegades from the camp of the proletariat but also—and this is the main point at issue— it is unable to dispense with the scientific method of the proletariat, admittedly in a distorted form. The existence of the theoretical renegades from Bernstein to Parvus is doubtless the symptom of an ideological crisis within the proletariat; but at the same time it signifies the capitulation of the bourgeoisie before historical materialism.

For the proletariat fought capitalism by forcing bourgeois society into a self-knowledge which would inevitably make that society appear problematic to itself. *Parallel with the economic struggle a battle was fought for the consciousness of society. Now, to become conscious is synonymous with the possibility of taking over the leadership of society.* The proletariat is the victor in the class struggle not only on the level of power but, at the same time, in the battle for social consciousness, for in the last 50–60 years it has had increasing success in eroding bourgeois ideology and in evolving its own consciousness to the point where it becomes decisive for the whole of society.

Historical materialism is the most formidable weapon in this struggle. It is consequently just as much a function of the growth and disintegration of capitalist society as are other ideologies. This point has often been made with regard to historical materialism by bourgeois thinkers. A common argument against the validity of historical materialism and one regarded by bourgeois thought as decisive, is that the methods of historical materialism must be applied to itself. For it to be a valid system of thought it must be the case that every so-called ideological formation is a function of economic realities: and (as the ideology of the embattled proletariat) it, too, is *a fortiori* just such an ideology, and just such a function of capitalist society.

I believe that this objection can be upheld in part, but to concede it is not to the detriment of the scientific status of historical materialism. Historical materialism both can and must be applied to itself. But this must not be allowed to lead to total relativism, let alone to the conclusion that historical materialism is not the correct historical method. The substantive truths of historical materialism are of the same type as were the truths of classical economics in Marx's view: they are truths within a particular social order and system of production. As such, but only as such, their claim to validity is absolute. But this does not preclude the emergence of societies in which by virtue of their different social structures other categories and other systems of truth prevail. To what conclusion should we then come? Above all we must investigate the social premises of the substance of historical materialism just as Marx himself scrutinised the social and economic pre-conditions of the truths of classical economics.

The answer to this question can likewise be found in Marx. Historical materialism in its classical form (which has unfortunately only penetrated the general consciousness in a vulgarised form) means the *self-knowledge of capitalist society*. And this not only in the ideological sense outlined above. Rather is it the case that this ideological problem is itself nothing other than the intellectual expression of the objective economic situation. In this sense the decisive result of historical materialism is that the totality and the driving forces of capitalism cannot be grasped or conceptualised by the crude, abstract, unhistorical and external categories of the science of the bourgeoisie. Thus historical materialism is, in the first instance, a theory of bourgeois society and its economic structure. "But in theory," Marx observes, "it is assumed that the laws of capitalist production operate in their pure form. In reality there exists only approximation; but this approximation is the greater, the more developed the capitalist mode of production and the less it is adulterated and amalgamated with survivals of former economic conditions."[2]

This correspondence of theory with reality can be seen in the fact that, on the one hand, the laws of economics inform the whole of society, but, on the other hand, they are able to function as pure 'laws of nature' by virtue of their purely economic power, i.e. without the aid of non-economic factors. Marx frequently emphasises the distinction between capitalist and pre-capitalist societies as being the difference between a capitalism which is only just emerging and is therefore locked in struggle for the control of society and a capitalism which is already dominant. He says: "the law of supply and demand of labour . . . the dull compulsion of economic relations completes the subjection of the labourer to the capitalist. Direct, *extra-economic* force is of course still used, but *only exceptionally*. In the ordinary run of things, the labourer can be left to the 'natural laws of production'. . . . *It is otherwise during the historical genesis of capitalist production.*"[3]

From this economic structure (which is found, of course, only as a tendency, but as a tendency which decisively conditions every theory), it follows that the different aspects of the social structure can and must become independent of each other and, thereby, conscious of themselves. The great upsurge of the theoretical sciences at the end of the eighteenth and the beginning of the nineteenth centuries, classical economics in England and classical philosophy in Germany show that these partial systems, these aspects of the structure and evolution of bourgeois society, have gained a consciousness of their autonomy. Economics, law and the state appear here as *closed* systems which control the whole of society by virtue of the perfection of their own power and by their own built-in laws. So that when individual scholars, such as Andler, attempt to prove that all the particular truths attributed to historical materialism were in fact discovered before Marx and Engels they miss the essential point and would be mistaken even if their demonstration were valid on all points; and this is, of course, far from being the case. For, as far as *method* is concerned, historical materialism was an epoch-making achievement precisely because it was able to see that these apparently quite independent, hermetic and autonomous systems were really aspects of a comprehensive whole and that their apparent independence could be transcended.

This semblance of independence, however, is no mere 'error' simply to be 'corrected' by historical materialism. It is rather the intellectual and conceptual expression of the objective social structure of capitalist society. To annul it and to transcend it means, therefore, to transcend capitalist society—in thought. It means anticipating its annulment by the accelerating power of thought. For this very reason, however, the annulled independence of the special systems is preserved within the rightly understood totality. That is to say, the right understanding of their lack of autonomy, their dependence on the economic structure of the whole of society entails the knowledge that this 'semblance' of independence, of cohesion and autonomy is a necessary part of the way in which they manifest themselves in capitalist society.

In pre-capitalist society the particular aspects of the economic process (as, for instance, interest-bearing capital and the production of commodities itself) remain separate from each other in a completely abstract way which permits neither an immediate interaction nor one that can be raised to the level of social consciousness. On the other hand, some of these aspects join with each other or with non-economic factors in the economic process to form—within such social structures—an indissoluble unity (for example, handicraft and agriculture on the feudal manor, or tax and rent in Indian serfdom).

In capitalism, however, all the elements of the structure of society interact dialectically. Their apparent independence of each other, their way of concentrating themselves into self-regulating systems, the fetishistic semblance of autonomy, all this is—as an essential aspect of capitalism as understood by the bourgeoisie—the necessary transition to a proper and complete understanding of them. Only by taking these tendencies towards independence to their logical conclusion (a thing which bourgeois science, of course, never managed to do even during its best periods) can they be understood as being mutually interdependent and as belonging to and fitting into the totality of the economic structure of society.

The Marxist point of view which regards, e.g. the economic problems of capitalism no longer from the standpoint of the individual capitalist but from that of the classes, could be reached subjectively, in the context of the history of dogma, only as the continuation and the dialectic reversal of the purely capitalist outlook. On the other hand, the 'obedience of the phenomena to natural laws', which is claimed here, i.e. their complete independence of human will, knowledge and purpose, forms the objective precondition for their reshaping at the hands of materialist dialectics. Problems like accumulation or average profit-rates, but also the relation of the state and the law to the total economy, show quite clearly how appearances which are constantly unmasking themselves are the historical and methodical precondition of the construction and application of historical materialism.

It is therefore no accident—as indeed it could hardly be otherwise when we are concerned with real truths about society—that historical materialism evolved into a scientific method around the middle of the nineteenth century. It is not the result of chance that social truths are always found when the soul of an age is revealed in them; the age in which the reality corresponding to the method becomes incarnate. For, as we have already explained, historical materialism is simply the self-knowledge of capitalist society.

Nor is it an accident that economics became an independent dicipline under capitalism. Thanks to its commodity and communications arrangements capitalist society has given the whole of economic life an identity notable for its autonomy, its cohesion and its exclusive reliance on immanent laws. This was something quite unknown in earlier forms of society. For this reason, classical economics with its system of laws is closer to the natural sciences than to any other. The economic system whose essence and laws it investigates does in fact show marked similarities with the objective structure of that Nature which is the object of study of physics and the other natural sciences. It is concerned with relations that are completely unconnected with man's humanity and indeed with any anthropomorphisms—be they religious, ethical, aesthetic or anything else. Man appears in it only as an abstract number, as something which can be reduced to number or to numerical relations. Its concern, as Engels put it, is with laws that are only understood, not controlled, with a situation in which—to quote Engels again—the producers have lost control of the conditions of life of their own society. As a result of the objectification, the reification of society, their economic relations have achieved complete autonomy, they lead an independent life, forming a closed, self-validating system. Hence it is no accident that capitalist society became the classical terrain for the application of historical materialism.

If we now consider historical materialism as a scientific method it is evident that it can also be applied to earlier societies antedating capitalism. This has indeed been done and not without success; at any rate it has resulted in some very interesting discoveries. But if we do bring historical materialism to bear upon pre-capitalist periods a very essential and weighty methodological difficulty makes itself felt, one which did not appear in the critique of capitalism.

This difficulty has been noted by Marx in countless places in his main works; Engels then formulated it clearly in the *Origin of the Family*: it lies in the *structural* difference between the age of civilisation and the epochs that preceded it. And with regard to the latter, Engels emphasises that "as long as production was maintained on this basis it could not grow beyond the control of the producers and it could not raise any strange, phantom powers against them, as is the case regularly and inevitably under civilisation".[4] For here "the producers have lost control of the aggregate production of the conditions of their own life. . . . Products and production become the playthings of chance. But chance is only one pole of a nexus whose other pole is necessity." And Engels then demonstrates how, from the resultant structure of society, consciousness follows in the shape of 'natural laws'. And indeed this dialectical interaction of chance and necessity, i.e.

the classical ideological form of the pre-eminence of economics, becomes more intense in proportion to the degree in which social phenomena escape the control of men and become autonomous.

The purest, indeed one might say the only pure form of the control of society by its natural laws is found in capitalist production. For is it not the world-historical mission of the process of civilisation that culminates in capitalism, to achieve control over *nature*? These 'natural laws' of society which rule the lives of men like 'blind forces' (even when their 'rationality' is recognised and indeed all the more powerfully when that is the case) have the task of subordinating the categories of nature to the process of socialisation. In the course of history they have performed this function. However, it was a lengthy process and one full of setbacks. While it was still taking place, i.e. during the time when these natural forces of society had *not yet* become dominant, it is evident that natural relations—both in the case of the 'metabolic changes' between man and nature and also in the relations between men—retained the upper hand and dominated man's social being and hence also the forms in which this existence was expressed intellectually and emotionally, etc. (as in religion, art and philosophy). "In all forms of society where landed property predominates," Marx observes, "the natural relation is paramount. In those where capital is predominant the social, historically created element prevails."[5] And Engels, in a letter to Marx, gives the same idea an even sharper formulation: "It just proves that at this stage the mode of production is less decisive than the degree to which the old blood bonds and the old mutual community of the sexes in the tribe have been dissolved."[6] So that in his opinion monogamy is the first form of the family "which was based not upon natural conditions but on economic ones".[7]

Of course, we have to do here with a lengthy process whose various stages are not mechanically separated from each other but which merge insensibly. But the general trend is clear enough: "The receding of natural limits"[8] in all areas; from which follows — *e contrario* and for our present problem—that these natural limits existed in all pre-capitalist societies and that they decisively conditioned all the social manifestations of man. Marx and Engels have demonstrated this so often and so convincingly with reference to economic categories that it must suffice here simply to point to their work. (Consider, for example, the development of the division of labour, the forms of surplus labour, of ground rent, etc.) Engels adds in several places[9] that when dealing with primitive stages of society it is quite wrong to speak of law in our sense.

This difference of structure appears even more decisively in those areas which Hegel designates those of the absolute spirit, in contrast to the forms of the objective spirit (economics, law and the state) which shape social, purely human interrelations.[10] For the former (art, religion and philosophy) are also essentially, although in ways that differ from each other, involvements of man with nature, both with the nature that surrounds him and with that which he finds within himself. Of course, this distinction too should not be understood mechanically. Nature is a societal category. That is to say, whatever is held to be natural at any given stage of social development, however this nature is related to man and whatever form his involvement with it takes, i.e. nature's form, its content, its range and its objectivity are all socially conditioned.

From this it follows, on the one hand, that the question whether in any given society a direct confrontation with nature is at all possible is one that can only be answered from within historical materialism, because the objective possibility of such a confrontation depends upon the "economic structure of society". But on the other hand, when these connections do exist in this socially conditioned form they develop according to their own inner laws and they preserve a much greater independence of their basis in the life of the society from which they (necessarily) spring than do the formations of the 'objective spirit'. Even these often manage to survive the demise of the social foundations to which they owe their existence. But in that event they survive as obstacles to progress which have to be swept away or by changing their functions they adapt themselves to the new economic circumstances. (The history of law is rich in instances of both possibilities.) In contrast to these, the survival of the formations of the absolute spirit—and to a certain extent this justifies the Hegelian terminology—can be due to their value, their continued relevance or even exemplary status. That is to say, the relations between origin and validity are much more complex here than in the case of the forms of the objective spirit. Marx saw the problem clearly: "But the difficulty does not consist in realising that Greek art and epic are bound to certain social forms of development. The difficulty is that they still give us artistic pleasure and that, in a sense, they stand out as norms and as models that cannot be equalled."[11]

This stability in the value of art, the semblance of its nature as something wholly above history and society, rests upon the fact that in art we find above all a dialogue between man and nature. This tendency goes so far that even the social relations between men to which it gives shape are transformed back into a kind of 'nature'. And if—as we have emphasised—even these natural relations are socially conditioned, if in consequence they change when society changes, this is still not the whole story. For they are based on factors which in contrast to the uninterrupted succession of purely social forms preserve the—subjectively— valid appearance of 'eternity'[12] since they are able to survive the manifold and very profound changes in the forms of society and since (sometimes) even more profound social changes, changes which mark off whole epochs from each other, are necessary to render them invalid.

It might seem as if the issue turned on a merely quantitative distinction between immediate and mediated relations to nature, or alternatively between immediate and mediated effects of the 'economic structure' upon the various social institutions. However, it is only from the point of view of capitalism that these quantitative distinctions constitute quantitative approximations to its own system of social organisation. From the standpoint of an understanding of how the pre-capitalist societies were *really constituted* these quantitative gradations signify qualitative differences which are expressed epistemologically as the hegemony of completely different systems of categories and as the completely different functions of particular sectors within the framework of society as a whole. Even in economics qualitatively *new* laws come into being. And this not only in the sense that laws are modified in accordance with the requirements of the subject matter to which they are applied. Over and above this, different laws are seen to obtain in different social milieus and the validity of any given type of law is tied to quite definite social presuppositions. It is only necessary to compare the conditions of the exchange of commodities at their value and the conditions of the exchange of commodities at their price of production in order to gain a clear picture of the way laws change even in the realm of pure economics.[13]

Of course, it is self-evident that a society based on the simple exchange of commodities is already, in one sense, close to the capitalist type, while in another sense it exhibits a qualitatively different structure. These qualitative differences increase in proportion to the hold of the natural relation over a given society (or over a particular form, such as art, within a given society). Thus as long as, within the framework of a close correlation in the mode of the division of labour, the bond between handicraft (the production of the consumer goods of daily life, including furniture, clothes but also house construction) and art in the narrower sense is very close, as long as the aesthetic and conceptual boundaries between the two cannot be disentangled (as is the case for instance with folk art), then the laws determining the evolution of the handicrafts (whose technique and organisation often remain immobile for centuries) in their relation to art (which develops according to its own immanent laws), are qualitatively different from those that operate under capitalism. For there the production of commodities advances purely economically 'of itself' in an unbroken revolutionary process. It is evident that in pre-capitalist societies the positive influence of art on handicraft production must be quite decisive. (As in the transition from Romanesque architecture to Gothic.) Under capitalism the scope of art is much more narrowly confined; it can exercise no determining influence upon the production of consumer goods and indeed the question of its own existence is decided by purely economic factors and the problems of technical production governed by them. (As in modern architecture.)

What has been outlined above with reference to art holds good also—though with important modifications—for religion. Here, too, Engels emphasises very strongly the distinction between the two periods.[14] However, religion is never able to express with such purity the relation of man to nature as was art and moreover its practical social functions play a much more direct role. But the variety of its functions, the qualitative distinction between the laws governing its historical role in an oriental theocratic society and in a 'state religion' under Western European capitalism are too obvious to require a commentary. For this reason Hegel's philosophy found itself confronted by the most difficult and indeed (for it) insuperable problems arising from the relation between state and religion (or alternatively society and religion). Hegel stood at the divide between two ages and when he undertook his systematisation he was faced with the problems of a world becoming capitalist while being rooted in a milieu in which, to use Marx's description, "one could speak neither of estates nor of classes but at most of past estates and unborn classes".[15]

The 'receding of natural limits' was already starting to reduce everything to the social level and to the reified relations of capitalism without yielding the possibility of a clear insight into the situation. For the contemporary state of knowledge made it impossible to look behind the two concepts of nature created by capitalism, viz. nature as the 'sum of the laws of nature' (the nature of modern mathematical science) and nature as a mood, as the model for a humanity 'ruined' by society (the nature of Rousseau and the Kantian ethic) and to glimpse their social unity, namely capitalist society with its dissolution of every natural bond.

To the degree to which capitalism carried out the socialisation of all relations it became possible to achieve self-knowledge, the true, concrete self-knowledge of man as a *social being*. And this not merely in the sense that earlier, undeveloped thought had been unable to grasp this fact (which existed then also), just as it is clear that Copernican astronomy was true before Copernicus but had not been recognised as such. But the absence of such self-knowledge on the part of society is itself only the intellectual reflex of the fact that objective, economic socialisation in this sense had not yet been established. The umbilical cord between man and nature had not yet been cut by the process of civilisation. For every piece of historical knowledge is an act of self-knowledge. The past only becomes transparent when the present can practise self-criticism in an appropriate manner; "as soon as it is ready for self-criticism to a certain extent, *dynamei* so to speak".[16] Until that time the past must either be naïvely identified with the structure of the present or else it is held to be wholly alien, barbaric and senseless, beyond all understanding. Thus we see that the road to an understanding of pre-capitalist societies with a non-reified structure could not be opened up until historical materialism had perceived that the reification of all man's social relations is both a product of capitalism and hence also an ephemeral, historical phenomenon. (The connection between the scientific exploration of primitive society and Marxism is no mere accident.) For only now, with the prospect opening up of re-establishing non-reified relations between man and man and between man and nature, could those factors in primitive, pre-capitalist formations be discovered in which these (non-reified)

forms were present—albeit in the service of quite different functions. And only now could the essential nature of these forms be
understood without their being distorted by the mechanical
application of the categories of capitalist society.

It was, therefore, no error to apply historical materialism in its
classical form rigorously and unconditionally to the history of
the nineteenth century. For in that century all the forces which
impinged upon society functioned in fact purely as the forms
of the 'objective spirit' become manifest. In pre-capitalist societies
this was not really the situation. In such societies economic life
did not yet possess that independence, that cohesion and imman-
ence, nor did it have the sense of setting its own goals and being
its own master that we associate with capitalist society.

It follows from this that historical materialism cannot be
applied in quite the same manner to pre-capitalist social formations as to capitalism. Here we need much more complex and
subtle analyses in order to show, on the one hand, what role was
played from among all the forces controlling society by the *purely*
economic forces in so far as they can be said to have existed in a
'pure' state in the strict sense of the word. And on the other hand
to show the impact of these economic forces upon the other
institutions of society. For this reason much greater caution is
required when applying historical materialism to earlier societies
than to changes in society in the nineteenth century. Connected
with this is the fact that while the nineteenth century could only
achieve self-knowledge by means of historical materialism,
research into the structure of older societies conducted on historical
materialist principles, e.g. into early Christianity or the early
history of the Orient such as Kautsky has undertaken, has shown
itself to be insufficiently subtle when compared with more recent
scientific studies, and their analyses have generally not been able
to do justice to their subject. Historical materialism has had its
greatest successes in the analysis of social formations, of law and
of related phenomena, e.g. strategy. For this reason studies such
as those of Mehring's—one thinks here of the *Lessing Legend*—
are profound and subtle when they are dealing with Napoleon's
or Frederick the Great's organisation of the army and the state.
But they become much less definitive and exhaustive when he
turns to the literary, scientific and religious institutions of the
same epoch.

Vulgar Marxism has wholly neglected this distinction. Its

application of historical materialism has succumbed to the same error that Marx castigated in the case of vulgar economics: it mistook purely historical categories, moreover categories relevant only to capitalist society, for eternally valid ones.

In the context of historical research this was no more than a scientific error and thanks to the fact that historical materialism was a weapon in the class struggle and not merely an instrument of scientific knowledge it had no further consequences. After all, even if we must recognise that Mehring's works have faults and that some of Kautsky's historical writings are not beyond reproach, it is still true that both men have merited undying fame for their achievements in awakening the class consciousness of the proletariat; as the instruments of the class struggle and as a driving force in that struggle their books have brought their authors an immortal renown which does more than compensate for any scientific errors—and this will be the judgement of later generations too.

However, the view of history favoured by the vulgar Marxists has also been a decisive influence on the actions of the workers' parties and on their political theory and tactics. The point at which the disagreement with vulgar Marxism is most clearly expressed is the question of *violence*; the role of violence in the struggle to gain and reap the fruits of victory in the proletarian revolution. It is, of course, not the first time that conflict has arisen between the organic evolution of historical materialism and its mechanical application; one recalls the debates about whether imperialism was a definite new phase in the history of capitalism or whether it was merely a transient episode. But the debates on the question of violence have contrived—unconsciously for many people—to throw the aspects crucial to methodology into high relief.

The position is that vulgar Marxist economism denies that violence has a place in the transition from one economic system to another. It bases itself on the 'natural laws' of economic development which are to bring about these transitions by their own impetus and without having recourse to a brute force lying 'beyond economics'. Almost always they cite the well-known sentence of Marx's: "No social order ever disappears before all the productive forces, for which there is room in it, have been developed; and new higher relations of production never appear before the material conditions of their existence have matured in the womb of the old society."[17] But intentionally, of course, they forget to add the explanation in the course of which Marx determined the point in history when this 'maturity' was to be achieved: "Of all the instruments of production, the greatest productive power is the revolutionary class itself. The organisation of revolutionary elements as a class *presupposes the existence of all the productive forces which could be engendered in the womb of the old society.*"[18]

It is evident from these sentences alone that to Marx the 'maturity' of the relations of production required for the transition from one form of production to another meant something quite different than to the vulgar Marxists. For the organisation of the revolutionary elements as a class not merely "as against Capital but also for itself",[19] the conversion of mere productive power into the lever of social change is not just a problem of class consciousness and the practical efficacy of conscious action, but at the same time it signals the beginning of the end for the 'natural laws' of economism. It means that the "greatest productive power" is in a state of rebellion against the system of production in which it is incorporated. A situation has arisen which can only be resolved by violence.

This is not the place to give even in outline a theory of violence and its role in history; nor to demonstrate that the radical separation of the concepts of violence and economics is an inadmissible abstraction and that an economic relation unconnected with violence whether latent or overt cannot be imagined. For example, it should not be forgotten that according to Marx[20] even in 'normal' times only the framework in which the relations between profits and wages are determined is established by pure and objective economic factors. "The fixation of its actual degree is only settled by the continuous struggle between capital and labour." It is evident that the chances of winning this struggle are themselves to a great extent conditioned by economic factors. However, this conditioning is subject to great variations due to 'subjective' factors connected with questions of 'violence', such as the organisation of the workers. The radical and mechanical separation of the concepts of violence and economics could only arise at all because, on the one hand, the growth of the fetish of the pure objectivity of economic relations obscures the fact that they are really relations between men and so transforms them into a second nature which envelops man with its fatalistic laws.

On the other hand, there is the circumstance that the—likewise fetishistic—legal form of organised violence distracts attention from its potential presence in and behind every economic relation; that distinctions like law and violence, order and insurrection, legal and illegal force cause the common foundation in violence of every institution of class societies to fade into the background. (For the process of 'metabolism' connecting primitive man with nature is no more economic in the strict sense of the word than the human relations of the time are regulated by law.)

Of course, there is a distinction between 'law' and force as also between latent and overt violence. However, it is not susceptible to an analysis in terms of jurisprudence, ethics or metaphysics, but only as the social and historical difference between different types of society. In some societies the order of production has acquired such complete mastery that it functions (as a rule) unproblematically and without conflict by virtue of its own immanent laws. In other societies, as the result of a conflict between different modes of production or the failure to achieve the (always relative) stabilisation of the shares apportioned to the various classes within a system of production, the use of naked 'extra-economic' violence must be the rule.

This stabilisation takes on a conservative form in non-capitalist societies and is expressed ideologically as the rule of tradition and of an order 'pre-ordained by God'. Only under capitalism, where this stabilisation means the stable hegemony of the bourgeoisie within an uninterrupted, revolutionary and dynamic economic process, does it take the shape of the 'natural rule' of the 'eternal iron laws' of political economy. And because every society tends to 'mythologise' the structure of its own system of production, projecting it back into the past, this past—and even more *the future*—appear likewise to be determined and controlled by such laws. It is then forgotten that the *birth* and the triumph of this system of production is the fruit of the most barbaric, brutal and naked use of 'extra-economic' violence. "Tantae molis erat," Marx exclaims at the end of his account of the growth of capitalism, "to give birth to the 'eternal laws of Nature' of the capitalist mode of production."[21]

However, seen from the perspective of world history, it is no less clear that the conflict between competing systems of production is decided as a rule by the social and economic superiority of one system. This superiority does not necessarily coincide with

K

its superiority in production technique. We know already that economic superiority takes the form of a series of violent measures and it is self-evident that the effectiveness of these measures depends on whether the class gaining supremacy in this way has the—world historical—preparedness and the mission to advance society.

But the question arises: how is the situation in which different systems of production compete to be understood socially? That is to say, to what extent is such a society to be perceived as a unified society in the Marxist sense when it lacks the objective precondition of such unity, namely a unified 'economic structure'? It is revealing that we are dealing here with marginal cases. Certainly, societies with a wholly unified, homogeneous structure are rare in history. (Capitalism has never been one of them and according to Rosa Luxemburg never can be.) In every society, therefore, the dominant system of production will put its stamp on those subordinated to it and will decisively modify their real economic structure. One may recall here the absorption of 'industrial' labour by the ground rent at the time of a predominantly natural economy and its control of the forms of its economy;[22] on the other hand, one may recall the forms taken by agriculture at the peak of capitalist development.

However, in the actual periods of transition society is governed by *none* of the systems of production; the struggle is still unresolved, no system has managed to impose its own economic structure upon society and—at least in tendency—to make it advance in the direction it desires. In such situations it is evidently not possible to speak of economic laws that determine the whole of society. The older system of production has lost control of society as a whole but the new system is not yet in the saddle. It is a situation of acute power struggles or of a latent balancing of opposing forces in which the laws of economics 'intermit' as one might say: the old law is *no longer valid* and the new law has *not yet* gained general acceptance.

To my knowledge the theory of historical materialism has not yet considered this question from the economic side. But the question did not escape the attention of the founders of historical materialism as we can see quite clearly in Engels' theory of the state. Engels points out that the state is "*as a rule* the state of the most powerful, *economically dominant class*". . . . "*By way of exception*, however, periods occur in which the warring classes *balance each other so nearly* that the state power, as ostensible mediator, acquires, for the moment, a certain degree of independence of both. Such was the absolute monarchy of the seventeenth and eighteenth centuries, which held the balance between the nobility and the class of burghers."[23]

It must not be forgotten, however, that the transition from capitalism to socialism will bring to light an economic structure different in principle from that of the transition from feudalism to capitalism. The rival systems of production will not *co-exist* as already perfected systems (as was seen in the beginnings of capitalism within the feudal order). But their rivalry is expressed as the insoluble contradiction *within* the capitalist system itself: namely as crisis. This structure makes capitalist production antagonistic from the very beginning. And the fact that in the crises of the past a solution was found within capitalism itself does nothing to mitigate the antagonism that arises when capital appears in the crises as a barrier to production "in a purely economic way, i.e. from the bourgeois point of view".[24]

A general crisis always signifies a point of—relative—suspension of the immanent laws of capitalist evolution; except that in the past the *capitalist class* has always been able to force production back *once again* into the path laid down by capitalism. It is not possible here to examine the question whether and to what extent the means used involved a deviation from the laws of 'normal' production and what role was played by conscious forces of organisation, 'extra-economic' factors, the non-capitalist basis, i.e. the expandibility of capitalism.[25] What must be made clear, however, is that explanations of crisis must—as was shown in Sismondi's debate with Ricardo and his school—go beyond the immanent laws of capitalism itself; that is to say, an economic theory that shows crises to be inevitable must, by the same token, point beyond capitalism. Nor can the 'solution' to a crisis ever mean that pre-crisis conditions can simply be resumed, advancing in conformity with their own immanent 'laws'. It always means a new line of development leading to yet another crisis. Marx formulates this pattern quite unambiguously: "This process would soon bring about the collapse of capitalist production if it were not for counteracting tendencies, which have a continuous decentralising effect alongside the centripetal one."[26]

Each crisis signifies a deadlock in the ordered evolution of capitalism, but it is only from the vantage-point of the proletariat that these deadlocks appear as a *necessary* aspect of capitalist production. Moreover, the distinctions, the degrees of intensity in the crisis, the dynamic significance of the points at which the laws of development are suspended, the impetus of the forces needed to bring the economy into action once more are likewise factors beyond the ken of the (self-contained) economics of the bourgeoisie; they can be understood only by historical materialism.

For it is evident that the greatest emphasis must be laid on whether the "greatest productive power" of the capitalist production system, namely the proletariat, experiences the crisis as object or as the subject of decision. For the crisis is always determined by the "antagonistic conditions of distribution", by the contradiction between the river of capital which flows on "in proportion to the impetus it already possesses" and "the narrow basis on which the conditions of consumption rest",[27] i.e. by the objective economic *existence of the proletariat*. But because of the immaturity of the proletariat and because of its inability to play any role in the process of production other than that of a "power of production" passively integrated into the economy and subordinated to its 'laws', this side of the antagonism never emerges into the open. This gives rise to the delusion that the 'laws' of economics can lead the way out of a crisis just as they lead into it. Whereas what happened in reality was that—because of the passivity of the proletariat—the capitalist class was in a position to break the deadlock and to start the machine going again. When compared to earlier crises the qualitative difference in the decisive, the 'last' crisis of capitalism (which obviously can consist of a whole age of successive individual crises) is, then, not merely that its extent and depth, its quantity, is simply transformed into a change in quality.

Or more accurately: this transformation is distinguished by the fact that the proletariat ceases to be merely the object of a crisis; the internal antagonisms of capitalist production which had already by definition implied a struggle between bourgeois and proletarian systems of production, the conflict between socialised forces of production and its individual anarchistic forms, now flourish openly. The proletariat had always striven "to destroy the ruinous effects of this natural law of capitalist production on their class";[28] it now leaves behind it the stage of negativity in which its effect was merely to impede, weaken or restrain, and it proceeds to a stage of greater activity. It is this that brings about the decisive qualitative change in the structure of the crisis. The measures taken by the bourgeoisie to break the deadlock of the crisis and which in the abstract (i.e. but for the intervention of the proletariat) are as available to it as in former crises, now become the arena where class warfare is openly waged. Violence becomes the decisive economic factor in the situation.

It appears then once again that these 'eternal laws of nature' are only valid for a particular epoch. They are not only the form in which the laws of social development of a particular sociological type become manifest (where, namely, the economic predomin-ance of a class is no longer contested); but even within that type they are relevant only for the specific mode of capitalist hege-mony. However, as we have pointed out, the connection between historical materialism and capitalist society is anything but an accident and so it is easy to understand why it regards the struc-ture of capitalism as paradigmatic and normal, as classical and canonical for its total view of world history. It is true that we have adduced examples that show clearly how cautious and critical Marx and Engels were in their judgements upon the specific structures and the specific laws governing the evolution of past, non-capitalist societies. But the internal nexus between the two factors did affect Engels at least to such an extent that, for example, in his interpretation of the dissolution of gentile societies he gives prominence to Athens as "an especially typical model" because its dissolution proceeds "quite purely without the interference of internal or external violence";[29] whereas the facts of the matter are that this is probably not quite true of Athens and is certainly not characteristic of the transition to this stage of development.

It is, however, on this very point that vulgar Marxist theory has concentrated: it denies the importance of violence as an 'economic power'. The underestimation by theorists of the importance of violence in history and the systematic denial of the role it played in the past form the basis in theory for the tactics of opportunism of vulgar Marxism. By elevating the laws of development specific to capitalist societies to the status of universal laws it lays the theoretical foundations essential to its aim of conferring immortality upon capitalist society in practice.

For a straightforward logical progression, as the vulgar Marxists understand it, the demand that socialism should be realised by virtue of the immanent laws of economics without recourse to 'extra-economic' violence is effectively synonymous with the

eternal survival of capitalist society. Nor is it the case that feudal
society gave birth to capitalism organically. It merely "brought
forth the material agencies for its own dissolution".[30] It freed
"forces and passions within the womb of society which feel themselves to be fettered by it". And in the course of a development
which includes "a series of forcible methods", these forces laid the
social foundations of capitalism. Only *after* this transition was
completed did the economic laws of capitalism come into
force.

It would be unhistorical and very naïve to expect more from
capitalism for its successors, the proletariat, than it received
itself at the hands of feudalism. The question of the propitious
moment for the transition has already been mentioned. What is
significant about this theory of 'maturity' is that it would like
to achieve socialism without the active participation of the proletariat. It thus forms a belated counterpart to Proudhon who also—
according to the *Communist Manifesto*—wished to retain the existing order 'without the proletariat'. This theory goes one step
further when it rejects the notion of violence in the name of
'organic evolution'. In so doing it forgets once again that the
whole 'organic evolution' is nothing but the theoretical expression
of capitalism as it has already evolved: it is its own historical
myth. It forgets likewise that its own real genesis had pro-
ceeded in quite the opposite manner. "These methods", Marx
says, "depend in part *on brute force*, e.g. the colonial system. But
they all employ the power of the State, the concentrated and
organised force of society, *to hasten, hothouse fashion*, the process of
transformation of the feudal mode of production into the capitalist
mode, *and to shorten the transition*."[31]

Thus, even if the function of violence in the transition from a
capitalist to a proletarian society were identical with its role in the
changeover from feudalism to capitalism, the actual course of
events teaches us that the 'unorganic', 'hothouse' and violent
nature of the transition proves nothing against the historical fact,
against the necessity and the 'healthiness' of the society thus
created. However, the question takes on another complexion
when we look a little more closely at the nature and function of
violence in this transition which signifies something fundamentally
and qualitatively new when compared to earlier transitions. We
repeat: the decisive importance of violence as an 'economic
power' is always relevant in the transitions from one system of

production to another; or in sociological terms: in periods when different competing systems of production exist side by side.

The nature of the conflicting systems of production will, however, determine the character and function of violence as an 'economic power' during these periods of transition. At the birth of capitalism there was a struggle between a static system and a dynamic one, between a 'natural' system and one striving for complete socialisation, between an ordered system with bounded territories and an anarchistic one which tended to expand beyond all limits. By contrast, in proletarian production there is a conflict, as is well known, between an ordered economic system and an anarchistic one.[32] And just as the systems of production determine the nature of the classes, so, too, the resulting antagonisms determine the kind of violence necessary to bring about change. "For," as Hegel says, "weapons are nothing but the essence of the combatants themselves."

At this point the disagreement goes beyond the controversies raging between genuine and vulgar Marxists within the framework of a critique of capitalism. What is at stake is the need to advance in the spirit of the dialectical *method* beyond the *results* previously achieved by historical materialism; to apply it to an area to which, because of its historical character, it *could* not be applied before; and to do this with all the modifications which a fundamentally and qualitatively novel subject matter must entail for any unschematic method such as the dialectic. Of course, the breadth of vision of Marx and Engels did much to prepare the ground. Not merely in predicting the probable stages of this process (in the *Critique of the Gotha Programme*), but also methodologically. The "leap from the realm of necessity into the realm of freedom", the conclusion of the "prehistory of mankind" were to Marx and Engels more than beautiful but abstract and empty visions providing resounding ornamental phrases with which to round off the critique of the present, but entailing no systematic commitment. They were rather the clear and conscious intellectual anticipation of the path history was to take and their methodological implications reach deeply into the interpretation of current problems. "Men make their history themselves," writes Engels, "but *not as yet* with a collective will according to a collective plan."[33] And at many points in *Capital* Marx makes use of the structure thus anticipated, on the one hand, in order to shed a sharper light upon the present and, on the other hand, to make the qualitatively novel character of the approaching future stand out more fully and clearly by contrast. For us the crucial element of this contrast is that "in capitalist society . . . social reason always asserts itself only post festum"[34] with regard to phenomena which require only ordinary foresight to destroy the reified veil of capitalism and to reduce appearances to their true underlying reality.

For as the *Communist Manifesto* states: "In bourgeois society the past dominates the present, in communist society the present dominates the past." And this radical unbridgeable contrast cannot be softened by the 'discovery' of certain 'tendencies' in capitalism that seem to make an 'organic change' feasible. It is inseparable from the nature of capitalist production. The past which rules over the present, the consciousness after the fact with which this rule becomes explicit is only the intellectual expression of the fundamental economic condition of capitalist society and of that society alone: it is the reified expression of the possibility, contained in the relations of capital, renewing itself and of expanding through the constant contact with living labour. It is, however, clear that "the domination of the products of past labour over living surplus-labour lasts only as long as the relations of capital; these rest on the particular social relations in which past labour independently and overwhelmingly dominates over living labour".[35]

The social significance of the dictatorship of the proletariat, socialisation, means in the first instance no more than that this domination will be taken out of the hands of the capitalists. But as far as *the proletariat*—regarded as a class—is concerned, *its own labour now ceases objectively to confront it in an autonomous, objectified manner.* Through the fact that the proletariat takes over simultaneously both all labour which has become objectified and also labour in the process of becoming so, this opposition is objectively abolished in practice. With it disappears also the corresponding opposition in capitalist society of past and present whose relation must now be changed structurally.

However lengthy the objective process of socialisation may be, however long it takes the proletariat to become conscious of the changed inner relationship of labour to its objectified forms (the relation of present to past) with the dictatorship of the proletariat the decisive *turning* has been taken. A turning which cannot be approached via 'socialisation' as an 'experiment', or by such devices as a planned economy *within* bourgeois society. For these are—at best—organisational concentrations *within* the capitalist system which do not affect the fundamental cohesion of the economic structure or the fundamental relation between the consciousness of the proletarian class and the production process as a whole. Conversely, even the most modest or most 'chaotic' socialisation which takes the form of appropriating property or power overturns *this very structure* and thereby prepares the course of development for an objective leap forward. When the economistic vulgar Marxists attempt to replace this leap by gradual transitions they forget that capitalism is not merely a matter of production techniques, it is not 'purely' economic (as in bourgeois economics) but is in the true sense of the word *social* and economic. They overlook the fact that "capitalist production as a continuous connected process, a process of reproduction, produces not only commodities, not only surplus-value, *but it also produces and reproduces the capitalist relation*; on the one side the capitalist, on the other the wage-labourer".[36]

Hence, a change in the course of social development is only possible if it prevents the self-reproduction of the capitalist relation and gives the self-reproduction of society another, new direction. The fundamental novelty of this structure is not in the least compromised by the economic impossibility of socialising small businesses which brings about a renewed reproduction of capitalism and of the bourgeoisie "unceasingly, daily, hourly, spontaneously and on a massive scale".[37] This greatly complicates the process, of course; the tension caused by the existence side by side of two social structures increases, but the *social significance* of socialisation, its function in the process of the evolution of proletarian consciousness, remains unchanged. The fundamental tenet of the dialectical method that "it is not the consciousness of men that determines their existence, but, on the contrary, their social existence determines their consciousness", has the necessary consequence—when rightly understood—that at the revolutionary turning-point the category of the radically new, the standing of the economic structure on its head, the change in the direction of the process, i.e. the category of the leap must be taken seriously *in practice*.

It is just this contrast between the 'wisdom that arrives post festum' and a simple and true foresight, between a 'false' and the correct social consciousness that indicates the point at which the leap becomes effective economically and objectively. Obviously, this leap does not consist of one unique act which without a transition brings about with lightening speed this, the greatest transformation in the history of mankind. Even less does it follow the schema of past history and take the form of a mere change of a slow and gradual quantitative development into a change of quality in which the 'eternal laws' of economics carry out the transformation behind men's backs by a sort of 'ruse of reason'. For in that case the leap would mean no more than that mankind would become aware (post festum) of the new situation, perhaps all at once. The leap is rather a lengthy, arduous process. Its essence is expressed in the fact that on every occasion it denotes *a turning in the direction of something qualitatively new*; conscious action directed towards the comprehended totality of society comes to the surface; and therefore—in intention and basis—its home is the realm of freedom.

For the rest it merges in form and content with the slow process of social change. Indeed, it can only genuinely preserve its character of a leap if it becomes fully identified with this process, if it is nothing more than the conscious meaning of every moment, its relation to the whole elevated to consciousness, the conscious acceleration of the process in the inevitable direction. An acceleration which is *one* step ahead of the process, which would impose on it no alien goals or self-made utopias but merely illuminates its own immanent purpose whenever the revolution takes fright at the "indefinite enormity of its own aims" and threatens to totter and lapse into compromise.

The leap seems then to be absorbed into the process without remainder. But the 'realm of freedom' is not a gift that mankind, groaning under the weight of necessity, receives from Fate as a reward for its steadfast endurance. It is not only the goal, but also the means and the weapon in the struggle. And here the fundamental and qualitative novelty of the situation is revealed: for the first time mankind consciously takes its history into its own hands—thanks to the class consciousness of a proletariat summoned to power. This does not negate the 'necessity' of the objective economic process, but it does confer on it another, new function. If, hitherto, the task was to deduce from the objective course of history what was going to come anyway in order to turn it to the advantage of the proletariat, if 'necessity' was until then the positive guiding element in the process, it now becomes an impediment which has to be fought. Step by step it is pushed back in the process of transformation until—after long, arduous struggles—it can be totally eliminated. The clear and relentless knowledge of what really is the case, of what must—inevitably—happen is not diminished by all this; indeed it is the decisive premise and the most potent weapon in the struggle. For every failure to realise what power still remains at necessity's command would reduce the knowledge that revolutionises the world to an empty utopia and would strengthen the power of the enemy. But recognition of the tendencies of economic compulsion no longer serves the purpose of accelerating this, *its own* process or of profiting from it. On the contrary, its function is to combat it effectively, to force it back and, where possible, to turn it in another direction or—in so far as it has really become necessary—to elude it.

The transformation thus accomplished is economic (together with the realignment of classes that it entails). But the 'economy' no longer has the function that every economy has had hitherto: for it is to be the servant of a consciously directed society; it is to lose its self-contained autonomy (which was what made it an economy, properly speaking); as an economy it is to be annulled. This tendency is expressed during the transition above all as a change in the relationship between economy and violence. For however great the economic importance of violence was in the transition to capitalism, the economy always had the upper hand while violence served and advanced its cause, removing obstacles from its path. But now violence is placed at the disposal of principles that could occur only as 'superstructure' in previous societies, that is only as factors accompanying the inevitable process and determined by it. Violence is now put to the service of man and the flowering of man.

It has frequently been stated with justification: socialisation is a question of power. The question of violence here takes precedence over the question of economics. (Of course, any use of power which neglects the resistance of the actual is madness; so it must take resistance into account—in order to overcome it and not to be borne along by it.) With this it might seem as though violence, naked and undisguised, were to emerge into the light of day and into the foreground of social action. But this is a delusion. For violence is no autonomous principle and never can be. And this violence is nothing but the will of the proletariat which has become conscious and is bent on abolishing the enslaving hold of reified relations over man and the hold of economics over society.

This abolition, this leap is a process. And it is just as vital to keep in mind the fact that it is a leap as that it is a process. The leap consists in the unmediated turning to the radically new character of a consciously ordered society whose 'economy' is subordinated to man and his needs. Characteristic of the process is the fact that this subordination of the economy qua economy, this tendency to annul its autonomy is expressed as the exclusive domination of the consciousness of those who perform this annulling operation by economic *contents*, the like of which had never been experienced before. This is true not merely because of the falling production of the transitional period, the greater difficulty of keeping the machine going and gratifying the needs (however modest) of men, and the increasingly bitter material need—all of which forces economic contents and economic anxiety into the minds of men. It is due also and essentially to this change in function. When the economy was the dominant form of society, the real motor force of evolution propelling society behind the backs of men, it had to enter men's minds in non-economic, ideological forms. If the principles of human existence are about to break free and take control of mankind for the first time in history, then economics and violence, the objects and the instruments of struggle, stand in the foreground of interest. Just because those contents which were before called 'ideology' now begin—changed, it is true, in every way—to become the real goals of mankind, it becomes superfluous to use them to adorn the economic struggles of violence which are fought for their sake. Moreover, their reality and actuality appear in the very fact that all interest centres on the real struggles surrounding their realisation, i.e. on economics and violence.

Hence it can no longer appear paradoxical that this transition is an era almost exclusively preoccupied with economic interests and characterised by the frank use of naked force. Economics and violence have started to act out the last stage of their historical existence, and if they seem to dominate the arena of history, this cannot disguise the fact that this is their last appearance. As Engels says: "The first act in which the state (organised force) really appears as the representative of the whole of society—the seizing of the means of production in the name of society—is at the same time its last independent act as the state . . . it withers away. . . ." "Men's own socialisation which appeared before as something imposed on them by nature and history now becomes their own free deed. The objective, alien powers which controlled history hitherto now come under the control of men themselves."[38] What until then had been merely 'Ideology', accompanying the inevitable evolution of mankind, the life of man as man in his relation to himself, his fellow men and to nature can now become the authentic content of human life. Socially, man is now born as man.

In the era of transition which has already begun to lead us to this goal even though we still face a long and painful journey, historical materialism will still preserve unchanged for a long time its importance as the pre-eminent weapon of the embattled proletariat. After all, by far the largest part of society is still under the sway of purely capitalist forms of production. And on the few islands where the proletariat has established its rule it can do no more than laboriously force capitalism to retreat step by step and consciously to call into being the new order of society—which is no longer amenable to such categories. But the mere fact that the struggle has entered this stage points incidentally to two very important changes in the function of historical materialism.

Firstly, it is necessary to use materialist dialectics to show the path that leads to the conscious control and domination of production and to the liberation from the compulsion of reified social forces. No analysis of the past, however careful and exact, is able to give satisfactory answer to this problem. Only the— unprejudiced—application of the dialectical method to this wholly novel material will suffice. Secondly, as every crisis represents the objectification of a self-criticism of capitalism, the extremely acute present crisis enables us to make use of this process of self-criticism now approaching completion to consolidate historical materialism as a method of studying the 'prehistory of mankind' more clearly and completely than has been possible up to now. That is to say, not merely because we shall need the constantly improving tool of historical materialism in battle for a long time to come, but also from the standpoint of consolidating our scientific knowledge, it is essential for us to use the victory of the proletariat to erect this home and this workshop for historical materialism.

June 1919.

NOTES

1   *The Eighteenth Brumaire of Louis Bonaparte*, in S.W. I, p. 260.
2   *Capital* III, p. 172.
3   *Capital* I, p. 737 (my italics).
4   *The Origin of the Family*, in S.W. II, pp. 292–3.
5   *A Contribution to the Critique of Political Economy*, p. 303.
6   8 December, 1882, in *Briefwechsel* IV, p. 495.
7   *The Origin of the Family*, in S.W. II, p. 204.
8   *Capital* I, p. 515.
9   *The Origin of the Family*, in S.W. II, p. 279.
10 To forestall any misunderstanding we would hasten to point out, firstly, that this Hegelian distinction is introduced only in order to differentiate clearly between these spheres. It is not our intention to apply his (very problematic) theory of the spirit. Secondly, it would be an error to suggest that the concept of the spirit had any psychological or metaphysical meaning even for Hegel himself. He defines spirit as the unity of consciousness and its object, a definition very close indeed to Marx's view of the categories. (See, for example, *The Poverty of Philosophy*, p. 117 and *A Contribution to the Critique of Political Economy*, p. 302.) This is not the place to discuss the *difference* between them, which I have not overlooked, but which is to be found in a quite different place from the one in which it is usually sought.
11 *A Contribution to the Critique of Political Economy*, pp. 311–12.
12 Cf. Marx on labour as the creator of use-values. *Capital* I, p. 41.
13 Cf., e.g. *Capital* III, p. 174.
14 *Anti-Dühring*, pp. 346–7.
15 *Der heilige Max, Dokumente des Sozialismus*, III, p. 171.
16 Cf. *A Contribution to the Critique of Political Economy*, pp. 301 et seq.
17 Cf. *A Contribution to the Critique of Political Economy*, p. 13.
18 *The Poverty of Philosophy*, p. 196 (my italics).
19 Ibid., p. 195.
20 *Wages, Price and Profit*, in S.W. I, pp. 401–2.
21 *Capital* I, p. 760.
22 *Capital* III, p. 767.
23 *The Origin of the Family*, in S.W. II, p. 290 (my italics).
24 *Capital* III, p. 254.
25 Cf., e.g. the reaction of English capitalists to the problems of crises, unemployment and emigration, *Capital* I, p. 574 et seq. The ideas outlined here are similar in some respects to the acute remarks made by Bukharin on the notion of 'balance' as a methodological postulate, *Ökonomie der Transformationsperiode*, pp. 159–60. It is unfortunately not possible to enter into a discussion with him here.
26 *Capital* III, p. 241.
27 Ibid., pp. 239–40.
28 *Capital* I, p. 640.

29 *The Origin of the Family*, in S.W. II, p. 248.
30 *Capital* I, p. 762.
31 *Capital* I, p. 751 (my italics).
32 In this confrontation imperialist capitalism, too, appears necessarily as anarchistic.
33 Letter to H. Starkenberg, in S.W. II, p. 458 (my italics).
34 *Capital* II, p. 315.
35 *Capital* III, p. 391.
36 *Capital* I, p. 578 (my italics).
37 Cf. Lenin, *"Left-Wing" Communism—An infantile disorder*, p. 518.
38 *Anti-Dühring*, pp. 309, 311–12.

Legality and Illegality

> The materialist doctrine that men are the
> product of circumstances and education, that
> changed men are therefore the products of
> other circumstances and of a different
> education, forgets that circumstances are
> in fact changed by men and that the educator
> must himself be educated.
>
> Marx: *Theses on Feuerbach.*

To gain an understanding of legality and illegality in the class struggle of the proletariat, as with any question touching on modes of action, it is more important and more illuminating to consider the motives and the tendencies they generate than merely to remain at the level of the bare facts. For the mere fact of the legality or illegality of one part of the workers' movement is so dependent on 'accidents' of history that to analyse it is not always to guarantee a clarification of theory. A party may be opportunistic even to the point of total betrayal and yet find itself on occasion forced into illegality. On the other hand, it is possible to imagine a situation in which the most revolutionary and most uncompromising Communist Party may be able to function for a time under conditions of almost complete legality.

As this criterion cannot provide an adequate basis for analysis we must go beyond it and examine the motives for choosing between legal and illegal tactics. But here it does not suffice to establish—abstractly—motives and convictions. For if it is significant that the opportunists always hold fast to legality *at any price*, it would be a mistake to define the revolutionary parties in terms of the reverse of this, namely illegality. There are, it is true, periods in every revolution when a *romanticism of illegality* is predominant or at least powerful. But for reasons which we shall discuss in what follows, this romanticism is quite definitely an infantile disorder of the communist movement. It is a reaction against legality at any price and for this reason it is vital that every mature movement should grow out of it and this is undoubtedly what actually happens.

256

1

What, then, is the meaning of the concepts of legality and illegality for Marxist thought? This question leads us inevitably to the general problem of organised power, to the problem of law and the state and ultimately to the problem of ideology. In his polemic against Dühring, Engels brilliantly disposes of the abstract theory of force. However, the proof that force (law and the state) "was originally grounded in an economic, social function"[1] must be interpreted to mean—in strict accordance with the theories of Marx and Engels—that in consequence of this connection a corresponding ideological picture is found projected into the thoughts and feelings of men who are drawn into the ambit of authority. That is to say, the organs of authority harmonise to such an extent with the (economic) laws governing men's lives, or seem so overwhelmingly superior that men experience them as natural forces, as the necessary environment for their existence. As a result they submit to them *freely*. (Which is not to say that they *approve* of them.)

For if it is true that an organisation based on force can only survive as long as it is able to overcome the resistance of individuals or groups by force, it is equally true that it could not survive if it were compelled to use force every time it is challenged. If this becomes necessary, then the situation will be revolutionary; the organs of authority will be in contradiction with the economic bases of society and this contradiction will be projected into the minds of people. People will then cease to regard the existing order as given in nature and they will oppose force with force. Without denying that this situation has an economic basis it is still necessary to add that a change can be brought about in an organisation based on force only when the belief of both the rulers and the ruled that the existing order is the only possible one has been shaken. Revolution in the system of production is the *essential precondition* of this. But the revolution itself can only be accomplished by people; by people who have become intellectually and emotionally emancipated from the existing system.

This emancipation does not take place mechanically parallel to and simultaneously with economic developments. It both anticipates these and is anticipated by them. It can be present and mostly is present at times when the economic base of a social system shows nothing more than a *tendency* to become problematical. In such cases the theory will think out what is merely a tendency and take it to its logical conclusion, converting it into what reality ought to be and then opposing this 'true' reality to the 'false' reality of what actually exists. (A case in point is the role played by natural law as a prelude to the bourgeois revolutions.) On the other hand, it is certainly true that even those groups and masses whose class situation gives them a direct interest, only free themselves inwardly from the old order *during* (and very often only *after*) a revolution. They need the evidence of their own eyes to tell them which society really conforms to their interests before they can free themselves inwardly from the old order.

If these remarks hold good for every revolutionary change from one social order to another they are much more valid for a social revolution than for one which is predominantly political. A political revolution does no more than sanction a socio-economic situation that has been able to impose itself at least in part upon the economic reality. Such a revolution forcibly replaces the old legal order, now felt to be 'unjust' by the new 'right', 'just' law. There is no radical reorganisation of the social environment. (Thus conservative historians of the Great French Revolution emphasise that 'social' conditions remained relatively unchanged during the period.)

Social revolutions, however, are concerned precisely to change this environment. Any such change violates the instincts of the average man so deeply that he regards it as a catastrophic threat to *life as such*, it appears to him to be a blind force of nature like a flood or an earthquake. Unable to grasp the essence of the process, his blind despair tries to defend itself by attacking the *immediate manifestations* of change that menace his accustomed existence. Thus in the early stages of capitalism, proletarians with a petty-bourgeois education rose up against machines and factories. Proudhon's doctrines, too, can be seen as one of the last echoes of this desperate defence of the old, accustomed social order.

It is here that the revolutionary nature of Marxism can be most easily grasped. Marxism is the doctrine of the revolution precisely because it understands the essence of the process (as opposed to its manifestations, its symptoms); and because it can demonstrate the decisive line of future development (as opposed to the events of the moment). This makes it at the same time the ideological expression of the proletariat in its efforts to liberate itself. This liberation takes the form at first of actual rebellions against the most oppressive manifestations of the capitalist economy and the capitalist state. These isolated battles which never bring final victory even when they are successful can only become truly revolutionary when the proletariat becomes *conscious* of what connects these battles to each other and to the process that leads ineluctably to the demise of capitalism. When the young Marx proposed the "reform of consciousness" he anticipated the essence of his later activity. His doctrine is not utopian, because it builds on a process which is actually taking place. It does not contemplate realising 'ideals' but merely wishes to uncover the inherent meaning of the process. At the same time it must go beyond what is merely given and must focus the consciousness of the proletariat on what is essential and not merely ephemerally the case. "The reform of consciousness", says Marx, "consists in no more than causing the world to become aware of its own consciousness, in awakening it from its dream about itself, in *explaining its own actions to it.* . . . It will then be seen that the world has long possessed a dream of things *which it only has to possess in consciousness in order to possess them in reality.*"[2]

This reform of consciousness is the revolutionary process itself. For the proletariat can become conscious only gradually and after long, difficult crises. It is true that in Marx's doctrine all the theoretical and practical consequences of the class situation of the proletariat were deduced (long before they became historical 'fact'). However, even though these theories were not unhistorical utopias but insights into the historical process itself, it by no means follows that the proletariat has incorporated in its own consciousness the emancipation achieved by the Marxian theory—even if in its *individual actions* it *acts* in accordance with that theory. We have drawn attention to this process in a different context[3] and emphasised that the proletariat can become conscious of the need to combat capitalism on the economic plane at a time when politically it remains wholly within the ambience of the capitalist state. How very true this was can be seen from the fact that it was possible for Marx and Engels' whole critique of the state to fall into oblivion and that the most important theoreticians of the Second International could accept the capitalist state as *the* state without more ado and so could regard their own activity and their conflict with that state as 'opposition'. (This can be seen at its clearest in the polemic between Pannekoek and Kautsky in 1912.) For to adopt the stance of 'opposition' means that the existing order is *accepted in all essentials as an immutable* foundation and all the efforts of the 'opposition' are restricted to making as many gains as possible for the workers *within* the existing system.

Admittedly, only fools and innocents would have remained blind to the real power of the bouregeois state. The great distinction between revolutionary Marxists and pseudo-Marxist opportunists consists in the fact that for the former the capitalist state counts *merely as a power factor against which* the power of the organised proletariat is to be mobilised. Whilst the latter regard the state as an institution *standing above the classes* and the proletariat and the bourgeoisie conduct their war *in order to* gain control of it. But by viewing the state as the object of the struggle rather than as the enemy they have mentally gone over to bourgeois territory and thereby lost half the battle even before taking up arms. For every system of state and law, and the capitalist system above all, exists in the last analysis because its survival, and the validity of its statutes, are simply accepted as unproblematic. The *isolated* violation of those statutes does not represent any particular danger to the state as long as such infringements figure in the general consciousness merely as isolated cases. Dostoyevsky has noted in his Siberian reminiscences how every criminal feels himself to be guilty (without necessarily feeling any remorse); he understands with perfect clarity that he has broken laws that are no less valid for him than for everyone else. And these laws retain their validity even when personal motives or the force of circumstances have induced him to violate them.

The state will never have difficulty in keeping such isolated infringements under control just because it is not threatened in its foundations for a single moment. To adopt the stance of being in 'opposition' implies a similar attitude to the state: it concedes that the essence of the state is to stand outside the class struggle and that the validity of its laws is not *directly* challenged by the class struggle. This leaves the 'opposition' with two alternatives: either it will attempt to revise the laws by legal means and then, of course, the old laws remain in force until the new laws take their place. Or else it will promote the isolated infringement of the laws. Hence, when the opportunists attempt to conflate the Marxist critique of the state with that of the Anarchists, they are merely indulging their low taste for demagogy. For Marxism is concerned neither with anarchistic illusions nor with utopias.

What is essential is to realise that the capitalist state *should be seen and evaluated as a historical phenomenon even while it exists.* It should be treated, therefore, purely as a power structure which has to be taken into account only to the extent to which its actual power stretches. On the other hand, it should be subjected to the most painstaking and fearless examination in order to discover the points where this power can be weakened and undermined. *This strong point, or rather weak point in the state is the way in which it is reflected in the consciousness of people.* Ideology is in this case not merely a consequence of the economic structure of society but also the precondition of its smooth functioning.

2

The clearer it becomes that the crisis of capitalism is ceasing to be a piece of knowledge gleaned by Marxist analysis and is in the process of becoming palpable reality, the more decisive will be the role played by ideology in determining the fate of the proletarian revolution. In an age when capitalism was still quite secure inwardly it was understandable that large sections of the working class should have taken up an *ideological* position wholly within capitalism. For a thorough-going Marxism required a posture they could not possibly sustain. Marx says: "In order to understand a particular historical age we must go beyond its outer limits."

When this dictum is applied to an understanding of the *present* this entails a quite extraordinary effort. It means that the whole economic, social and cultural environment must be subjected to critical scrutiny. And the decisive aspect of this scrutiny, its Archimedean point from which alone all these phenomena can be understood, can be no more than an aspiration with which to confront the reality of the present; that is to say it remains after all something 'unreal', a 'mere theory'. Whereas when we attempt to understand the past, the present is itself the starting-point. Of course, this aspiration is not merely petty bourgeois and utopian in character, yearning for a 'better' or 'more beautiful' world. It is a proletarian aspiration and does no more than discern and describe the direction, the tendency and the meaning of the social process in whose name it actively impinges on the present. Even so this just increases the difficulty of the task. For just as the

very best astronomer disregards his knowledge of Copernicus
and continues to accept the testimony of his senses which tells
him that the sun 'rises', so too the most irrefutable Marxist
analysis of the capitalist state can never abolish its empirical reality.

Nor is it designed to do so. Marxist theory is designed to put
the proletariat into a very particular frame of mind. The capitalist
state must appear to it as a link in a chain of historical development. Hence it by no means constitutes 'man's natural environment' but merely a real fact whose actual power must be reckoned
with but which has no inherent right to determine our actions.
The state and the laws shall be seen as having no more than an
empirical validity. In the same way a yachtsman must take
exact note of the direction of the wind without letting the wind
determine his course; on the contrary, he defies and exploits it in
order to hold fast to his original course. The *independence* which
man in the course of a long historical development has gradually
wrested from the hostile forces of nature, is still very largely lacking in the proletariat when it confronts the manifestations of
society. And this is easily understood. For the coercive measures
taken by society in individual cases are often hard and brutally
materialistic, but *the strength of every society is in the last resort a*
spiritual strength. And from this we can only be liberated by
knowledge. This knowledge cannot be of the abstract kind
that remains in one's head—many 'socialists' have possessed that
sort of knowledge. It must be knowledge that has become flesh of
one's flesh and blood of one's blood; to use Marx's phrase, it
must be "practical critical activity".

The present acute crisis in capitalism makes such knowledge
both possible and necessary. Possible because as a result of the
crisis even the ordinary social environment can be seen and felt to
be problematical. It becomes decisive for the revolution and
hence necessary because the actual strength of capitalism has been
so greatly weakened that it would no longer be able to maintain
its position by force if the proletariat were to oppose it consciously
and resolutely. Only ideology stands in the way of such opposition.
Even in the very midst of the death throes of capitalism broad
sections of the proletarian masses still feel that the state, the laws
and the economy of the bourgeoisie are the only possible environment for them to exist in. In their eyes many improvements would
be desirable ('organisation of production'), but nevertheless it
remains the 'natural' basis of society.

This is the ideological foundation of legality. It does not always entail a conscious betrayal or even a conscious compromise. It is rather the natural and instinctive attitude towards the state, which appears to the man of action as the only fixed point in a chaotic world. It is a view of the world that has to be overcome if the Communist Party wishes to create a healthy foundation for both its legal and illegal tactics. For all revolutionary movements begin with the romanticism of illegality, but hardly any succeed in seeing their way beyond the stage of opportunist legality. That this romanticism, like every kind of Putschism, should underestimate the actual strength possessed by capitalism even at a moment of crisis is, of course, often very dangerous. But even this is no more than a symptom of the disease from which this whole tendency suffers.

The disease itself is the inability to see the state as nothing more than a power factor. And in the last resort this indicates a failure to see the connections we have just mapped out. For by surrounding illegal means and methods of struggle with a certain aura, by conferring upon them a special, revolutionary 'authenticity', one endows the existing state with a certain legal validity, with a more than just empirical existence. For to rebel against the law *qua law*, to prefer certain actions *because* they are illegal, implies for anyone who so acts that the law has retained its binding validity. Where the total, communist, fearlessness with regard to the state and the law is present, the law and its calculable consequences are of no greater (if also of no smaller) importance than any other external fact of life with which it is necessary to reckon when deciding upon any definite course of action. The risk of breaking the law should not be regarded any differently than the risk of missing a train connection when on an important journey.

Where this is not the case, where it is resolved to break the law with a grand gesture, this suggests that the law has preserved its authority—admittedly in an inverted form—that it is still in a position *inwardly* to influence one's actions and that a genuine, inner emancipation has not yet occurred. At first sight this distinction may perhaps seem pedantic. But to realise that it is no empty and abstract invention but, on the contrary, a description of the true situation one need only recall how easy it was for typical illegal parties like the Socialist Revolutionaries in Russia to find their way back in to the bourgeois camp. One need only recall the first truly revolutionary illegal acts which had ceased to be the romantically heroic infringements of isolated laws and had become the rejection and destruction of the whole bourgeois legal system. One need only recall the way in which these acts exposed the ideological attachment of the 'heroes of illegality' to bourgeois concepts of law. (Today Boris Savinkov is fighting in the White Polish camp against proletarian Russia. In the past he was not only the celebrated organiser of almost all the great assassinations under Czarism but also one of the first theoreticians of romantic illegality.)

The question of legality or illegality reduces itself then for the Communist Party to *a mere question of tactics*, even to a question to be resolved on the spur of the moment, one for which it is scarcely possible to lay down general rules as decisions have to be taken on the basis of *immediate expediencies*. In this wholly unprincipled solution lies the only possible practical and principled rejection of the bourgeois legal system. Such tactics are essential for Communists and not just on grounds of expediency. They are needed not just because it is only in this way that their tactics will acquire a genuine flexibility and adaptability to the exigencies of the particular moment; nor because the alternate or even the simultaneous use of legal and illegal methods is necessary if the bourgeoisie is to be fought effectively.

Such tactics are necessary in order to complete the revolutionary self-education of the proletariat. For the proletariat can only be liberated from its dependence upon the life-forms created by capitalism when it has learnt to act without these life-forms inwardly influencing its actions. As motive forces they must sink to the status of matters of complete indifference. Needless to say, this will not reduce by one iota the hatred of the proletariat for these forms, nor the burning wish to destroy them. On the contrary, only by virtue of this inner conviction will the proletariat be able to regard the capitalist social order as an abomination, dead but still a lethal obstacle to the healthy evolution of humanity; and this is an indispensable insight if the proletariat is to be able to take a conscious and enduring revolutionary stand. The self-education of the proletariat is a lengthy and difficult process by which it becomes 'ripe' for revolution, and the more highly developed capitalism and bourgeois culture are in a country, the more arduous this process becomes because the proletariat becomes infected by the life-forms of capitalism.

The need to establish just what is appropriate to revolutionary action coincides fortunately—though by no means adventitiously—with the exigencies of this educational task. To take but one example, the Second Congress of the Third International laid down in its Supplementary Theses on the question of parliamentarism that the Parliamentary Party should be completely dependent on the Central Committee of the C.P. even where this latter should be proscribed by law. Now this decision is not only absolutely indispensable for ensuring unified action. It also has the effect of visibly lowering the prestige of parliament in the eyes of broad sections of the proletariat (and it is upon this prestige that the freedom of action of that bastion of opportunism, the Parliamentary Party, is based). How necessary this is, is shown by the fact that, e.g. the English proletariat has constantly been diverted into the paths of opportunism because of its *inner subservience* to such authorities. And the sterility of the exclusive emphasis upon the 'direct action' of anti-parliamentarism no less than the barrenness of the debates about the superiority of either method constitutes proof that both are still enmeshed in bourgeois prejudices, albeit in ways that are diametrically opposed.

There is yet another reason for insisting upon the simultaneous and alternating use of both legal and illegal methods. Only this will bring into being the precondition for an untrammelled revolutionary attitude towards law and the state, namely the exposure of the system of law as the brutal power instrument of capitalist oppression. Where one or other of the two methods is used exclusively, or predominantly, even though within certain restricted areas, the bourgeoisie will be able to maintain the fiction in the minds of the masses that its system of law is the only system. One of the cardinal aims of every Communist Party must be to force the government of the country to violate its own system of law and to compel the legal party of social traitors to connive openly at this 'violation'. In certain cases, especially where nationalist prejudices obscure the vision of the proletariat, a capitalist government may be able to turn this to its own advantage. But at times, when the proletariat is gathering its forces for the decisive battle, such violations will prove all the more risky. It is here, in this caution of the oppressors which springs from considerations such as these, that we find the origin of those fatal illusions about democracy and about the peaceful transition to socialism. Such illusions are encouraged above all by the fact that the opportunists persist in acting legally at any price and thereby render possible the policy of prudence adopted by the ruling class.

This work of educating the proletariat will only be directed into fruitful channels when sober, objective tactics are adopted that are prepared for every legal and every illegal method and that decide which is to be used solely on grounds of its utility.

3

However, the struggle for power will only begin this education; it will certainly be unable to complete it. Many years ago Rosa Luxemburg drew attention to the fact that a seizure of power is essentially 'premature' and this is especially true in the context of ideology. Many of the phenomena that make their appearance in the first stage of every dictatorship of the proletariat can be ascribed to the fact that *the proletariat is forced to take power at a time and in a state of mind in which it inwardly still acknowledges the bourgeois social order as the only authentic and legal one.* The basis of a soviet government is the same as that of any lawful system: it must be acknowledged by such large sections of the population that it has to resort only in exceptional cases to acts of violence.

Now it is self-evident from the very outset that under no circumstances will such recognition be forthcoming from the bourgeoisie at the beginning. A class accustomed by a tradition going back for many generations to the enjoyment of privileges and the exercise of power will never resign itself merely because of a *single* defeat. It will not simply endure the emergence of a new order without more ado. It must first be *broken ideologically* before it will voluntarily enter the service of the new society and before it will begin to regard the statutes of that society as legal and as existing of right instead of as the brutal facts of a temporary shift in the balance of power which can be reversed tomorrow. Whether or not the resistance of the bourgeoisie takes the form of open counter-revolution or of covert acts of sabotage, it is a naïve illusion to imagine that it can be disarmed by making some sort of concession to it. On the contrary, the example of the soviet dictatorship in Hungary demonstrates that all such concessions which in this case were without exception also concessions to the Social Democrats, served only to strengthen the power consciousness of the former ruling class and to postpone and even put an end to their inner willingness to accept the rule of the proletariat.

This retreat of the power of the soviets before the bourgeoisie had even more disastrous implications for the ideology of the broad masses of the petty bourgeoisie. It is characteristic of them that they regard the state as something general and universal, as an absolute supreme institution. Apart from an adroit economic policy which is often enough to neutralise the individual groups of the petty bourgeoisie it is evident, then, that much depends on the proletariat itself. Will it succeed in giving its state such authority as to meet half-way the faith in authority of such strata of the population and to facilitate their inclinations to subordinate themselves voluntarily to 'the' state? If the proletariat hesitates, if it lacks a sustaining faith in its own mission to rule, it can drive these groups back into the arms of the bourgeoisie and even to open counter-revolution.

Under the dictatorship of the proletariat the relationship between legality and illegality undergoes a change in function, for now what was formerly legal becomes illegal and vice versa. However, this change can at most accelerate somewhat the process of emancipation begun under capitalism; it cannot complete it at one stroke. The bourgeoisie did not lose the sense of its own legality after *a single* defeat, and similarly the proletariat cannot possibly gain a consciousness of its own legality through the fact of *a single* victory. This consciousness only matured very slowly under capitalism and even now, under the dictatorship of the proletariat, it will only ripen by degrees. In the first period it will even suffer a number of setbacks. For only now will the proletariat, having once gained control, be able to appreciate the mental achievements which created and sustained capitalism. Not only will it acquire a far greater insight into bourgeois culture than ever before; but also the mental achievements essential to the conduct of the economy and the state will only become apparent to large sections of the proletariat after it has come to power.

Furthermore, it must not be forgotten that to a great extent the proletariat has been deprived of the practice and the tradition of acting independently and responsibly. Hence it may often experience the need to act thus as a burden rather than as a liberation. And finally there is the fact that petty bourgeois and even bourgeois attitudes have come to permeate the habits of life of those sections of the proletariat that will occupy leading positions. This has the effect of making precisely what is new about the new society appear alien and even hostile to them.

All these obstacles would be fairly harmless and might easily be overcome were it not for one fact. This is that the bourgeoisie for whom the problem of legality and illegality has undergone a comparable change of function, is even here much more mature and much further advanced than the proletariat. (This remains true as long as it is fighting against a proletarian state that has not yet properly established itself.) With the same naïve complacency with which it formerly contemplated the legality of its own system of law it now dismisses as illegal the order imposed by the proletariat. We have made it a requirement for the proletariat struggling for power that it should view the bourgeois state merely as a fact, a power factor; this requirement is now instinctively fulfilled by the bourgeoisie.

Thus, despite the victory gained by the proletariat, its struggle with the bourgeoisie is still unequal and it will remain so until the proletariat acquires the same naïve confidence in the exclusive legality of its own system of law. Such a development is, however, greatly impeded by the attitude of mind imposed on the proletariat by the opportunists. Having accustomed itself to surrounding the institutions of capitalism with an aura of legality it finds it difficult to view with detachment the surviving remains which may endure for a very long time. Once the proletariat has gained power it still remains enmeshed intellectually in the trammels woven by the course of capitalist development. This finds expression, on the one hand, in its failure to lay hands on much that ought to be utterly destroyed. On the other hand, it proceeds to the labour of demolition and construction not with the sense of assurance that springs from legitimate rule, but with the mixture of vacillation and haste characteristic of the usurper. A usurper, moreover, who inwardly, in thought, feeling and resolve, anticipates the inevitable restoration of capitalism.

I have in mind here not only the more or less overt counterrevolutionary sabotage of the process of socialisation perpetrated throughout the Hungarian soviet dictatorship by the trade-union bureaucrats with the aim of restoring capitalism as painlessly as possible. I am thinking here also of the widely noted phenomenon of corruption in the soviets which has one of its chief sources here. Partly in the mentality of many soviet officials who were inwardly prepared for the return of a 'legitimate' capitalism and who were therefore intent on being able to justify their own actions when it became necessary. Partly also because many who had been involved in necessarily 'illegal' work (smuggling propaganda abroad) were intellectually and above all morally unable to grasp that from the only legitimate standpoint, the standpoint of the proletarian state, their activities were just as 'legal' as any other. In the case of people of unstable moral character this confusion was translated into open corruption. Many an honest revolutionary lapsed into a romantic hypostatisation of 'illegality', into the unprofitable search for 'illegal' openings, and these tendencies exhibit *a deficient sense of the legitimacy of the Revolution* and of the right of the Revolution to establish its own lawful order.

In the period of the dictatorship of the proletariat this feeling and this sense of legitimacy should replace the requirement of the previous stage of the revolution, namely the stage of unfettered independence *vis-à-vis* bourgeois law. But notwithstanding this change *the evolution of the class consciousness of the proletariat advances homogeneously and in a straight line*. This can be seen most clearly in the foreign policies of proletarian states which, when confronted by the power structures of capitalist states, have to do battle with the bourgeois state just as they did when they seized power in their own state, though now the methods have partly changed.

The peace negotiations at Brest–Litovsk have already testified to the high level and the maturity of the class consciousness attained by the Russian proletariat. Although they were dealing with the German imperialists they recognised their oppressed brothers all over the world as their truly legitimate partners at the negotiating table. Even though Lenin's judgement of the actual power relationships was notable for its supreme intelligence and realistic toughness, his negotiators were instructed to address themselves to the proletariat of the world and primarily to the proletariat of the Central Powers. His foreign policy was less a negotiation between Germany and Russia than the attempt to promote proletarian revolution and revolutionary consciousness in the nations of Central Europe. Since then the home and foreign policies of the Soviet Government have undergone many changes and it has been necessary to adapt them to the exigencies of the real power situation. But notwithstanding this the fundamental principle, the principle of the legitimacy of its own power which at the same time entails the principle of the need to advance the revolutionary class consciousness of the proletariat of the world, has remained a fixed point throughout the whole period.

The whole problem of the recognition of Soviet Russia by the bourgeois states must not be regarded in isolation as involving no more than the question of the advantages accruing to Russia. It must be seen also as the question of whether the bourgeoisie will recognise the legitimacy of the proletarian revolution. The significance of this recognition changes according to the concrete circumstances in which it takes place. Its effect on the vacillating sections of the petty bourgeoisie in Russia as well as on those of the proletariat of the world remains the same in all essentials: it sanctions the legitimacy of the revolution, something of which they stand in great need if they are to accept as legal its official exponents, the Soviet Republic. All the various methods of Russian politics serve this purpose: the relentless onslaught on the counter-revolution within Russia, the bold confrontation of the powers victorious in the war to whom Russia has never spoken in tones of submission (unlike the bourgeoisie of Germany), and the open support granted to revolutionary movements, etc. These policies cause sections of the counter-revolutionary front in Russia to crumble away and to bow before the legitimacy of the Revolution. They help to fortify the revolutionary self-consciousness of the proletariat, its awareness of its own strength and dignity.

The ideological maturity of the Russian proletariat becomes clearly visible when we consider those very factors which have been taken as evidence of its backwardness by the opportunists of the West and their Central European admirers. To wit, the clear and definitive crushing of the internal counter-revolution and the uninhibited illegal and 'diplomatic' battle for world revolution. The Russian proletariat did not emerge victoriously from its revolution because a fortunate constellation of circumstances played into its hands. (This constellation existed equally for the German proletariat in November 1918 and for the Hungarian proletariat at the same time and also in March 1919.) It was victorious because it had been steeled by the long illegal struggle and hence had gained a clear understanding of the nature of the capitalist state. In consequence its actions were based on a genuine reality and not on ideological delusions. The proletariat of Central and Western Europe still has an arduous road before it. If it is to become conscious of its historical mission and of the legitimacy of its rule it must first grasp the fact that the problem of legality and illegality is purely tactical in nature. It must be able to slough off both the cretinism of legality and the romanticism of illegality.

July 1920.

NOTES

1 *Anti-Dühring*, p. 205.
2 Nachlass I, pp. 382–3. [Correspondence between Marx and Ruge, 1843.] The italics are mine.
3 Cf. the essay "Class Consciousness".

Critical Observations on Rosa Luxemburg's "Critique of the Russian Revolution"

PAUL LEVI has felt impelled to publish a pamphlet that Comrade Rosa Luxemburg composed hurriedly while in Breslau gaol and that has survived as an incomplete fragment. Publication took place in the midst of the most violent struggles against the German C.P. and the Third International; it thus represents a stage in this struggle no less than the 'Vorwärts' revelations and Friesland's pamphlet—though it serves other deeper purposes. The aim this time is not to undermine the standing of the German C.P. or to weaken confidence in the policy of the Third International; it is to strike a blow at the theoretical basis of Bolshevik organisation and tactics. This is the cause in whose support the revered authority of Rosa Luxemburg is to be enlisted. The theory that would justify the liquidation of the Third International and its sections is to be quarried from her posthumous works.

Hence it is not enough to point out that Rosa Luxemburg later revised her views. It is necessary to see to what extent she was in the right. For—seen abstractly—it might well be the case that she had continued to develop her views in the wrong direction in the first months of the Revolution; and that the revision of her position noted by Comrades Warski and Zetkin could mean she had taken the wrong turning. Hence—independently of Rosa Luxemburg's later attitude to the opinions set down here—it is with these opinions that the discussion must come to grips. All the more as some of the differences of opinion between Rosa Luxemburg and the Bolsheviks had already come to light in the Junius Pamphlet and Lenin's criticism of that, and indeed as early as the criticism of Lenin's book *One Step Forwards, Two Steps Back* which Rosa Luxemburg published in the "Neue Zeit" in 1904. These differences were still influential in the formulation of the Spartacus programme.

272

1

What is at issue, then, is the substantive content of the pamphlet. But even here the principle, the method, the theoretical foundation, the general view of the character of the revolution which determines the stand to be taken on individual questions, is more important than the attitude adopted to particular problems of the Russian Revolution. For to a great extent these have been superseded by the passage of time.

Even Levi admits this in the case of the agrarian problem. A polemic on that point, then, is superfluous. It is necessary only to indicate the methodological point which takes us one step nearer to the central problem of this study: *to the false view of the character of the proletarian revolution.* Rosa Luxemburg emphasises: "A socialist government which has come to power must in any event do one thing: it must take measures which lead in the direction of those fundamental prerequisites for a later socialist reform of agriculture; it must at least avoid everything which may bar the way to those measures." And so she reproaches Lenin and the Bolsheviks with having omitted to do this, indeed, with having done the opposite. If this opinion stood in isolation one might confine oneself to pointing out that Comrade Luxemburg—like almost everyone else in 1918—was inadequately informed of the true events in Russia. But when we look at this opinion in the context of her other views we can see at once that she overestimates by a long chalk the actual power which the Bolsheviks had at their disposal for choosing the form in which to settle the agrarian question. The agrarian revolution was a given fact and one wholly independent of the will of the Bolsheviks and even of the proletariat. The peasants would have divided up the land in any circumstances in accordance with the elementary expression of their class interests. And had the Bolsheviks resisted them they would have been swept away by this elemental movement just as the Mensheviks and the Socialist Revolutionaries had been swept away by it.

The correct way to put the question about the agrarian problem is not to ask whether the Bolshevik's land reform was a socialist measure or at least one that would lead in the direction of socialism. But whether, in the situation as it then existed, when the rising revolutionary movement was striving towards the point of decision, all the elemental forces of the dissolving bourgeois

L

society could be marshalled against a bourgeoisie that was preparing for the counter-revolution. (And this regardless of whether they were 'purely' proletarian or petty bourgeois, regardless of whether they were heading in the direction of socialism.) In the face of an elemental peasant movement striving after the distribution of land a decision had to be taken. And this decision could only be a clear, unambiguous Yes or No. Either one had to place oneself at the head of the movement, or else to smash it by force of arms. And in that event one would have become the prisoner of the necessarily united bourgeoisie, as in fact happened to the Mensheviks and the Socialist Revolutionaries. *At that moment* there could be no thought of a gradual "deflection" of the peasant movement "in the direction of socialism". This could and had to be attempted later. How far these attempts really failed (and in my view the dossier on this is far from complete; there are 'failures' which nevertheless bear fruit in later contexts) and what the causes of this failure were cannot be investigated here. The issue here is the decision of the Bolsheviks *at the moment when they seized power*. And it must be firmly stated that the Bolsheviks simply were not given the choice between an agrarian reform leading in the direction of socialism and one leading away from it. The only choice they had was *either to mobilise the liberated energies of the elemental peasant movement in the service of the proletarian revolution; or, by pitting itself against the peasants, to isolate the proletariat hopelessly and thus to help the counter-revolution to victory.*

Rosa Luxemburg herself admits this candidly: "As a political measure to fortify the proletarian socialist government, it was an excellent tactical move. Unfortunately, however, it had two sides to it; and the reverse side consisted in the fact that the direct seizure of the land by the peasants has in general nothing at all in common with socialist economy." But when, despite this, she links her correct appreciation of the Bolsheviks' *political tactics* to her criticism of their *socio-economic* mode of action, we can already glimpse the nature of her evaluation of the Russian, of the proletarian Revolution.

It consists in the *overestimation* of its purely proletarian character, and therefore the overestimation both of the external power and of the inner clarity and maturity that the proletarian class can possess and in fact did possess in the first phase of the revolution. And at the same time we see as a corollary the *underestimation* of the importance of the non-proletarian elements in the revolution. And this includes the non-proletarian elements *outside* as well as the power wielded by such idologies *within* the proletariat itself. And this false assessment of the true driving forces leads to the decisive point of her misinterpretation: to the *underplaying of the role of the party* in the revolution and of its conscious political action, as opposed to the necessity of being driven along by the elemental forces of economic development.

2

Some readers may find it exaggerated to turn this into a question of principle. But to make the justice of our assessment stand out more clearly we must return to the particular questions raised in the pamphlet. Rosa Luxemburg's attitude to the nationalities problem in the Russian Revolution leads back to the critical discussions of the war-period, to the Junius pamphlet and to Lenin's criticism of it.

The thesis which Lenin always stubbornly contested (not only on the occassion of the Junius pamphlet, although this is where it was formulated most clearly and succinctly) went thus: "In the era of rampant imperialism there can no longer be any national wars."[2] It might seem as if the divergence of views here were merely theoretical. For Junius and Lenin were in complete agreement about the imperialist character of the World War. Even to the point of seeing that even those sectors of the war which taken in isolation were national wars, had to be considered as imperialist phenomena because of their connections with the total imperialist complex. (As in the case of Serbia and the correct behaviour of the Serbian comrades.) But in practice substantive questions of the first importance immediately present themselves.

In the first place, a situation in which national wars once again become possible is not indeed likely but neither is it wholly out of the question. Its realisation depends on the speed of the transition from the phase of imperialist war into the phase of civil war. So that it is wrong to universalise the imperialist character of the present to the point of denying absolutely that national wars are possible. For if that is done the socialist politician might find himself in a situation where his adherence to principle would lead him to behave in a reactionary manner.

In the second place, the revolts of the colonial and semi-colonial peoples must necessarily be national wars to which the revolutionary parties must by all means lend their support; to be indifferent to them would be directly counter-revolutionary. (See Serrati's attitude to Kemal.)

In the third place, it must not be forgotton that nationalist ideologies still survive and not only in the stratum of the petty bourgeoisie (whose behaviour can be very favourable to the Revolution in certain circumstances) but in the proletariat itself and especially in the proletariat of oppressed nations. And their interest in true internationalism cannot be aroused by intellectual utopians who behave as if the socialist world to come had already arrived and the nationality problem no longer existed. It can be aroused only by the *practical proof that the victorious proletariat of an oppressor nation has broken with the oppressive tendencies of imperialism with all its consequences to the point where it accepts the right of self-determination "including national independence"*. Of course, this slogan must be counterbalanced by the slogan of 'belonging together', of federation. But the mere fact of victory does not free the proletariat from contamination by capitalist and nationalist ideologies, and if it is to pass successfully through the transitional ideological phase, then it will need both slogans *together*. Notwithstanding the setbacks of 1918, the policy of the Bolsheviks on this issue has turned out to have been the right one. For after Brest–Litovsk, even without the notion of the right of complete self-determination, Soviet Russia would have lost the frontier states and the Ukraine. But in the absence of that policy, it would never have been able to recover the latter territories nor the Caucasian Republics, etc.

Rosa Luxemburg's criticism has been refuted on this point by history itself. And we should not have concerned ourselves with it so extensively (Lenin having already refuted the theory of it in his critique of the Junius pamphlet, *Against the Current*) if we had not perceived in it the same view of the character of the proletarian revolution that we have already analysed in the case of the agrarian problem. Here, too, Rosa Luxemburg overlooks the choice between 'impure' socialist necessities which fate forced upon the proletarian revolution right from the start. She overlooks the necessity for the revolutionary party of the proletariat to mobilise all forces which were revolutionary at that moment and so to consolidate the revolutionary front as clearly and powerfully as possible against the moment when the clash with the counter-revolution would come. She constantly opposes to the exigencies of the moment the principles of future stages of the revolution. This practice forms the basis of the ultimately crucial arguments of this pamphlet: concerning force and democracy, the Soviet system and the party. It is therefore important to understand the real tenor of the opinions expressed.

3

In this pamphlet Rosa Luxembourg joins the ranks of those who emphatically disapprove of the dispersal of the Constituent Assembly, the setting-up of the system of soviets, the denial of civil rights to the bourgeoisie, the lack of 'freedom' and the use of terror. We are therefore faced with the task of showing what fundamental theoretical beliefs brought Rosa Luxemburg—the unsurpassed prophet, the unforgettable teacher and leader of revolutionary Marxism—into such a sharp conflict with the revolutionary policy of the Bolsheviks. I have already indicated the most important factors in her appraisal of the situation. It is now essential to take one further step into Rosa Luxemburg's essay so as to be able to grasp the point from which these beliefs follow logically.

This point is the overestimation of *the organic character* of the course of history. In the debate with Bernstein, Rosa Luxemburg has incisively demonstrated that the idea of an organic 'growth' into socialism is untenable. She showed convincingly that history advances dialectically and that the internal contradictions of the capitalist system are constantly intensified; and this is so not merely in the sphere of pure economics but also in the relations between economics and politics. Thus at one point we find clearly stated: "The relations of production of capitalist society become increasingly socialist but its political and legal arrangements erect an ever loftier wall between capitalist and socialist society."[3] This implies the necessity of a violent, revolutionary break with prevailing social trends. Admittedly we can already see here the seeds of a belief that the Revolution was needed only to remove the 'political' obstacles from the path of economic developments. But such a glaring light is thrown upon the dialectical contradictions in capitalist production that it is hardly possible to justify such a conclusion in this context. Moreover, Rosa Luxemburg does not deny the necessity of violence in connection with the Russian Revolution. She declares: "Socialism presupposes a series of acts of violence—against property, etc." And later, in the Spartacus Programme it is recognised that "the violence of the bourgeois counter-revolution must be opposed by the revolutionary violence of the proletariat".[4]

However, this recognition of the role of violence refers only to the *negative* aspect, to the sweeping away of obstacles; it has no relevance to social construction. This cannot be "imposed or introduced by ukase". "The socialist system of society," Rosa Luxemburg claims, "should only be and can only be a historical product, born of the school of its own experiences; and—just like organic nature of which, in the last analysis, it forms a part— it has the fine habit of always producing, along with any real social need, the means to its satisfaction, along with the task simultaneously the solution."

I shall not pause to dwell on the singularly undialectical nature of this line of thought on the part of an otherwise great dialectician. It is enough to note in passing that the rigid contrast, the mechanical separation of the 'positive' and the 'negative', of 'tearing down' and 'building up' directly contradicts the actuality of the Revolution. For in the revolutionary measures taken by the proletarian state, especially those taken directly after the seizing of power, the 'positive' cannot be separated from the 'negative' even conceptually, let alone in practice. The process of struggling against the bourgeoisie, of seizing from its hands the instruments of power in economic conflict coincides—especially at the beginning of the revolution—with the first steps towards organising the economy. It is self-evident that these first attempts will have to be extensively revised later on. Nevertheless, as long as the class struggle persists—that is to say, for a long time—even the later forms of organisation will preserve the 'negative' quality of the struggle, i.e. the tendency to tear down and keep down. Even though the economic forms of the victorious proletarian revolutions to come in Europe may be very different from those in Russia, it yet remains very doubtful that the stage of 'war-communism' (to which Rosa Luxemburg's criticism refers) will be wholly avoidable.

Even more significant than the historical aspects of the passage just quoted is the method it reveals. We can perceive in it a tendency that can be summed up perhaps most clearly as *the ideological organic growth into socialism*. I know that Rosa Luxemburg was one of the first people to advance the opposite view and point to the fact that the transition from capitalism to socialism was characterised by frequent crises and reversions to earlier stages.[5] In this work, too, there is no lack of such passages. If I nevertheless speak of such a tendency I obviously do not mean to accuse her of a kind of opportunism, or of imagining that economic development would bring the proletariat to an adequate ideological maturity so that it merely has to pluck the fruits of this development and violence is needed only to remove 'political' obstacles from its path. Rosa Luxemburg had no illusions about the inevitable relapses, corrective measures and errors of the revolutionary period. Her tendency to overestimate the organic element in history appears only in the—dogmatic—conviction that history produces "along with any real social need the means to its satisfaction, along with the task simultaneously the solution".

This *overestimation of the spontaneous, elemental forces of the Revolution*, above all in the class summoned by history to lead it, determines her attitude to the Constituent Assembly. She reproaches Lenin and Trotsky with having a "rigid, schematic view" because they concluded from the composition of the Assembly that it was unsuited to be the organ of the proletarian revolution. She exclaims: "Yet how all historical experience contradicts this! Experience demonstrates quite the contrary: namely that the living fluid of the popular mood continuously flows around the representative bodies, penetrates them, guides them." And in fact, in an earlier passage, she appeals to the experience of the English and French Revolutions and points to the transformations undergone by their parliamentary bodies. This fact is perfectly correct. But Rosa Luxemburg does not sufficiently emphasise that the 'transformations' were devilishly close to the dispersal of the Constituent Assembly. The revolutionary organisations of those elements of the revolution that constituted the most powerful driving force at the time (the "soldiers' councils" of the English army, the Paris Sections, etc.) *always used force to evict recalcitrant elements from the parliamentary bodies* and it was in this way that they brought such bodies into line with the state of the revolution. Such transformations *in a bourgeois revolution* could for the most part amount only to shifts *within* the parliament, the fighting organ of the bourgeois class. Moreover, it is very noteworthy how much greater was the impact of extra-parliamentary (semi-proletarian) elements in the Great French Revolution in comparison to the English Revolution. Via 1871 and 1905 the Russian Revolution of 1917 brings the *transformation of these intensifications of quantity into changes of quality*. The soviets, the organisations of the most progressive elements of the Revolution were not content this time with 'purging' the Assembly of all parties other than the Bolsheviks and the left-wing Socialist Revolutionaries (and on the basis of her own analysis Rosa Luxemburg would presumably have no objection to this). But they went even further and put themselves in their place. Out of the proletarian (and semi-proletarian) organs for the control and the promotion of the bourgeois revolution developed the governing battle organisations of the victorious proletariat.

4

Now, Rosa Luxemburg absolutely refuses to take this 'leap'. Not merely because she greatly underestimates the abrupt, violent, 'inorganic' character of those past transformations of parliamentary bodies. But *because she rejects the soviet as the chief weapon in the period of transition, as the weapon by which to fight for and gain by force the presuppositions of socialism*. She sees in the soviets the 'superstructure' of that period in which the socialist transformation has been largely accomplished. "It makes no sense to regard the right of suffrage as a utopian product of fantasy, cut loose from social reality. And it is for this reason that it is not a serious instrument of the proletarian dictatorship. It is an anachronism, an anticipation of the juridical situation which is proper on the basis of an already completed socialist economy, but not in the transition period of the proletarian dictatorship."

With the imperturbable logic characteristic of her thought even when it is in error, Rosa Luxemburg here touches upon one of the questions most vital to a theoretical understanding of the period of transition. This is the question of the role to be played by the state (the soviets, the form of state of the victorious proletariat) in the socio-economic transformation of society.

Is it merely the case that a condition of society brought about by economic forces beyond the control of consciousness or, at best, reflected in a 'false' consciousness is to be sanctioned and protected *post facto* by the proletarian state and by its laws? Or do these, the organising forms of the proletariat, exercise a *consciously determining* influence on the economic structure of the period of transition? No doubt, Marx's statement in the *Critique of the Gotha Programme* to the effect that "Law can never be higher than the economic structure of society . . ." remains wholly valid. But this does not mean that *the social function of the proletarian state* and hence its place within the whole framework of proletarian society, *should be the same as that of the bourgeois state within bourgeois society*. In a letter to Konrad Schmidt, Engels assigns the state an essentially negative role within bourgeois society.[6] The state can help an existing economic development to advance, it can work against it or it can "cut it off from certain paths and prescribe certain others". And he adds: "But it is obvious that in cases two and three the political power can do great damage to the economic development and result in the squandering of great masses of energy and material." We may ask, therefore, is the economic and social function of the proletarian state the same as that of the bourgeois state? Can it do no more than—in the most favourable case—accelerate or retard an economic development independent of it (i.e. does the economic situation have *total primacy* vis-à-vis *the state?*). It is obvious that an answer to Rosa Luxemburg's objections to the Bolsheviks depends on the answer to this question. If it is in the affirmative, then Rosa Luxemburg is right: the proletarian state (the soviet system) can only arise as an ideological 'superstructure' *after and in consequence of* a socio-economic revolution that has *already taken place*.

However, the situation looks quite different if we see that the function of the proletarian state is to lay the foundations for the socialist, i.e. the conscious organisation of the economy. This is not to suggest that anyone (and least of all the Russian C.P.) believes that socialism can simply be 'created by decree'. The foundations of capitalist modes of production and with them their 'necessary natural laws' do not simply vanish when the proletariat seizes power or even as a result of the socialisation, however thoroughgoing, of the means of production. But their elimination and replacement by a consciously organised socialist economics must not be thought of only as a lengthy process but as a consciously conducted, stubborn battle. Step by step the ground must be *wrested* from this 'necessity'. Every overestimation of the ripeness of circumstances or of the power of the proletariat, every underestimation of the strength of the opposing forces has to be paid for bitterly in the form of crises, relapses and economic developments that inexorably revert to the situation before the point of departure. Yet the observation that the power of the proletariat and the possibility of conscious economic planning are often extremely limited should not lead us to conclude that the 'economics' of socialism will prevail—just as under capitalism—by virtue of their own momentum and through the 'blind laws' of the forces behind them. As Lenin remarks in his interpretation of the letter to Kautsky of 12 September, 1891, "Engels does not mean that 'economics' would of itself clear every obstacle out of the way. . . . The adaptation of politics to economics will follow inevitably but not all at once, not straightforwardly, not smoothly and not directly."[7]

The conscious, the organised planning of the economy can only be introduced consciously and the organ which will introduce it is in fact the proletariat, the soviet system. Thus the soviets signify in effect "the anticipation of the legal position" of a later phase of class stratification; however, they are not a utopia suspended in mid-air but, on the contrary, *the only instrument that is suitable really to call this anticipated situation into existence*. For socialism would never happen 'by itself', and as the result of an inevitable natural economic development. The natural laws of capitalism do indeed lead inevitably to its ultimate crisis but at the end of *its* road would be the destruction of all civilisation and a new barbarism.

It is this that constitutes the most profound difference between bourgeois and proletarian revolutions. The ability of bourgeois revolutions to storm ahead with such brilliant *élan* is grounded socially, in the fact that *they are drawing the consequences of an almost completed economic and social process in a society whose feudal and absolutist structure has been profoundly undermined politically, governmentally, juridically, etc., by the vigorous upsurge of capitalism*. The true revolutionary element is the economic transformation of the feudal system of production into a capitalist one so that it would be possible in theory for *this* process to take place *without a bourgeois revolution*, without political upheaval on the part of the revolutionary bourgeoisie. And in that case those parts of the feudal and absolutist superstructure that were not eliminated by 'revolutions from above' would collapse of their own accord when capitalism was already fully developed. (The German situation fits this pattern in certain respects.)

No doubt, a proletarian revolution, too, would be unthinkable if its economic premises and preconditions had not already been nurtured in the bosom of capitalist society by the evolution of the capitalist system of production. But the enormous difference between the two types of process lies in the fact that *capitalism already developed within feudalism, thus bringing about its dissolution.* In contrast to this, it would be a utopian fantasy to imagine that anything tending towards socialism could arise within capitalism apart from, on the one hand, the *objective economic premises that make it a possibility* which, however, can only be *transformed* into the true elements of a socialist system of production after and in consequence of the collapse of capitalism; and, on the other hand, the development of the proletariat as a class. Consider the development undergone by manufacture and the capitalist system of tenure even when the feudal social system was still in existence. As far as these were concerned it was only necessary to clear away the legal obstacles to their free development. By contrast, the concentration of capital in cartels, trusts, etc., does constitute, it is true, an unavoidable premise for the conversion of a capitalist mode of production into a socialist one. But even the most highly developed capitalist concentration will still be qualitatively different, even economically, from a socialist system and can neither change into one 'by itself' nor will it be amenable to such change 'through legal devices' within the framework of capitalist society. The tragi-comic collapse of all 'attempts to introduce socialism' in Germany and Austria furnishes ample proof of this.

The fact that after the fall of capitalism a *lengthy and painful process* sets in that makes this very attempt is no contradiction. On the contrary, it would be a totally undialectical, unhistorical mode of thought which, from the proposition that socialism could come into existence only as a *conscious transformation of the whole of society*, would infer that this must take place at one stroke and not as the end product of a process. This process, however, is *qualitatively* different from the transformation of feudalism into bourgeois society. And it is this very qualitative difference that is expressed in the different function of the state in the revolution (which as Engels says "is no longer a state in the true sense"); it is expressed most plainly in the qualitatively different relation of politics to economics. The very fact that the proletariat is aware of the role of the state in the proletarian revolution, in contrast to the ideological masking of it in bourgeois revolutions, an awareness that *foresees* and overturns in contrast to the *post festum* recognitions of the bourgeoisie, points up the difference sharply enough. In her criticism of the replacement of the Constituent Assembly by the soviets Rosa Luxemburg fails to note this: *she imagines the proletarian revolution as having the structural forms of bourgeois revolutions.*

5

This sharp antithesis between an 'organic' and a dialectical, revolutionary appraisal of the situation can lead us even more deeply into Rosa Luxemburg's train of thought, namely to the problem of the role of the party in the revolution and from there to the Bolshevik conception of the party and its consequences for organisation and tactics.

The antithesis between Lenin and Luxemburg has its roots quite a long way in the past. As is well known, at the time of the first conflict between the Mensheviks and the Bolsheviks on the question of organisation, Rosa Luxemburg took sides against the latter. Her opposition was not dictated by political tactics but purely by organisational considerations. In almost all tactical issues (mass strikes, appraisal of the Revolution of 1905, imperialism, struggle against the coming World War, etc.), Rosa Luxemburg was in harmony with the Bolsheviks. In Stuttgart at the time of the decisive resolution on the war she was in fact the Bolsheviks' representative.

Nevertheless, the antagonism is much less episodic than the long history of tactical political agreement would make it appear; even though, on the other hand, it is not enough to justify inferring a strict parting of the ways. Lenin and Rosa Luxemburg were agreed *politically* and *theoretically* about the need to combat opportunism. The conflict between them lay in their answers to the question whether or not the campaign against opportunism should be conducted as an *intellectual* struggle *within* the revolutionary party of the proletariat or whether it was to be resolved on the level of *organisation*.

Rosa Luxemburg opposes the latter view. Firstly, because she finds exaggerated the central role assigned by the Bolsheviks to questions of organisation as the guarantees of the spirit of revolution in the workers' movement. She maintains the opposite view that real revolutionary spirit is to be sought and found exclusively in the elemental spontaneity of the masses. Unlike them the central party organisations have always a conservative, braking function. She believes that with a really thorough centralisation "the differ-

ence between the eager attack of the mass and the prudent position of Social Democracy"[8] could only be exacerbated.

Secondly, she regards the form of organisation itself as something which grows and not as something 'made'. "In the social-
democratic movement organisation too . . . is a historical product
of class struggle and to it social democracy *has only to add political
consciousness*."[9] And this belief in turn is based *on her overall view of
the probable course of the revolutionary movement.* We have already seen
the practical consequences of this view in her critique of the
Bolshevik agrarian reform and her slogan of the right to self-
determination. She states: "Social Democracy has always con-
tended that it represents not only the class interests of the proletariat but also the progressive aspirations of the whole of contemporary society. It represents the interests of all who are oppressed
by bourgeois domination. This must not be understood merely
in the sense that all these interests are ideally contained in the
socialist programme. Historical evolution translates the given
proposition into reality. In its capacity as *a political party* Social
Democracy gradually becomes the haven of all discontented elements in our society and thus of the entire people, as contrasted
to the tiny minority of the capitalist masters."[10]

It is apparent from this that in her view the development of
revolutionary and counter-revolutionary fronts proceeds 'organically' (even before the revolution itself becomes imminent). *The
party becomes the organisational focus of all the strata whom the processes
of history have brought into action against the bourgeoisie.* It is necessary only to ensure that the idea of class struggle does not become
adulterated and infected by petty-bourgeois notions. In this the
centralised organ can and should help. But only in the sense that
it should be "at most a coercive instrument enforcing the will of
the proletarian majority in the party".[11]

Thus, on the one hand, Rosa Luxemburg starts from the premise that the working class will enter the revolution as a unified
revolutionary body which has been neither contaminated nor led
astray by the democratic illusions of bourgeois society.[12] On the
other hand, she appears to assume that the petty-bourgeois strata
that are mortally threatened in their social existence by the
revolutionary aggravation of the economic situation will join the
ranks of the fighting proletariat even to the extent of establishing
organisational, party bonds. If this assumption is correct its
illuminating corollary will be the rejection of the Bolshevik con-

ception of the party. For the political basis of that conception is the recognition that the proletariat must indeed carry out the revolution *in league* with the other classes that are in conflict with the bourgeoisie, but not as part of the same organisation. In the process it will necessarily *come into conflict with certain proletarian strata* who are fighting on the side of the bourgeoisie against the revolutionary proletariat. In this context it must not be forgotten that the cause of the first breach with the Mensheviks was not just the question of the regulations governing organisation. It involved also the problem of an alliance with the 'progressive' bourgeoisie and the problem of a coalition in order to carry out and secure the bourgeois revolution (which among other things meant in practice the betrayal of the revolutionary peasant movement).

In all questions of political tactics Rosa Luxemburg was at one with the Bolsheviks against their opportunist enemies; she was always not merely the most penetrating and passionate but also the most profound and radical unmasker of every kind of opportunism. But we see clearly here why *when it came to appraising the danger represented by opportunism, and the methods needed to combat it, she had to choose another path.* For if the war with opportunism is conceived exclusively as an intellectual conflict *within* the party it must obviously be waged so as to put the whole emphasis on convincing the supporters of opportunism and on achieving a majority *within* the party. Naturally, it follows that the struggle against opportunism will disintegrate *into a series of individual skirmishes* in which the ally of yesterday can become the opponent of today and vice versa. A war against *opportunism as a tendency* cannot crystallise out: the terrain of the 'intellectual conflicts' changes from one issue to the next and with it changes the composition of the rival groups. (Thus Kautsky in conflict with Bernstein and in the debate on the mass strike; Pannekoek in this and also in the dispute about accumulation; Lensch's attitude on this question and in the war, and so on.) This unorganised course of events was naturally not completely able to prevent the emergence of a right wing, a centre and a left wing, even in the non-Russian parties. But the merely episodic nature of these coalitions meant that in intellectual and organisational (i.e. party) terms the disagreements could not be clearly defined and this led necessarily to quite false groupings. When these did become fixed organisationally they became major obstacles to clarification in the working class. (Thus Ströbel in the 'Internationale' Group; 'Pacifism' as a factor causing a breach with the right wing; Bernstein in the Independent Socialist Party; Serrati in Zimmerwald; Klara Zetkin at the International Conference of Women.) These dangers were increased by the fact that—as in Western and Central Europe the party apparatus was mainly in the hands of the centre or the right wing—the unorganised, merely intellectual war against opportunism easily and frequently became an assault on the party-form as such. (Pannekoek, Rühle, etc.)

At the time of the first Lenin–Luxemburg debate and directly after, these dangers could not yet be clearly seen, at least not by those who were not in a position to evaluate critically the experience of the first Russian Revolution. Although Rosa Luxemburg was one of the greatest experts on Russian affairs she nevertheless adopted in all essentials the position of the non-Russian Left which was recruited chiefly from that radical stratum of the workers' movement that had had no practical revolutionary experience. That she did so can only be explained in terms of her 'overall organic view'. In view of what has been said, it is illuminating to see that in her otherwise magisterial analysis of the mass-strike movements of the first Russian Revolution she makes no mention whatever of the role played by the Mensheviks in the political movements in those years. At the same time she was perfectly aware of the tactical and political dangers implicit in every opportunistic attitude and she fought them vigorously. But she held to the opinion that swings to the Right should be and are dealt with—more or less spontaneously—by the 'organic' development of the workers' movement. Hence she ends her polemic against Lenin with the words: "Let us speak plainly. Historically, the errors committed by a truly revolutionary movement are infinitely more fruitful and more valuable than the infallibility of the best of all possible 'Central Committees'."[13]

6

With the outbreak of the World War, with the emergence of the civil war this quondam 'theoretical' question became a burning issue in practice. *The problem of organisation was converted into one of political tactics.* The problem of Menshevism became the crucial issue for the proletarian revolution. The walkover victory gained by the imperialist bourgeoisie over the whole of the Second International in the period of mobilisation in 1914, and the fact that this victory could be extended and consolidated during the World War, cannot possibly be understood as a 'misfortune' or as the inevitable consequence of 'betrayal'. If the revolutionary workers' movement wished to recover from this defeat and even turn it into the foundation of the victorious battles still to come *it was absolutely essential for it to see this failure, this 'betrayal' in the context of the history of the workers' movement; social chauvinism and pacifism, etc., would have then to be recognised as logical extensions of opportunism.*

To have seen this is one of the permanent gains resulting from Lenin's activity during the war. And his criticism of the Junius Pamphlet begins at that very point, namely with the failure to engage with opportunism as a general tendency. Admittedly, the Junius Pamphlet and the 'Internationale' were both full of *theoretically correct* polemics against the treachery of the Right and the vacillations of the Centre of the German workers' movement. But this polemic remained on the level of theory and propaganda rather than organisation because it was still informed by the belief that the debate was concerned only with 'differences of opinion' *within* the revolutionary party of the proletariat. It is true that the Guiding Principles attached to the Junius Pamphlet did include the organisational proposal for the founding of a new International (Theses 10–12). But this proposal was left suspended in mid-air as the intellectual and therefore the organisational backing needed to put it into practice were not forthcoming.

At this point the problem of organisation is transformed into a political one which concerns the whole of the revolutionary proletariat. The failure of all the workers' parties when confronted with the World War must be seen as a world historical fact, i.e. as the inevitable consequence of the previous history of the workers' movement. The fact was that almost without exception an influential section of the leadership in the workers' parties openly went over to the side of the bourgeoisie while another group was tacitly and secretly in league with it. *That both these groups have succeeded in retaining their hold on the crucial strata of the proletariat both intellectually and organisationally must be made the point of departure for the analysis of the situation and of the tasks of the revolutionary workers' party.* It must be clearly understood that as two fronts gradually crystallise out in the civil war the proletariat will at first enter the struggle deeply divided. This division cannot be made to disappear by discussions. It is a vain hope to rely on the fact that in time even these groups of leaders will be 'convinced' by the correctness of revolutionary beliefs; and that therefore the workers' movement will be able to construct its—revolutionary— unity 'organically' and from 'within'.

The problem arises: how can the great mass of the proletariat which is *instinctively* revolutionary but has *not reached the stage of clear consciousness* be rescued from the hands of this leadership? And it is obvious that it is precisely the 'organic' theoretical character of the conflict that has made it so easy for the Mensheviks to conceal from the proletariat for so long the fact that in the hour of decision they stand on the side of the bourgeoisie.

That part of the proletariat that spontaneously rebels against its leaders' behaviour in this respect and that longs for revolutionary leadership *must assemble in an organisation*. The genuine revolutionary parties and groups which thus arise must contrive to win the confidence of the great masses and remove them from the power of the opportunists by their *actions* (and furthermore it is absolutely essential that they acquire their *own revolutionary party organisations*). Until this is accomplished there is no question of a civil war taking place despite the fact that the overall situation is consistently and increasingly revolutionary.

And the world situation is—objectively—consistently and increasingly revolutionary. In her classical work *The Accumulation of Capital*, a book which the revolutionary movement, to its own great detriment, has neither appreciated nor profited from adequately, Rosa Luxemburg herself has provided the theoretical basis for understanding the—objectively—revolutionary character of the situation. She shows there that as capitalism develops it destroys those strata which are neither capitalist nor proletarian. This analysis *contains the socio-economic theory that suggests what the revolutionary tactics of the Bolsheviks ought to be* vis-à-vis *the non-proletarian strata of workers*. As the point approaches where capitalism reaches the apex of its development this destructive process must take more and more violent forms. Broader and broader strata separate out from the—seemingly—solid edifice of bourgeois society; they then bring confusion into the ranks of the bourgeoisie, they unleash movements which do not themselves proceed in the direction of socialism but which through the violence of the impact they make do hasten the realisation of the preconditions of socialism: namely, the collapse of the bourgeoisie.

In this situation which causes ever wider rifts in bourgeois society and which drives the proletariat on to revolution whether it would or not, *the Mensheviks have openly or covertly gone over to the camp of the bourgeoisie.* They stand behind enemy lines opposed to the revolutionary proletariat and the other instinctively rebellious strata (and perhaps nations). But to recognise this is to see that *Rosa Luxemburg's view of the course of the revolution collapses* and it was this view upon which her opposition to the Bolshevik form of organisation was based. In *The Accumulation of Capital* Rosa Luxemburg provided the most profound economic foundations for this understanding. As Lenin points out, she was only a step away from the clear formulation of it at many points in the Junius Pamphlet. But in her criticism of the Russian Revolution she was not yet able to draw the necessary conclusions from it. Even in 1918, even after the experiences of the first stage of the Revolution in Russia, she seems to have regarded the problem of Menshevism with unchanged eyes.

7

This explains why she takes it upon herself to defend the 'rights of freedom' against the Bolsheviks. "Freedom," she says, "is always freedom for the one who thinks differently." Which means freedom for the other 'currents' in the workers' movement: for the Mensheviks, and the Socialist Revolutionaries. It is obvious that Rosa Luxemburg is never at pains to offer a banal defence of democracy 'in general'. Her attitude here is no more than the logical consequence of her false estimate of the distribution of power in the present stage of the revolution. For the attitude adopted by a revolutionary to the so-called problems of freedom in the age of the dictatorship of the proletariat depends in the last analysis entirely on whether he regards *the Mensheviks as the enemies of the revolution or as one 'current' of the revolution,* one that simply has a divergent opinion in isolated questions of tactics and organisation, etc.

Everything which Rosa Luxemburg has to say about the necessity of criticism and about public control would be subscribed to by every Bolshevik and by Lenin above all—as Rosa Luxemburg herself emphasises. The only question is how is all this to be realised, how is *'freedom'* (and everything it entails) *to be given a revolutionary and not a counter-revolutionary function*? Otto Bauer, one of the cleverest opponents of the Bolsheviks, has grasped this problem with some clarity. He combats the 'undemocratic' nature of the Bolshevik state not merely with the aid of abstract reasons of natural law à la Kautsky, but because the Soviet system prevents the 'real' consolidation of the classes in Russia, because it prevents the peasants from asserting themselves and hence the peasants are dragged along in the wake of the proletariat. In saying this he bears witness—against his will—to the revolutionary character of the Bolshevik 'suppression of freedom'.

Rosa Luxemburg's exaggeration of the organic nature of the course of the revolution forces her into the most startling contradictions. The Spartacus Programme had provided the basis in theory for the centrist quibbles about the distinction between 'terror' and 'violence' in which the latter was affirmed while the former was rejected. And here too, in this pamphlet we find the contrast made by the Dutch Communist Workers' Party and the 'KAP' between the dictatorship of the party and the dictatorship of the class. Of course, when two people do the same thing (and even more when two people say the same thing) the result is not the same. However, even Rosa Luxemburg—just because she was becoming more and more remote from an understanding of the real structure of the opposing forces—comes dangerously close to exaggerating utopian expectations and to anticipating later phases in the process. Such distinctions did in fact lead to utopianism, a fate from which her, unfortunately too brief, practical activity in the revolution mercifully preserved her.

According to Rosa Luxemburg in her article against Lenin, the dialectical contradiction in the social-democratic movement consists in the fact that "for the first time in the history of civilisation the people are expressing their will consciously and in opposition to all ruling classes. But this will can only be satisfied *beyond the limits* of the existing system. Now the masses can only acquire and strengthen this will in the course of the day-to-day struggle against the existing social order—that is, *within the limits of capitalist society*. On the one hand, we have the masses; on the other, their historic goal, located outside existing society. On the one hand, we have the day-to-day struggle; on the other, the social revolution. Such are the terms of *the dialectical contradiction* in the social democratic movement. . . .[14]

This dialectical contradiction does not become any the less acute with the coming of the dictatorship of the proletariat: only its terms, the existing framework of action and that goal existing 'beyond' it, change their content. And the very problem of freedom and democracy that had seemed so simple while the war was fought out within bourgeois society because every foot of territory gained *was won from the bourgeoisie*, now advances *dialectically* to its crisis point. Even the actual process of wresting 'freedoms' from the bourgeoisie does not proceed in a straight line though, to be sure, the tactical goals which the proletariat set themselves did so and in an increasingly concentrated fashion. But now even this attitude must be modified. Lenin says of capitalist democracy that "developments do not always lead smoothly and directly to further democratisation".[15] Nor can they, because socially the revolutionary period is marked by the constant, abrupt and violent changes that occur as a result of the economic crisis both in a dying capitalism and in a proletarian society striving to establish itself.

From this it follows that the *continuous regrouping of revolutionary energies is a matter of life and death for the revolution*. It is evident that the overall economic situation will sooner or later drive the proletariat to create a revolution on a global scale. This revolution must first be in a position to adopt economic measures that are truly socialist. In the interests of the further progress of the revolution and acting with full confidence in this knowledge it is essential for *the proletariat to use all the means at its disposal to keep the power of the state in its own hands under all circumstances*. The victorious proletariat must not make the mistake of dogmatically determining its policy in advance either economically or ideologically. It must be able to manoeuvre freely in its economic policy (socialisation, concessions, etc.) depending on the way the classes are restratified and also upon how possible and necessary it is to win over certain groups of workers for the dictatorship or at least to induce them to preserve their neutrality.

Similarly, it must not allow itself to be pinned down on the whole complex issue of freedom. During the period of the dictatorship the nature and the extent of freedom will be determined by the state of the class struggle, the power of the enemy, the importance of the threat to the dictatorship, the demands of the classes to be won over, and by the maturity of the classes allied to and influenced by the proletariat. Freedom cannot represent a value in itself (any more than socialisation). *Freedom must serve the rule of the proletariat, not the other way round*. Only a revolutionary party like that of the Bolsheviks is able to carry out these often very sudden changes of front. Only such a party is sufficiently adaptable, flexible and independent in judgement of the actual forces at work to be able to advance from Brest–Litovsk and the war-communism of the fiercest civil wars to the new economic policy. Only the Bolsheviks will be able to progress from that policy (in the event of new shifts in the balance of power) to yet other power-groupings while preserving unimpaired the essential dominance of the proletariat.

However, in this flux one fixed pole has remained: the counter-revolutionary attitude of the other currents within the working-class movement. There is a straight line here running from Kornilov to Kronstadt. Their 'critique' of the dictatorship is not a self-criticism performed by the proletariat—the possibility of which must be kept open institutionally even under the dictatorship. It is a corrosive tendency in the service of the bourgeoisie. Engels' remark to Bebel may rightly be applied to such tendencies: "So long as the proletariat still *uses* the state, it does not use it in the interests of freedom but in order to hold down its adversaries."[16] And the fact that in the course of the revolution Rosa Luxemburg revised the views here analysed is certainly connected with the few months granted to her to experience intensively the actual progress of the revolution. This experience will undoubtedly have brought home to her the fallacies inherent in her earlier conception of its nature and in particular her mistaken view of the role played by opportunism, of the method of combating it and thence of the structure and function of the revolutionary party itself.

January 1922.

NOTES

1 Rosa Luxemburg, *The Russian Revolution*, ed. Bertram D. Wolfe, University of Michigan Press, 1961.
2 *Leitsätze über die Aufgaben der internationalen Sozialdemokratie.* These 5. Futurus Verl. 105.
3 *Soziale Reform oder Revolution?* Vulkan Verlag, p. 21.
4 *Bericht über den Gründungsparteitag der K.P.D.*, p. 53.
5 *Soziale Reform oder Revolution?* p. 47.
6 *Dokumente des Sozialismus* II, pp. 67–8.
7 Lenin/Zinoviev, *Gegen den Strom*, p. 409.
8 *Leninism or Marxism*, ed. Bertram D. Wolfe, University of Michigan Press, 1961, p. 92.
9 Ibid., p. 85 et seq. (my italics).
10 Ibid., p. 92

11   Ibid., p. 104.
12   *Massentreik, Partei und Gewerkschafte* 2nd edition, p. 51.
13   *Leninism or Marxism*, p. 108.
14   Ibid., p. 105 (my italics).
15   *The State and Revolution*, p. 327.
16   Ibid., p. 309.

Towards a Methodology of the Problem of Organisation

> Politics cannot be separated mechanically from organisation.
>
> Lenin: Speech concluding the 11th Congress of the Russian C.P.

ALTHOUGH there have been times when problems of organisation stood in the forefront of debate (e.g. when the conditions of amalgamation were under discussion), it nevertheless remains true that theorists have paid less attention to such questions than to any others. The idea of the Communist Party, opposed and slandered by all opportunists, instinctively seized upon and made their own by the best revolutionary workers, has yet often been seen purely in *technical* terms rather than as one of the most important *intellectual* questions of the revolution. It is not that materials were lacking for such a theoretical deepening of the problem of organisation. The theses of the 2nd and 3rd Congresses, the debates on policy within the Russian Party and the practical lessons of recent years provide a plethora of material. But the theoretical interest of the Communist Parties (always excepting the Russian C.P.) seems to have been too much absorbed by the problems presented by the economic and political situation, by their tactical implications and their foundation in theory. With the result that no really vital theoretical energy seemed to be left over for the task of anchoring the problem of organisation in communist theory. If much activity in this sphere is correct, this is due more to correct revolutionary instincts than to any clear theoretical insight. On the other hand, there are many false tactical attitudes, e.g. in the debates on a united front, which derive from a mistaken view of the problems of organisation.

Such 'unconsciousness' in these matters is quite definitely a sign of the immaturity of the movement. For the question of maturity and immaturity can only be resolved by asking whether the attitudes of the class and the party that leads it towards action are abstract and immediate, or concretely mediated. That is to say, as long as an objective still lies beyond reach, observers with particularly acute insight will be able to a certain extent to envisage the goal itself, its nature and its social necessity. They will, however, be unable to discern clearly either the concrete steps that would lead to that goal or the concrete means that could be deduced from their doubtlessly correct insight.

The utopians, it is true, can clearly see the situation that must constitute the point of departure. What makes them utopians is that they see it as a fact or at best as a problem that requires a solution but are unable to grasp the fact that the problem itself contains both the solution and the path leading to it. Thus "they see in poverty nothing but poverty without recognising in it the revolutionary, subversive side which will overturn the old society".[1] The antagonism emphasised here between a doctrinaire and a revolutionary science goes beyond the case analysed by Marx and broadens out into a typical antagonism in the evolution of the consciousness of the revolutionary class. As the proletariat advanced along the road to revolution, poverty ceased to be merely something given: it became integrated into the living dialectics of action. But—depending on the stage of development attained by the class—its place was taken by other phenomena which were regarded by proletarian theory in a way that closely resembled the *structure* analysed here by Marx. It would be a utopian illusion to infer that utopianism had been overcome by the revolutionary workers' movement merely because Marx refuted its first primitive manifestation.

In the last analysis this question is the same as that of the dialectical relation between 'final goal' and 'movement', i.e. between theory and practice. At every crucial stage of the revolution it reappears, always in a more advanced form and with reference to different phenomena. For a problem always makes its appearance first as an abstract possibility and only afterwards is it realised in concrete terms. And it only becomes meaningful to discuss whether questions are rightly or wrongly conceived when this second stage has been reached, when it becomes possible to recognise that concrete totality which is destined to constitute the environment and the path to the realisation of the goal in question. Thus, in the early debates of the Second International, the general strike was a purely abstract utopia which only acquired a concrete form with the first Russian Revolution and the Belgian general strike. Likewise, only after years of acute revolutionary conflict had elapsed was it possible for the Workers' Council to shed its utopian, mythological character and cease to be viewed as the panacea for all the problems of the revolution; it was years before it could be seen by the non-Russian proletariat for what it really was. (I do not mean to suggest that this process of clarification has been completed. In fact I doubt it very much. But as it is being invoked only by way of illustration I shall not enter into discussion of it here.)

It is precisely the problems of organisation which have languished longest in the half-light of utopianism. This is no accident. The great workers' parties grew up for the most part in periods when the problem of revolution was only conceived as influencing programmes in a theoretical way rather than as something which informed all the actions of daily life. Thus it did not seem necessary to spell out in theoretically concrete terms the nature and the probable course of the revolution in order to infer the manner in which the conscious sector of the proletariat should consciously act. However, the question of how to organise a revolutionary party can only be developed organically from a theory of revolution itself. Only when the revolution has entered into quotidian reality will the question of *revolutionary* organisation demand imperiously to be admitted to the consciousness of the masses and their theoreticians.

And even then only gradually. Even when the revolution became a fact, even when the necessity of taking up an immediate attitude towards it became unavoidable, as was the case during and after the first Russian Revolution, no real insight emerged. Part of the reason for this lay in the circumstance that opportunism had already taken root so deeply in the proletarian parties as to render a correct theoretical understanding of the revolution impossible. But even where this was not the case, even where the driving forces behind the revolution were clearly understood, this insight could not develop into a theory of revolutionary organisation. What stood in the way of that was, in part at least, the ununconscious, theoretically undigested, merely 'organic' character of the existing organisations.

The Russian Revolution clearly exposed the limitations of the West European organisations. Their impotence in the face of the spontaneous movements of the masses was clearly exposed on the issues of mass actions and the mass strike. A fatal blow was dealt to the opportunistic illusion implicit in the notion of the 'organisational preparation' for such actions. It was plainly demonstrated that such organisations always limp behind the real actions of the masses, and that they impede rather than further them, let alone lead them.

Rosa Luxemburg saw the significance of mass actions more clearly than anyone and her view goes much deeper than this criticism. She locates the defects of the traditional notion of organisation in its false relation to the masses: "The overestimation of or the misapprehensions about the role of organisation in the class struggle of the proletariat are usually accompanied by feelings of contempt for the unorganised proletarian masses and for their political immaturity."[2] Her own conclusions lead her, on the one hand, to a polemic against this overemphasis on organisation and, on the other hand, to an analysis of the function of the party. This is seen to lie "not in the technicalities of the preparations for the mass strike and in supplying its leadership but first and foremost in the *political leadership* of the whole movement".[3]

This was a great step forward in understanding the whole problem of organisation. By destroying its status of an abstraction in isolation (by correcting the tendency to 'overestimate' organisation) Rosa Luxemburg made it possible to define its *true function* within the revolutionary process. It was necessary, however, to go one step further and to look at the question of political leadership in the context of organisation. That is to say, she should have elucidated those *organisational factors* that render the party of the proletariat capable of assuming political leadership. We have elsewhere discussed in detail the considerations that prevented her from taking this step. It is only necessary to point out here that this step had in fact been taken some years earlier, namely in the debate about organisation in the Russian Social Democratic Party.

Rosa Luxemburg had clearly understood the issue but on this one question she sided with the retrograde party (of the Mensheviks). It is no accident that the factors responsible for the split in Russian Social Democracy included, on the one hand, the division of opinion about the nature of the coming revolution and the tasks it would impose (coalition with the 'progressive' bourgeoisie or else a struggle alongside the peasants' revolution), and on the other hand, the problems of organisation. What turned out to be disastrous for the movement outside Russia was that no one (not even Rosa Luxemburg) realised that the *two issues* really belonged together and were bound up in an indivisible dialectical *unity*. In consequence the opportunity was missed to disseminate information about the problems of revolutionary organisation among the proletariat with a view to preparing it intellectually for coming events; (at the time this was the most that could be expected). Moreover, even the correct political insights of Rosa Luxemburg, Pannekoek and others could not become sufficiently concrete—even as political trends. In Rosa Luxemburg's words they remained latent, merely theoretical, their links with the concrete movement were still infected with Utopianism.[4]

Organisation is the form of mediation between theory and practice. And, as in every dialectical relationship, the terms of the relation only acquire concreteness and reality in and by virtue of this mediation. The ability of organisation to mediate between theory and practice is seen most clearly by the way in which it manifests a much greater, finer and more confident sensitivity towards divergent trends than any other sector of political thought and action. On the level of pure theory the most disparate views and tendencies are able to co-exist peacefully, antagonisms are only expressed in the form of discussions which can be contained within the framework of one and the same organisation without disrupting it. But no sooner are these same questions given organisational form than they turn out to be sharply opposed and even incompatible.

Every 'theoretical' tendency or clash of views must immediately develop an organisational arm if it is to rise above the level of pure theory or abstract opinion, that is to say, if it really intends to point the way to its own fulfilment in practice. However, it would be an error to suppose that every instance of organised action can constitute a real and a reliable index of the validity of conflicting opinions or even of their compatibility or incompatibility. Every organised action is—in and for itself—a tangle of individual deeds on the part of individuals and groups. It is equally false to interpret it either as a socially and historically adequately motivated 'necessary' happening, or as the consequence of 'erroneous' or 'correct' decisions on the part of individuals. This tangle, confused in itself, can only acquire meaning and reality if it is comprehended within a historical totality. That is to say, it must possess a function within the historical process and its mediating role between past and future must be understood. However, an analysis that would see an organised action in terms of the lessons it contained for the future, as an answer to the question 'what then shall we do?' sees the problem in terms of organisation. By gauging the situation, by preparing for the action and by leading it such an analysis attempts to isolate those factors that lead with *necessity* from theory to the most appropriate action possible. It seeks out the *essential determinants* that connect theory and practice.

It is evident that only an investigation along these lines will make possible a truly seminal self-criticism and a truly seminal analysis of past 'errors'. The belief that events are generated by a 'necessity' leads to fatalism; similarly, the empty assumption that the 'errors' or the adroitness of individuals were the source of failure or success will yield no decisively creative doctrines for future action. From such a point of view it will always seem more or less 'adventitious' that this or that person should have been positioned at this point or that and made this or that mistake. The discovery of such a mistake can only go to show that the person concerned was unfit to hold his position. This insight is not without value, if correct, but as far as the essential self-criticism is concerned it can only be of secondary importance. The very fact that such a point of view so exaggerates the importance of individuals shows that it is incapable of objectifying the roles played by these individuals and their ability to determine an organised action decisively and in a particular manner. From this viewpoint individuals are regarded as fatalistically as objective fatalism regarded the whole process. But if the question is seen to involve more than merely isolated and chance phenomena, if it is granted that the right or wrong lines of action pursued by individuals are not without influence on the whole complex of events but that over and above this, and while accepting as given that these specific people were occupying these posts, etc., it is legitimate to investigate the objective range of possibilities for action open to them—in that case the problem will once again have entered the realm of organisation.[5] For this would be to direct attention towards the unity, holding the actors together and examine its appropriateness for a particular action. It would be to ask whether the right organisational methods have been chosen for transforming theory into practice.

Of course, the 'error' can lie in the theory, in the choice of objective or in the appraisal of the situation. But only an analysis orientated towards organisation can make possible a genuine criticism of theory from the point of view of practice. If theory is directly juxtaposed to an organised action without its being made clear how it is supposed to affect it, i.e. without clearly expressing their connectedness in terms of organisation, then the theory can only be criticised with regard to its own internal contradictions. This aspect of the problems of organisation enables us to understand why opportunism has always shown the very greatest reluctance to deduce organisational consequences from any theoretical disagreements.

The attitude of the German right-wing (Socialist) Independents and the followers of Serrati towards the conditions of admission laid down by the Second Congress, their attempt to shift the ground of the debate about their material disagreements with the Communist International from the realm of organisation to that of 'pure politics', sprang from their correct opportunistic instinct to the effect that in that realm the disagreements would endure for a very long time in a latent, and for practical purposes, unresolved state. By contrast, the Second Congress put the problem on the organisational level and thus forced an immediate and clear decision.

However, such an attitude is by no means new. The whole history of the Second International is full of such attempts to synthesise the most disparate, the most sharply divergent and incompatible views in the 'unity' of a decision, of a resolution that would do justice to them all. Inevitably these resolutions could not provide any guidance for concrete action and remained ambivalent and open to the most divergent interpretations. Just because the Second International studiously avoided all implications for organisation it was able to commit itself to many things in theory without feeling in the least compelled to bind itself to any particular line in practice. Thus it was possible to approve the very radical Stuttgart resolution about the war, although it contained no organisational obligations to take any definite concrete action, no organisational guide lines about what action should be taken and no organisational guarantees about whether the resolution could be implemented in practice. The opportunist minority felt no need to draw organisational conclusions from its defeat because it realised that the resolution would have no organisational consequences. This is why after the collapse of the International every shade of opinion was able to appeal to this resolution.

The weak point of all the non-Russian radical groups in the International lay in the fact that while their revolutionary positions diverged from the opportunism of the open Revisionists and the Centre they were neither able nor willing to give them any concrete organisational form. In consequence their opponents, and above all the Centre, were able to blur these distinctions in the minds of the revolutionary proletariat. The fact that they were in opposition in no way prevented the Centre from posing before the revolutionarily-minded section of the proletariat as the guardians of the true Marxism. It cannot possibly be our task here to offer a theoretical and historical explanation for the dominance of the Centre in the pre-war period. We wish only to point out once again that the attitudes of the Centre were viable because in the daily life of the movement, revolution and the reaction to the problems of revolution were not matters of immediate concern. These attitudes included a polemic both against an open Revisionism and against the demand for revolutionary action; the theoretical rejection of the former without making any serious efforts to eliminate it from the praxis of the party; the theoretical affirmation of the latter while denying its immediate application to the situation. With all this it was still possible, e.g. for Kautsky and Hilferding, to insist on the generally revolutionary nature of the age and on the idea that the *time was ripe for revolution* without feeling the compulsion to apply this insight to *decisions of the moment.*

The upshot was that for the proletariat these differences of opinion simply remained differences of opinion *within* workers' movements that were nevertheless revolutionary movements. And so it became impossible to draw a firm distinction between the various groups. However, this lack of clarity had repercussions on the views of the Left. Because these views were denied any interaction with practice they were unable to concretise themselves or to develop through the productive self-criticism entailed by the attempt to realise themselves in practice. Even where they came close to the truth they retained a markedly abstract and utopian strain. One is reminded for instance of Pannekoek's polemic against Kautsky on the issue of mass actions. And for the same reason Rosa Luxemburg, too, was unable to develop further her real insights into the *leading role* played by the organisation of the revolutionary proletariat. Her correct polemic against the mechanical forms of organisation in the workers' movement as in, e.g. the question of the relationship between the party and the trade unions and between the organised and unorganised masses, led her, on the one hand, to overestimate the importance of spontaneous mass actions. On the other hand she was never wholly able to free her view of leadership from the taint of being merely theoretical and propagandistic.

2

We have already shown elsewhere[6] that we are dealing with no mere chance or 'error' on the part of this important and pioneering thinker. In this context what is significant about such arguments can be summed up by saying that they are rooted in the illusion of an 'organic', *purely proletarian* revolution. In the course of the struggle against the opportunistic, 'organic' theory of evolution which imagined that the proletariat would by a slow expansion gradually conquer the majority of the population and so gain power by purely legal means, there arose a revolutionary 'organic' theory of spontaneous mass conflict.[7] Despite all the ingenious reservations of its best advocates, this theory ultimately implied the view that the constant exacerbation of the economic situation, the imperialist world war inevitably produced by this, and the approaching period of revolutionary mass conflict would issue with social and historical inevitability in the outbreak of spontaneous mass actions on the part of the proletariat. In the process, the leaders' clear appreciation of the goals and the methods of the revolution would be fully vindicated. However, this theory tacitly assumes that the revolution will be purely proletarian in character.

Of course, Rosa Luxemburg's notion of the range of the concept 'proletariat' was very different from that of the opportunists. It was she who showed so incisively how the revolutionary situation would mobilise great masses of the proletariat who had hitherto not been organised and indeed were inaccessible to the organs of the proletariat (farm labourers, etc.). It was she who showed how those masses exhibit in their actions an incomparably higher degree of class consciousness than even the party and the unions which presume to treat them with condescension, regarding them as immature and 'backward'. Notwithstanding this her view is still based on the assumption of the purely proletarian character of the revolution. According to this view, the proletariat presents a united front on the field of battle; the masses whose actions are being studied are purely proletarian masses. And it cannot be otherwise. For only in the class consciousness of the proletariat do we find that the correct view of revolutionary action is so deeply anchored and so deeply rooted in the instincts that this attitude need only be made conscious, for it to provide a clear lead. Action will then advance of itself along the right road. If, however, other strata of the population become decisively involved in the revolution they may advance it under certain circumstances. But it is just as easy for them to deflect it in a counter-revolutionary direction. For in the class situation of these strata (petty bourgeoisie, peasants, oppressed nationalities, etc.) there is nothing, nor can there be anything to make their actions lead inevitably towards the proletarian revolution. A revolutionary party so conceived must necessarily fail to accommodate such strata; it will be thwarted both by the impetus of their movement in favour of the proletarian revolution and by the obstacle represented by the fact that their action furthers the cause of counter-revolution.

Such a party will also be thwarted in its dealings with the proletariat itself. For its organisation corresponds to a stage in the class consciousness of the proletariat which does not aspire to anything more than making conscious what was hitherto unconscious and making explicit what hitherto had been latent. More accurately: it corresponds to a stage in which the process of acquiring consciousness does not entail a terrible *internal ideological crisis* for the proletariat. We are not concerned here to refute the anxiety of the opportunists concerning the proletariat's 'unpreparedness' to assume power and to retain it. Rosa Luxemburg has already dealt this objection a decisive blow in her debate with Bernstein.

Our aim here is to point out that the class consciousness of the proletariat does not develop uniformly throughout the whole proletariat, parallel with the objective economic crisis. Large sections of the proletariat remain intellectually under the tutelage of the bourgeoisie; even the severest economic crisis fails to shake them in their attitude. With the result that *the standpoint of the proletariat and its reaction to the crisis is much less violent and intense than is the crisis itself.*[8]

This state of affairs, which makes possible the existence of Menshevism, is doubtless not lacking in objective economic bases. Marx and Engels noted very early on that those sections of the

workers who obtained a privileged place *vis-à-vis* their class comrades thanks to the monopoly profits of the England of that time
tended to acquire bourgeois characteristics.[9] With the entry of
capitalism into its imperialist phase this stratum came into being
everywhere and is without a doubt an important factor in the
general trend in the working class towards opportunism and anti-
revolutionary attitudes.

In my opinion, however, this fact alone does not provide an
adequate explanation of Menshevism. In the first place, this
privileged position has already been undermined in many respects
while the position of Menshevism has not been correspondingly
weakened. Here too, the subjective development of the proletariat
has in many ways lagged behind the tempo of the objective crisis.
Hence we cannot regard this factor as the *sole* cause of Menshevism
unless we are to concede it also the comfortable theoretical position
arrived at by inferring the absence of an objective revolutionary
situation from the absence of a thorough-going and clear-cut
revolutionary fervour in the proletariat. In the second place, the
experiences of the revolutionary struggles have failed to yield any
conclusive evidence that the proletariat's revolutionary fervour
and will to fight corresponds in any straightforward manner to
the economic level of its various parts. There are great deviations
from any such simple, uniform parallels and there are great
divergencies in the maturity of class consciousness attained by
workers within economically similar strata.

These truths only acquire real significance in the context of a
non-fatalistic, non-'economistic' theory. If the movement of history
is interpreted as showing that the economic process of capitalism
will advance automatically and inexorably through a series of
crises to socialism then the ideological factors indicated here are
merely the product of a mistaken diagnosis. They would then
appear simply as proof that the objectively decisive crisis of
capitalism has not yet appeared. For in such a view there is
simply no room for the idea of an ideological crisis of the proletariat in which proletarian ideology lags behind the economic
crisis.

The position is not so very different where, while retaining the
basic economic fatalism, the prevailing view of the crisis becomes
revolutionary and optimistic: i.e. where it is held that the crisis is
inevitable and that for capitalism there can be no way out. In this
case, too, the problem examined here is not admitted to be a

M

problem at all. What before was 'impossible' is now 'not yet' the case. Now, Lenin has very rightly pointed out that there is no situation from which there is no way out. Whatever position capitalism may find itself in there will always be some 'purely economic' solutions available. The question is only whether these solutions will be viable when they emerge from the pure theoretical world of economics into the reality of the class struggle. For capitalism, then, expedients can certainly be thought of in and for themselves. Whether they can be put into practice *depends, however, on the proletariat.* The proletariat, the actions of the proletariat, block capitalism's way out of the crisis. Admittedly, the fact that the proletariat obtains power *at that moment* is due to the 'natural laws' governing the economic process. But these 'natural laws' only determine the crisis itself, giving it dimensions which frustrate the 'peaceful' advance of capitalism. However, if left to develop (along capitalist lines) they would not lead to the simple downfall of capitalism or to a smooth transition to socialism. They would lead over a long period of crises, civil wars and imperialist world wars on an ever-increasing scale to "the mutual destruction of the opposing classes" and to a new barbarism.

Moreover, these forces, swept along by their own 'natural' impetus have brought into being a proletariat whose physical and economic strength leaves capitalism very little scope to enforce a purely economic solution along the lines of those which put an end to previous crises in which the proletariat figured only as the *object* of an economic process. The new-found strength of the proletariat is the product of objective economic 'laws'. The problem, however, of converting this potential power into a real one and of enabling the proletariat (which today really is the mere object of the economic process and only potentially and latently its co-determining subject) to emerge as its subject in reality, is no longer determined by these 'laws' in any fatalistic and automatic way. More precisely: the automatic and fatalistic power of these laws no longer controls the essential core of the strength of the proletariat. In so far as the proletariat's reactions to the crisis proceed according to the 'laws' of the capitalist economy, in so far as they limit themselves at most to *spontaneous mass actions*, they exhibit a structure that is in many ways like that of movements of pre-revolutionary ages. They break out spontaneously almost without exception as a defence against an economic and more rarely, a political thrust by the bourgeoisie, against the attempts of the latter to find a 'purely economic' solution to the crisis. (The spontaneity of a movement, we note, is only the subjective, mass-psychological expression of its determination by pure economic laws.) However, such outbreaks come to a halt no less spontaneously, they peter out when their immediate goals are achieved or seem unattainable. It appears, therefore, as if they have run their 'natural' course.

That such appearances may prove to be deceptive becomes clear if these movements are regarded not abstractly but in their true context, in the historical totality of the world-crisis. This context is the *extension of the crisis to every class* and not just the bourgeoisie and the proletariat. Where the economic process provokes a spontaneous mass-movement in the proletariat there is a fundamental qualitative distinction to be made between a situation in which the society as a whole is basically stable and one in which a profound regrouping of all social forces and an erosion of the bases of the power of the ruling class is taking place.

It is for this reason that an understanding of the significant role played by non-proletarian strata during a revolution and an understanding of its non-proletarian character is of such decisive importance. The exercise of power by a minority can only perpetuate itself if it can contrive to carry the classes that are not directly and immediately affected by the revolution along with it ideologically. It must attempt to obtain their support or at least their neutrality. (It goes without saying that there is also an attempt to neutralise sections of the revolutionary class itself.)

This was especially true of the bourgeoisie. The bourgeoisie had far less of an *immediate* control of the actual springs of power than had ruling classes in the past (such as the citizens of the Greek city–states or the nobility at the apogee of feudalism). On the one hand, the bourgeoisie had to rely much more strongly on its ability to make peace or achieve a compromise with the opposing classes that held power before it so as to use the power-apparatus they controlled for its own ends. On the other hand, it found itself compelled to place the actual exercise of force (the army, petty bureaucracy, etc.) in the hands of petty bourgeois, peasants, the members of subject nations, etc. If, following a crisis, the economic position of these strata were to alter and if their naïve, unthought-out loyalty to the social system led by the bourgeoisie were shaken, then the whole apparatus of bourgeois

M*

domination might collapse, as it were, at a single blow. In that event the proletariat might emerge as the only organised power, as the victor without its having fought a serious battle let alone having really gained a victory.

The movements of these intermediate strata are truly spontaneous and they are nothing but spontaneous. They really are nothing more than the fruits of the natural forces of society obedient to 'natural laws'. As such they are themselves—socially —blind. These strata have no class consciousness that might have any bearing on the remoulding of society.[10] As a result of this they always represent particular class interests which do not even pretend to be the objective interests of the whole of society. The bonds that join them to the whole objectively are only causal, i.e. they are *caused* by movements within the whole but they cannot be *directed* towards changing it. Hence both their concern with the whole and the ideological form it assumes have something adventitious about them even though their origins can be conceived in terms of causal necessities. Because of the nature of these movements their actions are determined by factors external to themselves. Whatever direction they finally choose, whether they attempt to hasten the dissolution of bourgeois society, whether they again acquiesce in their own exploitation by the bourgeoisie, whether they sink back into passivity as the result of the frustration of their efforts, nothing that they do is implicit in their inner nature. Instead everything hinges on the behaviour of the classes capable of consciousness: the bourgeoise, and the proletariat. Whatever form their later fate may take the very explosion of such movements can easily lead to the paralysis of all the machinery that holds bourgeois society together and enables it to function. It is enough to reduce the bourgeoisie to immobility at least for a time.

From the Great French Revolution on, all revolutions exhibit the same pattern with increasing intensity. When revolution breaks out the absolute monarchy and later the semi-absolute, semi-feudal military monarchies upon which the economic hegemony of the bourgeoisie was based in Central and Eastern Europe, tend 'all at once' to lose their hold over society. Social power lies abandoned in the street, without an owner so to speak. A Restoration only becomes possible in the absence of any revolutionary class to take advantage of this ownerless power.

The struggles of a nascent absolutism against feudalism were on very different lines. For there the opposing classes could create organs of force much more directly from their own ranks and hence the class struggle was much more a struggle of one power against another. One recalls, for instance, the battles of the Fronde at the birth of absolutism in France. Even the downfall of English absolutism ran a similar course, whereas the collapse of the Protectorate and even more the—much more bourgeois— absolutism of Louis XVI were closer to the pattern of modern revolutions. There direct force was introduced from 'outside', from absolute states that were still intact or from territories that had remained feudal (as in La Vendée).

By contrast, purely 'democratic' power complexes may easily find themselves in a similar position in the course of a revolution: whereas at the moment of collapse they came into being of their own accord, as it were, and seized the reigns of power, they now find themselves no less suddenly stripped of all power—in consequence of the receding movement on the part of the inchoate strata that bore them up and onward. (Thus Kerensky and Károlyi.) It is not yet possible to discern with complete clarity the pattern of future developments in the bourgeois and democratically progressive states of the West. Despite this Italy has found itself in a very similar situation since the end of the war and up to about 1920. The power organisation that it devised for itself since that time (Fascism) constitutes a power apparatus which is relatively independent of the bourgeoisie. We have as yet no experience of the effects of the symptoms of disintegration in highly developed capitalist countries with extensive colonial possessions. And in particular, we do not know what will be the effects of colonial revolts, which to a certain extent play the part of internal peasant uprisings, upon the attitude of the petty bourgeoisie, the workers' aristocracy (and hence, too, the armed forces, etc.).

In consequence the proletariat finds itself in an environment which would assign a quite different function to spontaneous mass movements than they had possessed in the stable capitalist system. This holds good even where these mass movements, when viewed in isolation, have preserved their former characteristics. Here, however, we observe the emergence of very important quantitative changes in the opposing classes. In the first place, the concentration of capital has made further advances and this in turn results in a further concentration of the proletariat

—even if the latter is unable wholly to keep pace with this trend in terms of its consciousness and its organisation. In the second place, the crisis-ridden condition of capitalism makes it increasingly difficult to relieve the pressure coming from the proletariat by making minute concessions. Escape from the crisis, the 'economic' solution to the crisis can only come through the intensified exploitation of the proletariat. For this reason the tactical theses of the Third Congress very rightly emphasise that "every mass strike tends to translate itself into a civil war and a direct struggle for power".

But it only tends to do do. And the fact that this tendency has not yet become reality even though the economic and social preconditions were often fulfilled, *that precisely is the ideological crisis of the proletariat.* This ideological crisis manifests itself on the one hand in the fact that the objectively extremely precarious position of bourgeois society is endowed, in the minds of the workers with all its erstwhile stability; in many respects the proletariat is still caught up in the old capitalist forms of thought and feeling. On the other hand, the bourgeoisification of the proletariat becomes institutionalised in the Menshevik workers' parties and in the trade unions they control. These organisations now consciously labour to ensure that the merely spontaneous movements of the proletariat (with their dependence upon an immediate provocation, their fragmentation along professional and local lines, etc.) should remain on the level of pure spontaneity. They strive to prevent them from turning their attention to the totality, whether this be territorial, professional, etc., or whether it involves synthesising the economic movement with the political one. In this the unions tend to take on the task of atomising and de-politicising the movement and concealing its relation to the totality, whereas the Menshevik parties perform the task of establishing the reification in the consciousness of the proletariat both ideologically and on the level of organisation. They thus ensure that the consciousness of the proletariat will remain at a certain stage of relative bourgeoisification. They are able to achieve this only because the proletariat is in a state of ideological crisis, because even in theory the natural—ideological—development into a dictatorship and into socialism is out of the question for the proletariat, and because the crisis involves not only the economic undermining of capitalism but, equally, the ideological transformation of a proletariat that has been reared in capitalist society under the influence of the life-forms of the bourgeoisie. This ideological transformation does indeed owe its existence to the economic crisis which created the objective opportunity to seize power. The course it actually takes does not, however, run parallel in any automatic and 'necessary' way with that taken by the objective crisis itself. *This crisis can be resolved only by the free action of the proletariat.*

"It is ridiculous," Lenin says in a statement that only caricatures the situation formally, not essentially, "to imagine an army taking up battle positions somewhere and saying: 'We are for Socialism' while somewhere else another army will stand and declare: 'We are for Imperialism' and that such a situation should constitute a social revolution."[11] The emergence of revolutionary and counter-revolutionary fronts is full of vicissitudes and is frequently chaotic in the extreme. Forces that work towards revolution today may very well operate in the reverse direction tomorrow. And it is vital to note that these changes of direction do not simply follow mechanically from the class situation or even from the ideology of the stratum concerned. They are determined decisively by the constantly changing relations with the totality of the historical situation and the social forces at work. So that it is no very great paradox to assert that, for instance, Kemal Pasha may represent a revolutionary constellation of forces in certain circumstances whilst a great 'workers' party' may be counter-revolutionary.

Among the factors that determine the direction to be taken, *the proletariat's correct understanding of its own historical position is of the very first importance.* The course of the Russian Revolution in 1917 is a classic illustration of this. For we see there how at a crucial moment, the slogans of peace, self-determination and the radical solution to the agrarian problem welded together an army that could be deployed for revolution whilst completely disorganising the whole power apparatus of counter-revolution and rendering it impotent. It is not enough to object that the agrarian revolution and the peace movement of the masses would have carried the day without or even against the Communist Party. In the first place this is absolutely unprovable: as counter-evidence we may point e.g. to Hungary where a no less spontaneous agrarian uprising was defeated in October 1918. And even in Russia it might have been possible to crush the agrarian movement or allow it to dissipate itself, by achieving a 'coalition' (namely a counter-revolutionary coalition) of all the 'influential' 'workers' parties'. In the second place, if the 'same' agrarian movement had prevailed against the urban proletariat it would have become counter-revolutionary in character in the context of the social revolution.

This example alone shows the folly of applying mechanical and fatalistic criteria to the constellation of social forces in acute crisis-situations during a social revolution. It highlights the fact that the proletariat's correct insight and correct decision is *all-important*; it shows the extent to which the resolution of the crisis *depends upon the proletariat itself*. We should add that in comparison to the western nations the situation in Russia was relatively simple. Mass movements there were more purely spontaneous and the opposing forces possessed no organisation deeply rooted in tradition. It can be maintained without exaggeration, therefore, that our analysis would have an *even greater validity* for western nations. All the more as the undeveloped character of Russia, the absence of a long tradition of a legal workers' movement—if we ignore for the moment the existence of a fully constituted Communist Party—gave the Russian proletariat the chance to resolve the ideological crisis with greater dispatch.[12]

Thus the economic development of capitalism places the fate of society in the hands of the proletariat. Engels describes the transition accomplished by mankind *after* the revolution has been carried out as "the leap from the realm of necessity into the realm of freedom".[13] For the dialectical materialist it is self-evident that despite the fact that this leap is a leap, or just because of it, it must represent in essence a *process*. Does not Engels himself say in the passage referred to that the changes that lead in this direction take place "at a constantly increasing rate"? The only problem is to determine the *starting-point* of the process. It would, of course, be easiest to take Engels literally and to regard the realm of freedom simply as a *state* which will come into being after the completion of the social revolution. This would be simply to deny that the question had any immediate relevance. The only problem then would be to ask whether the question would really be exhausted by this formulation, which admittedly does correspond to Engels' literal statement. The question is whether a situation is even conceivable, let alone capable of being made social reality, if it has not been prepared by a lengthy *process* which has contained and developed the elements of that situation, albeit in a form that is inadequate in many ways and in great need of being subjected to a series of dialectical reversals. If we separate the 'realm of freedom' sharply from the process which is destined to call it into being, if we thus preclude all dialectical transitions, do we not thereby lapse into a utopian outlook similar to that which has already been analysed in the case of the separation of final goal and the movement towards it?

If, however, the 'realm of freedom' is considered in the context of the process that leads up to it, then it cannot be doubted that even the earliest appearance of the proletariat on the stage of history indicated an aspiration towards that end—admittedly in a wholly unconscious way. However little the final goal of the proletariat is able, even in theory, to influence the initial stages of the early part of the process directly, it is a principle, a synthesising factor and so can never be completely absent from any aspect of that process. It must not be forgotten, however, that the difference between the period in which the decisive battles are fought and the foregoing period does not lie in the extent and the intensity of the battles themselves. These quantitative changes are merely symptomatic of the fundamental differences in quality which distinguish these struggles from earlier ones. At an earlier stage, in the words of the *Communist Manifesto*, even "the massive solidarity of the workers was not yet the consequence of their own unification but merely a consequence of the unification of the bourgeoisie". Now, however, the process by which the proletariat becomes independent and 'organises itself into a class' is repeated and intensified until the time when the final crisis of capitalism has been reached, the time when the decision comes more and more within the grasp of the proletariat.

This state of affairs should not be taken to imply that the objective economic 'laws' cease to operate. On the contrary, they will remain in effect until long *after the victory* of the proletariat and they will only wither away—like the state—when the classless society wholly in the control of mankind comes into being. What is novel in the present situation is merely—merely!!—that the blind forces of capitalist economics are driving society towards the abyss. The bourgeoisie no longer has the power to help society, after a few false starts, to break the 'deadlock' brought about by its economic laws. And the proletariat has the *opportunity* to turn events *in another direction* by the conscious exploitation of existing trends. This other direction is the conscious regulation of the productive forces of society. To desire this *consciously*, is to desire the 'realm of freedom' and to take the *first conscious step* towards its realisation.

This step follows 'necessarily' from the class situation of the proletariat. However, this necessity has itself the character of a leap.[14] The *practical* relationship to the whole, the real unity of theory and practice which hitherto appeared only unconsciously, so to speak, in the actions of the proletariat, now emerges clearly and consciously. At earlier stages, too, the actions of the proletariat were driven to a climax in a series of leaps whose continuity with the previous development could only subsequently become conscious and be understood as the necessary consequence of that development. (An instance of this is the political form of the Commune of 1871.) In this case, however, the proletariat must take this step *consciously*. It is no wonder, therefore, that all those who remain imprisoned within the confines of capitalist thought recoil from taking this step and with all the mental energy at their disposal they hold fast to necessity which they see as a law of nature, as a 'law of the repetition' of phenomena. Hence, too, they reject as impossible the emergence of anything that is radically new of which we can have no 'experience'. It was Trotsky in his polemics against Kautsky who brought out this distinction most clearly, although it had been touched upon in the debates on the war: "For the fundamental Bolshevist prejudice consists precisely in the idea that one can only learn to ride when one is sitting firmly on a horse."[15] But Kautsky and his like are only significant as symptoms of the state of affairs: they symbolise the ideological crisis of the working class, they embody that moment of its development when it "once again recoils before the inchoate enormity of its own aims", and when it jibs at a task which it must take upon itself. Unless the proletariat wishes to share the fate of the bourgeoisie and perish wretchedly and ignominiously in the death-throes of capitalism, it must accomplish this task *in full consciousness*.

3

If the Menshevik parties are the organised form of the ideological crisis of the proletariat, the Communist Party is the organised form of the conscious approach to this leap and hence the first *conscious* step towards the realm of freedom. We have already clarified the general notion of the realm of freedom and shown that its nearness by no means signifies that the objective necessities of the economic process suddenly cease to operate. It is essential for us to follow this up with an examination of the relationship between the realm of freedom and the Communist Party.

Above all one thing must be made clear: freedom here does *not* mean the freedom of the individual. This is not to say that the fully developed communist society will have no knowledge of the freedom of the individual. On the contrary, it will be the first society in the history of mankind that really takes this freedom seriously and actually makes it a reality. However, even this freedom will not be the same as the freedom that bourgeois ideologists have in mind today. In order to achieve the social preconditions necessary for real freedom battles must be fought in the course of which present-day society will disappear, together with the race of men it has produced.

"The present generation," says Marx, "resembles the Jews whom Moses led through the wilderness. It must not only conquer a new world, it must also perish in order to make room for people who will be equal to a new world."[16] For the 'freedom' of the men who are alive now is the freedom of the individual isolated by the fact of property which both reifies and is itself reified. It is a freedom *vis-à-vis* the other (no less isolated) individuals. A freedom of the egoist, of the man who cuts himself off from others, a freedom for which solidarity and community exist at best only as ineffectual 'regulative ideas'.[17] To wish to breathe life into this freedom means in practice the renunciation of real freedom. This 'freedom' which isolated individuals may acquire thanks to their position in society or their inner constitution regardless of what happens to others means then in practice that the unfree structure of contemporary society will be perpetuated in so far as it depends on the individual.

The *conscious* desire for the realm of freedom can only mean consciously taking the steps that will really lead to it. And in the awareness that in contemporary bourgeois society individual freedom can only be corrupt and corrupting because it is a case of unilateral privilege based on the unfreedom of others, this desire must entail the renunciation of individual freedom. It implies the conscious subordination of the self to that collective will that is destined to bring real freedom into being and that today is earnestly taking the first arduous, uncertain and groping steps towards it. This conscious collective will is the Communist Party. And like every aspect of a dialectical process it too contains the seeds, admittedly in a primitive, abstract and undeveloped form, of the determinants appropriate to the goal it is destined to achieve: namely freedom in solidarity.

The unifying factor here is *discipline*. Only through discipline can the party be capable of putting the collective will into practice, whereas the introduction of the bourgeois concept of freedom prevents this collective will from forming itself and so transforms the party into a loose aggregate of individuals incapable of action. More importantly, even for the individual it is only discipline that creates the opportunity of taking that first step to the freedom that is already possible even though it is freedom of a very primitive sort, corresponding as it does to the stage of societal development. This is the freedom that works at overcoming the present.

Every Communist Party represents a higher type of organisation than every bourgeois party or opportunist workers' party, and this shows itself *in the greater demands made by the party on its individual members*. This emerged very clearly as early as the first split in Russian Social Democracy. Whereas for the Mensheviks (as for every fundamentally bourgeois party) the simple acceptance of the Party Programme was an adequate qualification for membership, for the Bolsheviks, party membership was synonymous with active personal participation in the work of revolution. This principle underlying party structure did not alter in the course of the revolution. The theses of the Third Congress that deal with organisation state: "To accept a communist programme is to announce one's intention of becoming a Communist . . . the first prerequisite for the serious implementation of the programme is that all members should be involved in constant, day-to-day collaboration." Of course, in many cases this principle exists only on paper even to this day. But this does not in the least detract from its fundamental importance. For just as the realm of freedom cannot be given to us as a present all at once, as a *gratia irresistitibilis*, just as the 'final goal' is not simply waiting for us somewhere outside the process but inheres in every particular aspect of the process, so too the Communist Party as the revolutionary form of consciousness of the proletariat is a *process by nature*. Rosa Luxemburg saw very clearly that "the organisation must come into being as the product of struggle". Her mistake was merely to overestimate the organic nature of the process while underestimating the importance of conscious organisation.

But now that the error has been seen for what it is we should not take it so far as to overlook the process element in the forms of organisation. Despite the fact that the non-Russian parties, with the Russian experiences before them, were fully aware of the principles of organisation right from the start, it would be wrong to let their organisational measures obscure the process-like nature of their birth and growth. Where the organisational measures are the right ones, they can speed up the process immeasurably and can perform the greatest service towards clarifying consciousness, and they are therefore an indispensable precondition for the existence of any organisation. A communist organisation, however, can only be created through struggle, it can only be realised if the justice and the necessity of this form of unity are accepted by every member as a result of his own experience.

What is essential, therefore, is the interaction of spontaneity and conscious control. In itself this is nothing new in the history of organisations. On the contrary, it is typical of the way in which new organisations arise in the first place. Thus, Engels describes how certain forms of military action originated spontaneously in the instincts of the soldiers as a reaction to the objective exigencies of the situation.[18] This happened without any theoretical preparation, and indeed often conflicted with the prevalent theories and hence with the existing military organisations. Despite this they prevailed and only afterwards were they incorporated into the organisations concerned.

What was novel in the formation of the Communist Parties was the new relation between spontaneous action and conscious, theoretical foresight, it was the permanent assault upon and the gradual disappearance of the purely *post festum* structure of the merely 'contemplative', reified consciousness of the bourgeoisie. This altered relationship has its origins in the *objective possibility*, available to the class consciousness of the proletariat at this stage of its development, of an insight into its own class situation which is no longer *post festum* in character and in which the correspondingly correct line of action is already contained. This remains true despite the fact that *for each individual worker*, because his own consciousness is reified, the road to achieving the objectively possible class consciousness and to acquiring that inner attitude in which he can assimilate that class consciousness must pass through the process of comprehending his own immediate experience only after he has experienced it; that is to say, in each individual the *post festum* character of consciousness is preserved. This conflict between individual and class consciousness in every single worker is by no means a matter of chance. For the Communist Party shows itself here to be superior to every other party organisation in two ways: firstly, for the first time in history the active and practical side of class consciousness *directly* influences the specific actions of every individual, and secondly, at the same time it *consciously* helps to determine the historical process.

This twofold meaning of activity—its simultaneous impact upon the individual who embodies proletarian class consciousness and upon the course of history, i.e. *the concrete mediation between man and history*—this is the decisive characteristic of the organisation now being born. In the older type of organisation, regardless of whether we include bourgeois parties or opportunist workers' parties under this heading, the individual can only occur as 'the masses', as follower, as cipher. Max Weber gives an apt definition of this type of organisation: "What is common to them all is that a nucleus of people who are in active control gather around them the 'members' whose role is essentially more passive while the mass of the membership are mere objects."[19] Their role as objects is not mitigated by the fact of formal democracy, by the 'freedom' that obtains in these organisations; on the contrary, this freedom only fixes and perpetuates it. The 'false consciousness', the objective impossibility of intervening in the process of history by means of conscious action is reflected on the level of organisation in the inability to form active political units (parties) that could mediate between the action of every member and that of the whole class. As such classes and parties are not active in the objective historical sense of the word, as their ostensible activity is only a reflex of the way in which they are borne along fatalistically by historical forces they do not comprehend, they must manifest all the symptoms that arise out of the structure of the reified consciousness and from the separation between consciousness and being, between theory and practice. That is to say, as *global complexes* they take up a purely *contemplative* position towards the course of events.

Corresponding to this is the necessary appearance simultaneously of two complementary but equally false views of the course of history: the voluntaristic overestimation of the active importance of the individual (the leader) and the fatalistic underestimation of the importance of the class (the masses). The party is divided into an active and a passive group in which the latter is only occasionally brought into play and then only at the behest of the former. The 'freedom' possessed by the members of such parties is therefore nothing more than the freedom of more or less peripheral and never fully engaged *observers* to pass judgement on the fatalistically accepted course of events or the errors of individuals. Such organisations never succeed in encompassing the total personality of their members, they cannot even attempt to do so. Like all the social forms of civilisation these organisations are based on the exact mechanised division of labour, on bureaucratisation, on the precise delineation and separation of rights and duties. The members are only connected with the organisation by virtue of abstractly grasped aspects of their existence and these abstract bonds are objectivised as rights and duties.[20]

Really active participation in every event, really practical involvement of all the members of an organisation can only be achieved by engaging the whole personality. Only when action within a community becomes the central personal concern of everyone involved will it be possible to abolish the split between rights and duties, the organisational form of man's separation from his own socialisation and his fragmentation at the hands of the social forces that control him. Engels, in his description of the gentile constitution, lays great weight on this point: "In the realm of the internal, there was as yet no distinction between rights and duties."[21] According to Marx it is typical of the nature of law that "Right by its very nature can consist only in the application of an equal standard", but that necessarily unequal individuals "are measurable only by an equal standard in so far as they are brought under an equal point of view and nothing more is seen in them, everything else being ignored".[22]

Hence every human relationship which breaks with this pattern, with this abstraction from the total personality of man and with his subsumption beneath an abstract point of view, is a step in the direction of putting an end to the reification of human consciousness. Such a step, however, presupposes the *active engagement of the total personality*. With this it becomes completely clear that the forms of freedom in bourgeois organisations are nothing but a 'false consciousness' of an actual unfreedom; that is to say, a pattern of consciousness in which man contemplates from a position of formal freedom his own integration in a system of alien compulsions and confuses this formal 'freedom' of his contemplation with an authentic freedom.

Only when this is understood can our earlier paradox be resolved. We said then that the discipline of the Communist Party, the unconditional absorption of the total personality in the praxis of the movement, was the only possible way of bringing about an authentic freedom. And this not merely for the whole movement which only acquires a purchase on the objective societal preconditions for this freedom by means of such an organisation, but even for the single individual, for the single member of the party who by this means alone can hope to obtain freedom *for himself too*.

The question of discipline is then, on the one hand, an elementary practical problem for the party, an indispensable precondition for its effective functioning. On the other hand it is no mere technical and practical question: it is one of the most exalted and important *intellectual* problems in the history of revolution. This discipline can only come into being as the free and conscious deed of the most conscious element, of the vanguard of the revolutionary class. Without the intellectual foundations of that class it cannot be realised. Without an at least instinctive understanding of the link between total personality and party discipline on the part of every single party member this discipline must degenerate into a reified and abstract system of rights and duties and the party will relapse into a state typical of a party on the bourgeois pattern. Thus it becomes evident that objectively the organisation will react with the greatest sensitivity to the revolutionary worth or worthlessness of theoretical views and tendencies. Subjectively, the revolutionary organisation presupposes a very high degree of class consciousness.

4

Important though it is to clarify in theory the relation between the Communist Party organisation and its individual members, it would be disastrous to stop at the treatment of the problem of organisation from its formal, ethical side. For the relationship as we have described it between the individual and the aspirations of the whole movement to which he subordinates his whole personality is, if regarded in isolation, not the prerogative of the Communist Party alone. It has been, on the contrary, the characteristic of many utopian sects. Indeed many sects regarded this formal, ethical aspect as the sole or at least as the decisive principle and not as a mere aspect of the *whole* problem of organisation. In consequence of this they were often able to reveal its importance more clearly than the Communist Parties.

However, where the formal, ethical principle is given such a one-sided emphasis it annuls itself: its truth is not achieved, consummate being but only *the correct pointer* towards the goal to be reached. It ceases to be correct when that relationship to the whole of the historical process is dissolved. It was for this reason that we placed such emphasis upon the party as the concrete principle of mediation between man and history when we elaborated the relationship between the organisation and the individual. It is essential that the collective will embodied in the party should intervene actively and consciously in the course of history and that it should exist in a state of constant, vital interaction with the process of social revolution. Its individual components should likewise interact with the process and its repository, the revolutionary class. And only if this takes place can the demands made on the individual lose their formal and ethical dimension. This is why Lenin, when discussing how to maintain the revolutionary discipline of the Communist Party, stressed the importance not only of the dedication of its members but also of the relation of the party to the masses and the correctness of its political leadership.[23]

However, these three factors cannot be conceived in isolation from each other. The formal, ethical view of the sects breaks down precisely because it cannot understand that these factors are unified, that there is a vital interaction between the party organisation and the unorganised masses. However hostile a sect may be towards bourgeois society, however deeply it may be convinced —subjectively—of the size of the gulf that separates it from the bourgeoisie, it yet reveals at this very point that its view of history coincides with that of the bourgeoisie and that, in consequence, the structure of its own consciousness is closely related to that of the bourgeoisie.

This affinity can ultimately be traced back to a similar view of the duality of existence and consciousness, viz. to the failure to comprehend their unity as a dialectical process, as *the* process of history. From this point of view it is a matter of indifference whether this unity appears in the distorting mirror of the sects as existence frozen into immobility, or as less immobile non-existence. It makes no difference whether, by a process of mythologising, a correct flair for revolutionary action is unreservedly attributed to the masses or whether it is argued that the 'conscious' minority has to take action on behalf of the 'unconscious' masses. Both these extremes are offered here only as illustrations, as even the most cursory attempt to give a typology of the sects would be well beyond the scope of this study.

But it can be seen that they resemble each other and the consciousness of the bourgeoisie in that they all regard the real process of history as something separate from the growth of the consciousness of the 'masses'. If the sect acts as the representative of the 'unconscious' masses, instead of them and on their behalf, it causes the historically necessary and hence dialectical separation of the party organisation from the masses to freeze into permanence.

If, on the other hand, it attempts to merge entirely with the spontaneous instinctive movement of the masses, it is forced into making a simple equation between the class consciousness of the proletariat and the momentary thoughts and feelings, etc., of the masses. In consequence it sacrifices every criterion by which to judge correct action objectively. It succumbs to the bourgeois dilemma of voluntarism and fatalism. It adopts a vantage point from which neither the objective nor the subjective stages of the course of history can be effectively judged. Hence it is led to the extravagant overestimation of organisation, or else to the no less extravagant underestimation of it. It is forced to treat the problem of organisation in isolation from the general questions of historical praxis and equally from the problems of strategy and tactics.

The criterion for and the guide to the correct relationship between class and the party can be found nowhere but in the class consciousness of the proletariat. On the one hand, the real, objective unity of class consciousness forms the basis of a dialectical alliance despite the organisational separation of class from the party. On the other hand, the prevailing disunity, the differing degrees of clarity and depth to be found in the consciousness of the different individuals, groups and strata of the proletariat make the organisational separation of the party from the class inevitable.

Bukharin rightly points out that if a class were inwardly unified the formation of a party would be superfluous.[24] It only remains to ask: does the organisational independence of the party, the freeing of this part from the whole class correspond to an objective

stratification within the class? Or is the party separated from the class only as the result of the development of its consciousness, i.e. as the result of its conditioning by and its reaction upon the growth of the consciousness of its members?

Of course, it would be foolish wholly to overlook the existence of objective economic stratifications within the proletariat. But it must not be forgotten that these stratifications are by no means based upon objective differences even remotely similar to those which determine the division into classes. Indeed, in many respects they cannot even be regarded as sub-sections within the general context of the principles governing that division. When, for instance, Bukharin points out that "a peasant who has just entered a factory is quite different from a worker who has worked in a factory from childhood", this is without a doubt an 'ontological' distinction. But it exists on quite a different plane from the other distinction which Bukharin also makes between a worker in modern large-scale industry and one in a small workshop. For in the latter case we find an objectively different position within the process of production.

In the first case there is merely a change (however typical) in the place of an individual within the production process. The problem therefore turns on the speed with which the consciousness of the individual (or the stratum) becomes adapted to its new situation and on the length of time during which the psychological inheritance from his previous class situation has a retarding effect on the formation of his class consciousness. In the second example, however, the question is raised whether the class interests arising from the objective economic situations of the differing strata within the proletariat are sufficiently distinct to bring about divergencies within the objective interests of the whole class. What is at issue, therefore, in this later case is whether the objective, imputed class consciousness[25] must itself be thought of as differentiated and stratified. By contrast, in the first instance the question is only which particular—or even typical—life situations will act as obstacles to the successful development of this objective class consciousness.

It is clear that only the second case presents an important problem in theory. For, since Bernstein, the opportunists have striven constantly to portray the objective economic stratifications in the proletariat as going so deep and to lay such emphasis on the similarity in the 'life situations' of the various proletarian,

semi-proletarian and petty-bourgeois strata that *in consequence the unity and the autonomy of the class was lost.* (The Görlitz Programme of the S.P.D. was the last formulation of this trend and there it had already acquired a clear implication for organisation.)

Of course, the Bolsheviks will be the last to overlook the existence of such divergences. The only point at issue is what is their ontological *status*, what is their function within the totality of the socio-historical process? How far should an understanding of them lead to (predominantly) tactical and how far to (predominantly) organisational analyses and measures? Such questions seem at first to lead to a sterile debate about concepts. It must be remembered, however, that an organisation—in the sense of the Communist Party—presupposes unity of consciousness, the unity of the underlying social reality. A tactical union, by contrast, can be achieved and can even be inevitable between different classes whose social existence is objectively different.

This occurs when historical circumstances conjure up movements that are determined by a variety of causes but which from the point of view of the revolution move for a time in the same direction. If, however, their social existence is really different, then the direction of these movements cannot be attended by the same degree of necessity as in the case of movements with a unified class basis. That is to say, the fact of a unified direction is the determining element only in the first 'kind of organisation. Its emergence into empirical reality can be delayed by various circumstances but in the long run it will prevail. In the second type of organisation, however, the convergence of a number of different trends occurs as the result of the combination of a variety of historical circumstances. Fortune smiles and her favours must be tactically exploited or else they will be lost, perhaps irretrievably.

Of course, it is no accident that it should be possible for the proletariat to collaborate with semi-proletarian strata. But such collaboration has a necessary foundation *only* in the class situation of the proletariat. For, as the proletariat can liberate itself only by destroying class society, it is *forced* to conduct its war of liberation *on behalf of* every suppressed and exploited sector of the population. But whether the *latter* find themselves fighting on the side of the proletariat or in the camp of its opponents is more or less 'fortuitous' when judged from the standpoint of strata with an ill-defined class consciousness. It depends, as has been shown,

very much upon whether the revolutionary party of the proletariat has chosen the correct tactics. In this case, then, where the
active classes have a different existence in society, where they are
linked only by the universal mission of the proletariat, collaboration on the level of *tactics* (which is never more than haphazard in
terms of concepts, though often of long duration in practice) can
only serve the interests of revolution if the different organisations
are kept separate. For the process by which semi-proletarian
strata become aware that their own emacipation depends on the
victory of the proletariat is so lengthy and is subject to so many
setbacks that anything more than a tactical collaboration might
jeopardise the fate of the revolution.

It is now clear why we had to formulate our question so sharply:
Is there a comparable (if weaker) stratification of society, i.e. of
the class structure, and hence also of the objective, imputed class
consciousness, that corresponds to the strata within the proletariat? Or do these stratifications owe their existence merely to
the relative ease or difficulty with which this true class consciousness is able to penetrate the individual strata, groups and individuals in the proletariat? That is to say, do the undeniably very
real stratifications within the proletariat determine only the
perspectives from which to judge the momentary interests—where
these *interests* appear no doubt to diverge considerably but in
fact *coincide objectively*? And do they determine these perspectives
not only from a world-historical point of view but actually and
immediately, even if not every worker can recognise them? Or
can these interests themselves diverge as the consequence of
objective differences in society?

If the question is put thus, there can be no doubt as to the
answer. The words of the *Communist Manifesto* which are repeated
almost word for word in the Theses of the Second Congress concerning "the role of the Communist Party in the proletarian
revolution", can be understood meaningfully only if the proletariat's objective economic existence is acknowledged to be a
unity. "The Communist Party has no interests separate and apart
from those of the proletariat as a whole, it is distinguished from the
rest of the proletariat by the fact that it has a clear understanding of the historical path to be taken by the proletariat as a
whole. It is concerned through all the turns that path may take
to defend the interests not of isolated groups or professions but of
the proletariat in its entirety."

N

In that case, however, the stratifications within the proletariat that lead to the formation of the various labour parties and of the Communist Party are no objective, economic stratifications in the proletariat but simply stages in the development of its class consciousness. Individual proletarian strata are no more predestined to become Communists by virtue of their economic existence than the individual worker is born a Communist. Every worker who is born into capitalist society and grows up under its influence has to acquire by a more or less arduous process of experience a correct understanding of his own class situation.

The struggle of the Communist Party is focused upon the class consciousness of the proletariat. Its organisational separation from the class does not mean in this case that it wishes to do battle *for* its interests *on its behalf and in its place*. (This is what the Blanquists did, to take but one instance.) Should it do this, as occasionally happens in the course of revolution, then it is not in the first instance an attempt to fight for the objective goals of the struggle in question (for in the long run these can only be won or retained by the class itself), but only an attempt to advance or accelerate the development of class consciousness. The process of revolution is—on a historical scale—synonymous with the process of the development of proletarian class consciousness. The fact that the organisation of the Communist Party becomes detached from the broad mass of the class is itself a function of the stratification of consciousness within the class, but at the same time the party exists in order to hasten the process by which these distinctions are smoothed out—at the highest level of consciousness attainable.

The Communist Party must exist as an independent organisation so that the proletariat may be able to see its own class consciousness given historical shape. And likewise, so that in every event of daily life the point of view demanded by the interests of the class as a whole may receive a clear formulation that every worker can understand. And, finally, so that the whole class may become fully aware of its own existence as a class. While the organisations of the sects artificially separate 'true' class consciousness (if this can survive at all in such abstract isolation) from the life and development of the class, the organisations of the opportunists achieve a compromise between these strata of consciousness on the lowest possible level, or at best, at the level of the average man. It is self-evident that the actions of the class

are largely determined by its average members. But as the average is not static and cannot be determined statistically, but is itself the product of the revolutionary process, it is no less self-evident that an organisation that bases itself on an existing average is doomed to hinder development and even to reduce the general level. Conversely, the clear establishing of the highest possibility *objectively* available at a given point in time, as represented by the autonomous organisation of the conscious vanguard, is itself a means by which to relieve the tension between this objective possibility and the actual state of consciousness of the average members in a manner advantageous to the revolution.

Organisational independence is senseless and leads straight back to sectarianism if it does not at the same time constantly pay heed *tactically* to the level of consciousness of the largest and most retrograde sections of the masses. We see here the importance of a correct theory for the organisation of the Communist Party. It must represent the highest objective possibility of proletarian action. But the indispensable prerequisite for this is to have correct theoretical insight. An opportunistic organisation is less sensitive to the consequences of a false theory than is a Communist organisation because it consists of heterogeneous elements more or less loosely combined for the purpose of taking occasional action, because it is not given true leadership by the party but rather finds itself pushed by the uncontrollable movements of the masses and because the party is held together by a fixed hierarchy of leaders and functionaries in a rigid division of labour. (The fact that the constant misapplication of false theories must lead inevitably to the collapse of the party is a separate issue.)

The pre-eminently practical nature of the Communist Party, the fact that it is a fighting party presupposes its possession of a correct theory, for otherwise the consequences of a false theory would soon destroy it. Moreover, it is a form of organisation that produces and reproduces correct theoretical insights by consciously ensuring that the organisation has built into it ways of adapting with increased sensitivity to the effects of a theoretical posture. Thus the ability to act, the faculty of self-criticism, of self-correction and of theoretical development all co-exist in a state of constant interaction. The Communist Party does not function as a stand-in for the proletariat even in theory. If the class consciousness of the proletariat viewed as a function of the thought and action of the class as a whole is something organic and in a state of constant flux, then this must be reflected in the organised form of that class consciousness, namely in the Communist Party. With the single reservation that what has become objectivised here is a higher stage of consciousness. The more or less chaotic ups and downs in the evolution of consciousness, the alternation of out-breaks which reveal a maturity of class consciousness far superior to anything foreseen by theory with half-lethargic conditions of stasis, of passivity, of a merely subterranean progress finds itself opposed by a conscious effort to relate the 'final goal' to the immediate exigencies of the moment.[26] Thus in the theory of the party the process, the dialectic of class consciousness becomes a dialectic that is consciously deployed.

In consequence, this uninterrupted dialectical interaction between theory, party and class, this concentration of theory upon the immediate needs of the class does not by any means imply that the party is absorbed into the mass of the proletariat. The debates about a United Front demonstrated that almost all the opponents of such a tactical manoeuvre suffered from a lack of dialectical grasp, of appreciation of the true function of the party in develop-ing the consciousness of the proletariat. To say nothing of those misunderstandings that led to the United Front being thought of as leading to the immediate reunification of the proletariat at the level of organisation.

But the fear that the party might sacrifice its communist character because of too close a familiarity with the—seemingly— 'reformist' slogans of the day and because of the occasional tactical collaboration with the opportunists, shows that even now there are large numbers of Communists who do not place sufficient trust in correct theory, in the view that the self-knowledge of the prole-tariat is a knowledge of its objective situation at a given stage of historical development, and in the 'final goal' as present dialecti-cally in every slogan of the day when seen from a true revolution-ary point of view. It shows that they still frequently follow the sects by acting for the proletariat instead of letting their actions advance the real process by which class consciousness evolves.

To adapt the tactics of the Communist Party to those facets of the life of the class where—even though in a false form—a genuine class consciousness appears to be fighting its way to the surface, does not at all imply an unconditional willingness to implement the momentary desires of the masses. On the contrary, just be-cause the party aspires to the highest point that is objectively and revolutionarily attainable—and the momentary desires of the masses are often the most important aspect, the most vital symptom of this—it is sometimes forced to adopt a stance opposed to that of the masses; it must show them the way by rejecting their immediate wishes. It is forced to rely upon the fact that only *post festum*, only after many bitter experiences will the masses understand the correctness of the party's view.

But such opportunities for collaborating with the masses must not be erected into a general tactical scheme. The growth of proletarian class consciousness (i.e. the growth of the proletarian revolution) and that of the Communist Party are indeed one and the same process—seen from a world-historical standpoint. Therefore in everyday praxis they condition each other in the most intimate way. *But despite this their concrete growth does not appear as one and the same process. Indeed there is not even a consistent parallel.* For the way in which the process develops, the changes undergone by certain objective-economic developments in the consciousness of the proletariat and, above all, the shape assumed within this process by the interaction between party and class, cannot be reduced to any schematic 'laws'.

The party's process of maturation, its inner and outer consolidation does not, of course, take place in the vacuum we find in the case of the sects; it takes place within the bounds of historical reality, in an unbroken, dialectical interaction with the objective economic crisis and the masses which the latter has revolutionised. It can happen—as in Russia between the two revolutions—that the course of events gives the party the chance to work its way to complete inner clarity before the decisive battles are joined. But it can also be the case—as in some countries in Central and Western Europe—that the crisis revolutionises the masses so widely and so quickly that sections of them even become organised Communists before they have achieved the stage of consciousness which is the indispensable precondition of organisation. With the result that communist mass parties come into existence that only become true Communist Parties in the course of their struggles. However complex the typology of the birth of parties may be, however much it may appear in certain extreme cases that a Communist Party grows organically from an economic crisis in obedience to 'laws', it nevertheless remains true that the decisive steps, the conscious welding together of the revolutionary vanguard into a coherent whole, i.e. the emergence of an authentic

Communist Party *always remains the conscious, free action of the conscious vanguard itself.*

To take two extreme instances, the position is no different where a relatively small, inwardly coherent party develops into a great mass party through interaction with the broad mass of the proletariat, nor where, after many internal crises, a mass party that has arisen spontaneously develops into a communist mass party. The theoretical basis of all these alternatives remains the same: the overcoming of the ideological crisis, the struggle to acquire the correct proletarian class consciousness. From this point of view it is dangerous for the revolution to overestimate the element of inevitability and to assume that the choice of any particular tactic might unleash even a series of actions (to say nothing of determining the course of the revolution itself), and trigger off a chain reaction leading to even more distant goals by some ineluctable process. And it would be no less fatal to believe that the most successful action of the largest and best-organised Communist Party could do more than lead the proletariat correctly into battle in pursuit of a goal to which it itself aspires—if not with full awareness of the fact. It would likewise be folly to regard the concept of the proletariat purely in static and statistical terms; "the concept of the masses changes in the course of the struggle," Lenin observes. The Communist Party is an *autonomous form* of proletarian class consciousness serving the interests of the revolution. It is essential to gain a correct theoretical understanding of it in its twofold dialectical relation: as both the *form* of this consciousness and the form of *this* consciousness, i.e. as both an independent and a subordinate phenomenon.

5

The separation of tactics and organisation in the party and the class is, then, precise, even though it is constantly changing and adapting itself to changed circumstances. The separation gives rise within the party to the problem of the form that the attempt to harmonise tactical and organisational questions might take. For our experience of the internal life of the party we have to rely, of course, even more strongly than in the issues already discussed, on the Russian Party with its real and conscious measures to create a genuine communist organisation.

In the period of their 'infantile disorders' the non-Russian parties often tended towards a sectarian view of the party. And similarly later on they combined 'external' activity, i.e. the party's propagandistic and organisational efforts with regard to the masses, with the neglect of their 'internal' life. Evidently, this too is an 'infantile disorder' brought about in part by the swift growth of the great mass parties, by the almost continuous succession of vital decisions and actions and by the need for the party to direct its energies 'outwards'. But to understand the chain of causes that led to an error does not mean that one should become reconciled to it. Especially when the correct way to direct one's actions 'outwards' makes it perfectly plain how senseless it is to make a sharp distinction between tactics and organisation in the internal life of the party, and when it is obvious how powerfully this internal unity informs the intimate bonds between the 'inner-directed' life of the party and its 'outer-directed' activities. (This holds good even though at present the empirical separation that every Communist Party has inherited from the environment from which it sprang appears almost insuperable.)

Thus everyone must learn from his immediate experience of day-to-day praxis that the centralisation of the party organisation (with all the problems of discipline that follow from it and are no more than its other aspect) and the capacity to take tactical initiatives are concepts that mutually modify each other. On the one hand, the fact that it is possible for tactics desired by the party to have an effect on the masses presupposes that they can impose themselves within the party. And not merely mechanically, through having resort to discipline to ensure that the individual parts of the party should be firmly controlled by the central authority and that they should function *vis-à-vis* the outside world as real limbs of the collective will. But rather it should mean that the party would be such a homogeneous formation that every change of direction would mean the regrouping of all one's forces, every change of attitude would be reflected in every party member. In short, the organisation's sensitivity to changes in direction, increases in the pressure of the active struggle and to the need to retreat, etc., would be raised to its highest pitch. I trust that it is not necessary to argue the case that this does not imply a demand for 'mechanical obedience' [Kadavergehorsam]. For it is plain that this sensitivity on the part of the organisation will be the very best method by which to expose the falsities of individual slogans as they work out in practice, and will do most to bring about a situation where a healthy and productive self-criticism will be possible.[27]

On the other hand, it goes without saying that the firm organisational cohesion of the party not only gives it the objective capacity for action. It also creates the inner atmosphere within the party essential for vigorous intervention in practical matters and the exploitation of the opportunities they present. So that when all the resources of the party are thoroughly centralised they must by virtue of their own dynamics urge the party forward in the direction of action and initiatives. Conversely, the feeling that the organisation is insufficiently cohesive must necessarily have an inhibiting and crippling effect on the tactical decisions and even on the basic theoretical positions of the party. (As was the case, e.g. in the German Communist Party at the time of the Kapp Putsch.)

"For a communist party," it says in the theses on organisation approved by the Third Congress, "there is no period in which the party organisation could not be politically active." Thus revolutionary preparedness and revolutionary action itself are permanent tactical and organisational possibilities, but this can only be understood correctly if the unity of tactics and organisation is fully grasped.

If tactics are divorced from organisation and if it is not realised that both are involved in the identical process by which the class consciousness of the proletariat is evolved, then the concept of tactics will inevitably succumb to the dilemma of opportunism and Putschism. In that event 'organised action' will either be the isolated deed of the 'conscious minority' in its efforts to seize power or else it will be a 'reformist' measure designed to satisfy the short-sighted wishes of the masses, whereas the organisation will simply be assigned the technical role of 'preparing' for action. (This is true of the views both of Serrati and his supporters and also of Paul Levi.)

The revolutionary situation may be permanent but this does not mean that the proletariat could seize power at any moment. It means only that in consequence of the objective overall economic situation every change, every movement of the masses induced by the state of the economy contains a tendency that can be given a revolutionary twist which the proletariat can exploit for the advancement of its own class consciousness. In this context the inner evolution of the independent expression of that class consciousness, viz. the Communist Party, is a factor of the very first importance. What is revolutionary in the situation is seen in the first instance and most strikingly in the constantly increasing instability of social institutions, and this is brought about in turn by the increasing imbalance in the powers and forces that create the equilibrium upon which bourgeois society rests. The fact that proletarian class consciousness becomes autonomous and assumes objective form is only meaningful for the proletariat if at every moment *it really embodies for the proletariat the revolutionary meaning of precisely that moment.*

In an objectively revolutionary situation, then, the correctness of revolutionary Marxism is much more than the 'general' correctness of its theory. Precisely because it has become wholly practical and geared to the latest developments the theory must become the guide to every day-to-day step. And this is only possible if the theory divests itself entirely of its purely theoretical characteristics and becomes purely dialectical. That is to say, it must transcend in practice every tension between the general and the particular, between the rule and the individual case 'subsumed' under it, between the rule and its application and hence too every tension between theory and practice. The tactics and organisation of the opportunists are based on a Realpolitik that abandons all pretention to dialectical method; they do just enough to placate the demands of the moment to sacrifice their solid basis in theory, while on the other hand, in their daily practice, they succumb to the rigid stereotypes of their reified forms of organisation and to their tactical routines.

By contrast, the Communist Party must keep exactly to the demands of the moment and thus preserve and keep alive within itself the dialectical tension between them and the 'ultimate goal'. For individuals this would mean the possession of a 'genius', a thing with which a revolutionary Realpolitik can never reckon. In fact it is never forced to do so as the conscious development of the communist principle of organisation is the best way to initiate the process of education in practical dialectics in the vanguard of the revolution. The unity of tactics and organisation, the need for every application of theory and every tactical step to be given immediate organisational backing is the prophylactic, to be consciously applied as a defence against dogmatic rigidity. For this rigidity is a constant threat to every theory adopted by men with a reified consciousness who have grown up under capitalism.

This danger is all the greater as the same capitalist environment that creates the stereotyped consciousness continually assumes new forms in its present crisis-ridden state and is thus placed even more beyond the reach of any stereotyped outlook. Therefore, what was right today can be wrong tomorrow. What is medicinally curative when the right dose is taken can be fatal if the dose is too large or too small. As Lenin observes in connection with certain forms of communist dogmatism, "One need only go one small step further" a step that seems to lead in the same direction— "and truth is transformed into error."[28]

The struggle against the effects of reified consciousness is itself a lengthy process full of stubborn battles and it would be a mistake to assume that the form of those effects or the contents of particular phenomena could be determined in advance. But the domination of reification over men living today does in fact have that kind of effect. If reification is overcome at one point the danger immediately arises that the state of consciousness that led to that victory might itself atrophy into a new form of reification. For example, the workers who live under a capitalist system have to conquer the delusion that the economic or juridical forms of bourgeois society constitute the 'eternal', the 'rational' and the 'natural' environment for man. They must cease to feel the excessive respect they have had for their accustomed social environment.

But after they have taken power, after they have overthrown the bourgeoisie in an open class war it may turn out that what Lenin called 'communist arrogance' will be just as dangerous for the workers as their Menshevist timidity when facing the bourgeoisie had been earlier on. For the very reason that historical materialism, correctly understood and in sharp contrast to opportunist theories, proceeds from the assumption that the development of society constantly produces *new* phenomena, i.e. new in a qualitative sense,[29] every communist organisation must be prepared to increase as far as possible its own sensitivity and its own ability to *learn* from every aspect of history. It must make sure that the weapons used to gain a victory yesterday do not become an impediment in future struggles. "We must learn from the common soldiers," Lenin remarks in the speech we have just quoted concerning the tasks of the Communists in the NEP.

Flexibility, the ability to change and adapt one's tactics and a tightly knit organisation are just two sides of one and the same thing. The whole trajectory of this, the deepest meaning of the communist form of organisation is rarely grasped in its entirety even in communist circles. And this despite the fact that both the possibility of right action and the Communist Party's inner capacity for development depend on it. Lenin stubbornly insists on rejecting every utopian view of the human material with which the revolution must be made and with which the victory must be won: it consists necessarily of men who have been brought up in and ruined by capitalist society.

However, to reject utopian hopes or illusions is not to imply that fatalism is the only alternative. But as it is a utopian illusion to hope that man can be inwardly transformed as long as capitalism still exists, we must discover *organisational devices and guarantees* that will mitigate the catastrophic effects of this situation, that can correct them as soon as they make their inevitable appearance and destroy the malignant growths they produce. Theoretical dogmatism is only a special case of those tendencies towards fossilisation to which every man and every organisation is incessantly exposed in a capitalist environment. The capitalist process of reification both over-individualises man and objectifies him mechanically.[30] The division of labour, alien to the nature of man, makes men ossify in their activity, it makes automata of them in their jobs and turns them into the slaves of routine. As against this it simultaneously overdevelops their individual consciousness which has been turned into something empty and abstract by the impossibility of finding satisfaction and of living out their personalities in their work, and which is now transformed into a brutal egoism greedy for fame or possessions. These tendencies will necessarily persist in the Communist Party which after all has never claimed to be able to reform the inner nature of its members by means of a miracle. And this is all the truer for the fact that the requirements of purposeful action also compel the Party to introduce the division of labour to a considerable degree and this inevitably invokes the dangers of ossification, bureaucratisation and corruption.

The inner life of the party is one unceasing struggle against this, its capitalist inheritance. The only decisive weapon it possesses is its ability to draw together all the party members and to involve them in activity on behalf of the party *with the whole of their personality*. A man's function in the party must not be seen as an office whose duties can be performed conscientiously and devotedly but only as official duties; on the contrary, the activity of every member must extend to every possible kind of party work. Moreover this activity must be varied in accordance with what work is available so that party members enter with their whole personalities into a living relationship with the whole of the life of the party and of the revolution so that they cease to be mere specialists necessarily exposed to the danger of ossification.[31] Here, once again, we see the indissoluble union of tactics and organisation. Every hierarchy in the party (and while the struggle is raging it is inevitable that there should be a hierarchy), must be based on the suitability of certain talents for the objective requirements of the particular phase of the struggle. If the revolution leaves a particular phase behind, it would not be possible to adapt oneself to the exigencies of the new situation merely by changing one's tactics, or even by changing the form of the organisation (e.g. exchanging illegal methods for legal ones). What is needed in addition is a reshuffle in the party hierarchy: the selection of personnel must be exactly suited to the new phase of the struggle.[32] Of course, this cannot be put into practice without 'errors' or crises. The Communist Party would be a fantastical utopian island of the blessed reposing in the ocean of capitalism if its progress were not constantly attended by such dangers. The decisively novel aspect of its organisation is only that it struggles with a steadily growing awareness against this inner threat.

If every member of the party commits his whole personality and his whole existence to the party in this way, then the same centralising and disciplinary principle will preside over the living interaction between the will of the members and that of the party leadership, and will ensure that the will and the wishes, the proposals and the criticisms of the members are given due weight by the party leaders. Every decision of the party must result in actions by all the members of the party and every slogan leads to deeds in which the individual members risk their whole physical and moral existence. For this very reason they are not only well placed to offer criticism, they are forced to do so together with their experiences and their doubts.

If the party consists merely of a hierarchy of officials isolated from the mass of ordinary members who are normally given the role of passive onlookers, if the party only occasionally acts as a whole then this will produce in the members a certain indifference composed equally of blind trust and apathy with regard to the day-to-day actions of the leadership. Their criticism will at best be of the *post festum* variety (at congresses, etc.) which will seldom exert any decisive influence on future actions.

Whereas the active participation of all members in the daily life of the party, the necessity to commit oneself with one's whole personality to all the party's actions is the only means by which to compel the leadership to make their resolutions really comprehensible to the members and to convince members of their correctness. For where this is not done they cannot possibly be carried out satisfactorily. (The more thorough-going the organisation of the party is and the more important are the functions that devolve upon every member—e.g. as member of a trade-union delegation, etc.—the more urgent does this necessity become.) But also, even before action is taken and certainly during it, these dialogues must lead to precisely this living interaction between the will of the whole party and that of the Central Committee; they must correct and modify the actual transition from resolution to deed. (And here too the interaction increases in proportion to the degree of centralisation and discipline.)

The more deeply ingrained these tendencies become, the sooner the harsh unrelenting contrast between leader and the masses, that has survived as a vestige of bourgeois party politics, will disappear. This will be accelerated by reshuffles in the official hierarchy. And the *post festum* criticism—which is inevitable at the moment—will be transformed into an exchange of *concrete and general*, tactical and organisational experiences that will be increasingly oriented towards the future. Freedom—as the classical German philosophers realised—is something practical, it is an activity. And only by becoming a world of activity for every one of its members can the Communist Party really hope to overcome the passive role assumed by bourgeois man when he is confronted by the inevitable course of events that he cannot understand. Only then will it be able to eliminate its ideological form, the formal freedom of bourgeois democracy. The separation of rights and duties is only feasible where the leaders are divorced from the masses, and act as *their representatives*, i.e. where the stance adopted by the masses is one of contemplative fatalism. True democracy, the abolition of the split between rights and duties is, however, no formal freedom but the *activity* of the members of a collective will, closely integrated and collaborating in a spirit of solidarity.

The much vilified and slandered question of party 'purges' is only the negative side of the same issue. Here, as with every problem, it was necessary to progress from utopia to reality. For example, the demand contained in the 21 Conditions of the Second Congress that every legal party must initiate such purges from time to time proved to be a utopian requirement incompatible with the stage of development reached by the newly-born mass parties in the West. (The Third Congress formulated its views on this issue with much greater caution.) However, the fact that this clause was inserted was nevertheless no 'error'. For it clearly and unmistakably points to the *direction* that the Communist Party must take in its internal development even though the *manner* in which the principle is carried out will be determined by historical circumstances. Just because the question of organisation is the most profound intellectual question facing the revolution it was absolutely vital that such problems should be borne in upon the consciousness of the revolutionary vanguard even if for the time being they could not be realised in practice. The development of the Russian Party magnificently demonstrates the practical importance of this question. And as is implied by the indissoluble unity of tactics and organisation, its importance extends beyond the inner life of the party to the relation between the party and the broad mass of all workers. The purging of the party in Russia has taken many different forms according to the different phases of the revolution. In the case of the most recent one, in the autumn of last year, we witnessed the frequent application of the interesting and significant principle that the views and experiences of workers and peasants who were not party members were made use of so that these masses were drawn into the labour of purging the party. Not that the party was prepared henceforth to accept the judgement of these masses blindly. But it was willing to take their suggestions and rejections into account when eliminating corrupt, bureaucratised and revolutionarily unreliable elements estranged from the masses.[33]

Thus, this most intimate internal problem illustrates the most intimate internal relation between party and class at a higher stage of development of the Communist Party. It shows that the sharp split in the organisation between the conscious vanguard and the broad masses is only an aspect of the homogeneous but dialectical process of development of the whole class and of its consciousness. But at the same time, it shows that the more clearly and energetically the process mediates the necessities of the moment by putting them in their historical perspective, the more clearly and energetically will it be able to absorb the individual in his isolated activity; the more it will be able to make use of him, bring him to a peak of maturity and judge him.

The party as a whole transcends the reified divisions according to nation, profession, etc., and according to modes of life (economics and politics) by virtue of its action. For this is oriented towards revolutionary unity and collaboration and aims to establish the true unity of the proletarian class. And what it does as a whole it performs likewise for its individual members. Its closely-knit organisation with its resulting iron discipline and its demand for total commitment tears away the reified veils that cloud the consciousness of the individual in capitalist society. The fact that this is a laborious process and that we are only just beginning cannot be allowed to prevent us from acknowledging as clearly as we can the *principle* that we perceive here and demand for the class-conscious worker: the approach of the 'realm of freedom'. Precisely because the rise of the Communist Party can only be the conscious achievement of the class-conscious workers every step in the direction of true knowledge is at the same time a step towards converting that knowledge into practical reality.

September 1922.

NOTES

1 *The Poverty of Philosophy*, p. 140.
2 *Massenstreik, Partei und Gewerkschaften*, p. 47.
3 Ibid., p. 49. On this question as well as on others to be discussed below see the very interesting article by J. Révai, "Kommunistische Selbstkritik und der Fall Levi", *Kommunismus* II, 15/16. I cannot, of course, enter into a detailed discussion of his conclusions here.
4 On the consequences of this position cf. Lenin's criticism of the Junius Pamphlet as well as of the attitude of the German, Polish and Dutch Left in the World War (*Gegen den Strom*). But even the Spartacus Programme still contains a highly utopian and unmediated account of the tasks facing the proletariat in its outline sketch of the course of the revolution. See the *Bericht über den Gründungsparteitag der K.P.D.*, p. 51.
5 For an exemplary instance of a methodologically correct critique bearing on questions of organisation cf. Lenin's speech at the 11th Congress of the Russian C.P., where he focuses centrally on

the failure of tried and tested communists in economic matters and demonstrates the symptomatic nature of particular errors. It is obvious that this is not allowed to *blunt* his criticism of individuals.

6   Cf. the preceding essay.

7   Cf. Rosa Luxemburg's polemic against the Mainz Resolution of David, *Massenstreik, Partei und Gewerkschaften*, p. 59 as well as her arguments concerning the 'Bible' of Legalism, viz. Engels' Preface to the *Class Struggles in France, Programmrede am Gründungsparteitag der K.P.D.*, pp. 22 et seq.

8   This view is not simply the consequence of the so-called slow development of the Revolution. As early as the 1st Congress Lenin expressed his anxiety lest "the struggles become so stormy that the consciousness of the masses of the workers will not be able to keep pace with events". Similarly, the standpoint of the Spartacus Programme that the C.P. should refuse to assume power merely because bourgeois and social-democratic 'democracy' has become bankrupt rests on the belief that the objective collapse of bourgeois society can precede the establishment of a revolutionary class consciousness in the proletariat. *Bericht über den Gründungsparteitag der K.P.D.*, p. 56.

9   A good selection of their statements here can be found in *Gegen den Strom*, pp. 516–17.

10   Cf. the essay "Class Consciousness".

11   *Gegen den Strom*, p. 412.

12   This does not mean that the question is finally solved as far as Russia is concerned. On the contrary, it will last as long as the struggle against capitalism. But it will take other (and presumably weaker) forms in Russia than in Europe, corresponding to the more feeble influence exerted by capitalist modes of thought and feeling upon the proletariat. On the subject of this problem, see Lenin, *"Left-Wing" Communism—An Infantile Disorder*, p. 589.

13   *Anti-Dühring*, p. 312.

14   Cf. the essay "The Changing Function of Historical Materialism".

15   *Terrorsismus und Kommunismus*, p. 82. I hold it to be no mere coincidence that Trotsky's polemic against Kautsky in the sphere of politics should have repeated the essential arguments adduced by Hegel in his attack on Kant's theory of knowledge (there is of course no philological connection). Cf. Hegel's *Werke* XV, p. 504. Kautsky, incidentally, later claimed that the laws of capitalism were unconditionally valid for the future, even though it was not possible to attain to a concrete knowledge of the actual trends. Cf. *Die proletarische Revolution und ihr Programm*, p. 57.

16   *Class Struggles in France*, in S.W. I, p. 193.

17   Cf. the *methodology* of the ethics of Kant and of Fichte; this individualism is considerably diluted in the actual exposition. But e.g. Fichte emphasises that (in his system) the formulation "limit your freedom so that your neighbour may also be free", which

is so close to that of Kant, is to have no absolute validity but only a 'hypothetical' one. *Die Grundlage des Naturrechts*, § 7, IV, Werke (new edition), Vol. II, p. 93.

18 *Anti-Dühring*, pp. 189 and especially p. 191–2.
19 *Wirtschaft und Gesellschaft*, p. 169.
20 A good description of these types of organisation can be found in the Theses on Organisation of the 3rd Congress (II, 6). A valid comparison is made there between them and the organisation of the bourgeois state.
21 *Origin of the Family, Private Property and the State*, S.W. II, p. 279.
22 *Critique of the Gotha Programme*, S.W. II, p. 22.
23 *"Left-Wing" Communism—An Infantile Disorder*, pp. 518–9.
24 Bukharin, *Klasse, Partei, Führer*, Die Internationale, IV, p. 22, Berlin, 1922.
25 For a definition of this concept, see the essay "Class Consciousness".
26 On the relation between ultimate goal and particular action, cf. the essay "What is Orthodox Marxism?"
27 "With some reservations we may say of politics and parties what we may say of individuals. A clever man is not one who makes no mistakes, such people do not and cannot exist. A clever man is one who does not make very significant mistakes and who, once he has made them, knows how to correct them quickly and easily." Lenin, *"Left-Wing" Communism—An Infantile Disorder*, p. 527.
28 Ibid., p. 581.
29 Already the debates about accumulation focus on this point. It is emphasised even more sharply in the controversies about war and imperialism. Cf. Zinoviev against Kautsky in *Gegen den Strom*, p. 321. And even more trenchantly in Lenin's speech on state capitalism at the 11th Congress of the Russian C.P.: "State capitalism in the form in which we possess it has not been analysed by any theory and in any literature for the simple reason that all ideas normally associated with the term are related to bourgeois government and bourgeois society. We, however, possess a social order that has left the track laid down by capitalism but has not yet acquired a track of its own. For our state is directed not by the bourgeoisie but by the proletariat. And the kind of state capitalism we shall have depends on us, on the Communist Party and the working class."
30 On this point, cf. the essay "Reification and the Consciousness of the Proletariat".
31 See the very interesting section on the party press in the Theses on Organisation of the 3rd Congress. This requirement is quite clearly stated in Point 48. But the whole techique of organisation, e.g. the relation of the parliamentary party to the Central Committee, the alternation of legal and illegal work, etc., is based on this principle.
32 See Lenin's speech of 6 March, 1922 at the All-Russian Metal Workers' Congress, as well as that made at the 11th Congress

of the Russian C.P. on the implications of the new economic policy for party organisation.

33 Cf. Lenin's article in *Pravda*, 21 September, 1921. It requires no further discussion to perceive that this organisational measure is also a brilliant tactical device whereby to increase the authority of the C.P. and to strengthen its relations with the mass of the workers.

Notes to the English Edition

WHEREVER possible English sources have been given, particularly in the case of Marx and Engels. Available translations of quotations have been used but with frequent alterations to fit the context. Lukács' own references have been retained where translations were hard to find or non-existent. An exception is the *Nachlass* (see below) where the titles are added in English.

1 *Capital* (3 vols.), Foreign Language Publishing House, Moscow, 1961, 1962.

2 S.W. = Marx/Engels, *Selected Works* (2 vols.), Lawrence and Wishart, London, 1950.

3 *Nachlass = Aus dem literarischen Nachlass von Karl Marx, Friedrich Engels and Ferdinand Lassalle.* Herausgegeben von Franz Mehring (4 vols), Stuttgart, 1902.

4 *A Contribution to a Critique of Political Economy,* trans. by N. I. Stone, New York and London, 1904.

5 *Anti-Dühring,* Lawrence and Wishart, London, n.d.

6 *The Poverty of Philosophy,* Foreign Languages Publishing House, Moscow, n.d.

7 *Antikritik* = Rosa Luxemburg, *Die Akkumulation des Kapitals oder Was die Epigonen aus der Marxschen Theorie gemacht haben. Eine Antikritik.* Leipzig, 1921.

8 Rosa Luxemburg, *The Russian Revolution* and *Leninism or Marxism,* introd. by Bertram D. Wolfe, Ann Arbor Paperbacks, Michigan, 1961.

9 V. I. Lenin, *Selected Works,* Lawrence and Wishart, London, 1969.

Square brackets in the text indicate insertions by the Translator.

The following notes are not intended to be comprehensive. In Section A explanations are only given of terms that presented difficulties in translation. In Sections B & C comment is limited to difficult points in the text and to historical events or persons important for the general argument.

A. *Terminology*

Lukács' language is strongly influenced by German Idealism

and the Neo-Kantian, vitalist and Weberian thought of the early years of this century. The impact of Hegel is particularly powerful: concepts like 'totality', 'mediated'/'unmediated' and even 'abstract' and 'concrete' are used in their Hegelian senses. No protracted analysis of them is possible here but it should be remembered that what we tend to think of as immediate (sense) perceptions are in Hegel's view the product of complicated mediations. Furthermore, ideas that commonsense regards as concrete, because particular, are normally abstract for him, because they are unmediated; the truly concrete is not a particular, isolated phenomenon, but an aspect or 'moment' of a totality. Thus in his usage 'concrete' pertains more properly to 'totality', while 'abstract' is related to the partial and one-sided, the individual and unmediated.

Reflexionsbestimmungen,-kategorien, etc. 'Reflection' is one of the most difficult and complex concepts in Hegel. On the one hand, there is the 'philosophy of reflection', which refers generally to empiricist or rationalist philosophies, to what Kant called 'dogmatism'. In such philosophies thought is an unmediated reflection of existence and the duality of thought and existence is never overcome. Hegel rejects this as undialectical. On the other hand, reflection has a positive function; it transcends mere Being. Moreover, to his dialectical way of thinking, reflection is also constitutive of Being, thought and existence interpenetrate.

The Determinants of Reflection are to be found in the section on Essence in the Science of Logic. They are concerned with identity, difference and contradiction. For Marcuse the positive aspect is so strong that he claims that "the laws of reflection are the fundamental laws of the dialectic". By contrast for Lukács they are largely negative: they are the forms of thoughts that will be overcome by dialectics. They are treated, therefore, as roughly the same as the 'philosophy of reflection' (p. 17 and the quotation from Hegel on p. 177). In line with this the phrases containing reflection have been translated variously as 'unmediated' or 'abstract mental categories', and more neutrally as the 'categories' or 'determinants of reflection' (see pp. 13–15, 163–206 *passim*). In addition, we may remark that in the discussion of the 'reflection theory' (p. 199 f.) reflection means the mirroring of reality, rather than meditation upon it, or the dialectical interaction of Essence and Being.

Imputed class consciousness (zugerechnetes Klassenbewusstsein).

'Zurechnen' means to impute, or attribute. Its technical use by Lukács seems to derive from Max Weber (and, ultimately, Kant). Weber used it to supplant the crude notions of causality prevalent in socio-historical explanation in the nineteenth century (see *Basic Concepts of Sociology*, Section 11). In the present work an 'imputed' class consciousness refers neither to the *actual* consciousness of a class, nor to the consciousness it ought ideally to have. It refers instead to the consciousness that may be 'imputed' to it as being logically (rather than causally) appropriate to its situation. For G.L.'s own definition, see pp. xviii–xix, 51.

'*Creation*' (Erzeugung) (see Reification and the Consciousness of the Proletariat, Section II); *genesis* (e.g. pp. 140 etc., 204). It may help to understand the debate between history and genesis if it is seen that it is related to the argument about 'creation'. If bourgeois thought is essentially passive and contemplative, if it only views history *post festum* and if its actions are non-creative and the mere manipulations of existing phenomena, then the problem is how to dissolve 'facts' into processes and arrive at a true 'creativity', one which is active and not just reactive. In this sense the search for 'genesis' is the search for the truly creative subject of a genuinely active action.

The identical subject-object (e.g. pp. 123, 205). This concept is related to those of creation and genesis. For classical German philosophy man is a subject in a world of objects. But also men are in fact objects to each other. Both Humean scepticism and scientific determinism appeared to deny the subjectivity, the freedom of man and his power to control and create his world. Hence the task of German Idealism was to overcome dualism and show that, for example, freedom was more than a subjective whim within a world dominated by scientific laws. It was necessary to prove both that freedom had an objective reality and that the seemingly objective 'facts' were 'produced', 'created' by man himself. This was the search for the identical subject-object. Lukács sets out to fulfil the programme of German Idealism in a Marxist sense by demonstrating that the proletariat is the true subject-object of history, and hence the goal that idealism itself could not reach.

Classical philosophy is used frequently to mean classical *Gernam* philosophy, i.e. the idealist tradition from Kant to Hegel.

'*Critical*' is used ironically in a double sense. It refers to attempts, e.g. by Bernstein or Struve and Tugan-Baranovsky, to revise or refine Marxism critically while in fact undermining it; that is to say it refers to revisionism. A further irony stems from the fact that Lukács opposes his Hegelian standpoint to that of Kantians or Neo-Kantians. Thus 'critical' refers to the Kantian Critiques and and the irony is that their advocates have often reverted to pre-Critical positions.

Science. It is well known that *Wissenschaft* includes both natural and humane sciences. It would normally be easier to limit the word 'science' to physics and chemistry, etc. Here, however, the usual difficulty is increased because Lukács, following Dilthey, bases an important argument on the distinction. He is concerned to demonstrate that what we think of as science is the reified thought of the bourgeoisie. To this he opposes the dialectic. Since he wishes to retain the dignity of science for the dialectic the word has normally been retained in translation.

B. *Notes on the Text*

pp. xiii–xiv   *The March Action*: Rioting in Mansfeld led on 16 March, 1921, to the intervention of the Reichswehr. On the following day the German C.P., lately given a new lease of life by the merger with the left wing of the Independent Socialists, called for open insurrection. There was little response and it was followed by a call for a general strike. This brought members of the C.P. into conflict with fellow-workers as well as police and troops. There were many casualties and thousands of arrests. The action was called off on 31 March. The failure had disastrous consequences for the German C.P. whose membership fell from over 400,000 to 180,000. The Third International was also involved as there was some evidence that Béla Kun and others had urged vigorous action to bolster up morale following the Kronstadt revolt in Russia. It triggered off a debate on putschism.

pp. xiii, 332   *The Kapp Putsch* of 13 March, 1920 was a revolt of the Freikorps against the Ebert government. Berlin was occupied by the Ehrhardt Brigade, and Wolfgang Kapp, a civil servant and Junker, and General von Lüttwitz were declared heads of the new government. Ebert appealed in vain to the army for help. The putsch was defeated by a four-day-long general strike organised by the S.P.D.

p. xlv *synthetic unity of apperception:* the principle according to
which the manifold of intuitions and representations are
united in one self-consciousness. "The principle of apperception is the highest principle in the whole sphere of
human knowledge." ... "Indeed this faculty of the apperception is the understanding itself." Kant, *Critique of
Pure Reason*, §16.

p. 44 Gustav Noske and Philipp Scheidemann were two of the
prominent socialist leaders of the German government
in 1919. Scheidemann was Prime Minister, Noske was
Minister for War. Both together bear responsibility for
the organised suppression of the Spartacus League by
the army and the Freikorps, in the course of which Liebknecht and Rosa Luxemburg were murdered.

p. 125 The Kantian argument attacked here by Hegel is as
follows: "The commonest understanding can distinguish
without instruction what form of maxim is adapted for
universal legislation, and what is not. Suppose, for example, that I have made it my maxim to increase my
fortune by every safe means. Now, I have a deposit in
my hands, the owner of which is dead and has left no
writing about it. This is just the case for my maxim. I
desire, then, to know whether that maxim can also hold
good as a universal practical law. I apply it, therefore,
to the present case, and ask whether it could take the
form of a law, and consequently whether I can by my
maxim at the same time give such a law as this, that
everyone may deny a deposit of which no one can produce a proof. I at once become aware that such a principle, viewed as a law, would annihilate itself, because
the result would be that there would be no deposits."
Critique of Practical Reason, Chapter I, §IV, Theorem III.
(Abbott's translation, London, 1967, p. 115.)

p. 147 The restored Prussian state: this refers to the restoration
of Prussia within the new German Confederation after
the defeat of Napoleon in 1815.

p. 161 Infinite progression: the idea of an infinite progression
or approximation towards holiness is advanced by Kant
in the *Critique of Practical Reason*, Book I, Chapter I, §VII,
2nd Remark. (Abbott's translation, London, 1967, p.
121.) Lukács' point here is that "the indefinite progress

of one's maxims and of their steady disposition to advance" does nothing at all to bridge the gap between the 'is' and the 'ought'.

p. 240   *Economism:* the view that workers should concentrate on advancing their economic interests rather than on revolutionary action. Social Democrats should champion the practical demands of the workers: higher wages, shorter hours, better factory conditions, etc. Lenin analyses it in detail in *What is to be done?* (Section II).

p. 272   *the Vorwärts revelations and Friesland's pamphlet:* The collapse of the March Action had a serious effect on the new unified German C.P. Paul Levi accused the Third International of having engineered a putsch in Germany. Among his supporters was Clara Zetkin who assembled material with which to confront the Third Congress. On her way there the Prussian police confiscated her papers at the frontier (in July 1921). The contents of these papers were then published by the Vorwärts on December 25, 1921. This was followed by a number of resignations in the German Party.

Friesland was the party name of Ernst Reuter, who had opposed Levi on the March Action and succeeded him as General Secretary of the Central Committee. From this vantage point he soon decided that there was no way to combat the growing Russian influence in the German Party and so left and joined the Social Democrats at the end of 1921.

Both these incidents show that the choice was seen as a decision either to support the International or to opt for reformism and social democracy.

pp. 284, 301   *The Stuttgart Resolution.* This refers to the declarations against war made at the Stuttgart congress of the Second International in 1907. The resolution strengthened by amendments by Rosa Luxemburg and Lenin, proclaimed that war should be opposed by the mass strike. It was carried in the teeth of opposition from Bebel. Nevertheless, it was essentially a statement of good intentions rather than a definite commitment, and this became all too obvious on the outbreak of the war in 1914.

p. 287   Zimmerwald: The Zimmerwald conference, convened

5–8 September, 1915 was the first attempt by socialists to come together and discuss policy on the war. It was also the scene of a major confrontation between the Centrists, who aimed at peace with no annexations and no reparations, and Lenin, who saw such formulae as a hypocritical mask for social patriots and chauvinists and who argued instead for the need to turn an imperialist war into civil war.

p. 288   *The 'Internationale'*: a journal edited by Rosa Luxemburg and Franz Mehring whose one and only issue appeared in April 1915 with an article by Karl Liebknecht. The journal gave its name to the group around Rosa Luxemburg, but was gradually superseded by the Spartacus League. The Guiding Lines referred to became the programme of the Spartacus League when it was officially constituted on 1 January, 1916.

p. 291   *KAP* Kommunistische Arbeiterspartei Deutschlands: Following the assassinations of Rosa Luxemburg and Karl Liebknecht, Paul Levi became head of the German C.P. He soon became embroiled with the ultra-left who opposed participation in trade unions and elections. In April 1920 there was a split and the ultra-left formed the KAP, taking the majority of the membership in Berlin and Hamburg with them. They lined up with the Dutch Communist Herman Gorter who had written an Open Letter, attacking Lenin's conception of the party and its relation to the working class. To Lenin their revolt came under the heading of an 'infantile disorder', but he nevertheless gave them a special sympathisers' status in the Comintern. They ceased to play a role after 1922.

p. 293   Kornilow to Kronstadt: Kornilow (1870–1918) was a general both in the Czarist army and in the Russian army after the February Revolution. He was even Commander-in-Chief, July/August 1917. He then led the counter-revolutionary revolt in August 1917. After the revolt was crushed he was arrested and sent to gaol. He escaped and fled to the Don where he organised and led a white guard volunteer army. He was killed in battle near Krasnodar.

Kronstadt: an uprising by the sailors of Kronstadt early in March 1921, in protest against the rigours of 'war-communism' and the effects of the Civil War. According to Lenin, the sailors were the 'tools of former Czarist generals' and their revolt the 'work of entente interventionists and French spies'. The revolt was crushed by Tukhachevsky (by March 17). The same month saw the start of the New Economic Policy.

p. 295 The Second Congress was opened on 19 July, 1921 at Petrograd and was then adjourned to Moscow where it was held from 23 July to 7 August. The Third Congress was held from 22 June to 12 July 1921.

Much relevant material (including the Theses on communist parties and parliament mentioned on p. 265) can be found in *The Communist International 1919–1943*. Documents selected and edited by Jane Degras, O.U.P., 1956.

C. *Biographical Notes*

Bauer, Otto (1881–1938)

Bauer was one of the leading figures in the Austrian Social Democratic Party and one of the most eminent of the revisionist thinkers. He became leader of the Party together with Friedrich Adler after World War I. He stood on the left wing, in opposition to Karl Renner who led the patriots.

Dilthey, Wilhelm (1833–1911)

Dilthey's influence on German thought in the late nineteenth century is profound and pervasive. He was the first to attempt a systematic confrontation of history with the natural sciences. Although in many respects a positivist his ideas on hermeneutics were an important stage in the overcoming of positivism. His emphasis on actual 'experience' led him finally in the directions of subjective irrationalism. His book on Hegel (1906) helped to bring about a revival of interest in Hegel of which the present work is one of the offshoots.

Lask, Emil (1875–1915)

Pupil of Windelband and Rickert, professor of philosophy in Heidelberg. His main work, *The Logic of Philosophy and the Doctrine of the Categories*, furnished the logical foundation for a sort of neo-platonism. He had a profound influence on Lukács' early work.

Lassalle, Ferdinand (1825–64)

One of the great leaders of German socialism. The German Social Democratic Party was formed by a merger of his supporters with the so-called Eisenacher led by August Bebel. At first he was on friendly terms with Marx and Engels who, however, became increasingly critical of his ideas such as state socialism and the so-called 'iron law of wages'. Killed in a duel.

Levi, Paul

Member of the Spartacus League and leader of the German C.P. after the death of Rosa Luxemburg and Karl Liebknecht. He denounced the International for its part in instigating the March Action (1921) and was expelled. In 1922 he led his group into the Independent Socialists and so back into the Social Democratic Party.

Mach, Ernst

Professor of physics and the philosophy of science in Prague and Vienna. He criticised the crude positivism of his day from a sophisticated neo-Kantian position. Thus mechanistic and materialist theories were attacked by denying their underlying assumptions of the existence of matter and 'substance'. This eventually led him towards philosophical subjectivism. His thought had an important impact on the Austrian Social Democrats who used it to undermine the materialist basis of Marxism.

Marburg School

Marburg was the centre of neo-Kantian philosophy whose leading exponents were Hermann Cohen and Paul Natorp, and later Ernst Cassirer. Unlike the Heidelberg thinkers (Rickert, etc.) the Marburgers concentrated less on history and the distinction elaborated by Dilthey between the natural and the cultural sciences. Their attention was focused on epistemology and they saw it as their task to maintain and strengthen Kant's own critique of metaphysics.

Pannekoek, Anton (1873–1960)

Dutch social democrat and member of the Dutch C.P. (1918–21) and the Comintern. He held ultra-left, sectarian views. The debate with Kautsky mentioned on p. 302 is discussed in detail by Lenin in *State and Revolution*, Chapter 6.

Parvus (Alexander Helphand)

Joined the S.P.D. in the 1890s; took part in the 1905 revolution; exiled to Siberia. He took a prominent part in the revisionist debate, attacking Bernstein with great verve, and, as was thought, lack of tact. Later he evolved the idea of permanent revolution with Trotsky. Later still he became one of the leaders of the pro-war faction.

Rickert, Heinrich

Professor of philosophy at Freiburg, student of Windelband. He accepted Dilthey's distinction between the 'cultural' and the natural sciences and applied it above all to history. Where Ranke had offered little more than 'contemplation' of the panorama of events Rickert argued that the historian discerns patterns based on his own value-judgements. These judgements are based ultimately on his own system of values. In the attempt to avoid total relativism Rickert retreated into metaphysical assumptions: values could not be verified but only 'intuited'; nevertheless, they were saved from arbitrariness because they were rooted in the 'normal consciousness' of humanity.

Serrati, Giacinto Menotti (1872–1926)

One of the leaders of the Italian Socialist Party, especially of the Centrist wing. During World War I he took an internationalist stand. Afterwards he headed the Italian delegation to the Second Congress.

p. 301, The 21 Conditions of Admission to the International, laid down by Lenin and presented to the Congress by Zinoviev and Meyer insisted on the need to break with reformists and centrists. Both Serrati and the German Independent Socialists took the line that the time was inopportune: a new reaction was on the way and to expel members would mean alienating supporters they could ill afford to lose. Lenin replied that there could never be a moment when it would be inappropriate to break with the MacDonalds and Kautskys.

Simmel, Georg (1838–1918)

Simmel is one of the chief representatives of classical German sociology, together with Max Weber and Ferdinand Tönnies. In *The Philosophy of Money* he examined the effect of the money economy on human behaviour and the relationship between capitalism and the philosophy of the natural sciences. The influence of the Neo-Kantians can be seen in his emphasis on the "endless variety of the *forms* of social life" and his belief that sociology must abstract from the 'content' of those forms.

Socialist Revolutionaries

Left-wing Russian party formed from a merger of various populist groups. First Congress December 1905-January 1906. It aimed at united revolutionary action by peasants, workers and intelligentsia; proposed the abolition of private ownership of land and setting up of peasant communes. It was criticised by Lenin for blurring the lines of class struggle and for denying precedence to the proletariat. He also attacked their affirmation of terrorism. After the February Revolution they formed the mainstay of the provisional government.

Struve, Peter (1870–1944)

'Legal' Marxist; anticipated some of Bernstein's 'critical' revisions of Marxism. He worked at first on *Iskra* but soon left and founded his own, liberal, organ *Osvobozhdenie*. Henceforth he was treated as a renegade by Lenin. Associated with him was M. I. Tugan-Baranovsky (1865–1919).

Windelband, Wilhelm

Neo-Kantian philosopher. His rectoral address at Strasbourg in 1894 sounded to his contemporaries like "a declaration of war against positivism", i.e. it was the opening shot in the counteroffensive of German Idealism.

Index